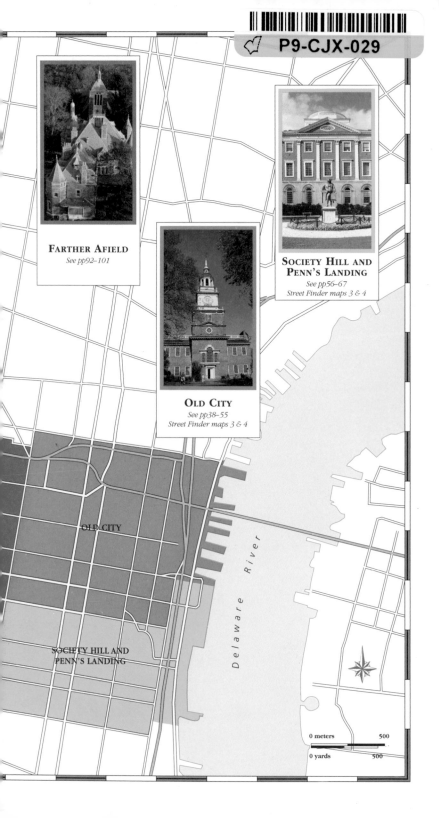

FARTHER AFIELD
See pp92–101

**SOCIETY HILL AND
PENN'S LANDING**
See pp56–67
Street Finder maps 3 & 4

OLD CITY
See pp38–55
Street Finder maps 3 & 4

OLD CITY

Delaware River

SOCIETY HILL AND
PENN'S LANDING

0 meters   500
0 yards   500

PHILADELPHIA
AND THE PENNSYLVANIA
DUTCH COUNTRY

EYEWITNESS TRAVEL GUIDES

PHILADELPHIA
AND THE PENNSYLVANIA DUTCH COUNTRY

Main Contributor: RICHARD VARR

LONDON, NEW YORK,
MELBOURNE, MUNICH AND DELHI
www.dk.com

MANAGING EDITOR Aruna Ghose
ART EDITOR Benu Joshi
EDITORS Ankita Awasthi, Bhavna Seth Ranjan
DESIGNERS Mathew Kurien, Divya Saxena, Shruti Singhi
SENIOR CARTOGRAPHER Uma Bhattacharya
CARTOGRAPHIC RESEARCHER Suresh Kumar
PICTURE RESEARCHER Taiyaba Khatoon
DTP COORDINATOR Shailesh Sharma
DTP DESIGNER Vinod Harish

MAIN CONTRIBUTOR
Richard Varr

PHOTOGRAPHER
Demetrio Carrasco

ILLUSTRATORS
Arun Pottirayil, T. Gautam Trivedi, Mark Warner

Reproduced by Colourscan (Singapore)
Printed and bound in China by L. Rex Printing Co. Ltd

First American Edition 2005
05 06 07 08 09 10 9 8 7 6 5 4 3 2 1

Published in the United States by
DK Publishing, Inc., 375 Hudson Street,
New York, New York 10014

Copyright © 2005 Dorling Kindersley Limited, London
A Penguin Company

Published in Great Britain by Dorling Kindersley Limited.

A CATALOGING IN PUBLICATION RECORD IS AVAILABLE FROM THE
LIBRARY OF CONGRESS.

ISSN: 1542-1554
ISBN-13: 978-0-75661-355-6
ISBN-10: 0-75661-355-8

**The information in this
Dorling Kindersley Travel Guide is checked regularly**.
Every effort has been made to ensure that this book is as up-to-date as
possible at the time of going to press. Some details, however, such as
telephone numbers, opening hours, prices, gallery hanging
arrangements and travel information are liable to change. The
publishers cannot accept responsibility for any consequences arising
from the use of this book, nor for any material on third party websites,
and cannot guarantee that any website address in this book will be a
suitable source of travel information. We value the views and
suggestions of our readers very highly. Please write to:
Publisher, DK Eyewitness Travel Guides,
Dorling Kindersley, 80 Strand, London WC2R 0RL, Great Britain.

◁ **Philadelphia's skyscrapers towering over the Schuylkill River**

CONTENTS

HOW TO USE THIS
GUIDE *6*

**The Liberty Bell, one of the world's
greatest symbols of freedom**

INTRODUCING PHILADELPHIA AND THE PENNSYLVANIA DUTCH COUNTRY

FOUR GREAT DAYS IN
PHILADELPHIA *10*

PUTTING PHILADELPHIA
ON THE MAP *12*

THE HISTORY OF
PHILADELPHIA *16*

PHILADELPHIA
AT A GLANCE *24*

PHILADELPHIA THROUGH
THE YEAR *32*

**The relaxing environs of tree-
shaded Rittenhouse Square**

A panoramic view of the Camden waterfront at dusk

PHILADELPHIA AREA BY AREA

OLD CITY 38

SOCIETY HILL AND PENN'S LANDING 56

CENTER CITY 68

LOGAN SQUARE AND THE MUSEUM DISTRICT 80

FARTHER AFIELD 92

TWO GUIDED WALKS AND A DRIVE 102

BEYOND PHILADELPHIA 110

Delicate bloom at the Magnolia Garden in Society Hill

TRAVELERS' NEEDS

WHERE TO STAY 132

RESTAURANTS AND CAFÉS 142

SHOPS AND MARKETS 154

ENTERTAINMENT IN PHILADELPHIA 162

CHILDREN'S PHILADELPHIA 170

The 18th-century Independence Hall

SURVIVAL GUIDE

PRACTICAL INFORMATION 174

TRAVEL INFORMATION 182

PHILADELPHIA STREET FINDER 190

Trademark horse and buggy in the Pennsylvania Dutch Country

GENERAL INDEX 198

ACKNOWLEDGMENTS 207

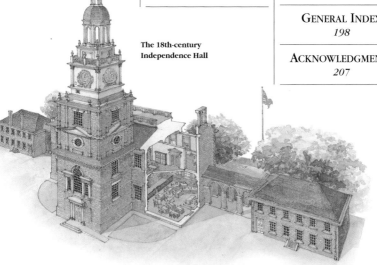

HOW TO USE THIS GUIDE

THIS DORLING KINDERSLEY travel guide helps you get the most from your visit to Philadelphia. It provides detailed practical information and expert recommendations. *Introducing Philadelphia* maps the city and the region, sets it in its historical and cultural context, and describes events through the entire year. *Philadelphia at a Glance* is an overview of the city's main attractions. The main sightseeing section of the book is *Philadelphia Area by Area*, which covers all the important sights, with photographs, maps, and illustrations. *Farther Afield* suggests sights just outside the city core, while *Beyond Philadelphia* describes Dutch Country and historic Gettysburg among other areas. Information about hotels, restaurants, shopping, entertainment, and sports is found in *Travelers' Needs*. The *Survival Guide* has practical advice on everything from using Philadelphia's medical services and transport system to public telephones and post offices.

FINDING YOUR WAY AROUND THE SIGHTSEEING SECTION

Each of the four sightseeing areas in Philadelphia is color-coded for easy reference. Every chapter opens with an introduction to the area of the city it covers, describing its history and character, and has a

Street-by-Street map illustrating an interesting part of that area. Finding your way around the chapter is made simple by the numbering system used throughout. Sights outside Philadelphia have a regional map.

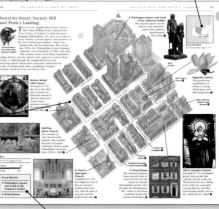

Each area has color-coded thumb tabs.

1 Introduction to the Area
For easy reference, the sights in each area are numbered and plotted on an area map. This map also shows SEPTA subway stops and regional rail stations, as well as indicating the area covered by the Street-by-Street map. The area's key sights are listed by category.

Locator map

A locator map shows where you are in relation to other areas in the city.

A suggested route takes in some of the most interesting and attractive streets in the area.

2 Street-by-Street Map
This gives a bird's-eye view of the most interesting and important parts of each sightseeing area. The numbering of the sights ties in with the preceding area map and with the fuller descriptions of the entries on the pages that follow.

The list of star sights indicates the places that no visitor should miss.

PHILADELPHIA AREA MAP

The colored areas shown on this map *(see inside front cover)* are the four main sightseeing districts used in this guide. Each area is covered in detail in *Philadelphia Area by Area (see pp36–109)*, as are sights located outside the city center and the walks. These areas are also highlighted on other maps throughout the book. In *Philadelphia at a Glance (see pp24–31)*, for example, they help locate the top sights.

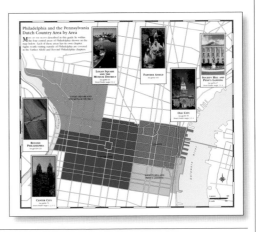

Numbers refer to each sight's position on the area map and its place in the chapter.

Practical information provides everything you need to know to visit each sight. Map references pinpoint the sight's location on the *Street Finder* maps *(see pp190–97)*.

3 Detailed Information

All the important sights in Philadelphia are described individually. They are listed in order, following the numbering on the area map at the start of the section. Practical information includes telephone numbers, opening hours, and map reference. The key to the symbols used is on the back flap.

The visitors' checklist provides all the practical information needed to plan your visit.

Story boxes provide information about historical or cultural topics relating to the sights.

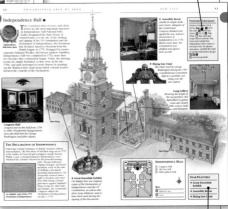

4 Philadelphia's Major Sights

These are given two or more full pages in the sightseeing area where they are found. Historic buildings are dissected to reveal their interiors; color-coded floor plans in museums and galleries help you find important exhibits.

Stars recommend the features that no visitor should miss.

INTRODUCING PHILADELPHIA

FOUR GREAT DAYS IN PHILADELPHIA 10-11

PUTTING PHILADELPHIA ON THE MAP 12-15

THE HISTORY OF PHILADELPHIA 16-23

PHILADELPHIA AT A GLANCE 24-31

PHILADELPHIA THROUGH THE YEAR 32-35

FOUR GREAT DAYS
IN PHILADELPHIA

YOU COULD EASILY spend a few weeks enjoying all the historic sights and attractions in Philadelphia, not to mention separate excursions to the Pennsylvania Dutch Country and Gettysburg. Most visitors, however, only have a few days and will want to make the most of their time. Outlined here are ideas for four separate days of sightseeing and

Grave, Christ Church Burial Ground

enjoyment – three of them in Philadelphia and one in the Pennsylvania Dutch Country. They include suggestions on what to see, where to eat, and what to do for entertainment. Of course, the suggestions are just that, and can be modified to suit your requirements. The prices are indicative of the cost of transport and admission (if any) for two adults or a family of four.

Interior of Congress Hall, adjacent to Independence Hall

HISTORIC PHILADELPHIA

- **Tour Independence Hall and National Constitution Center**
- **Lunch at Bourse Building**
- **Tour historic Old City**
- **Watch the Lights of Liberty Show**

TWO ADULTS allow at least $60

Morning
It is best to arrive at the **Independence Visitor Center** *(see p45)* when it opens at 8:30am to pick up your free, timed tickets to **Independence Hall** *(see pp42–3)*. The earlier you arrive, the better the chances of being admitted quickly. Note that tickets are usually gone by noon. Once you have your tickets the day can be planned accordingly. Visitors are first guided through the **Liberty Bell Center** *(see p44)*, and

should spend the remainder of the morning visiting the **National Constitution Center** *(see pp48–9)*. Stop for lunch at the satisfying food court in **The Bourse** *(see p145)* in Independence Mall East.

Afternoon
Start off by visiting the **Christ Church Burial Ground** *(see p46)* where Benjamin Franklin is buried. Allow 15 to 30 minutes here, and then go on to take a half-hour tour of the **Betsy Ross House** *(see p52)*. Visit the Colonial portrait gallery at the **Second Bank of the US** *(see p47)* and pass by the imposing façades of the **First Bank of the US** *(see p53)* and the **Merchants' Exchange** *(see p54)*. The **City Tavern** *(see p55)* is a good place to stop for some refreshment.
In the evening, take in the **Lights of Liberty Show** *(see p175)*, which features

spectacular images flashed onto historic buildings. Reservations are needed for this one-hour show.

A SHOPPING DAY

- **Browse boutiques along Rittenhouse Row**
- **Lunch at Rittenhouse Square**
- **Visit King of Prussia Mall**

TWO ADULTS allow at least $40

Morning
Start by browsing through the elegant boutiques on **Rittenhouse Row** *(see p156)*, which has such high-fashion names as Jones New York and Ann Taylor. Also visit the nearby **Shops at Liberty Place** *(see p156)*. As noon approaches, check out the specialty shops at the **Bellevue Building** *(see p156)*.

Mural at Italian Market, famous for specialty foods and eateries

---

◁ **Artist's impression of street life near the former State House (now known as Independence Hall) c.1800**

and then have a quick bite at the building's upbeat food court. For restaurants with outdoor seating, head toward **Rittenhouse Square** *(see p78)*. **Pietro's Coal Oven Pizzeria** and **Devon Seafood Grill** are good choices *(see p149)*.

Afternoon
Visit **The Gallery at Market East** mall *(see p156)* for some more shopping. Do not miss the nearby **Reading Terminal Market** *(see p73)*, and if you have time left over, head to the **Italian Market** *(see p97)* for coffee and Italian pastries. End your spree with a visit to the colossal **King of Prussia Mall** *(see p156)*.

Franklin Institute Science Museum features hands-on exhibits

A FAMILY DAY

- **Visit museums around Logan Square**
- **Walk along Penn's Landing**
- **Take the RiverLink Ferry**
- **Visit the Adventure Aquarium**

FAMILY OF FOUR allow at least $165

Morning
Depending on time and budget, you may choose to visit one or more of the three fascinating museums on Logan Square – **Franklin Institute Science Museum** *(see p85)*, **Academy of Natural Sciences** *(see p85)*, or the **Please Touch Museum** *(see p170)* for

children up to seven. Enjoy lunch at one of the fun cafeterias inside the Academy of Natural Sciences or the Franklin Institute.

Afternoon
Head over to **Penn's Landing** *(see p66)* and visit the **Independence Seaport Museum** *(see pp64–5)*. Later, take the RiverLink Ferry to the **Camden Waterfront** *(see p101)*. The ferry runs from April through mid-November. Make it a point to head to the **Adventure Aquarium** *(see p171)*, as the kids will love the aquatic life there.

Evening
In the warmer months, the **Ghost Tour of Philadelphia** *(see p175)* is a great option. In winter, ice skate on the **Blue Cross RiverRink** *(see pp168–9)*.

PENNSYLVANIA DUTCH COUNTRY

- **Tour Landis Valley Museum**
- **Have an Amish-style lunch**
- **Visit the Amish Experience**
- **Hop on board the Strasburg Railroad**

FAMILY OF FOUR allow at least $130

Morning
Arrive at **Lancaster Central Market** *(see p114)* by 8am to eat a hearty country breakfast. Only steps away are the **Lancaster Cultural History Museum** and the **Lancaster**

The Blacksmith Shop at the Landis Valley Museum

Quilt & Textile Museum *(see p114)*. Go on to the **Landis Valley Museum** *(see pp116–17)* off Route 272 and spend some time exploring this living history village. Head east on Route 340 through Bird-in-Hand and stop for a family-style lunch at the **Plain and Fancy Farm Restaurant** *(see p153)* next to the **Amish Experience** *(see p118)*.

Afternoon
Visit the Amish Experience and wander through the Country Homestead, a typical Amish home. Then watch the multimedia cultural presentation, *Jacob's Choice*, at the Amish Experience Theater. Spend the second part of the afternoon at Kitchen Kettle Village in **Intercourse** *(see p118)*, shopping for crafts and jarred foods.

Evening
During the summer months, after an early dinner, hop onto the 7pm train on the **Strasburg Railroad** *(see p119)* for the day's last ride through miles of farmland.

Tourists shopping for art and antiques in Lancaster

hiladelphia on the Map

ortheast region of the United States, its on the southeastern edge of Pennsylvania re River, which separates Pennsylvania from ded by William Penn in the late 17th century, Philadelphia is now the nation's fifth largest city and the second largest on the East Coast. Close to 1.5 million people live within the city's 135 sq mile (350 sq km) area.

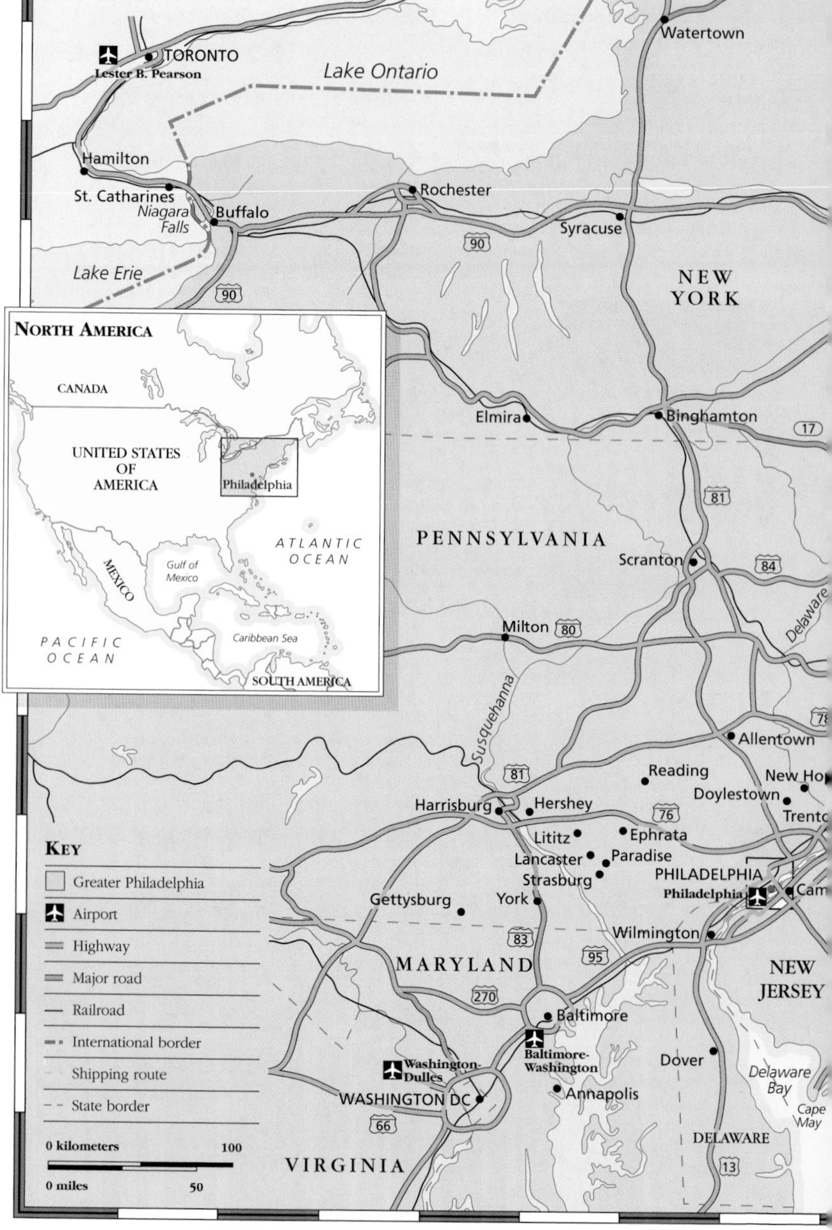

CANAD
TORONTO
Lester B. Pearson
Lake Ontario
Watertown
81
Hamilton
St. Catharines
Niagara Falls
Buffalo
Rochester
Syracuse
90
Lake Erie
NEW YORK
NORTH AMERICA
CANADA
UNITED STATES OF AMERICA
Philadelphia
ATLANTIC OCEAN
Gulf of Mexico
MEXICO
PACIFIC OCEAN
Caribbean Sea
SOUTH AMERICA
Elmira
Binghamton
17
PENNSYLVANIA
Scranton
84
Delaware
Milton
80
Susquehanna
Allentown
Reading
New Ho
Doylestown
Trento
Harrisburg
Hershey
76
Lititz
Ephrata
Lancaster
Paradise
Strasburg
PHILADELPHIA
Philadelphia
Cam
Gettysburg
York
83
Wilmington
95
MARYLAND
NEW JERSEY
270
Baltimore
Baltimore-Washington
Washington-Dulles
Dover
Delaware Bay
WASHINGTON DC
Annapolis
Cape May
66
DELAWARE
13
VIRGINIA
KEY
Greater Philadelphia
Airport
Highway
Major road
Railroad
International border
Shipping route
State border
0 kilometers 100
0 miles 50

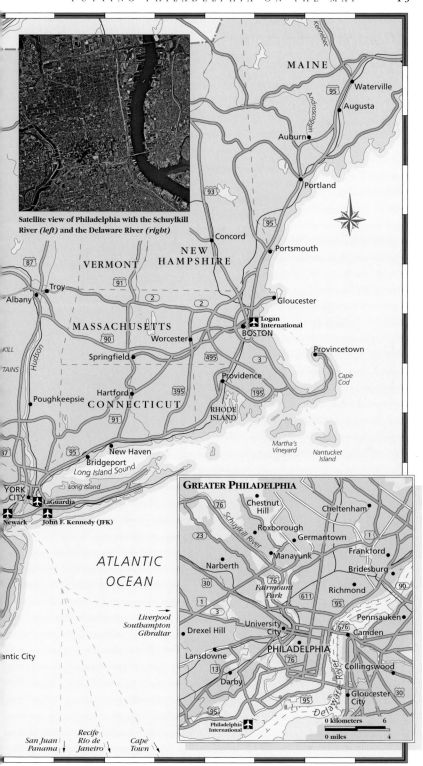

Satellite view of Philadelphia with the Schuylkill River *(left)* and the Delaware River *(right)*

MAINE

Waterville
Augusta
Auburn
Portland
95
93
95
Androscoggin
Kennebec

Concord
Portsmouth
NEW HAMPSHIRE
VERMONT
87
91
Troy
Albany
91
2
2
Gloucester
MASSACHUSETTS
90
Worcester
Logan International
BOSTON
Springfield
495
3
Provincetown
Cape Cod
Hudson
KILL
TAINS
Providence
195
Poughkeepsie
Hartford
395
CONNECTICUT
RHODE ISLAND
91
Martha's Vineyard
Nantucket Island
37
95
New Haven
Bridgeport
Long Island Sound
Long Island

YORK CITY
LaGuardia
Newark
John F. Kennedy (JFK)

ATLANTIC OCEAN

Liverpool
Southampton
Gibraltar

antic City

San Juan
Panama
Recife
Rio de
Janeiro
Cape Town

GREATER PHILADELPHIA

76
Chestnut Hill
Cheltenham
Roxborough
23
Germantown
1
Schuylkill River
Manayunk
Frankford
Narberth
Bridesburg
30
76
Fairmount Park
Richmond
90
1
611
95
3
University City
Pennsauken
Drexel Hill
676
Camden
Lansdowne
PHILADELPHIA
76
13
Collingswood
Darby
Gloucester City
30
Delaware River
95
95
Philadelphia International

0 kilometers 6
0 miles 4

Central Philadelphia

Fː{LANKED BY THE} Delaware and Schuylkill Rivers, central Philadelphia comprises four distinct neighborhoods, which together span more than three centuries of development. Much of the modern-day layout is based on city founder William Penn's original grid pattern – a crisscross of streets with five green squares. Four of these squares remain as pleasant, shaded parks today. The fifth, Penn's original Center Square, contains City Hall. The oldest districts are Old City and Society Hill.

Central Philadelphia
Center City (see pp68–79) skyscrapers can be seen along the Schuylkill River.

Statue of George Washington at Eakins Oval
A prominent equestrian statue pays tribute to America's founding father and first president against the backdrop of the imposing temple-like façade of the Museum of Art (see pp88–91).

Rittenhouse Square
One of William Penn's original five squares, this Center City park (see p78) is popular with downtown workers and residents. Extravagant high-rise buildings and upscale restaurants surround the square.

| 0 meters | | 500 |
| 0 yards | | 500 |

KEY

	Star sight
S	SEPTA subway stop
	SEPTA regional rail station
	Greyhound bus terminal
	Police station
P	Parking
	Hospital
	Visitor information
	Church
	Synagogue

Old City Hall
Located next to Independence Hall (see pp42–3) in the heart of Old City, where a new nation was born in 1776, Philadelphia's Old City Hall was home to the US Supreme Court from 1791 to 1800.

Penn's Landing
This waterfront area hosts summer festivals and is home to the city's tall ships, the submarine Becuna *and the USS* Olympia. *Also located here is the Independence Seaport Museum (see pp64–5).*

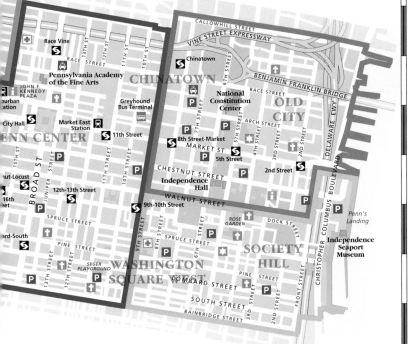

THE HISTORY OF PHILADELPHIA

W ILLIAM PENN *first landed in the New World in 1682. Armed with a land charter, he founded a colony based on religious freedom that just a century later, would give birth to a new nation. Penn named the new city Philadelphia, derived from Greek words meaning "City of Brotherly Love."*

Before William Penn's arrival, the Delaware River basin and the Schuylkill River watershed were inhabited by Algonquian-speaking Native Americans known as Lenni-Lenape. They were mostly peaceful hunters and gatherers, and many lived along the Delaware River and its tributaries. They were named "Delawares" for that reason by the first European settlers.

Chief Tammany, Delaware Indian chief

FIRST EUROPEAN EXPLORERS AND SETTLERS

Chartered by the Dutch East India Company, Englishman Henry Hudson's ship, the *Half Moon*, sailed into Delaware Bay in 1609 and claimed it for Holland. Dutch navigators followed shortly after: Captain Cornelius Hendricksen sailed up the Delaware in 1616 to where it meets the Schuylkill River; and in 1623, Cornelius Jacobsen explored the region further, leading to the establishment of a number of trading posts, including one on the Schuylkill in 1633.

The first settlement in what is now Pennsylvania, however, did not occur until 1643, when Swedish Lutheran settlers – who had first settled in Wilmington, Delaware, in 1638 – established their capital of New Sweden on Tinicum Island, near present-day Philadelphia. Eight years later, the Dutch, whose previous colonial efforts had been directed elsewhere, seized control and annexed the region as part of the Dutch Colony. From 1655 to 1664, the Dutch controlled the area until the English captured the Dutch colonies, calling them New York, after the Duke of York.

THE FOUNDING OF PENNSYLVANIA AND PHILADELPHIA

The son of a wealthy British admiral, William Penn was born in 1644. While attending Oxford University, Penn joined the Religious Society of Friends, the Quakers, a group who worshipped, without dogma or clergy, silently in unadorned meetinghouses. The faith was based on

TIMELINE

1600	1615	1630	1645	1660	1675

1609 Explorer Henry Hudson sails into Delaware Bay

Henry Hudson, English navigator

1638 Swedish Lutheran settlers arrive in Wilmington, Delaware

1644 Birth of William Penn

1664 England takes control of the Dutch colonies

1616 Dutch Captain Cornelius Hendricksen sails up the Delaware to the Schuylkill River

1623 Dutchman Cornelius Jacobsen explores the region further

1643 Swedes establish capital on Tinicum Island near present-day Philadelphia

1655 Dutch seize control of New Sweden

◁ **Detail from *Penn's Treaty with the Indians* by Edward Hicks, 1830–1840**

William Penn receiving the Charter for Pennsylvania from King Charles II of England

pacifism and equality. Expelled from university, Penn was later harassed and even imprisoned for his devotion to Quakerism. However, his wealth and social position allowed him to retain influence in the King's court.

The Charter for Pennsylvania was founded in 1681 as a result of a debt owed by King Charles II to Penn's father. The king repaid the £16,000 debt by granting the younger Penn land between Maryland and New York. In October 1682, Penn's ship, the *Welcome*, landed at New Castle in Delaware with many Quaker passengers. A few days later, Penn sailed up the Delaware to the capital of his new colony: Philadelphia.

As a Quaker, Penn espoused non-violence, and one of his first initiatives was to reach an agreement with the Delawares, thus forming treaties and enduring friendships with the Native Americans. The new colony also promised religious freedom, and was seen as a "Holy Experiment." More settlers followed, including both English and Dutch Quakers, German Mennonites, and the Amish, who settled in what is now called Pennsylvania Dutch Country.

Penn and surveyor Thomas Holmes designed Philadelphia in a grid pattern between the Delaware and Schuylkill Rivers. Their plan included five public spaces, as Penn and Holmes wanted to create a "green countrie towne." These tree-lined areas – Washington, Rittenhouse, Logan, and Franklin Squares – still remain today. City Hall now occupies the original "Center Square" at the junction of Market and Broad Streets.

Detail from *Peaceable Kingdom* by Edward Hicks (1780–1849), painted in 1826

TIMELINE

1683 Penn signs treaty with Delawares	**1684** Penn leaves Philadelphia and returns to England	**1699** Penn returns to Philadelphia	**1701** Penn grants charter to City of Philadelphia	**1718** Death of Penn in England

1680	**1690**	**1700**	**1710**

Gloria Dei Church

1677 Swedes establish Gloria Dei church

1682 Penn arrives in Pennsylvania and establishes Philadelphia

1701 Penn leaves America for good and returns to England

1710 Christ Church built at 2nd Street

COLONIAL EXPANSION

At the beginning of the 18th century, Philadelphia was already witnessing rapid growth. Penn had left Philadelphia in 1684 but returned in 1699 to find the population at more than 7,000. In October 1701, he granted a charter to the City of Philadelphia and left for England, never to return. As a port city, Philadelphia soon became an important center of commerce, with imports of sugar, rum, and molasses from the Caribbean. As trade flourished, so did manufacturing and shipbuilding. An increase in the number of homes led to a burgeoning community of craftsmen. The city also boasted a paper mill, furnaces, distilleries, tanneries, and a glass factory. One of its most famous residents, Benjamin Franklin *(see p53)*, arrived from Boston in 1723. His achievements as a scientist, inventor, printer, publisher, and statesman turned Philadelphia into a cultural center. In 1751, along with physician Thomas Bond, Franklin founded Pennsylvania Hospital, America's first public hospital.

The mid-1700s saw a clash between pacifist Quaker beliefs and the need to establish defenses for the colony. Pennsylvania was part of the British Empire and was involved in skirmishes against the French over land in North America. The conflicts climaxed with the French and Indian War, fought between the French and the British from 1754 to 1763, where a 21-year-old native of Virginia named George Washington

Franklin, famous Philadelphia resident

received his first command. Britain was eventually victorious, but the war's end signaled a turning point for colonists, who now craved independence from Britain.

NEW NATION TAKES SHAPE

On July 4, 1776, independence from Britain was declared in Philadelphia, and in 1789, George Washington was elected the first president of the fledgling nation. The city remained the political heart of the country for a decade, serving as the capital from 1790 until 1800. During this time, America's first bank was chartered in 1791 to unify the nation's currency and to pay off war debts. The US Mint was established the following year.

In 1793, Philadelphia suffered a yellow fever epidemic, resulting in a large loss of life. Despite this, immigrants continued to flock to the city, increasing its population to nearly 70,000 by 1800, making it America's largest city at the time.

Yellow fever epidemic in Philadelphia, 1793

1723 Benjamin Franklin arrives from Boston	1743 Franklin founds American Philosophical Society	1754 Start of the French and Indian War	1763 French and Indian War ends

| 1720 | 1730 | 1740 | 1750 | 1760 |

| 1724 Carpenters' Company founded | *Journal published by Franklin in 1741* | 1751 Pennsylvania Hospital founded | *Pennsylvania Hospital* |

Colonial Philadelphia and the American Revolution

T**HE YEARS LEADING UP TO**, including, and after the American Revolutionary War are arguably the most important years of the history of Philadelphia. Rebellion against British rule began as early as 1765 with opposition to taxation without representation in Parliament. A decade later, the colonists **Gunpowder** elected Washington to lead their army – **casket, 1800s** the Continental Army – in the war for independence. In 1776, the Declaration of Independence was signed in Philadelphia, though by 1777 the city was again occupied by British forces. Freedom was gained in 1781, and Britain at last recognized the colonies' independence with the 1783 Treaty of Paris. Five years later, the US Constitution (*see pp48–9*) was ratified at Independence Hall, Philadelphia.

George Washington
The Second Continental Congress elected Washington to lead the Continental Army against the British in 1775.

Drafting the Declaration
Thomas Jefferson wrote the first draft of the Declaration of Independence. Leaders of 13 North American colonies later ratified it at Independence Hall.

DECLARATION OF INDEPENDENCE (1776)
Delegates of the Continental Congress ratified the Declaration of Independence on July 4, 1776. This 1817 John Trumbull painting shows the presentation of the Declaration by the drafting committee. The signing of the Declaration was completed that August.

TIMELINE

1774 First Continental Congress held	**1775** Second Continental Congress in Philadelphia	**1781** British surrender at Yorktown, Virginia	*Postcard depicting George Washington*	**178** George Washingto elected nation' first presider
	1776 Signing of the Declaration of Independence			
	1775	1780		1785
		1777 Continental Army retreats after losing battles at Brandywine and Germantown	**1783** Signing of the Treaty of Paris	**1788** US Constitution ratified
		1776 Washington's army crosses Delaware River and defeats hired Hessian soldiers at Trenton		

Crossing the Delaware River
Washington's army crossed the Delaware River on Christmas Day in 1776, as depicted in this 1851 Emmanuel Leutze painting. They later defeated British troops at Princeton.

The Battle of Germantown (1777)
British troops barricaded themselves behind the stone walls of Cliveden, a Germantown mansion, forcing the Continental army to retreat.

Valley Forge, 1777–78
After losing the battles of Brandywine and Germantown in 1777, Washington's army lost over 2,500 men to exposure and disease during the winter encampment here.

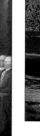

Adoption of the Constitution (1787)
In 1787, delegates from all 13 original states, except Rhode Island, gathered at the Constitutional Convention in Philadelphia to draft and adopt a Constitution for the new nation.

1790
Death of Benjamin Franklin

1793 Yellow fever epidemic kills 4,000

1800
Capital moves to Washington DC

White House, Washington DC

1790   **1795**   **1800**

1791 First Bank of the US chartered

The First Bank of the United States

1790 Philadelphia becomes the nation's capital

1799
Death of George Washington

The City & Port of Philadelphia (1800), engraving with watercolor by William Russell Birch

INDUSTRIALIZATION

By the 1830s, the city's financial and political prominence had begun to wane, as Washington DC, due to its location midway between the north and the south, became the nation's capital. Commercial activity and trade also diminished, as it could not compete with the more accessible port of New York City. Instead, Philadelphia turned to industry and manufacturing, becoming a regional center for textiles, iron and steel, and the shipping of coal. Shipbuilding continued along the Delaware. The city kept growing, with row houses built within the city limits and in surrounding boroughs and districts, including Germantown and Chestnut Hill. These areas soon became new neighborhoods by way of the city consolidation bill of 1854, under which they were incorporated within the city limits.

Growth also brought social clashes. For instance, there were rebellions against anti-slavery movements, and Pennsylvania Hall, the meeting place of the abolitionists, was set on fire in 1838. The 1840s saw violence against Catholics and immigrants, especially the Irish, with angry mobs burning down St. Augustine's Church, across from St. George's Church, in 1844.

POST CIVIL WAR PHILADELPHIA

The need for weapons, munitions, uniforms, and warships for the Union forces bolstered Philadelphia's economy during the Civil War years (1861–65). During the nation's centennial celebrations in 1876, the city held one of the first World Fairs and dedicated grand new buildings, some of which can be seen even today. These include Memorial Hall, a Beaux-Arts structure in Fairmount

Centennial Exhibition in 1876 at Fairmount Park, one of the oldest municipal parks in America

TIMELINE

Burning of St. Augustine	**1844** Anti-Catholic rioters burn churches	**1854** Surrounding boroughs incorporated	**1861** Civil War begins	*Wagons from the Civil War era*	**1907** First underground rail line commences
1830		**1855**		**1880**	**1900**
	1838 Anti-abolitionists burn Pennsylvania Hall	**1856** Completion of Pennsylvania Railroad to Pittsburgh	**1876** City celebrates centennial with nation's first World Fair	**1890s** Electric trolleys introduced	**1914** World War I begins

Park, and the Victorian-style Pennsylvania Academy of the Fine Arts. Politically, however, this was a time of corruption as Republican leaders controlled city contracts and thousands of jobs. Their influence only waned in the 1930s and 40s when voter support was lost due to allegations of corruption and financial mismanagement in city government.

Streetcar on 9th Street, Philadelphia, 1921

THE EARLY 20TH CENTURY

The city's infrastructure was well-established by the end of the 19th century. For instance, its streetcar system was run by electric power as early as the 1890s. There were further improvements in mass transit with the completion of its first underground rail line, the Market Street Subway, in 1907, and the completion of the Broad Street Subway in the 1920s. Economic and industrial activity in Philadelphia remained brisk during World War I (1914–18), though it registered a dip during the Great Depression of the 1920s and 30s. World War II (1939–45) revived steel, chemical, and petroleum production, but Philadelphia gradually lost most of its manufacturing sector to other regions of the US.

MODERN PHILADELPHIA

After World War II, the city lost jobs and population to the suburbs, and then underwent political restructuring in 1951, with a new city charter that called for a stronger mayor and new city departments. It was also a time of urban preservation efforts downtown, but some neighborhoods in the city's north and west deteriorated. Racial tensions mounted in the 1960s and through the mayoral terms of Frank Rizzo and W. Wilson Goode, the city's first African-American mayor, before eventually stabilizing in the late 1980s. In 1985, during Goode's term as mayor, the controversial bombing of the headquarters of the black radical group MOVE took place, resulting in the deaths of 11 persons and the destruction of over 60 homes.

Today, Philadelphia's economy is diversified. While some manufacturing units remain, corporate business has recently gained ground. Philadelphia is home to companies specializing in technology, banking, pharmaceuticals, and insurance. Tourism is also key to the local economy. The city has several universities, colleges, medical schools, and world-class hospitals. In 2000, it hosted the Republican National Convention, which nominated George W. Bush for president.

Celebrations at the Republican National Convention in 2000 in Philadelphia

1920s Broad Street Subway completed	1941 US enters World War II	1976 Bicentennial celebrations in Philadelphia	1985 Bombing of MOVE headquarters	2000 Philadelphia hosts Republican National Convention
1930	**1955**	**1980**		**2005**
1929 Great Depression begins	1951 New city charter provides strong mayoral leadership	*Wilson Goode, Philadelphia's first African-American mayor*	1990s Philadelphia becomes a model for urban renewal despite a declining population	

PHILADELPHIA AT A GLANCE

MANY OF Philadelphia's most popular sights are to be found in Old City, within what's called "America's most historic square mile." They include Independence Hall *(see pp42–3)* and the iconic Liberty Bell *(see p44)*. Outstanding museums, including the Pennsylvania Academy of the Fine Arts *(see pp74–5)* and the Philadelphia Museum of Art *(see pp88–91)*, are in the city center, while the Barnes Foundation *(see pp98–9)* is just beyond city limits. More than 100 places of interest are described in the *Area by Area* and *Beyond Philadelphia* sections of this book. To help you make the most of your stay, the following six pages are a guide to the best of Philadelphia, with a selection featured below.

PHILADELPHIA'S TOP TEN SIGHTS

Independence Hall
(see pp42–3)

Liberty Bell Center
(see p44)

Barnes Foundation
(see pp98–9)

Fairmount Park
(see p95)

National Constitution Center
(see pp48–9)

Pennsylvania Academy of the Fine Arts
(see pp74–5)

Philadelphia Museum of Art
(see pp88–91)

Reading Terminal Market
(see p73)

Penn's Landing
(see p66)

Liberty Place
(see p79)

◁ Staircase and Grand Foyer of the Pennsylvania Academy of the Fine Arts

Philadelphia's Best: Museums

PHILADELPHIA HAS SEVERAL world-famous museums that reflect its cultural diversity, as well as its maritime and colonial past. Many are sited along the Benjamin Franklin Parkway, including the Franklin Institute Science Museum, Academy of Natural Sciences, and the Philadelphia Museum of Art, which is the third-largest fine arts museum in the country. The Rodin Museum near Logan Square houses the largest collection of sculptor Auguste Rodin's works outside Paris, while the University of Pennsylvania Museum of Archaeology and Anthropology, just across the Schuylkill River, has an excellent collection of remnants from civilizations past and present. A few miles northwest of the city, the Barnes Foundation has an extraordinary collection of Impressionist and Postimpressionist art.

Philadelphia Museum of Art
This museum houses over 300,000 objects, including a 12th-century stone portal from a French Augustinian abbey (see pp88–91).

Rodin Museum
The Shade *is just one of nearly 130 plaster, bronze, and marble sculptures housed in an impressive temple-like structure along the Benjamin Franklin Parkway (see p86).*

Logan Square and the Museum District

Franklin Institute Science Museum
The Giant Walk-Through Heart *is a key exhibit of this children-friendly science museum named after statesman and inventor Benjamin Franklin (see p85).*

Center City

Academy of Natural Sciences
A favorite exhibit at Philadelphia's natural history museum is Dinosaur Hall, *home to fossil constructions of the largest carnivores to ever walk the earth (see p85).*

Pennsylvania Academy of the Fine Arts
An ornate, arched foyer is the entrance to the country's oldest art school and museum. It was founded in 1805 with a collection of American paintings by artists such as Benjamin West and Impressionist Mary Cassatt (see pp74–5).

The African American Museum in Philadelphia
This museum celebrates important aspects of African-American history through permanent and changing exhibitions (see p51).

Atwater Kent Museum
Philadelphia's official history museum has a collection of over 100,000 objects, including Norman Rockwell's Saturday Evening Post *covers depicting "vignettes of daily life" (see p50).*

Old City

National Museum of American Jewish History
Located in Old City, this museum has a collection of nearly 10,000 artifacts, some dating to the 18th century, showcasing the history of Jews in America (see p46).

Society Hill and Penn's Landing

Independence Seaport Museum
A prominent seafaring museum, showcasing the submarine Becuna *and the cruiser* Olympia. *This is a view of the interior of the submarine* Becuna *(see pp64–5).*

0 meters   500

0 yards   500

Philadelphia's Architecture

EARLY ARCHITECTURAL STYLES, derived from the colonists' native Britain, can still be seen in the older areas of Philadelphia. Colonial buildings incorporated simple Georgian and Palladian designs, which evolved into a bolder Federal style, with touches of Roman and Greek classical styles. The 19th century brought grander designs fueled by the Victorian era and the French-influenced Beaux-Arts style, which inspired many of the city's architectural wonders along the Benjamin Franklin Parkway. While modernist buildings crowd parts of Center City, it is the scattering of postmodernist skyscrapers that enliven the city skyline.

Philadelphia Merchants' Exchange, an example of the Greek Revival style

Betsy Ross House, a simple Georgian-style structure

GEORGIAN

NAMED AFTER three British kings called George, this architectural style proliferated in early 18th-century Britain and soon became popular in colonial Philadelphia. Developed from the Roman Palladian style and often with columned façades, many of the early Georgian-style designs in the colonies were less elaborate than their English counterparts.

Independence Hall (see pp42–3) is a Georgian structure influenced by the style of English master architect Christopher Wren, while Christ Church (see p52) is a bold example of Georgian ecclesiastical architecture. colonial Georgian-style homes include the Deshler-Morris House, which was George Washington's summer retreat, and Cliveden, both in Germantown (see pp106–107). Both houses

have columned doorways and nine front windows. A more simple home is the Betsy Ross House (see p52).

FEDERAL

IN COLONIAL America, the Georgian style quickly evolved into a more sophisticated Federal style, often with classical Greek and Roman influences. Particularly popular after the American Revolution until about 1820, this architectural style is characterized by oval and circular rooms, classical entryway detailing, rounded fanlights over doors, and Palladian windows. Also typical of this style are free-standing mansions and town houses with symmetrical brick façades and shuttered windows. Entrances are often cut from granite slabs and feature gently fluted columns. The largest and most elegant rooms of Federal houses are usually

found on the second floor. Some stately examples of such architecture are Old City Hall, Congress Hall, and the east and west wings of Independence Hall. Idyllic Fairmount Park, next to the Schuylkill River, has several mansions built with this architectural style, including Sweetbriar, Strawberry Mansion, and Lemon Hill, which has oval rooms on all three floors (see pp108–109).

GREEK REVIVAL

PHILADELPHIA'S MERCHANTS' Exchange (see p54), with a four-columned Corinthian portico at one end and an unusual, semi-circular portico at the other, testifies to the nation's infatuation with Greek Revival architecture in the 1830s. It was designed by the up-and-coming architect William Strickland, already noted for designing the steeple atop Independence Hall. He also

Strawberry Mansion, a Federal-style house in Fairmount Park

Parlor of the Victorian-style Ebenezer Maxwell House

drafted the architectural plan for another prominent Greek Revival structure, the imposing Second Bank of the US *(see p47)*, with sturdy stone columns on its Greek temple-like façade.

A smaller Greek Revival structure, which now houses the Atwater Kent Museum *(see p50)*, was designed by John Haviland, a contemporary of Strickland. This was the first home of the Franklin Institute *(see p85)*, where Strickland and other architects taught the new nation's first architecture classes.

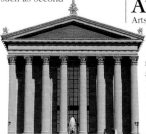

Detail of Philadelphia Museum of Art façade

VICTORIAN

Ornate, VICTORIAN-style façades were designed for Philadelphia buildings from the 1850s onwards. Victorian-era architecture is influenced by various styles, such as Second

Colonnaded entrance of the Beaux-Arts style Philadelphia Museum of Art

Empire, Italianate, and Gothic Revival. For example, City Hall *(see p72)*, with its colonnades and mansard roof, is a French Second Empire design. The Academy of Music *(see p76)*, designed by prominent 19th-century architect and Philadelphia native Napoleon LeBrun, is Italianate in style, with period gas lamps on its high-windowed façade and lavish interiors. The Italianate Revival Athenaeum also has gas lamps on its walls. The city's only authentically restored Victorian home is the Ebenezer Maxwell House in Germantown *(see pp106–107)*, which is capped with a high tower, a mansard, and gable roof design.

BEAUX-ARTS

AMERICAN architects trained at the École des Beaux-Arts in France brought home this Greek- and Roman-influenced style of architecture, with elaborate detailing, balustrades, and prominent columns. Due to the grandiosity and size of these structures, Beaux-Arts became the favored style for court houses, government buildings, museums, and railroad terminals, and was used in many

late 19th- and early 20th-century buildings. The 1876 centennial celebration in Philadelphia ushered in Fairmount Park's Memorial Hall *(see p109)*, dotted with bronze sculptures and topped by a glass and iron dome creating a spacious atrium.

With one of the city's most splendid Corinthian porticos, 30th Street Station *(see p184)* is an example of this grand style, as is the Philadelphia Museum of Art *(see pp88–91)*. Displaying much of the same grandeur is the Free Library of Philadelphia *(see p84)*, and the similar structure next to it, both with porticos sheltering imposing colonnaded façades. On a smaller scale, the nearby temple-like Rodin Museum *(see p86)* features columns and a portico topped with a balustrade.

Philadelphia's skyscrapers, Liberty One *(left)* and Mellon Bank Center

POSTMODERNIST

THE LATE 20th century witnessed a rebellion against the box-like glass and steel structures built after World War II. Thus was born the postmodern era in architecture, which featured sleek modernism tempered by conservative and historical design. This is evident in the shining twin towers of Liberty Place *(see p79)* with their pointed apexes. Also in the same style are the top floors of the red granite Bell Atlantic Tower that recede in a unique design, while the 54-story Mellon Bank Center building is crowned with a pyramid-like dome.

Philadelphia's Best: Parks and Gardens

WILLIAM PENN WANTED his city to be "a green countrie towne" and included five squares in his original city grid. Today, three of these, Logan, Rittenhouse, and Washington Squares, are pleasant areas with trees and park benches. Along the Schuylkill River on the outskirts of Center City is Fairmount Park, which has an extensive greenbelt and gardens and forms part of the city's park system. The park has biking and walking paths along the river and one of its tributaries, Wissahickon Creek, that runs within a gorge. Fairmount Park includes the peaceful Shofuso Japanese House and Garden and restored historic houses that were once the homes of the colonial elite. Beyond Philadelphia, near the Delaware state border, are the exquisite Longwood Gardens.

Morris Arboretum and Gardens
Located in the Chestnut Hill neighborhood, this scenic tract of land includes ponds, greenhouses, meadows, and gardens with thousands of rare plants and "trees-of-record" (see p95).

Longwood Gardens
22 miles (35 km)

Longwood Gardens
Industrialist Pierre S. du Pont designed this extravagant horticultural wonderland filled with spectacular choreographed fountains, whimsical topiaries, conservatories with exotic plants, and meadows and gardens replete with more than 11,000 varieties of indoor and outdoor plants (see p128).

0 kilometers 2

0 miles 2

Fairmount Park
This extensive greenbelt along the Schuylkill River and Wissahickon Creek is dotted with statues and features miles of running and biking paths (see p95).

Wissahickon Gorge
The country's only covered bridge within a major city is sited on a hiking trail in this gorge, whose forests and creek are home to over 100 bird species.

Logan Square
This grand square was once used as a burial ground and pastureland. Its centerpiece is a majestic circular, multi-spouted fountain designed by sculptor Alexander Stirling Calder (see p84).

Washington Square and Tomb of the Unknown Soldier
Named in honor of George Washington, the first president of the US, the centerpiece of this peaceful park is his statue, and the tomb of the unknown soldier of the Revolutionary War (see p60).

Welcome Park
Named after Penn's ship, this park was completed in 1982, three centuries after the founding of Philadelphia. Marble slabs depicting the city's original grid crisscross the park (see p55).

Rittenhouse Square
Center City's most popular park often fills with downtown workers who lunch under the trees. Reminiscent of New York's Central Park, it is flanked by upscale restaurants (see p78).

PHILADELPHIA THROUGH THE YEAR

MODERATING MID-ATLANTIC coastal waters often temper the effects of extreme heat and harsh cold, making Philadelphia's summers enjoyable and the winters bearable. Spring flowers and warmer temperatures breathe new life into the city, with restaurants and cafés setting up tables outdoors, while city residents head to parks and riverfronts, anticipating summer festivals and excursions to beaches and lakes. Activities continue outdoors in fall, which heralds a rush of cool air and colorful foliage to Philadelphia's forested greenbelts. After Thanksgiving, activities tend to move indoors with a rush of Christmas shoppers to quaint boutiques and shopping malls. Sports and cultural activities are in full swing during the winter months, right through to spring.

Phillies logo

School and college track teams compete at the Penn Relays

SPRING

CHERRY BLOSSOMS bloom along the Schuylkill River in early spring, as Philadelphians flock to the Kelly Drive river walk to enjoy the warmer weather. April also signals the start of the Philadelphia Phillies' baseball season.

MARCH

The Book and the Cook Festival *(mid-Mar)*, Fort Washington Expo Center. Local restaurants welcome cookbook authors for special dining events. It also features a culinary market.
Philadelphia Flower Show *(mid-Mar)*, Pennsylvania Convention Center. Largest indoor flower show in the United States.
St. Patrick's Day Parade *(mid-Mar)*, Center City. Celebrates Philadelphia's strong Irish heritage.

APRIL

Philadelphia Antiques Show *(mid-Apr)*, 33rd Street Armory. Dealers from across the United States gather to display their unique finds.
Philadelphia Film Festival *(mid-Apr)*. Showcases the best in independent and foreign cinema.
Philadelphia Furniture and Furnishings Show *(mid-Apr)*, Pennsylvania Convention Center. The country's premier exhibition and sale of artisan-designed and manufactured furniture and home furnishings.
Penn Relays *(late Apr)*, Franklin Field. High school and college track stars compete in the longest uninterrupted collegiate track meet in the nation.
Equality Forum *(late Apr)*. Begun in the 1960s, this week-long gathering celebrates the cultural and political legacy of the gay, lesbian, bisexual, and transgender communities.
International Children's Festival *(end Apr)*, Annenberg Center for the Performing Arts. Jugglers, folk singers, puppeteers, and dancers delight young audiences.
Philadelphia Phillies Baseball *(Apr–Sep)*, Citizens Bank Park. The season starts with many home games at the 43,500-capacity park.

Juggler in action

Blooms at the Philadelphia Flower Show, a spring-time celebration

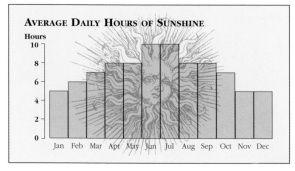

AVERAGE DAILY HOURS OF SUNSHINE

Hours

Sunshine Chart
This chart shows the average daily number of hours of sunshine in Philadelphia each month. June, July, and August have long days with lots of sunshine. Spring and fall have lesser hours of sunshine, with the shortest days in winter, which can still have ample hours of bright sun on clear, cold days.

MAY

Broad Street Run *(early May)*, Olney to south Philadelphia. This 10-mile (16-km) run raises funds for the American Cancer Society.
Dad Vail Regatta *(second weekend)*, Schuylkill River at Kelly Drive. Largest collegiate regatta in the United States with more than 100 colleges and universities participating.
Jam on the River *(last weekend)*, Penn's Landing. The biggest party on Memorial Day, it features rock and blues music.
Devon Horse Show and Country Fair *(late May and early Jun)*, Devon Show Grounds. Equestrian talents on display at the country's oldest and largest event of its kind. Features contests and an old-fashioned fair.
Mann Center for the Performing Arts *(May–Sep)*, Fairmount Park. Performances through the summer by the Philadelphia Orchestra, Philly Pops, and others.
Penn's Landing Festivals *(May–Sep)*. Concerts along with ethnic events for families.
Annual Student Exhibition *(May/Jun)*, Pennsylvania Academy of the Fine Arts. This century-old tradition displays the works of advanced and award-winning students.

SUMMER

Summer ushers in a variety of festivals and live music on Penn's Landing. Fairmount Park fills with

picnickers and thousands jam roadways to the New Jersey shore. Philadelphians celebrate the nation's birth, which took place in their own city, on the Fourth of July with remembrances, concerts, parades, and a massive display of fireworks near the Philadelphia Museum of Art.

JUNE

US Pro Cycling Championships *(first week)*. Philadelphia Museum of Art to Manayunk. The country's largest one-day professional cycling race.
Bloomsday *(Jun 16)*, Rosenbach Museum & Library. James Joyce fans celebrate the day on which Leopold Bloom, the protagonist of Joyce's *Ulysses*, made his "odyssey" through Dublin.
Odunde Afrikan American Street Festival *(mid-Jun)*, South Street. Celebrates the Yoruba New Year, beginning with a procession to the Schuylkill River and ending with a lively street fair.
Manayunk Arts Festival *(late Jun)*, Main Street. The region's largest outdoor arts and craft festival.

US Pro Cycling Championship on the 14.4-mile (23.2-km) circuit

Fourth of July fireworks over the Philadelphia Museum of Art

JULY

Sunoco Welcome America *(week leading up to Jul 4)*. A week-long celebration with free events for all ages.
Fourth of July Parade *(Jul 4)*, Center City. Parade with fireworks over the Philadelphia Museum of Art.
Let Freedom Ring *(Jul 4)*, Liberty Bell Center. Descendants of those who signed the Declaration of Independence tap the Liberty Bell.
Philadelphia International Gay & Lesbian Film Festival *(mid–late Jul)*. Largest show on the East Coast showcasing gay and lesbian films.

AUGUST

Philadelphia Folk Festival *(late Aug)*, Schwenksville. One of the oldest active folk festivals, this has folk music, dance, storytelling, and crafts.
Philadelphia Eagles Football *(Aug–Dec)*, Lincoln Financial Field. The season features several home games.

AVERAGE MONTHLY PRECIPITATION

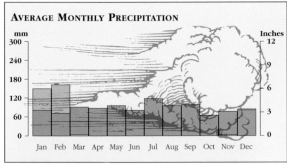

Rainfall Chart
This chart shows the average monthly rainfall and snowfall. The heaviest rain is in July and August, with a yearly average of 41 inches. Considerable snow falls in January and February. The annual snowfall average is 21 inches.

■ Rainfall (from baseline)

■ Snow (from baseline)

Rowers in Lancaster County in the fall

FALL

SUMMER GRADUALLY gives way to cooler temperatures by mid-September, as thousands of students flock to colleges and universities. The bright reds and yellows of fall foliage begin to make an appearance by the end of September, with dramatic colors in October and early November. Football season gets into high gear, as fans head out to watch the Philadelphia Eagles. Autumn also kicks off many cultural activities, signaling a new season for the city's world-class performing arts, opera, and symphony companies.

SEPTEMBER

Philadelphia Fringe Festival *(early–mid Sep).* Avant-garde performances and street theater for two weeks at various locations.
Von Steuben Day Gala and Parade *(late Sep),* Center City. Celebrates the city's German heritage and pays tribute to Baron Friedrich von Steuben, a general in the Revolutionary War.
Puerto Rican Day Parade *(last Sun),* Center City. Celebrating Puerto Rican heritage with a festival and parade.
Philadelphia College Festival *(late Sep or early Oct).* College Day concert in the Benjamin Franklin Parkway, plus various career fairs and cultural events.

OCTOBER

Pulaski Day Parade *(first Sun),* Center City. Pays tribute to the Polish Revolutionary War hero, General Casimir Pulaski.
Columbus Day Parade *(second Sun),* South Broad Street. The parade honors explorer Christopher Columbus and the Italian American community.
Philadelphia Open Studio Tours *(mid-Oct).* Local artists throughout the city open their workshops for two weekends.
Philadelphia 76ers Basketball *(Oct–Apr),* Wachovia Center. NBA basketball season begins with a number of home games.
Philadelphia Flyers Hockey *(Oct–May),* Wachovia Center. The NHL hockey season kicks off with home games.
Terror Behind the Walls *(mid-Oct through Oct 31),* Eastern State Penitentiary. A "haunted" house in the former prison celebrates Halloween.

NOVEMBER

Philadelphia Museum of Art Craft Show *(first week),* Pennsylvania Convention Center. Features handmade textiles, jewelry, household wares, and more.
Philadelphia Marathon *(third Sun).* A 26-mile (42-km) run through the city starts and ends at the Philadelphia Museum of Art.
Thanksgiving Day Parade *(fourth Thu).* Benjamin Franklin Parkway. The oldest such parade in the country.

Colorful floats and giant balloons at the Thanksgiving Day Parade

AVERAGE MONTHLY TEMPERATURE

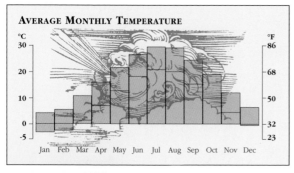

°C
30
20
10
0
-5

°F
86
68
50
32
23

Jan Feb Mar Apr May Jun Jul Aug Sep Oct Nov Dec

Temperature Chart
Spring is usually mild with some brisk days. Summer can be hot and muggy on certain days, although most days are comfortable. Fall brings clear and colder days. In winter, wind chills sometimes drop temperatures to below freezing, but many days are refreshingly chilly and bright.

Christmas lights at Lord and Taylor, Wanamaker Building

WINTER

STRINGS OF sparkling lights illuminate streets, buildings, and trees throughout Center City and beyond, as Christmas shoppers throng the city's main shopping districts. New Year's Day brings the Mummers Day Parade, one of Philadelphia's most honored traditions, in which costumed revelers and string bands march down the street. Sports enthusiasts spend the winter months attending Philadelphia 76ers basketball and Flyers hockey games.

DECEMBER

Christmas Tree Lighting
(Wed after Thanksgiving), City Hall. Signals the start of the holiday season.
Philadelphia Holiday Festival *(dates vary)*. Citywide performances by Mummers string bands, festivities, lighting events, and even tax-free shopping for shoes and clothing.

Washington Crossing the Delaware River Reenactment *(Dec 25)*, Washington Crossing. Reenactment of this historic turning point in the American Revolutionary War.
New Year's Eve *(Dec 31)*, Penn's Landing. A night of celebrations with fireworks along the Delaware River.
The Nutcracker *(dates vary)*, Academy of Music. Part of Pennsylvania Ballet's season, productions of this ballet are put on before Christmas.

JANUARY

Mummers Day Parade
(Jan 1), Center City. A Philadelphia tradition, where upto 20,000 people in decorative costumes parade to the music of string bands.
Chinese New Year Celebrations *(dates vary)*, Chinatown. Parades and festivities for two weeks.
Welcome Spring *(mid-Jan through Mar)*, Longwood Gardens. Indoor displays of bulbs, trees, and flowers create the illusion of spring during the winter months.

FEBRUARY

Philadelphia International Auto Show *(first week)*, Pennsylvania Convention Center. Highlights the latest in classic and luxury cars.
Mardi Gras *(Fat Tuesday before Ash Wednesday)*, South Street. Day-long revelry and celebration.
African American History Month *(all month)*. Various events throughout the city.

PUBLIC HOLIDAYS

New Year's Day (Jan 1)
Martin Luther King Day (3rd Mon in Jan)
Presidents' Day (3rd Mon in Feb)
Memorial Day (Last Mon in May)
Independence Day (Jul 4)
Labor Day (1st Mon in Sep)
Columbus Day (2nd Mon in Oct)
Veterans Day (Nov 11)
Thanksgiving Day (4th Thu in Nov)
Christmas Day (Dec 25)

Mummers Day Parade, a Philadelphia New Year's Day tradition

Georgian-style houses on Elfreth's Alley, the oldest continuously-occupied street in the US ▷

PHILADELPHIA AREA BY AREA

OLD CITY 38-55
SOCIETY HILL AND PENN'S LANDING 56-67
CENTER CITY 68-79
LOGAN SQUARE AND THE MUSEUM DISTRICT 80-91
FARTHER AFIELD 92-101
TWO GUIDED WALKS AND A DRIVE 102-109

OLD CITY

T HE FOUNDATIONS of Philadelphia, and all of the United States, are rooted in the neighborhood of Old City, which includes the Liberty Bell and Independence Hall, both of which form part of Independence National Historical Park. This area was settled by city founder William Penn and his fellow Quakers in the late

Plaque at Independence Hall

1600s. It later served as the seat of government for rebellious colonial patriots during the American Revolution in the 1770s. Today, well-preserved historical structures, buildings, and homes that date back to the 18th and 19th centuries, some still situated on narrow cobblestoned streets, stand alongside modern buildings and high-rises.

SIGHTS AT A GLANCE

Historical Buildings and Districts
Arch Street Friends
  Meeting House **7**
Betsy Ross House **20**
Bishop White House **27**
Carpenters' Hall **25**
Christ Church Burial Ground **8**
City Tavern **29**
Curtis Center and Dream
  Garden Mosaic **13**
Declaration House **15**
Elfreth's Alley **19**
First Bank of the US **24**
Franklin Court and B. Free
  Franklin Post Office **22**

Free Quaker Meeting House **4**
Independence Hall pp42–3 **1**
Philadelphia Merchants'
  Exchange **28**
Philosophical Hall and
  Library Hall **12**
Second Bank of the US **11**
Todd House **26**
US Mint **6**

Museums and Galleries
The African American Museum
  in Philadelphia **16**
Atwater Kent Museum **14**
Fireman's Hall Museum **18**
Independence Visitor Center **3**

Liberty Bell Center p44 **2**
*National Constitution
  Center pp48–9* **5**
National Liberty Museum **23**
National Museum of American
  Jewish History **9**

Places of Worship
Christ Church **21**
Mikveh Israel **10**
St. George's Church **17**

Parks and Gardens
Welcome Park **30**

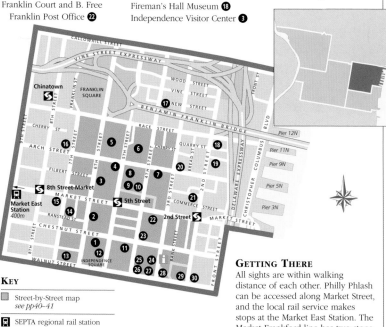

KEY

- Street-by-Street map
  see pp40–41
- **R** SEPTA regional rail station
- **S** SEPTA subway stop
- **i** Visitor information

0 meters 500
0 yards 500

GETTING THERE
All sights are within walking distance of each other. Philly Phlash can be accessed along Market Street, and the local rail service makes stops at the Market East Station. The Market-Frankford line has two stops in Old City, at 2nd and Market, and 5th and Market. SEPTA buses 21, 38, and 42 also have stops in Old City.

◁ **The south face of Georgian-style Independence Hall, formerly known as the State House**

Street-by-Street: Independence National Historical Park

K NOWN LOCALLY AS Independence Mall, this urban park encompasses several well-preserved 18th-century structures associated with the American Revolution. The Declaration of Independence that heralded the birth of a new nation was signed in this historic area. Dominated by the tall brick tower of Independence Hall, the park includes the oldest street in Philadelphia, the US Mint, and several special-interest museums that explore Philadelphia's colonial and seafaring past, as well as its ethnic heritage. At least 20 of the buildings are open to the public.

Plaque commemorating Independence Hall

US Mint
This mint, the oldest in the country, struck its first coins in 1793. It also mints commemorative coins such as the Eisenhower dollar ❻

Christ Church Burial Ground ❽

ARCH STREET

5TH STREET

7TH STREET

★ National Constitution Center
This museum features interactive exhibits explaining the US Constitution. Visitors can walk among life-sized statues of the delegates who were present when this document was adopted in 1787 ❺

Free Quaker Meeting House ❹

KEY

- – – Suggested route

STAR SIGHTS

- ★ National Constitution Center
- ★ Liberty Bell Center
- ★ Independence Hall

Independence Visitor Center
Located in what is called "America's most historic square mile," the Independence Visitor Center provides visitors with practical information and a cutural and historical orientation. Timed tickets for Independence Hall are available here ❸

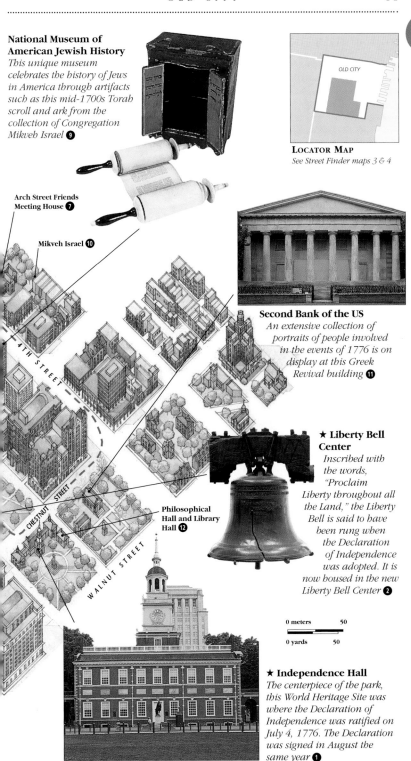

**National Museum of
American Jewish History**
*This unique museum
celebrates the history of Jews
in America through artifacts
such as this mid-1700s Torah
scroll and ark from the
collection of Congregation
Mikveh Israel* ⑨

LOCATOR MAP
See Street Finder maps 3 & 4

**Arch Street Friends
Meeting House** ⑦

Mikveh Israel ⑩

Second Bank of the US
*An extensive collection of
portraits of people involved
in the events of 1776 is on
display at this Greek
Revival building* ⑪

★ **Liberty Bell
Center**
*Inscribed with
the words,
"Proclaim
Liberty throughout all
the Land," the Liberty
Bell is said to have
been rung when
the Declaration
of Independence
was adopted. It is
now housed in the new
Liberty Bell Center* ❷

**Philosophical
Hall and Library
Hall** ⑫

0 meters   50

0 yards   50

★ **Independence Hall**
*The centerpiece of the park,
this World Heritage Site was
where the Declaration of
Independence was ratified on
July 4, 1776. The Declaration
was signed in August the
same year* ❶

Independence Hall ❶

Independence Hall tower clock

T HIS UNADORNED BRICK BUILDING and clock tower are the most important structures in Independence Hall National Park. Earlier designated the State House of Pennsylvania, it is the site of the drafting and signing of the US Constitution and the Declaration of Independence, the document that declared America's freedom from the British Empire in 1776. Designed by master carpenter Edmund Woolley and lawyer Andrew Hamilton, Independence Hall was completed in 1753, more than two decades after construction began. Today, the meeting rooms are simply furnished, as they were in the late 1700s, and park personnel re-create history by pointing out the Windsor-style chairs from which colonial leaders debated the contents of the Declaration.

West Wing

Congress Hall
Congress met in this hall from 1790 to 1800. Presidential inaugurations were also held here for George Washington and John Adams.

THE DECLARATION OF INDEPENDENCE

Following colonial resistance to British "taxation without representation," the first shots of rebellion rang out in 1775 at the battles of Concord and Lexington outside Boston. Within a year, a strong feeling for independence over-whelmed the colonies. Known for his powerful writing style, Thomas Jefferson, Virginia Delegate and future president, took on the task of drafting a document declaring independence. He eloquently asserted man's right to freedom and rebel-lion while listing colonial grievances against England's King George III. After making changes, the Continental Congress ratified the Declaration of Independence on July 4, 1776.

An original copy of the 1776 Declaration of Independence

★ **Great Essentials Exhibit**
On display here are original copies of the Declaration of Independence and the US Constitution, as well as this silver Syng inkstand, said to have been used during the signing of the documents.

★ Assembly Room

Amidst its simple desks and chairs, delegates of the Continental Congress debated and signed the new nation's Declaration of Independence in 1776. Eleven years later, the Constitution was drafted and signed here as well.

★ Rising Sun Chair

The chair used by George Washington during the 1787 Constitutional Convention depicts a symbolic sun rising over the new nation.

Long Gallery

Running the length of the second floor, this light-filled reception room also hosted 18th-century balls and banquets.

East Wing

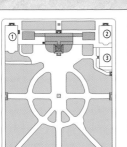

INDEPENDENCE HALL

① Congress Hall
② Old City Hall
③ Philosophical Hall

KEY

▢ Illustrated Area

▢ Lawn

STAR FEATURES

★ **Great Essentials Exhibit**

★ **Assembly Room**

★ **Rising Sun Chair**

Liberty Bell Center ❷

ORIGINALLY RUNG TO signal Pennsylvania Assembly meetings in the State House (now Independence Hall) in the mid-1700s, the Liberty Bell is one of the world's greatest symbols of freedom, bearing the inscription "Proclaim Liberty throughout all the Land unto all the Inhabitants thereof." Famous for its irreparable crack, the 2,080-lb (940-kg) bell was moved to its new home in the Liberty Bell Center in 2003. The center details the bell's history and significance, and how it became an icon for other freedom struggles. Clearly visible on the bell is the unsuccessful "stop drilling" repair, where, in 1846, the edges of the fracture were filed down to reduce friction and stress in an effort to slow the growth of the crack.

Multimedia Display Gallery
This gallery displays old newspaper reports, videos, and photographs of people who have fought for liberty, such as the Dalai Lama and Nelson Mandela.

The Liberty Bell
The bell cracked the first time it was rung in 1753. Recast twice by Philadelphia's Pass and Stow Foundry, it was placed in the steeple of the State House (now called Independence Hall). It is said to have been first referenced as "Bell of Liberty" by 19th-century abolitionists.

Curved wall

Entrance

Liberty Bell Center
The center is an elongated building where visitors first walk through a multimedia display gallery. This leads to the bell itself, set next to a large window with an excellent view of Independence Hall. Park rangers recount the bell's history, including how the crack was found and repaired in 1846. However, when it cracked once more, the bell could never be rung again.

LIBERTY BELL TIMELINE

1752 Pennsylvania Assembly orders the bell from Whitechapel Foundry in England	**1835** Termed "Bell of Liberty" by abolitionists	**1944** Tapped during Normandy Invasion on June 6		**1988** Liberty Bell Medal created	
	1841–45 Cracks again in this period				
1750	**1800**	**1850**	**1900**	**1950**	**2000**
1776 Possibly rung on July 8 after first public reading of the Declaration of Independence			**1976** Moved from Independence Hall to outside pavilion for country's bicentennial		
1753 It cracks when first rung, and is recast twice		**1915** Tapped when transcontinental telephone service started		**2003** Bell moved to new Liberty Bell Center	

Independence Visitor Center ❸

6th & Market Sts. **Map** 4 D2.
📞 (215) 965-7676. 🚇 Market
East Station. 🚊 5th St. 🚌 Philly
Phlash. 🕐 Oct– Jun: 8:30am–5pm
Mon–Sun; Jul–Sep: open later.
● Jan 1, Thanksgiving, Dec 25.
♿ 📷 🎁 Ⓦ www.
independencevisitorcenter.com

Ｏｎｅ of the first stops for
any visitor to Philadelphia
should be the Independence
Visitor Center. It was opened
in 2001 as part of the
Independence Mall redevelopment project, which also
included the Liberty Bell and
National Constitution Centers.

This expansive center offers
information on more than
4,000 attractions in the city
and its environs. Apart from
screening historical and orientation films, such as the short
film *Independence* directed
by John Huston, it has maps
and brochures, touch-screen
information kiosks, daily
listings of events, and trip
planning services. Both
National Park Service rangers
and City of Philadelphia
tourism specialists provide
assistance and advice about
historical sights, attractions,
shopping, and dining. A gift
shop has all manner of
souvenirs themed around
Philadelphia.

Of particular interest at the
center is a rotating exhibition
of original engravings of

**Plain brick façade of the 18th-century
Free Quaker Meeting House**

colonial Philadelphia by
William Russell Birch, which
were first published in 1800.
Prints of his original engravings line the entrance corridor
leading in from Market Street.

The center is the first stop
for visitors to Independence
Hall as well, since timed-entry
tickets for the hall are available here on a first-come-first-
served basis.

Free Quaker Meeting House ❹

Arch & 5th Sts. **Map** 4 D2.
🚇 Market East Station. 🚊 5th St.
🚌 Philly Phlash. 🕐 1–5pm Wed–
Sun. 📷 ♿

Ｔｈｉｓ ｓｉｍｐｌｅ Georgian brick
building was built in 1783
for Quakers who were com-
pelled to bear arms in the
American Revolution. Bearing
arms meant going against the
pacifist beliefs of the order,

which led inevitably to
expulsion from the main
Quaker community. A
group of about 200 such
people called themselves
the "Free Quakers" and
founded a meetinghouse
of their own. However, in
the years that followed,
attendance dropped to
perhaps a few dozen, and
by 1834, only two Free
Quakers, Betsy Ross and
John Price Wetherill, still
attended meetings. Shortly
thereafter, the meeting-
house was permanently
closed. Since then, the
building has served as a
school, a library, and a
warehouse.

Today, the building still
contains two benches and a
window from colonial
times. Also on
display is Betsy
Ross's five-
pointed star
tissue pattern,
which she is
said to have
used to shape
stars to make
the colonial-era
American flag.
Today, the
descendants of
the original Free Quakers
hold their annual meetings
here to decide how to dis-
tribute funds generated by
rental of the hall and how
best to invest income for
charitable purposes. Actors
dressed in colonial garb give
talks and interpretations of
the building's history, and
guides demonstrate how
to cut a five-pointed
star in one snip.

**Free Quaker
Meeting House**

The Independence Visitor Center, in the middle of "America's most historic square mile"

National Constitution Center 5

See pp48–9.

US Mint 6

5th & Arch Sts. **Map** 4 D2. ☎ *(215) 408-0112.* 🚆 *Market East Station.* 🚇 *5th St.* 🚌 *Philly Phlash.* ⛔ *closed to the public.* 🚶 *group tours by prior arrangement.* [W] www.usmint.gov
Federal Reserve Bank of Philadelphia 6th & Arch Sts. ☎ *(215) 574-6257.* 🕐 *Jun–Aug: 9:30am– 4:30pm Mon–Fri; 10am–4pm Sat– Sun; Sep–May: 9:30am–4:30pm Mon–Fri.*

The Philadelphia Mint, the oldest in the US, produces gold bullion coins and medals, and also makes most of the coins that Americans use everyday. The first US coins, minted in 1793, were copper pennies intended solely for commerce in the colonies. Today, 24 hours a day, five days a week, hundreds of machines and operators, in a room the size of a football field, blank, anneal, count, and bag millions of dollars worth of pennies, dimes, and quarters. The gift shop, open on a limited basis, sells commemorative coins and numismatic collectables.

A related exhibit, Money in Motion, is on display at the **Federal Reserve Bank of Philadelphia**, which is located one block west of the US Mint. It explains US monetary policy and history with the help of interactive computer screens and impressive exhibits.

Philadelphia's oldest Quaker meetinghouse, on Arch Street

Arch Street Friends Meeting House 7

320 Arch St. **Map** 4 E2. ☎ *(215) 627-2667.* 🚆 *Market East Station.* 🚇 *2nd St.* 🚌 *Philly Phlash.* 🕐 *10am–4pm Mon–Sat.* ✝ *10:30am Sun; 7pm Wed.* [W] www.archstreetfriends.org

This brick structure is the oldest Quaker meetinghouse still in use in Philadelphia. Built in 1804, the site first served as a Quaker burial ground, but later accommodated victims of the yellow fever epidemic in the 1790s. Today, the house has a central hall and two adjacent meeting rooms. The East Room features Quaker artifacts and six dioramas depicting William Penn's life as a Quaker. The West Room contains worn wooden benches and now serves as the main meeting and worship hall.

Headstone, Christ Church Burial Ground

Christ Church Burial Ground 8

5th & Arch Sts. **Map** 4 D2. ☎ *(215) 922-1695.* 🚆 *Market East Station.* 🚇 *5th St.* 🚌 *Philly Phlash.* 🕐 *10am– 4pm Mon–Sat; noon–4pm Sun.* 📷 🚶 [W] www.christchurchphila.org

This crammed cemetery dates back to 1719, and is an expansion of the church's original graveyard. More than 5,000 people are buried here, most from colonial times. The burial ground is the final resting place of Benjamin Franklin, his wife Deborah, and their daughter and son-in-law Sarah Franklin and Richard Bache. Four other signers of the Declaration of Independence – Dr. Benjamin Rush, Francis Hopkinson, George Ross, and Joseph Hewes – are also buried here. Franklin's grave is on the perimeter of the grounds, and is visible through an iron grating. Passers-by toss coins on the grave, both showing respect and following a tradition that is supposed to bring good luck. With headstones already deteriorating by the mid-19th century, all gravestone inscriptions were copied and published in 1864 in order to preserve records of people interred in this graveyard.

National Museum of American Jewish History 9

Independence Mall East, 55 N 5th St. **Map** 4 D2. ☎ *(215) 923-5986.* 🚆 *Market East Station.* 🚇 *5th St.* 🚌 *Philly Phlash.* 🕐 *10am–5pm Mon–Thur, 10am–3pm Fri, noon–5pm Sun.* ⛔ *Sat, Jewish holidays.* ♿ [W] www.nmajh.org

The museum's mission of preserving and exploring the history of American Jews is carried out through its large collection of artifacts. The museum had only 40 objects when it was founded in 1976. Since then, the collection has

Inspecting coins at the US Mint

grown to more than 10,000 artifacts, including posters, photographs, ritual objects, books, and paintings. Of particular note are a 1789 prayer manuscript composed by Richmond Jews on the adoption of the US Constitution and a selection of Jewish cookbooks dating to the mid-19th century. On the grounds can be seen the impressive *Religious Liberty*, a massive marble monument by American Jewish sculptor, Sir Moses Jacob Ezekiel, which was dedicated in 1876.

Federal-style façade of Library Hall, a reproduction of the 1789 original

Mikveh Israel ❿

44 N 4th St. **Map** 4 E2. ❓ (215) 922-5446. ⬛ Market East Station. Ⓢ 5th St. 🚌 Philly Phlash. ⏰ 10am–5pm Mon–Thu; 10am–3pm Fri; noon–5pm Sun. ✴ Fri evenings & Sat. ♿ Ⓦ www.mikvehisrael.org

PHILADELPHIA'S OLDEST Jewish congregation, Mikveh Israel, dates to before the 1740s, when services were held in a private home. The congregation built its first synagogue in 1782, and moved into its current redbrick building in 1976.

Mikveh Israel's archival collection includes two pairs of Torah finials crafted by silversmith Myer Myers in 1772 and letters written by US Presidents George Washington and Abraham Lincoln. Past congregation members included colonial patriot and financier Haym Salomon; Nathan Levy, whose ship brought the Liberty Bell to America; and Rebecca Gratz, who founded educational and social institutions. The synagogue still holds a traditional service, which has remained virtually unchanged since the colonial era.

Second Bank of the United States ⓫

420 Chestnut St. **Map** 4 D3. ❓ (215) 965-7676, (800) 537-7676. ⬛ Market East Station. Ⓢ 5th St. 🚌 Philly Phlash. ⏰ hours vary. ♿

BUILT BETWEEN 1819 and 1824, this is one of America's finest examples of Greek Revival architecture. Once a repository that provided credit for federal government agencies and private businesses, it now houses a collection of 185 paintings from the late 18th and early 19th centuries. On view are portraits of colonial and federal leaders, military officers, explorers, scientists, and founding fathers.

Many of the portraits are by Charles Willson Peale (1741–1827), his brother James, and their respective children, who together form America's most distinguished family of artists. Peale began collecting portraits after the Revolutionary War. Today, 94 of his paintings, including likenesses of George Washington, Thomas Jefferson, and the Marquis de LaFayette,

the Continental Army's French ally, are on display, along with portraits by other artists.

Philosophical Hall and Library Hall ⓬

5th St between Chestnut & Walnut Sts. **Map** 4 D3. ❓ (215) 440-3400. ⬛ Market East Station. Ⓢ 5th St. 🚌 Philly Phlash. ⏰ Philosophical Hall: 10am–4pm Thu–Sun, varies with exhibits; Library Hall: 9am–4:45pm Mon–Fri (lobby exhibit). Ⓦ www.amphilsoc.org

A COLONIAL-ERA "think tank," the American Philosophical Society was founded in 1743 by Benjamin Franklin to promote the study of government, nature, science, and industry. Built in 1789, the Federal-style Philosophical Hall was a meeting place for doctors, clergymen, and the founding fathers of the nation. Reopened in 2001 for the first time since the early 19th century, the hall today hosts art, history, and science exhibitions.

The society also owns Library Hall, once the home of the Library Company founded by Franklin in 1731. The company's vast collections served as the Library of Congress until 1800. The current building, a reconstruction of the 1789 original, stores some of the society's most precious works, including the title page of an 1859 manuscript of Darwin's *Origin of Species*, the journals of explorers Lewis and Clark, and Jefferson's handwritten Declaration of Independence.

Redbrick exterior of Congregation Mikveh Israel

National Constitution Center ❺

Engraved Façade
"We the People," part of the opening words of the US Constitution, engraved on the façade of the center.

T HE INSCRIPTION "We the People" is boldly engraved on the massive Indiana limestone façade of this sprawling center, which was opened on July 4, 2003. It explains the US Constitution through more than 100 interactive and multimedia exhibits, including artifacts, sculptures, photographs, video, and film. Visitors can listen to President Franklin Delano Roosevelt's speeches or to actual arguments from Supreme Court cases at a replica of the Supreme Court Bench, or walk through a re-creation of the 19th-century Senate floor. The circular main hall also contains displays that illuminate the text of the Constitution and highlight the themes of liberty and freedom.

Washington's statue in Signers' Hall

THE US CONSTITUTION

After the Revolutionary War, delegates from the original 13 states, except Rhode Island, gathered in Philadelphia for the Constitutional Convention in 1787. It took them nearly four months to draft a document creating a strong centralized government for the new nation. Adopted on September 17, the Constitution ensures individual liberties and defines distinct powers for Congress, the president, and the federal courts, while also establishing a system of "Checks and Balances" so that no branch of government can dominate the others.

A copy of the Constitution of the United States

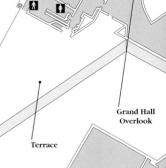

F.M. Kirby Auditorium and Theater

Grand Hall Overlook

Terrace

Grand Hall Lobby
Flags of US states hang from the Grand Hall's second floor overlook, from where the lobby's two-story glass windowpanes provide a stunning view of Independence Mall.

STAR EXHIBITS

★ "Freedom Rising"

★ American National Tree

★ Signers' Hall

Second
Floor

VISITORS' CHECKLIST

525 Arch St. **Map** 4 D2.
☎ (215) 409-6600. 🚇 Market
East Station. 🚋 5th St. 🚌 Philly
Phlash. ◻ 9:30am–5pm
Sun–Fri, 9:30am–6pm Sat.
● Thanksgiving, Dec 25.
🖼 ♿ 🚻 📷 🎁
Ⓦ www.constitutioncenter.org

★ "Freedom Rising"
*The circular, 350-seat
Kimmel Theater features
"Freedom Rising," a multimedia production that
narrates the story of the US Constitution. This
17-minute show is projected on a 360-degree screen.*

★ American National Tree
*With the "We the People" wall in the foreground,
the circular American National Tree features the
stories of 100 Americans who have influenced the
Constitution. Each story exemplifies tolerance,
diversity, and opportunity.*

Box Office

First Floor

Main Entrance

KEY

◻ Richard and Helen DeVos
Exhibit Hall

◻ Kimmel Theater

◻ Posterity Hall

◻ Signers' Hall

◻ F.M. Kirby Auditorium
and Theater

◻ First Public Printing of the
Constitution

◻ Non-exhibition space

CENTER GUIDE
*The Grand Hall Lobby
and Kimmel Theater are
on the ground floor.
Permanent displays and
interactive exhibits are
situated on the second
floor in the circular
DeVos Hall.*

★ Signers' Hall
*Walk among life-sized bronze
statues of the 39 men who
signed the Constitution
(including that of Benjamin
Franklin, seated in the front),
and the three who dissented.*

Curtis Center and Dream Garden Mosaic 13

6th & Walnut Sts. **Map** 4 D3. ☎ *(215) 238-6450.* 🚆 *Market East Station.* 🚇 *5th St.* 🚌 *Philly Phlash.* 🕒 *8am–6pm Mon–Fri, 10am–1pm Sat.* ♿

THIS BEAUX-ARTS building is where Cyrus Curtis kicked off his publishing empire in 1883 with the founding of the *Ladies Home Journal*. His publishing company also breathed new life into the *Saturday Evening Post*, and created popular magazines such as *American Home*, *Jack and Jill*, *Holiday*, and *Country Gentleman*.

Inside the building is the enormous *Dream Garden Mosaic*, a 49ft x 15ft (15m x 4.5m) glasswork that dominates the lobby. Designed by Maxfield Parrish, the mosaic was completed in 1916 by Louis Comfort Tiffany and Tiffany Studios. The artwork, depicting a garden with trees and streams, has more than 100,000 pieces of hand-fired favrile glass. In 1998, it was sold to a Las Vegas casino owner, but the people of Philadelphia resisted the move. Local artists and historians helped in raising $3.5 million for the Pennsylvania Academy of the Fine Arts *(see pp74–5)* to buy back the mosaic. It later underwent painstaking restoration.

Atwater Kent Museum 14

15 S 7th St. **Map** 4 D3. ☎ *(215) 685-4830.* 🚆 *Market East Station.* 🚇 *8th St.* 🚌 *Philly Phlash.* 🕒 *10am–5pm Wed–Mon.* ● *Jan 1, Thanksgiving, Dec 25.* 📷 🛍 [W] www.philadelphiahistory.org

PHILADELPHIA'S official history museum since 1938, the Atwater Kent Museum has a collection of 100,000 objects and images spanning 300 years. Designed by John Haviland in Greek Revival style and completed in 1826, this was the original home of the Franklin Institute. The nation's first architecture classes were taught here. The building was saved from demolition in 1935 when A. Atwater Kent purchased it for a museum. Today, a colorful walk-on map of the city of Philadelphia covers the entire first floor gallery. Objects displayed in past exhibitions have included furniture used by President George Washington while living in Philadelphia, Benjamin Franklin's wine glass, and the Wampum belt given to William Penn by the Lenni-Lenape *(see p18)*. The museum has an expansive collection of *Saturday Evening Post* covers showing "vignettes of daily life" in America by Norman Rockwell, who created 322 images for the Philadelphia-based magazine between 1916 and 1963.

Atwater Kent exterior detail

Declaration House, reconstructed in 1975 by National Park Service

Declaration House 15

7th & Market Sts. **Map** 4 D2. ☎ *(215) 965-7676, (800) 537-7676.* 🚆 *Market East Station.* 🚇 *8th St.* 🚌 *Philly Phlash.* 🕒 *hours vary, call to confirm.*

THE CURRENT brick structure of Declaration House is a 1975 reconstruction of the Georgian-style home where Thomas Jefferson drafted the Declaration of Independence *(see p42)* from June 11 to 28, 1776. He had rented two upstairs rooms from bricklayer Jacob Graff, who had built the house in 1775. Although only a few blocks from Independence Hall, the house faced a field and stable, and offered Jefferson a quieter setting to write the Declaration.

Today, along with a bust of the famous American statesman and third president, the house includes copies of Jefferson's rough drafts of the Declaration. The two

***Dream Garden Mosaic*, an enormous glass artwork gracing the Curtis Center lobby**

rooms upstairs contain period furnishings, and include re-creations of Jefferson's bedroom and parlor, where he wrote the document.

The African American Museum in Philadelphia

701 Arch St. **Map** 4 D2. ☎ (215) 574-0380. ▣ Market East Station. Ⓢ 5th St. ▦ Philly Phlash. ◯ 10am– 5pm Tue–Sat; noon–5pm Sun; Martin Luther King Day. ● Mon, public hols. ⬛ ▨ ◪ ⬛ ▦ www.aampmuseum.org

L'Ouverture by Ulrick Jean-Pierre, African American Museum

A SMITHSONIAN affiliate, this museum is one of several founded in Philadelphia during the nation's bicentennial year. The museum is dedicated to "collecting, preserving, and interpreting the material and intellectual culture of African Americans" in the local area and the Americas. Since opening in 1976, the museum's collection has swelled to more than 500,000 artifacts, including photographs, documents, fine and folk art, costumes, books, periodicals, and a number of other memorabilia.

Permanent and changing exhibitions recognize and celebrate important aspects of African-American life and history, including the Civil Rights movement, and contributions in diverse areas, such as the arts, entertainment, sports, medicine, politics, religion, law, and technology. A permanent exhibit features artifacts from and an overview of the ancient Nile Valley civilizations of Egypt, Nubia, and Aksum. Previous exhibitions at the museum have showcased African woodcarvings and textile designs while interpreting the traditions and ceremonies of several African countries. Others have focused on struggles against slavery and oppression, including the Haitian Revolution, which

Exhibit at the African American Museum

resulted in Haiti establishing the world's first Black republic in 1804. The museum also organizes regular workshops and demonstrations.

St. George's Church ⑰

235 N 4th St. **Map** 4 E2. ☎ (215) 925-7788. ▣ Market East Station. Ⓢ 5th St. ▦ Philly Phlash. ◯ 10am– 3pm Mon–Fri; Sun morning after worship; Sat by appt. ⬛

THE AMERICAN Methodist movement began in St. George's Church in 1769, making it the country's oldest Methodist church in continuous use. This simple brick structure, its inside walls adorned with a muted blue tint, has not changed much since it was remodeled in 1792. Colonial-era wooden pews and floorboards remain, as do the wrought iron candle chandeliers and candelabra, although now wired with electric lights. A two-room museum has 18th- and 19th-century artifacts, hymnals, bibles, and other important church keepsakes. They include a 1785 silver chalice from John Wesley, the founder of the movement, the original handwritten journals of Joseph Pilmoor, the first pastor of the church, and a bible from Francis Asbury, considered

the father of the American United Methodist Church.

St. Augustine's Church across the street dates back to 1796. Burned down in 1844 by anti-Catholic rioters, the current building was designed by architect Napoleon LeBrun and rebuilt in 1847.

Fireman's Hall Museum ⑱

147 N 2nd St. **Map** 4 E2. ☎ (215) 923-1438. ▣ Market East Station. Ⓢ 2nd St. ▦ Philly Phlash. ◯ 9am– 5pm Tue–Sat. ▦ www.mfrconsultants. com/pfd/museum.shtml

HOUSED IN AN old firehouse that was operational between 1902 and 1952, this unique museum narrates the history of firefighting in Philadelphia, back to colonial times. The building still contains the original brass sliding pole used for quick access to fire trucks. Several pieces of old equipment are on display, including an 1896 hook-and-ladder, a 1903 high-pressure Cannon Wagon, and a 1907 steam-powered pumper. Of special note are two well-preserved hand-pumpers, one from 1815, and the other from 1730, six years before Benjamin Franklin founded the nation's first fire department. Also on display are axes, saws, nozzles, old fire plaques indicating insured buildings, and leather fire hats from the early 19th century. A large stained-glass window memorializes fallen firefighters.

Façade of the Fireman's Hall Museum

's Alley ⓳

N 2nd St between Arch & Race Sts.
Map 4 E2. ▯ *Elfreth's Alley
Museum, 126 Elfreth's Alley, (215)
574-0560.* ▯ *Market East Station.*
▤ *2nd St.* ▤ *Philly Phlash.*
◯ *Mar–Oct: 10am–5pm Mon–Sat,
noon–5pm Sun; Nov–Feb: 10am–5pm
Thu–Sat, noon–5pm Sun.* ▨ ▯
▯ *www.elfrethsalley.org*

THE OLDEST continuously
occupied residential street
in the country, this narrow
cobblestoned lane is lined
with 33 historic homes, most
in simple Georgian style.
Named after Jeremiah Elfreth,
a blacksmith who built and
rented out some of the first
homes, the alley dates back
to 1702, when it was a path
used by carts hauling goods
from the Delaware River
docks. Its early occupants
were tradespeople, artisans,
and sea captains, while the
industrial boom later brought
in laborers and tailors.

The oldest homes are at 120
and 122, built between 1724
and 1728. The street's Museum
House, at 126, has been
restored to resemble the period between 1762 and 1794,
when it was owned by sisters-
in-law Mary Smith and Sarah
Milton, makers of mantuas
and dresses. The home at 124
is now a gift shop.

Halfway down the street is
yet another smaller alley,
Bladen Court, which includes
three houses and a charming
courtyard. Twice a year, in
June and December, many
Elfreth Alley residents open
their homes for tours.

**Betsy Ross House, where the first
American flag was sewn**

Betsy Ross House ⓴

239 Arch St. **Map** 4 E2. ▯ *(215)
686-1252.* ▯ *Market East Station.*
▤ *2nd St.* ▤ *Philly Phlash.*
◯ *Apr–Sep: 10am–5pm; Oct–Mar:
10am–5pm Tue–Sun.* ◯ *Jan 1,
Thanksgiving, Dec 25.* ▯ *limited
access.* ▯ *www.betsyrosshouse.org*

ONE OF PHILADELPHIA'S most
visited historic sites, this
simple colonial home was
where Quaker seamstress and
upholsterer Betsy Ross is said
to have sewn the first
American flag – although no
official documentation exists
to prove it. Instead, the story
was handed down through
generations of her family.
Nonetheless, the 1740 row
house has been restored to
around 1777, when Ross was
supposedly commissioned by
George Washington to
create the "Stars and Stripes"
for the struggling new nation.
The home, with narrow
stairwells and low ceilings,

is decorated with period
antiques and reproduction
pieces, but also has a few
original items that once
belonged to Ross, including
her eyeglasses, a family bible,
and an American Chippendale
walnut chest-on-chest.

Christ Church ⓴

2nd St above Market St. **Map** 4 E2.
▯ *(215) 922-1695.* ▯ *Market East
Station.* ▤ *2nd St.* ▤ *Philly Phlash.*
◯ *9am–5pm Mon–Sat; 1pm–5pm
Sun.* ◯ *Jan & Feb: Mon & Tue.*
▯ *9am & 11am Sun, noon Wed.*
▯ *www.christchurchphila.org*

FOUNDED IN 1695, Christ
Church was Philadelphia's
only Church of England parish
for 66 years. The existing
structure, built in 1754 in
Georgian style, after Wren's
London churches, was the
town's tallest building at the
time. Often called the "Nation's
Church," it was where revolu-
tionary leaders, including
Benjamin Franklin, Betsy
Ross, and George and Martha
Washington, once worshipped.
Plaques mark some pews
used by the colonial elite.

Inside is the baptismal font
in which William Penn was
baptized, dating from the 14th
century and donated by
London's All Hallows Church
in 1697. Bishop William White
(see p54), parish rector for 57
years, is buried in the chancel
of the church.

Franklin Court and B. Free Franklin Post Office ⓴

Between 3rd & 4th Sts and Chestnut
& Market Sts. **Map** 4 E3. ▯ *(215)
965-7676, (800) 537-7676.* ▯
Market East Station. ▤ *2nd St.* ▤
Philly Phlash. ◯ *court: hours vary;
post office: 9am–5pm Mon–Sat.* ▯

THIS EXPANSIVE court, which
cuts through an entire city
block, is where Benjamin
Franklin's home once stood.
Although razed in 1812, a
"Ghost House" frame depicts
the exact positions of the
house and adjacent print shop,
while excavations underneath

Elfreth's Alley, dating to the early 18th century

reveal the original foundations. An underground museum has exhibits explaining his accomplishments and features a few original family artifacts. On the court grounds are several former residences once owned by Franklin, which now house artifacts, replicas and demonstrations of colonial printing and bookbinding operations, and the B. Free Franklin Post Office and Museum, which has an active post office. Another building houses the restored offices of *The Aurora*, the newspaper published by Franklin's grandson, Benjamin Franklin Bache.

Classical façade of the First Bank, designed by Samuel Blodgett

Tribute to valor – the National Liberty Museum

National Liberty Museum 23

321 Chestnut St. **Map** 4 E3. ☎ *(215) 925-2800.* 🚉 *Market East Station.* 🚏 *2nd St.* 🚌 *Philly Phlash.* ○ *Jun–Aug: 10am–5pm; Sep–May: 10am–5pm Tue–Sun.* ● *Jan 1, Thanksgiving, Dec 25.* 💲 *for adults.* ♿ [W] www.libertymuseum.org

THROUGH EXHIBITS heralding freedom and diversity, the National Liberty Museum takes an unconventional approach to its mission of defusing violence and bigotry. Using various exhibits and displays, the museum honors 2,000 people worldwide who have stood up against repression. On display are life-sized dioramas of South Africa's Nelson Mandela in his jail cell, and concentration camp victim Anne Frank's Amsterdam bedroom, in which she hid from the Nazis. Another display has photographs of every rescue worker who died in the September 11, 2001 attacks. With over 100 glass artworks, the museum is the only one in the world to use glass as a symbol for freedom, and has a two-story structure, the *Flame of Liberty*, by Dale Chihuly, as its centerpiece.

First Bank of the United States 24

116 S 3rd St between Chestnut & Walnut Sts. **Map** 4 E3. ☎ *(215) 965-7676.* 🚉 *Market East Station.* 🚏 *2nd St.* 🚌 *Philly Phlash.* ● *closed to the public.*

THE DISPUTE over building the First Bank instigated the new nation's first debate on the interpretation of the US Constitution *(see pp48–9)*, which neither allowed nor prohibited the building of a federal bank. Alexander Hamilton, treasury secretary from 1789 to 1795, led the charge to provide the nation with a firm financial footing and a means to pay off the Revolutionary War debt. Chartered by President Washington and Congress in 1791, the bank building was completed six years later, with its classical design signifying culture and political maturity.

In 1811, Congress voted to withdraw the charter. The building was then occupied by Girard Bank through the 1920s, and finally taken over by the National Park Service in 1955. Original brick rooms and sheet iron vault doors still remain in the building, which is now used as storage and office space.

BENJAMIN FRANKLIN

Benjamin Franklin (1706–90)

Undoubtedly one of America's finest statesmen, Benjamin Franklin wore many hats as a printer, inventor, author, philosopher, postmaster, and diplomat. Born in Boston in 1706, Franklin moved to Philadelphia in 1723. He established the first library and fire department in the city, and upgraded its postal services. Franklin also founded the University of Pennsylvania and the Pennsylvania Hospital. During the Revolutionary War, he presided over the 1776 Constitutional Convention and helped draft the Declaration of Independence *(see p42)*. He traveled to Paris and won favor with the French who would come to America's aid against the British. In 1787, he signed the US Constitution, and died in Philadelphia three years later at the age of 84.

Carpenters' Hall 25

320 Chestnut St. **Map** 4 E3. *(215) 925-0167.* Market East Station. 5th St. Philly Phlash. Mar–Dec: 10am–4pm Tue–Sun; Jan–Feb: 10am–4pm Wed–Sun. Jan 1, Thanksgiving, Dec 25. www.carpentershall.org

AS THE NAME suggests, this two-story structure was built for the Carpenters' Company, the country's oldest trade guild, established in 1724. It played an important role in the Revolutionary War, secretly hosting the First Continental Congress in 1774.

Today, it displays original Windsor chairs, used during the Congress, and colonial-era carpenters' tools. Two rebuilt structures share the grounds – Pemberton House, named after a Quaker merchant, is now a gift shop, while the New Hall Military Museum displays weapons of the colonial army and navy. The original 1791 building housed War Department offices.

Georgian-style Carpenters' Hall, designed by Robert Smith in 1770

Todd House 26

4th & Walnut Sts. **Map** 4 D3. *(215) 965-7676.* Market East Station. 5th St. Philly Phlash. compulsory; free tickets available at Independence Visitor Center on first-come, first-served basis.

THIS GEORGIAN-STYLE home reflects the way the middle class lived in late 18th-century Philadelphia. What makes Todd House particularly interesting is its

Reconstructed dining room of Bishop White House

famous resident, Dolley Payne, who later married James Madison, the fourth president of the US. Built in 1775, the home was occupied by Dolley and her first husband, lawyer John Todd, both Quakers, from 1791 to 1793. Dolley lost Todd and their infant son in 1793 during the city's yellow fever epidemic. The following year, she met Madison during an arranged meeting.

Today, the three-story home has been restored to when John and Dolley Todd lived here, with furnishings that reflect subtle Quaker conservatism. Period items include replicas of Dolley's dressing table, and John Todd's first-floor law library, which contained more than 300 volumes.

Bishop White House 27

309 Walnut St. **Map** 4 E3. *(215) 965-7676.* Market East Station. 5th St. Philly Phlash. compulsory; free tickets available at Independence Visitor Center on first-come, first-served basis.

THE RESIDENCE OF Bishop William White for nearly 50 years, this three-story Federal structure, built in 1786, is an excellent example of a late 18th-century upper-class Philadelphia home. Dr. White, the first Episcopal Bishop of Pennsylvania and rector of Christ Church (see p52) and St. Peter's Episcopal Church (see p61), often entertained the colonial elite here, including George Washington

and Benjamin Franklin. The house has been restored, and period and original family pieces decorate the rooms, including whale oil lamps on the fireplace mantel and an assortment of silver pieces in the dining room. Chair placement and bookcases in Dr. White's upstairs study have been accurately reconstructed, thanks to a painting of the room commissioned after his death. An inside privy, which remains today, is indicative of the home's upper-class status.

Philadelphia Merchants' Exchange, designed in Greek Revival style

Philadelphia Merchants' Exchange 28

143 S 3rd St at Walnut St. **Map** 4 E3. *(215) 965-7676.* Market East Station. 2nd St. Philly Phlash. 9am–5pm (lobby exhibit). www.phlx.com

THE OLDEST STOCK exchange building in the country, this imposing edifice is one of

Old City's finest architectural gems. Completed in 1834, it was designed in Greek Revival style by the up-and-coming architect William Strickland, already noted for designing the new steeple atop Independence Hall (*see pp42–3*) and for his work on the Second Bank of the US (*see p47*). Strickland's admiration of classical Greek design is reflected by the columned Corinthian portico at one end and the unusual, semi-circular portico at the other.

With the financial district shifting to Center City in the late 19th century, the building soon became neglected. The National Park Service took it over in 1952, making it a part of Independence National Historical Park. Today, the Park Service maintains offices in the building. Although the exchange is closed to the public, visitors are permitted to enter the lobby and view a small exhibit that details the history and architecture of the exchange.

City Tavern ㉙

138 S 2nd St between Walnut & Chestnut Sts. **Map** 4 E3. ☎ *(215) 413-1443.* 🚇 *Market East Station.* 🚋 *2nd St.* 🚌 *Philly Phlash.* 🕐 *from 11:30am; reservations taken until 8:30pm* ♿ Ⓦ *www.citytavern.com*

RECALLING THE atmosphere of an authentic London tavern, the City Tavern also boasted the second largest ballroom in the colonies when it first opened in 1773.

City Tavern, still a popular dining spot in Philadelphia

However, just a year later, with the Revolutionary War in the offing, the three-story building was used by members of the First Continental Congress as an unofficial gathering place. Later, in 1777, when he became the leader of the Continental Army, Washington used the tavern as his headquarters.

After the Revolutionary War, the Constitutional Convention held its closing banquet here in 1787. Frequented by the likes of George Washington, Thomas Jefferson, and other colonial notables, it was once called "the most genteel tavern in America," by John Adams, the second president of the United States.

However, by the 1790s, the City Tavern had lost its prominence and served as a merchants' exchange until 1834, when it was partially destroyed by fire. The original structure was finally demolished in 1854 to make way for new brownstone buildings.

After careful research, the National Park Service reconstructed the tavern in 1975. Today, the inn is almost identical to the original, with serving staff in period dress and colonial-style dishes on the menu. These include such delicacies as sweet potato biscuits, said to be a favorite of Jefferson, turkey pot pie based on Martha Washington's recipe, West Indies pepperpot soup, and ales brewed according to Washington's and Jefferson's original recipes.

Welcome Park, dedicated to city founder William Penn

Welcome Park ㉚

S 2nd St at Walnut St. **Map** 4 E3. 🚇 *Market East Station.* 🚋 *2nd St.* 🚌 *Philly Phlash.*

NAMED AFTER the ship that ferried Penn and the first Quakers from England to the New World, the *Welcome*, this open city square is dedicated to the city's founder, William Penn. It was constructed in 1982 to commemorate the 300th anniversary of the founding of the colony of Pennsylvania. The centerpiece of the park is a smaller version of Penn's statue from City Hall (*see p72*). Emblazoned along the south wall of the park is a timeline of Penn's life and the events leading to the creation of the new colony. The park is located where the Slate Roof House – Penn's home and the Pennsylvania Seat of Government from 1700 to 1701 – once stood. This postmodernist square is made of concrete crisscrossed by marble slabs, depicting the main streets of the original city grid planned by William Penn and his surveyor Thomas Holmes.

Statue of William Penn

At the park's north end sits the Thomas Bond House, named after the physician and surgeon who, in 1751, along with Benjamin Franklin and others, founded Pennsylvania Hospital, America's first public hospital (*see p67*). The restored 1769 Georgian-style home is now a bed-and-breakfast inn (*see p134*).

SOCIETY HILL AND PENN'S LANDING

WILLIAM PENN FIRST stepped ashore on the banks of the Delaware River at what is today known as Penn's Landing, the eastern edge of this neighborhood. An elongated and tree-lined promenade, Penn's Landing includes a plaza for concerts, historic ships and dinner boats along the piers, and the Independence Seaport Museum.

Detail, Old St. Mary's Church

Heading west, several walkways lead to Society Hill, a well-preserved area with churches, synagogues, and 18th-century homes. The area's southern border, South Street, contrasts with the more serene Society Hill, indulging in the excitement derived from a trendy and eclectic mix of cafés, restaurants, shops, nightclubs, and bars.

SIGHTS AT A GLANCE

Historical Buildings and Districts

New Market and Head House Square 15
Penn's Landing 14
Pennsylvania Hospital 17
Physick House 6
Powel House 12
South Street and Walkway 16

Parks and Gardens

Rose Garden and Magnolia Garden 9
Washington Square 1

Places of Worship

Mikveh Israel Cemetery 18
Mother Bethel AME Church 2
Old Pine Street Church 3
Old St. Joseph's Church 10
Old St. Mary's Church 8
Society Hill Synagogue 7
St. Peter's Episcopal Church 4

Museums and Galleries

Independence Seaport Museum pp64–5 13
Polish American Cultural Center Museum 11
Thaddeus Kosciuszko National Memorial 5

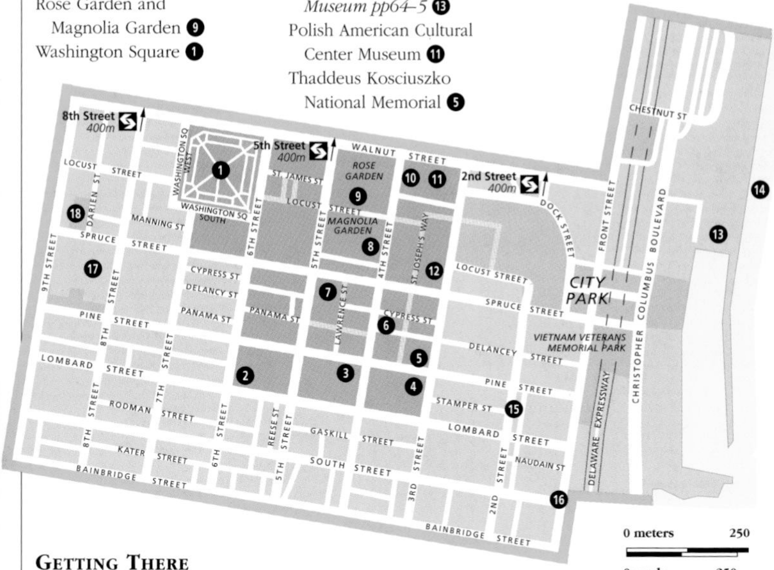

0 meters 250
0 yards 250

GETTING THERE

Most sights here are a 5- to 15-minute walk from Independence Mall. Philly Phlash buses are accessible on Market Street, while the Market-Frankford line has stops at 2nd and Market, 5th and Market, and 8th and Market. SEPTA bus 42 runs along Spruce and Walnut Streets.

KEY

Street-by-Street map *see pp58–9*

[S] SEPTA subway stop

◁ **Penn's statue outside Pennsylvania Hospital, founded in 1751**

Street-by-Street: Society Hill and Penn's Landing

Flowers laid at the Tomb of the Unknown Soldier

THIS HISTORIC neighborhood dates back to 1682 when William Penn chartered the "Free Society of Traders" to help develop a fledgling Philadelphia. The area was home to many notable colonial figures and members of the new Federal government, which was formed after the Revolutionary War. In the late 1950s, the Philadelphia Redevelopment Authority saved hundreds of 18th- and early 19th-century homes from likely demolition, selling them to private citizens who agreed to restore them. Today, a walk through the neighborhood reveals surviving narrow streets and courtyards, and houses in a mix of architectural styles, including Georgian, Federal, Greek Revival, and Beaux-Arts.

Mother Bethel AME Church
Founded in 1791, this site is the oldest piece of land continuously owned by African Americans. A lower level museum includes the tomb of founder Richard Allen ❷

Old Pine Street Church
The cemetery of "the Church of the Patriots" also contains the grave of Eugene Ormandy, director of the Philadelphia Orchestra from 1938 to 1980 ❸

KEY

− − − Suggested route

| 0 meters | 100 |
| 0 yards | 100 |

STAR SIGHTS

★ **Washington Square and Tomb of the Unknown Soldier**

★ **Powel House**

St. Peter's Episcopal Church
Completed in 1761, this Anglican church has an unusual double-ended interior, with the altar at one end, and the pulpit at the other ❹

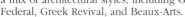

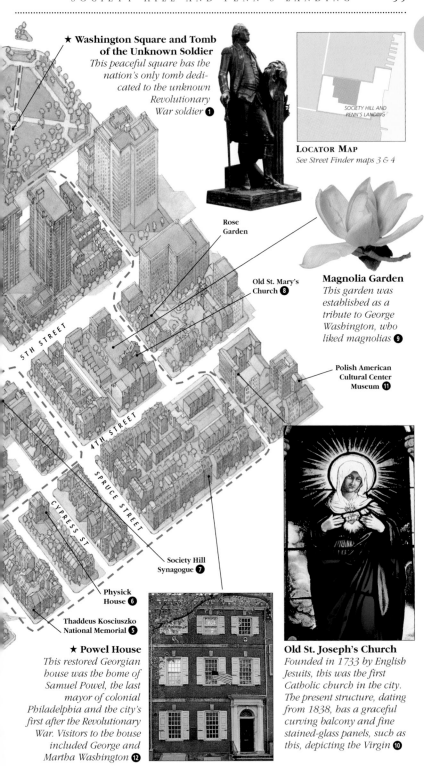

★ **Washington Square and Tomb of the Unknown Soldier**
This peaceful square has the nation's only tomb dedicated to the unknown Revolutionary War soldier ❶

LOCATOR MAP
See Street Finder maps 3 & 4

Rose Garden

Old St. Mary's Church ❽

Magnolia Garden
This garden was established as a tribute to George Washington, who liked magnolias ❾

Polish American Cultural Center Museum ⓫

5TH STREET

4TH STREET

SPRUCE STREET

CYPRESS ST

Society Hill Synagogue ❼

Physick House ❻

Thaddeus Kosciuszko National Memorial ❺

★ **Powel House**
This restored Georgian house was the home of Samuel Powel, the last mayor of colonial Philadelphia and the city's first after the Revolutionary War. Visitors to the house included George and Martha Washington ⓬

Old St. Joseph's Church
Founded in 1733 by English Jesuits, this was the first Catholic church in the city. The present structure, dating from 1838, has a graceful curving balcony and fine stained-glass panels, such as this, depicting the Virgin ❿

Washington Square, one of the five original squares in Penn's grid

Washington Square and Tomb of the Unknown Soldier ❶

Walnut St between 6th & 7th Sts. **Map** 4 D3. 🚇 *Market East Station.* 🚍 *5th, 8th, 9th-10th Sts.* 🚌 *42, Philly Phlash.*

ONE OF THE FIVE original squares in Penn's city grid, Washington Square, named after the nation's first president, is a pleasant park with benches and towering trees. This quiet space is also hallowed ground, having served as a cemetery for 90 years until the late 18th century. More than 2,000 Revolutionary War soldiers and prisoners of war were buried in massive pits here. Congressman John Adams described the pathos in a letter to his wife Abigail in 1777, writing that he spent an hour "in the Congregation of the dead" and that "I never in my whole life was affected with so much melancholy." In 1793, mass graves were again dug for victims of the city's yellow fever epidemic. Today, the park's centerpiece is the Tomb of the Unknown Soldier, with a statue of Washington, which was erected in the 1950s as a tribute to those who fought in the

Washington's statue at Washington Square

Revolutionary War. The tomb includes the remains of a revolutionary soldier who was buried on the site.

Mother Bethel AME Church ❷

419 Richard Allen Ave, corner of 6th & Lombard Sts. **Map** 4 D4. 📞 *(215) 925-0616.* 🚇 *Market East Station.* 🚍 *5th St.* 🚌 *42, Philly Phlash.* 🕐 *10am–3pm Tue–Sat only by appt.* Ⓦ *www.ame-today.com*

STANDING ON the oldest piece of land to be continuously owned by African Americans in the US, Mother Bethel traces its roots to former slave Richard Allen (1760–1831), the first Bishop of the African Methodist Episcopal Church. Allen began preaching in 1786 at St. George's Church *(see p51)*, where he successfully built up a black parish. He founded his own church in 1794, by buying and moving a blacksmith's shop to the current site, and using the anvil as his pulpit. The current structure, built in 1889, still contains the original curved pews and stained-glass windows.

In 1830, the church hosted the first national convention for African Americans, and for years was a stop along the Underground Railroad, the

system set up by abolitionists to transport fugitive slaves to Canada and the free states. Today, a museum in the lower level houses the tomb of Allen and his wife Sarah, along with historic church artifacts, including the original pews from the blacksmith shop.

Old Pine Street Church ❸

412 Pine St. **Map** 4 D4. 📞 *(215) 925-8051.* 🚇 *Market East Station.* 🚍 *2nd, 5th Sts.* 🚌 *42, Philly Phlash.* 🕐 *10am–3pm Mon–Sat, call in advance.* ⛪ *10:30am Sun.* ♿ *limited access.* Ⓦ *www.oldpine.org*

THE ONLY remaining colonial Presbyterian place of worship in Philadelphia today, Old Pine Street Church was founded in 1768. Designed in Georgian style by Robert Smith, it was later remodeled into an imposing columned Greek Revival building. George Duffield, the church's first pastor, served as chaplain to the Continental Congress of 1774 and second US President John Adams and Dr. Benjamin Rush, the "Father of American Psychiatry," were parishioners here, earning it the moniker "Church of the Patriots."

In 1777, occupying British forces used the church as a hospital and stable, also burying 100 Hessian soldiers in a mass grave outside the church wall. Today, there are more than 3,000 tombs in the surrounding cemetery, including that of Eugene Ormandy, conductor of the Philadelphia Orchestra from 1938 to 1985.

Detail of a gravestone from the Old Pine Street Church graveyard

Interior and altar of St. Peter's Episcopal Church

St. Peter's Episcopal Church ❹

313 Pine St. **Map** 4 D4. ☎ (215) 925-5968. ⚏ Market East Station. ⚡ 2nd, 5th Sts. ☒ 42, Philly Phlash. ⏰ 8am–4pm Mon–Fri; 11am–3pm Sat; 1–3pm Sun. ✝ 9am & 11am Sun. ♿ ⓦ www.stpetersphila.org

OPENED FOR worship in 1761, St. Peter's was founded by Society Hill Anglicans who were members of a then overcrowded Christ Church *(see p52)*, and who wanted a church closer to their homes. Christ Church and St. Peter's functioned as one parish until 1832, with Bishop White *(see p54)* serving as rector of both churches.

St. Peter's, built in Georgian style by Robert Smith, has a unique design. The placement of the wine-glass pulpit and altar at opposite ends of the building, and the seats in boxed pews facing either way, give the church no definitive front or back. In 1842, well-known architect William Strickland designed the landmark tower and spire that still house bells from London's Whitechapel Foundry, which had forged the first Liberty Bell in 1753 *(see p44)*.

Buried in the graveyard are several important colonial Americans, including portrait painter Charles Willson Peale, naval hero Stephen Decatur, and George M. Dallas, vice president of the US from 1845 to 1849, after whom counties were named in Texas, Iowa, Arkansas, and Missouri.

Thaddeus Kosciuszko National Memorial ❺

301 Pine St. **Map** 4 D4. ☎ (215) 597-9618. ⚏ Market East Station. ⚡ 2nd St. ☒ 42, Philly Phlash. ♿ limited access. ⏰ noon–4pm Wed–Sun.

REMEMBERED AS the "Hero of Two Continents," General Thaddeus Kosciuszko fought for freedom in both his native Poland and colonial America. During the Revolutionary War, he designed and built fortifications at Saratoga and West Point that proved critical to American victories over the British troops.

After the war, Kosciuszko returned to Poland in 1784 and took part in its fight for independence from Russia, but he was wounded and imprisoned by the Russians. He was released only upon the condition that he leave Poland. He then returned to Philadelphia to recuperate from his war wounds for nine months in this Society Hill house. His upstairs room has been restored and furnished with period pieces similar to those he owned. It also contains his medals, walking crutch, and a sable fur given to him on his release by Russia's Tsar Paul I. While nursing his injuries, Kosciuszko spent most of his time reading, sketching, and receiving guests, including his close friend and then US Vice President, Thomas Jefferson.

Physick House ❻

321 S 4th St. **Map** 4 D4. ☎ (215) 925-7866. ⚏ Market East Station. ⚡ 2nd, 5th Sts. ☒ 42, Philly Phlash. ⏰ noon–5pm Thu–Sat; 1–5pm Sun. ♿

NAMED AFTER Dr. Philip Syng Physick, the "Father of American Surgery" and grandson of silversmith Philip Syng, who designed the inkwell used during the signing of the Declaration of Independence *(see p42)*, this is one of the few free-standing colonial homes that remain today. Built in 1786 by wine importer Henry Hill, this Federal-style house has what was believed to be the largest fanlight in colonial Philadelphia over its door. After acquiring the home in 1815, Physick set up his medical practice, treating such prominent patients as Dolley Madison *(see p54)* and President Andrew Jackson.

Physick lived there until his death in 1837, and the house has been restored to that period. Original, locally quarried Pennsylvania Blue Marble can be seen in the hall and on fireplace mantels. Family pieces, such as an

Physick House entrance fanlight

unusual mid-18th-century oval wooden case that belonged to William Penn's grandson, a British Wagstaff grandfather clock belonging to Physick's father, and original silver items are also displayed. Physick's medical instruments can be seen in an upstairs room, and include surgical tools and medicine chests with bottles.

Interior of Physick House, containing original colonial-era furnishings

Society Hill Synagogue ❼

418 Spruce St. **Map** 4 D4. 📞 (215) 922-6590. 🚇 Market East Station.
🚊 5th St. 🚌 42, Philly Phlash.
🕐 9am–4pm Mon–Thu; call in advance. ⭐ Fri night & Sat morning.
♿ 🌐 www.societyhillsynagogue.org

ORIGINALLY BUILT as a Baptist church, this impressive structure was designed by 19th-century architect Thomas Ustick Walter, who was most noted for his design of the dome and House and Senate wings of the US Capitol in Washington DC. The original structure was built in Greek Revival style in 1830, but two decades later, Walter was again commissioned to design a new Italianate façade, much of which remains today. The building was home to Baptist worshippers for more than 80 years, until a group of Romanian Jews acquired it in 1912.

By 1916, the building was known as the Great Romanian Synagogue. The name, written in Yiddish, is still visible over the entrance. In the mid-1960s, it became the new home of Society Hill Synagogue, which is an active congregation rooted in the texts and practices of conservative Judaism.

Old St. Mary's Church ❽

252 S 4th St. **Map** 4 D4. 📞 (215) 923-7930. 🚇 Market East Station.
🚊 5th St. 🚌 42, Philly Phlash.
🕐 9am–4:30pm Mon–Sat. ⛪ Sun.
♿ 🌐 www.stmaryholytrinity.org

FOUNDED TO TAKE on parishioners from an overcrowded Old St. Joseph's Church, this redbrick church was built in 1763. Together, the two houses of worship served the city's Catholic population as one parish until the 1820s. Old St. Mary's witnessed several significant events in the years leading up to the birth of the nation. During the American Revolutionary War, members of the Continental Congress attended services here. The first public religious commemoration of the Declaration of Independence took place here in 1779, on the third anniversary of its adoption. Following the British surrender at Yorktown in 1781, the church held a thanksgiving service, with the flags of the conquered army laid on the altar steps. In 1810, Old St. Mary's was enlarged to its present size and became the first Catholic cathedral of the new diocese of Philadelphia. Its graveyard, dating to 1759, contains the tombs of Commodore John Barry, "Father of the American Navy," and the first to capture a British ship during the Revolutionary War, Thomas Fitzsimons, one of the signers of the Constitution, Mathew Carey, 18th-century American publisher and bookseller, and Michael Bouvier, the great-great-grandfather of first lady Jacqueline Kennedy Onassis.

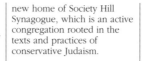

Detail from Old St. Mary's Church

Roses in full bloom in Society Hill's Rose Garden

Rose Garden and Magnolia Garden ❾

Locust St between 4th & 5th Sts.
Map 4 D3. 🚇 Market East Station.
🚊 5th St. 🚌 42, Philly Phlash.

THESE TWO public gardens, directly across each other on Locust Street, are nestled within shaded and quiet courtyards, characteristic of Society Hill's charm. The Rose Garden stretches through the center of the entire block, all the way up to Walnut Street. It commemorates the signers of both the Declaration of Independence and the US Constitution. The funding to plant roses, which flower during spring and summer, is povided by The Daughters of the American Revolution, an organization whose members are drawn from the direct descendants of those who fought in the Revolutionary War. Inside the garden is a section of a cobblestoned street dating back to 1800.

The Magnolia Garden was established as a tribute to George Washington, who had often expressed an interest in horticulture and, in particular, magnolia trees. Different varieties of magnolias are planted around the restful garden, whose centerpiece is a small fountain.

Italianate façade of Society Hill Synagogue

Interior of Old St. Joseph's Church with its unusual curving balcony

Old St. Joseph's Church ⑩

321 Willings Alley. **Map** 4 D3.
📞 (215) 923-1733. 🚇 Market East Station. 🚋 5th St. 🚌 42, Philly Phlash. 🕐 9:30am–4pm Mon–Fri; 9:30am–6:30pm Sat; 7:30am–2pm Sun. ♿ ⓦ www.oldstjoseph.org

Located in a narrow and historic alleyway, Old St. Joseph's was Philadelphia's first Catholic church. Reverend Joseph Greaton, an English Jesuit, founded it in 1733. In 1734, efforts were made to thwart Roman Catholic church services, but these were unsuccessful, with religious freedom for all assured by Penn's 1701 Charter of Privileges.

The old chapel was replaced by a larger building in 1757, and six years later, Old St. Mary's was built a block away to handle the growing number of members. St. Joseph's current structure dates from 1838 and features a grand columned altar and a curved balcony at the sanctuary's front end. On the ceiling is the fresco, *The Exaltation of Saint Joseph into Heaven*, painted by 19th-century Italian artist Filippo Costaggini, whose work can also be seen in the US Capitol in Washington DC.

Polish American Cultural Center Museum ⑪

308 Walnut St. **Map** 4 E3. 📞 (215) 922-1700. 🚇 Market East Station. 🚋 2nd, 5th Sts. 🚌 42, Philly Phlash. 🕐 May–Dec: 10am–4pm Mon–Sat; Jan–Apr: 10am–4pm Mon–Fri. ⬤ public hols. 🅿 ⓦ www. polishamericancenter.org

Through portraits and memorabilia from Poland, this small museum's mission is to promote awareness and appreciation of Polish culture and history. It honors Poles who have made significant contributions to history, ranging from figures such as Nicholas Copernicus, the astronomer, and composer Frédéric Chopin, to such modern-day luminaries as the late Pope John Paul II and politician and Nobel Peace Prize winner Lech Walesa. Of particular note are displays on the heroes of the American Revolutionary War, Thaddeus Kosciuszko and General Casimir Pulaski, the namesake of an annual city parade that celebrates Polish heritage *(see p34)*. Also on display is traditional Polish folk art – festive garb, Easter eggs, decorative paper cutouts, and wooden plates.

Portrait of General Pulaski, Polish American Cultural Center Museum

Powel House ⑫

244 S 3rd St. **Map** 4 E4. 📞 (215) 627-0364. 🚇 Market East Station. 🚋 2nd St. 🚌 42, Philly Phlash. 🕐 noon–5pm Thu–Sat, 1–5pm Sun. ♿ 🛈 compulsory.

This grand Georgian home built in 1765 is an exquisite example of how the colonial elite lived. Samuel Powel, one of the wealthiest men in colonial America, was its second owner, purchasing it in 1769 when he was about to marry Elizabeth Willing. Powel was Philadelphia's last mayor before the Revolutionary War and the first after the nation's birth. He died in 1793, a victim of the city's yellow fever epidemic.

The Powels used their lavish home to entertain the country's most important citizens, including Benjamin Franklin, George Washington, and John Adams, the second president of the US. Original features that remain today include a Pennsylvania Blue Marble fireplace on the first floor, the stairwell of Santo Domingo mahogany, and the cypress front door. Noteworthy furnishings include a small scale from Benjamin Franklin, original china and a sewing cabinet gifted to Mrs. Powel by the Washingtons, Gilbert Stuart portraits, and original silhouettes of Washington cut on cobalt blue paper by Samuel Powel at a social event. Outside the house is a peaceful garden dating back to the late 1700s.

Powel House, an elegant upper-class colonial-era residence

Independence Seaport Museum ⑬

Olympia exhibit

Located in a modern building on Penn's Landing waterfront, the mandate of this museum is to preserve US maritime history and traditions with a special focus on Delaware Bay and the Delaware River and its tributaries. Displays combine artifacts and paintings of naval encounters, along with computer games, large-scale ship models, and audiovisuals that include sounds of ship horns and accounts by sailors and shipbuilders. The museum recreates the Benjamin Franklin Bridge as a three-story replica that spans a carpeted Delaware River. Exhibits include a replica of the bridge of the destroyer USS *Lawrence*, and of steerage compartments in which many immigrants traveled to America. There is an active boatbuilding workshop, and berthed nearby are the World War II submarine *Becuna*, commissioned in 1944, and the *Olympia*, Admiral George Dewey's flagship in the 1898 Spanish-American War.

Waterfront Museum
This expansive facility is the centerpiece of Penn's Landing.

Museum Library

Submarine Becuna
This World War II vessel with torpedo launching tubes was the submarine flagship of the Southwest Pacific Fleet, which was under the command of General Douglas MacArthur.

First Floor

What Floats Your Boat? is an interactive exhibit exploring the science, art, and history of boats.

★ **Workshop on the Water**
Craftspeople build and restore traditional boats of the 19th century at this workshop dedicated to the skills and traditions of wooden boatbuilding and sailing in the Delaware River Valley and the New Jersey shore.

KEY

- ☐ Workshop on the Water
- ☐ What Floats Your Boat?
- ☐ Home Port Philadelphia
- ☐ Divers of the Deep
- ☐ River Gallery
- ☐ Quarterdeck Gallery
- ☐ On the Rivers, On the Shores
- ☐ Non-exhibition space

MUSEUM GUIDE
The first floor houses most of the exhibits, the museum shop, and visitor information. The second floor includes On the Rivers, On the Shores and the Quarterdeck Gallery with the Olympia exhibit. The Olympia and the Becuna are berthed outside the museum.

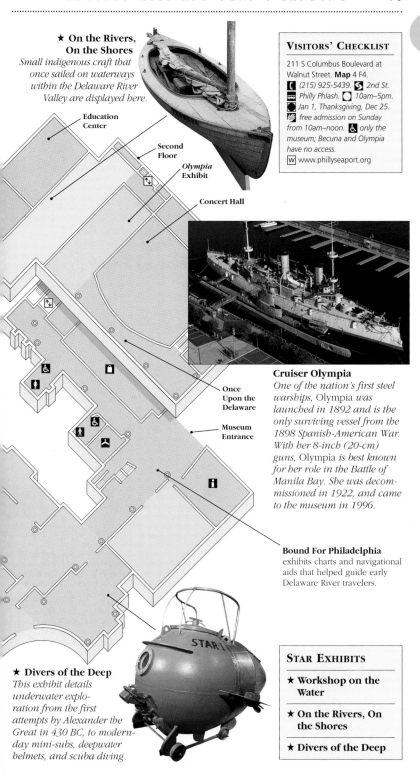

★ **On the Rivers, On the Shores**
Small indigenous craft that once sailed on waterways within the Delaware River Valley are displayed here.

Education Center

Second Floor

Olympia Exhibit

Concert Hall

Once Upon the Delaware

Museum Entrance

Cruiser Olympia
One of the nation's first steel warships, Olympia *was launched in 1892 and is the only surviving vessel from the 1898 Spanish-American War. With her 8-inch (20-cm) guns,* Olympia *is best known for her role in the Battle of Manila Bay. She was decommissioned in 1922, and came to the museum in 1996.*

Bound For Philadelphia
exhibits charts and navigational aids that helped guide early Delaware River travelers.

★ **Divers of the Deep**
This exhibit details underwater exploration from the first attempts by Alexander the Great in 430 BC, to modern-day mini-subs, deepwater helmets, and scuba diving.

STAR-I

STAR EXHIBITS

★ **Workshop on the Water**

★ **On the Rivers, On the Shores**

★ **Divers of the Deep**

Small boats at Penn's Landing marina with the Benjamin Franklin Bridge in the background

Penn's Landing ⑭

Western shore of the Delaware River between Market & South Sts. **Map** 4 F3. 🚉 *Market East Station.* Ⓢ *2nd St.* 🚌 *21, Philly Phlash.*

A POPULAR waterfront on the Delaware River, Penn's Landing is where city founder William Penn first stepped onto his new colony in 1682 *(see p18)*. Development of the docks seen today began in 1967, before which it was an unappealing stretch of land. Among its attractions are grassy areas with trees, walkways, and an amphitheater where summer festivals and concerts are held. Several vessels are anchored at the docks, Including the century-old sailing ship *Moshulu (see p148)*, the dinner cruise boat *Spirit of Philadelphia*, the 1883 three-masted barkentine *Gazela*, once a Portuguese fishing boat, and the paddleboat charter *Liberty Belle*.

Nearby is the Independence Seaport Museum *(see pp64–5)* with its two historic vessels – the cruiser *Olympia* and the submarine *Becuna* – docked in a small harbor.

Penn's Landing offers outstanding waterfront views of the Ben Franklin and Walt Whitman Bridges, and the Camden Waterfront, where *Battleship New Jersey* is moored. Along the Chestnut Street overpass is the impressive Irish Memorial, a bronze sculpture with 35 life-sized figures, which honors the more than one million people who died and the others who fled Ireland during the Great Hunger of the 1840s.

New Market and Head House Square ⑮

2nd St between Pine & Lombard Sts. **Map** 4 E4. 🚉 *Market East Station.* Ⓢ *2nd St.* 🚌 *42, Philly Phlash.*

O NE OF THE oldest in America, this covered marketplace was established in 1745. Called the "Shambles," meaning butcher shop, it was the second public marketplace in colonial Philadelphia – the first was located at the eastern end of High Street, now called Market Street. It was where vendors sold fresh produce, meat, poultry, and fish two days a week. The original New Market stretched two blocks from Pine Street to South Street and was flanked by two firehouses, known as head houses. The two firehouses once contained fire gear and apparatus for three volunteer fire companies.

Today, only the firehouse at 2nd and Pine Streets remains. Built in 1805, it is thought to be the country's oldest existing firehouse. New Market was restored in the 1960s, and has since housed the Crafts and Fine Arts Fair on summer weekends.

South Street and Walkway ⑯

South St. **Map** 4 E5. 🚉 *Market East Station.* Ⓢ *2nd St.* 🚌 *42, Philly Phlash.*

K NOWN AS Cedar Street in colonial times, and bordering on what was then New Market and Head House Square, South Street remains a marketplace of sorts today, but with an emphasis on pop culture and counterculture.

South Street, promising revelry and an exciting atmosphere

The South Street Head House District, which stretches from Front to 11th Streets and includes surrounding streets at some points, is an eclectic melting pot of over 300 shops, galleries, cafés, restaurants, bars, and more. Eateries range from pizzerias and sushi bars to vegetarian cafés and fine-dining restaurants, while shops sell everything from jewelry and fine art to funk culture items and grunge-style clothing. There are also body piercing and tattoo parlors, jazz clubs, and rocking nightclubs. The strip often overflows with younger revelers on weekend nights that usually extend into the early hours of the morning. A walkway over I-95 (also called the Delaware Expressway) links Columbus Boulevard to South Street, offering fine views of Penn's Landing, and *Battleship New Jersey* across the Delaware River.

Exterior of Pennsylvania Hospital with a statue of William Penn

Pennsylvania Hospital ⓱

800 Spruce St. **Map** 3 C4. 📞 (215) 829-3000. 🚇 Market East Station. Ⓢ 8th St. 🚌 42, Philly Phlash. 🕐 8:30am–4:30pm Mon–Fri. ♿ Ⓦ www.pahosp.com

Founded by surgeon Thomas Bond and Benjamin Franklin in 1751 to care for the "sick-poor and insane," Pennsylvania Hospital was the nation's first public hospital. The old section, the Pine Building, was built in stages. The wings are Georgian, the

Pennsylvania Hospital's surgical amphitheater

east wing being completed in 1755, and the west in 1796. The Federal center section was built in 1804 and includes the Great Court, the area open for self-guided tours.

Inside the center section is artist Benjamin West's masterpiece, *Christ Healing the Sick in the Temple*, which was delivered to the hospital in 1817, along with portraits of colonial physicians, including Dr. Philip Syng Physick *(see p61)* and Benjamin Rush, well-known for his contributions to the field of psychiatry. In the Great Court are the hospital's early fire pumper, purchased in 1803, and the musical planetarium clock constructed by colonial clockmaker and astronomer, David Rittenhouse, in 1780.

On the second floor is a medical library founded in 1762 with a collection of more than 13,000 volumes, some dating back to the 15th century. The library, located in this room since 1807, houses the country's most complete collection of medical books published between 1750 and 1850. Under a skylight on the top floor is the nation's first surgical amphitheater, called the "dreaded circular room," which was used for operations from 1804 to 1868. Outside, an 18th-century statue of William Penn stands over a peaceful courtyard overflowing with wisteria shrubbery.

Mikveh Israel Cemetery ⓲

Spruce St between 8th & 9th Sts. **Map** 3 C3. 📞 (215) 922-5446. 🚇 Market East Station. Ⓢ 8th St. 🚌 42, Philly Phlash. 🕐 summer: 10am–3pm Tues–Sat, and by appt. Ⓦ www.mikvehisrael.org

This burial ground, the oldest Jewish cemetery in the city and one of the oldest in America, was founded in 1740 after shipper and merchant Nathan Levy sought a place to bury one of his children according to Jewish law. Governor Thomas Penn, son of William Penn, granted land here and deemed it a Jewish graveyard. Levy, whose ship brought the Liberty Bell to Philadelphia, is also buried here. Other notables include members of the prominent Gratz family, including philanthropist Rebecca Gratz, the inspiration for the eponymous character in Sir Walter Scott's novel *Ivanhoe*, fur trader Aaron Levy, founder of Aaronsburg, Pennsylvania, rabbis of the congregation, and financier Haym Salomon. His grave is unmarked, only noted by a memorial at the entrance. Jewish soldiers of the Revolutionary War, the War of 1812, and the Civil War are also buried here. The cemetery was walled in the late 18th century to protect it from people "setting marks and firing shots."

Marker at Mikveh Israel cemetery

CENTER CITY

T HIS SPRAWLING, modern downtown district is Philadelphia's financial and business center. The city's tallest skyscrapers are situated west of City Hall along Market Street. At the neighborhood's eastern end is Chinatown, flanking the Pennsylvania Convention Center and the adjacent Reading Terminal Market, with Center City's major department stores nearby.

Classical urn at Rittenhouse Square

Along Broad Street, the central north-south artery, are 19th-century buildings that house the Masonic Temple and the Pennsylvania Academy of the Fine Arts in the north, while the theater district is located in the south. In Rittenhouse Square, some of the city's most extravagant apartment buildings and hotels tower over town homes that line quiet, shaded streets.

SIGHTS AT A GLANCE

Historical Buildings and Districts

Chinatown **7**
City Hall **4**
Liberty Place **15**
Library Company of
    Philadelphia **8**
Masonic Temple **3**
Reading Terminal Market **5**
Rittenhouse Square **13**

Places of Worship

Arch Street United
    Methodist Church **2**
St. Mark's Episcopal
    Church **14**

Museums and Galleries

The Civil War and Underground
    Railroad Museum of
    Philadelphia **11**
College of Physicians of
    Philadelphia/Mütter Museum **16**
Rosenbach Museum and
    Library **12**

Cultural Venues

Academy of Music **9**
Kimmel Center for the
    Performing Arts **10**
*Pennsylvania Academy of
    the Fine Arts pp74–5* **1**
Pennsylvania Convention
    Center **6**

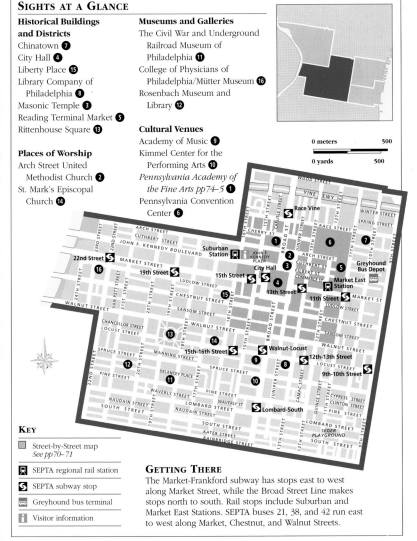

| 0 meters | | 500 |
| 0 yards | | 500 |

KEY

Street-by-Street map
See pp70–71

SEPTA regional rail station

SEPTA subway stop

Greyhound bus terminal

Visitor information

GETTING THERE

The Market-Frankford subway has stops east to west along Market Street, while the Broad Street Line makes stops north to south. Rail stops include Suburban and Market East Stations. SEPTA buses 21, 38, and 42 run east to west along Market, Chestnut, and Walnut Streets.

◁ **High-rise office buildings dominating the skyline in Center City, Philadelphia's business district**

Street-by-Street: Center City

CITY HALL SITS IN THE HEART of Center City, where Market Street and Broad Street – the city's main east-west and north-south arteries – converge. Most of this area, dominated by 19th- and 20th-century architecture, was developed well after the American Revolutionary War. Diagonally across from City Hall is JFK Plaza, where Philadelphia's famous LOVE artwork stands next to a pool and fountain, providing respite from the area's heavy commercial activity. Just a block north of City Hall are the landmark Masonic Temple and the Pennsylvania Academy of the Fine Arts.

The Union League of Philadelphia on Broad Street, is a classic French Renaissance-styled building.

★ City Hall
A 37-ft (11-m) high statue of William Penn stands atop this Beaux-Arts building, one of the largest and most elaborate city halls in the country ❹

JFK Plaza features Robert Indiana's iconic 1960s LOVE artwork.

0 meters	250
0 yards	250

KEY

--- --- Suggested route

STAR SIGHTS

★ City Hall

★ Pennsylvania Academy of the Fine Arts

★ Reading Terminal Market

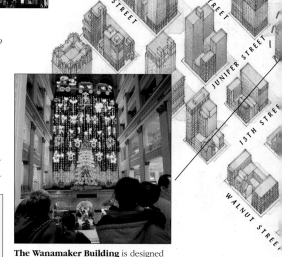

The Wanamaker Building is designed in Beaux-Arts style with a restrained Renaissance exterior. It is built around a soaring central atrium, which houses one of the world's largest pipe organs, with recitals twice a day and an annual Christmas light-and-sound show.

★ Pennsylvania Academy of the Fine Arts
America's oldest art museum was founded in 1805 by portrait artist Charles Willson Peale. Its collection spans three centuries ❶

LOCATOR MAP
See Street Finder maps 1, 2, & 3

Arch Street United Methodist Church
This Gothic Revival church is the square's oldest structure ❷

Masonic Temple
Home to the Grand Lodge of Freemasons, the building has an ornate Romanesque Revival façade ❸

Pennsylvania Convention Center
Opened in 1993, the center has vast amounts of exhibition and ballroom space ❻

★ Reading Terminal Market
Once the largest arched-roof train shed in the world, this is now one of the best farmers' markets in the country ❺

Pennsylvania Academy of the Fine Arts ❶

See pp74–5.

Arch Street United Methodist Church ❷

Broad & Arch Sts. **Map** 2 F4.
📞 *(215) 568-6250.* 🚉 *Suburban Station.* 🚊 *15th St, City Hall.*
🚌 *Philly Phlash.* ⏱ *10am–3pm Mon–Fri.* ✝ *8:30am & 11am Sun.*
♿ Ⓦ *www.archstreetumc.org*

T HIS GOTHIC REVIVAL marble building, constructed in two sections between 1864 and 1870, is the oldest structure on William Penn's original Center Square. The church was founded in 1862 during the American Civil War and was still being built when the funeral procession of President Abraham Lincoln passed by it in 1865. It was designed by Quaker Addison Hutton, whose architectural plan called for a radical change from the unadorned and plain Quaker meetinghouses of the 18th and 19th centuries.

The original construction included the installation of a 2,322-pipe organ by J.C.B. Standbridge, Philadelphia's leading builder of organs. The organ has been restored twice, once in 1916 and again in 1959. The sanctuary's spacious

Philadelphia's Masonic Temple, an architectural masterpiece

atrium is detailed with a Victorian stenciling pattern and stained glass. Today, a diverse congregation from the Center City neighborhood worships at the church.

Masonic Temple ❸

1 N Broad St. **Map** 2 F4. 📞 *(215) 988-1900.* 🚉 *Suburban Station.*
🚊 *15th St, City Hall.* 🚌 *Philly Phlash.* ● *Jul–Aug: Sat; Mon, public hols.* 🎟 *by donation.* 🎫 *11am, 2pm, & 3pm Tue–Fri, 10am & 11am Sat.*
♿ Ⓦ *www.pagrandlodge.org*

A N ARCHITECTURAL jewel, dedicated as the Grand Lodge of Free and Accepted Masons of Pennsylvania in 1873, this remarkable building contains a number of ornate meeting halls in various styles. Among them, the Oriental Hall's (1896) ornamentation

and coloring have been copied from the Alhambra in Granada, Spain; the Renaissance Hall (1908) follows an Italian Renaissance motif; while the Egyptian Hall (1889) takes its inspiration from the temples of Luxor, Karnak, and Philae. High arches, pinnacles, and spires form the Gothic Hall, and the cross-and-crown emblem of Sir Knights – "Under this sign you will conquer" – hangs over a replica of the Archbishop's throne in Canterbury Cathedral, Great Britain.

The halls, which are still in use, were created to honor the building trades, and much of the stone and tilework are imperceptibly faux finished – an attestation to the skill of the men who made them. President George Washington, a Freemason, wore his Masonic apron when he laid the cornerstone of the US Capitol in Washington DC. The apron is on display, along with other Masonic rarities, in a museum on the first floor.

City Hall ❹

Broad & Market Sts. **Map** 2 F4.
📞 *(215) 686-2840.* 🚉 *Suburban Station.* 🚊 *15th St, City Hall.* 🚌 *38, Philly Phlash.* 🎫 *building and tower:12:30pm Mon–Fri; tower: every 15 mins from 9:30am–4:15pm Mon–Fri.* ♿ Ⓦ *www.phila.gov*

B UILT ON Penn's original Center Square, this imposing marble, granite, and limestone landmark is the largest and perhaps the nation's most ornate city hall. The building, which took 30 years to build and was completed only in 1901, is designed in French Second Empire style with a mansard roof and prominent 548-ft (167-m) high tower. City Hall was the nation's tallest occupied building until 1909. The tower, with four clocks and a 37-ft (11-m) tall statue of Penn, was the city's highest structure until 1987 *(see box).*

Philadelphia artist Alexander Milne Calder designed the

City Hall with Penn's statue

NO BUILDING HIGHER THAN WILLIAM PENN'S STATUE

While skyscrapers sprang up across America in the 20th century, Philadelphia maintained a "gentlemen's agreement" not to build higher than 491 ft (150 m) – lower than the statue of William Penn on top of City Hall. Honoring Penn and the city's colonial heritage, the rule remained unchallenged for almost a century. But lured by new revenues and jobs – and despite much controversy – the agreement was broken in 1987 when the 61-story One Liberty Place *(see p79)* was built. It towers over City Hall by more than 400 ft (122 m). Within just five years, several other skyscrapers followed, including Two Liberty Place, the Mellon Bank Center, and the Bell Atlantic Tower.

Ornamental, French-influenced City Hall in the midst of Center City

60,000-lb (27-ton) statue, the largest atop any building in the world. Calder also designed over 250 other sculptures in the building, including the tower's bronze eagles, and the bronze figures of Native American and Swedish settlers.

Inside, rooms not to be missed include the Mayor's Reception Room, and Conversation Hall, which has statues of Washington and other colonial notables. The Council Caucus Room, with its grand domed ceiling, features carvings representing the four seasons as stages in life. A small elevator takes visitors to a deck on the tower that offers spectacular city views.

Reading Terminal Market ❺

12th & Arch Sts. **Map** 3 B2. ▌ (215) 922-2317. ▯ Market East Station. ▤ 11th St. ▥ Philly Phlash. ○ 8am–6pm Mon–Sat. ● Jan 1, Easter, Jul 4, Memorial Day, Thanksgiving, Dec 25. ♿ ⓦ www.readingterminalmarket.org

Once a Center City railroad terminal and market-place, Reading Terminal Market is now considered by

many to be one of the finest farmers' markets in the United States. It was created in 1892, after two farmers' markets on this site were leveled to make space for a new train terminal. These markets were relocated beneath the new train shed. So modern was the market for its time that people came from as far off as the New Jersey shore to buy fresh Lancaster County produce. Over the years, the market gradually declined and was nearly destroyed in the 1970s. New construction routed the city's trains around the old terminal in the 1980s, and the market was refurbished in the early 1990s.

Today, the revitalized Reading Terminal Market houses more than 80 vendors, six days a week, selling an extensive variety of free-range meats and poultry, seafood, country vegetables, pastas, Amish spe-cialties, and baked goods, as well as other items such as books, clothing, flowers, jewelry, crafts, unique spices, and hard-to-find specialties and ethnic foods. Several stands also offer freshly-made and prepared foods, ranging from Pennsylvania Dutch country breakfasts to soul food.

Jars of preserves at Reading Terminal Market

Pennsylvania Convention Center ❻

Between Market & Race Sts and 11th & 13th Sts. **Map** 2 F3. ▌ (215) 418-4700, (800) 428-9000. ▯ Market East Station. ▤ 11th St, 13th Sts. ▥ 38, Philly Phlash. ○ for conven-tions; Head House entrance open 24 hrs. ⓦ www.paconvention.com

A sprawling 1.3 million sq ft (120,774 sq m) of meeting and exhibition space make up one of the country's most unique convention centers. The building's Grand Hall, above Reading Terminal Market, was once a bustling train terminal for the Reading Railroad. Reopened in 1994, the hall retains its Victorian features, including the majestic ceiling that had once made it the largest single-arch train shed in the world. Much of the original wooden roof and milk-glass windows remain, now casting natural light onto the terrazzo marble floor with simulated tracks where com-muter trains once awaited passengers. Visitors can enter through the old railroad headhouse (now part of the Marriott Hotel) on the Market Street side for a peek at the Grand Hall, where a story-board outlines its history.

Scattered throughout the multiblock complex is a vast and diverse collection of con-temporary paintings, sculp-tures, and other artworks rendered by nearly 60 artists. Expansion plans are under-way to double convention space by 2008.

Colorful wares for sale at Reading Terminal Market

Pennsylvania Academy of the Fine Arts ❶

Founded by colonial painter and scientist Charles Willson Peale and sculptor William Rush in 1805, the Pennsylvania Academy of the Fine Arts is America's oldest art museum and fine arts school. Its galleries display works by some of the world's best-known artists. One of them, the classical stylist Benjamin West (1738–1820), a Quaker from Pennsylvania, helped organize the British Royal Academy in 1768. Former student, the Impressionist Mary Cassatt (1844–1926), and modern abstractionist Richard Diebenkorn (1922–93), among others, share its wall space. The academy's main building, the distinctive National Historic Landmark Building, with its ornate arched foyer, is considered one of the finest examples of Victorian architecture in America. The contemporary Samuel M.V. Hamilton Building, with new galleries, opened in 2005 as part of the museum's 200th anniversary celebrations.

National Historic Landmark Building
Designed by Furness and Hewitt, the academy's main building opened during the nation's cen- tennial in 1876.

Sculpture Exhibit
The 1873 marble sculpture Semiramis, *by William Wetmore Story (1819–95).*

National Historic Landmark Building Second Floor

★ **The Cello Player**
One of America's greatest painters, Thomas Eakins (1844–1916) taught at the academy from 1876 to 1886. This penetrating study of a cello player, capturing a moment of intense concen- tration, was painted in 1896. Rudolph Hennig, a leading musician, posed for it.

STAR EXHIBITS
★ The Cello Player
★ The Fox Hunt
★ Pantocrator

★ **The Fox Hunt**
This 1893 masterpiece by naturalist painter Winslow Homer (1836–1910), considered one of the greatest American artists of the 19th century, is among the academy's vast collections.

VISITORS' CHECKLIST

118 N Broad St at Cherry St.
Map 2 F3. 📞 (215) 972-7600.
🚊 Suburban Station. 🚇 City
Hall. 🚌 Philly Phlash. ⏰ 10am–
5pm Tue–Sat, 11am–5pm Sun.
● Mon, public hols. 📷 Morris
Gallery free. 🎟 11:30pm &
12:30pm Tue–Sat, noon & 1pm
Sat–Sun. ♿ Ⓦ www.pafa.org

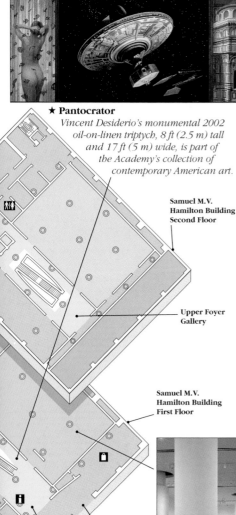

★ Pantocrator
*Vincent Desiderio's monumental 2002
oil-on-linen triptych, 8 ft (2.5 m) tall
and 17 ft (5 m) wide, is part of
the Academy's collection of
contemporary American art.*

**Samuel M.V.
Hamilton Building
Second Floor**

**Upper Foyer
Gallery**

**Samuel M.V.
Hamilton Building
First Floor**

Entrance

**Lower Foyer
Gallery**

Samuel M.V. Hamilton Building
*Adjacent to the National Historic
Landmark Building, this contemporary structure doubles the academy's
available display space, and
includes a sculpture study center
and a painting deck.*

Fisher Brooks Gallery
*This expansive new space on the first floor of the Samuel
M.V. Hamilton Building houses the academy's post-World
War II collection and also holds special exhibitions.*

KEY

☐	Fisher Brooks Gallery
☐	Foyer Galleries
☐	18th–20th century art
☐	Exhibit gallery
☐	Tuttleman Sculpture Gallery
☐	Non-exhibition space

GALLERY GUIDE

*The grand staircase of the National Historic Landmark
Building leads up to the gallery level on the second floor,
which displays sculpture and 18th- to early 20th-century
works, including portraiture, Impressionist, American genre,
and landscape paintings. The Samuel M.V. Hamilton building houses contemporary artworks after 1945.*

Ornamental gate at the entrance of Chinatown

Chinatown ❼

North of Arch St at 10th St.
Map 3 C1. 🚇 *Market East Station.*
🚊 *11th St.* 🚌 *Philly Phlash.*

THIS THRIVING neighborhood spans an area nearly four blocks wide and includes more than 50 restaurants, a score of grocery stores, and other shops and boutiques. Chinatown's origin dates to the 1860s when the first Chinese laundry was established in the area. It witnessed rapid growth after World War II owing to a huge influx of immigrants.

Although not as prominent as some of the larger Chinatowns in New York and San Francisco, visitors can still find a variety of Asian fare including traditional eel, squid, and duck dishes, and Chinese cultural gifts such as porcelain, wooden Buddhas, and dragons. The colorful Friendship Gate, with ornate dragons and Chinese art, is at 10th and Arch Streets and should not be missed.

Dragon figurine in a Chinatown shop

Library Company of Philadelphia ❽

1314 Locust St. **Map** 2 F5. 📞 *(215) 546-3181.* 🚇 *Suburban Station.*
🚊 *Walnut-Locust.* 🚌 *21, 42.*
🕐 *9am–4:45pm Mon–Fri.*
🌐 *www.librarycompany.org*

FOUNDED AS the country's first lending library by Benjamin Franklin in 1731, the Library Company has the distinction of being America's oldest cultural institution. Its extraordinary collection of historic books, papers and images – numbering more than 500,000 books, 75,000 graphics, and 160,000 manuscripts – documents American culture from the colonial era through the 19th century.

The **Historical Society of Pennsylvania**, housed on the same block as Library Company, was founded in 1824 and is one of the oldest historical societies in the US. Its stockpile has 600,000 printed items, and more than 19 million manuscripts and graphic materials from the 17th century onwards.

🏛 Historical Society of Pennsylvania

1300 Locust St. 📞 *(215) 732-6200.*
🕐 *12:30pm–5:30pm Tue & Thu, 12:30pm–8:30pm Wed; 10am–5:30pm Fri.* ⚫ *public hols.* ♿
🌐 *www.hsp.org*

Academy of Music ❾

S Broad & Locust Sts. **Map** 2 E5.
📞 *(215) 893-1999.* 🚇 *Suburban Station.* 🚊 *Walnut-Locust.*
🚌 *21, 42, Philly Phlash.* ⚫ *for performances.* 🎫 *tickets sold one hour before a performance & until half-an-hour after the last perfor- mance begins; tickets also sold at the Kimmel Center 10am–6pm.*
🎟 *by appt; call (215) 893-1935.*
🌐 *www. academyofmusic.org*

OFTEN REFERRED to as the "Grand Old Lady of Locust Street," the Academy of Music was the city's fore- most performing arts venue before the construction of the Kimmel Center in 2001. It remains the country's oldest grand opera house still in use.

Designed by Philadelphia architects Napoleon LeBrun and Gustavus Runge, the Victorian Italianate style struc- ture took two years to build and was completed in 1857. The interior's horseshoe design offers greater visibility to the audience seated on both sides of the balconies, which are supported by Corinthian-style columns. While the façade has ornate gas lamps, the main hall still has a glittering, 5,000-lb (2,300-kg) crystal chandelier, originally with 240 gas burners, and later wired for electricity. Statues representing Poetry and Music crown the prosce- nium arch. The former home of the Philadelphia Orchestra – which now performs in the Kimmel Center – the academy today hosts the Pennsylvania Ballet and the Opera Company of Philadelphia *(see p164).*

The Academy of Music, home to Philadelphia's opera and ballet

The Kimmel Center's glittering, modern façade

Kimmel Center for the Performing Arts ⑩

S Broad & Spruce Sts. **Map** 2 E5. *(215) 893-1999. Suburban Station. Walnut-Locust. 21, 42, Philly Phlash. 10am– 6pm; later for performances.* www.kimmelcenter.org

THE CENTERPIECE of the city's performing arts district, this modern complex opened in December 2001 after three years of construction. Covering an entire city block, it includes two separate venues in a spacious atrium under a 150-ft (46-m) high barrel-vaulted glass roof. The center is named after philanthropist and businessman Sidney Kimmel, who made the single-largest private donation for the complex.

The cello-shaped Verizon Hall, whose acoustics have been designed specifically for the Philadelphia Orchestra, seats more than 2,500 people. The Perelman Theater seats 650 people and has a rotating stage for chamber music, dance, and theatrical shows.

Other highlights include an expansive lobby with a stage for separate functions, an education center for performing arts classes, and a smaller studio and theater. The center's glass-enclosed roof garden offers great city views and an upper balcony houses a high-end restaurant.

The Civil War and Underground Railroad Museum of Philadelphia ⑪

1805 Pine St. **Map** 2 D5. *(215) 735-8196. Suburban Station. Lombard-South. 21, 42. 11am–4:30pm Thu–Sat; photo ID required.* www. civilwarmuseumphiladelphia.org

FOUNDED BY former Civil War Union officers in 1888, this museum and library has an impressive collection of Union artifacts. Housed in a 19th-century residence, it has over 5,000 photographs and 12,000 books and documents. Among its key holdings are items that belonged to General George Meade of Philadelphia, who commanded the Union Army in Gettysburg *(see pp120-23)*. These include his uniform, swords, spurs, and the stuffed head of his horse, Old Baldy. General, and later President, Ulysses S. Grant's original letters, signed photographs of President Lincoln, cavalry armaments, surgeons' kits and presentation swords are also on display. A small room with Confederate artifacts includes the jacket worn by President Jefferson Davis when he was captured by Union forces.

Exhibits at the Civil War and Underground Railroad Museum

Rosenbach Museum and Library ⑫

2008-2010 DeLancy Pl at 20th St. **Map** 2 D5. *(215) 732-1600. Suburban Station. Lombard-South. 21, 42. 10am–5pm Tue–Sun, 10am–8pm Wed. Mon, public hols.* www.rosenbach.org

HOME TO Dr. Rosenbach, one of America's most prominent rare book and manuscript dealers, this 1865 townhouse with a museum and research library sits on a quiet and shaded Rittenhouse street. Dr. Abraham Simon Wolf Rosenbach (1876–1952) and his brother Philip ran their company during the first half of the 20th century, combining great scholarship and business acumen. Apart from books, they also bought and sold 18th- and 19th-century artifacts such as silver, furniture, sculptures, drawings, and paintings.

So precious were many of their acquisitions that the brothers kept them for their own collection, which includes 30,000 books and 300,000 manuscripts and letters. Some of these are displayed today, including manuscript pages of James Joyce's *Ulysses*, over 100 personal letters of George Washington, and three of President Lincoln's speeches in manuscript form. In the house are the brothers' original possessions, including Chippendale furniture, gold-plated silver, and portraits by American artist Thomas Sully.

Shaded walkway and benches at Rittenhouse Square, a favored outdoor park

Rittenhouse Square ⑬

Walnut St between 18th & 19th Sts.
Map 2 D5. 🚇 Suburban Station.
Ⓢ Walnut-Locust. 🚌 21, 38, 42,
Philly Phlash.

ONE OF CENTER CITY'S most popular outdoor parks, on any sunny day shaded Rittenhouse Square teems with local residents and downtown workers relaxing under the trees. One of the five public areas planned by Penn in his 1682 city grid, it was originally known as Southwest Square. It was renamed in 1825 in honor of David Rittenhouse (1732–96), first director of the US Mint, astronomer, clockmaker, and a descendant of Wilhelm Rittenhouse, who established the nation's first papermill near Wissahickon Creek in 1690.

In the mid-19th century, the first house was built opposite the square, which soon became a prominent public garden. The park was given its present-day appearance in 1913 by French American Beaux-Arts architect Paul Cret, who also designed the Barnes Foundation's gallery building and the Valley Forge memorial arch. Benches line the many walkways that crisscross the park and lead to the small fountain and reflecting pool at its center. Flowers add color in spring and summer.

Since its development, the square has been a desirable address in town. Extravagant high-rise apartments and hotels, and upscale restaurants and cafés surround the square, reminiscent of a New York City park scene.

St. Mark's Episcopal Church ⑭

1625 Locust St. **Map** 2 E5. 📞 (215)
735-1416. 🚇 Suburban Station.
Ⓢ Walnut-Locust. 🚌 21, 38, 42,
Philly Phlash. 🕐 daily. 🎫 only by
appointment. 🌐 www.
saintmarksphiladelphia.org

FOUNDED BY A local group of Anglican worshippers in 1847, St. Mark's Episcopal Church is one of the nation's best examples of Gothic Revival architecture. The parishioners raised $30,000 and hired John Notman, a prominent Philadelphia architect, to design and build a new church in the medieval designs of the 14th- and 15th-century high Gothic period. The church was opened in 1849 during the early development of the Rittenhouse Square neighborhood.

Inside is a baptistry made of inlaid Italian marble and colorful panels in a spacious sanctuary that is reminiscent of an old English church.

Not to be missed is the adjoining structure, the spectacular Lady Chapel. It was donated by Rodman Wanamaker as a memorial to his wife, who died in 1900 and is buried in the chapel's crypt. The 12 panels in this chapel have ornate carvings depicting scenes from the life of St. Mary the Virgin. Its ornate and beautiful marble altar, encased in silver, was made by Carl Krall and is one of only three such in the world. Still used for mass, it is the most well-known of St. Mark's ecclesiastical treasures. In 1937, the organ, considered to be one of the best examples of tonal construction in the nation, was dedicated to the church.

Downtown Philadelphia's Gothic-style
St. Mark's Episcopal Church

Liberty Place 🄯

16th & Chestnut Sts. **Map** 2 E4.
📞 (215) 851-9055. 🚉 Suburban
Station. 🚇 Broad St. 🚌 Philly
Phlash. ⏰ 9:30am–7pm Mon–Sat;
noon–6pm Sun. ♿ Ⓦ www.
shopsatliberty.com

THIS GLEAMING, modern office complex, which sprawls over a vast area, is built on two city blocks and anchors Philadelphia's tallest skyscrapers. Designed by Murphy and Jahn Associates and built by Rouse & Associates, the two steel towers with sapphire blue glass sheathing have a postmodern architectural aesthetic. Built in 1987 with pyramidal tops and spires reminiscent of New York's Chrysler Building, the 945-ft (288-m) One Liberty Place tower was the first structure to break the 86-year gentlemen's agreement not to build higher than the height of the hat on Penn's statue on top of City Hall *(see p 72)*. The 61-story One Liberty Place stretches almost 100 ft (30 m) higher than its 58-story companion tower Two Liberty Place, which houses the national headquarters of the CIGNA Insurance Corporation.

The mall complex that connects the two towers houses 60 stores that cover the needs and fashion desires of Center City office workers, running the gamut from specialty food shops, chic boutiques, and trendy shoe shops to more practical outlets such as bookstores and newsstands. A food court has several vendors dishing up everything from spicy Cajun dishes to smoothies.

Joseph Hyrtl's collection of 139 skulls, Mütter Museum

College of Physicians of Philadelphia/Mütter Museum 🄰

19 S 22nd St. **Map** 1 C4. 📞 (215) 563-3737. 🚉 Suburban Station. 🚇 15th St. 🚌 21, 38, 42. ⏰ 10am–5pm. ⬤ Jan 1, Thanksgiving, Dec 25. 📷 Ⓦ www.collphyphil.org

A NON-PROFIT society founded in 1787 "to advance the Science of Medicine," the College of Physicians provides health education to medical professionals and the public through the C. Everett Koop Community Health Information Center, the Historical Medical Library, the Free Library, and computerized databases.

For a visitor, the college's most fascinating resource is the Mütter Museum. Named after professor of surgery Thomas Mütter, who in 1858 donated 2,000 specimens he had used for teaching, the museum displays some curious and unusual items, including preserved specimens and wax anatomical and pathological models. These were used for educational purposes in the mid-1800s, when diseases and genetic defects were identifiable only by their physical manifestations.

Key exhibits include the skull collection of Joseph Hyrtl, a 19th-century Viennese anatomist, a plaster cast of the original Siamese twins, Chang and Eng, who died in 1874, and When the President is the Patient, one of the only major exhibitions in the US to focus on the long, hidden history of illness in the White House. Memorabilia from famous scientists and physicians is also on display.

One Liberty Place, with Two Liberty Place behind it

LOGAN SQUARE AND THE MUSEUM DISTRICT

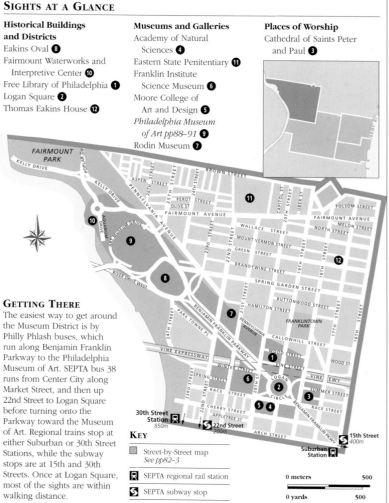

LOGAN SQUARE, with its multispouted Swann Memorial Fountain, is the centerpiece of the Museum District, bordered by the Schuylkill River on the west and the Cathedral of Saints Peter and Paul on the east. Benjamin Franklin Parkway, often referred to as the Champs Elysées of Philadelphia, is the route

Detail, Philadelphia Museum of Art façade

for most parades held in the city. It runs through the heart of this area and is flanked by buildings with imposing architectural styles, reminiscent of the ancient temples of Greece and Rome. To the north is the Eastern State Penitentiary, a fortress-turned-museum that once housed some of the country's most notorious criminals.

SIGHTS AT A GLANCE

Historical Buildings and Districts
Eakins Oval **8**
Fairmount Waterworks and Interpretive Center **10**
Free Library of Philadelphia **1**
Logan Square **2**
Thomas Eakins House **12**

Museums and Galleries
Academy of Natural Sciences **4**
Eastern State Penitentiary **11**
Franklin Institute Science Museum **6**
Moore College of Art and Design **5**
Philadelphia Museum of Art pp88–91 **9**
Rodin Museum **7**

Places of Worship
Cathedral of Saints Peter and Paul **3**

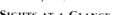

GETTING THERE
The easiest way to get around the Museum District is by Philly Phlash buses, which run along Benjamin Franklin Parkway to the Philadelphia Museum of Art. SEPTA bus 38 runs from Center City along Market Street, and then up 22nd Street to Logan Square before turning onto the Parkway toward the Museum of Art. Regional trains stop at either Suburban or 30th Street Stations, while the subway stops are at 15th and 30th Streets. Once at Logan Square, most of the sights are within walking distance.

KEY

▢	Street-by-Street map *See pp82–3*
🚉	SEPTA regional rail station
Ⓢ	SEPTA subway stop

0 meters   500
0 yards   500

◁ Boat crews row down the Schuylkill River past Fairmount Park's Boathouse Row

Street-by-Street: Logan Square and the Museum District

CENTRAL TO THIS NEIGHBORHOOD is the Benjamin Franklin Parkway – a grand boulevard lined with trees and grassy areas stretching from Center City to the Philadelphia Museum of Art. Statues and sculptures around the museum add to the area's European flair. Imposing structures housing many of the city's other key museums were built along the Parkway and around Logan Square in the 19th and early 20th centuries. Today, they hold some of the world's most prized antiquities, artworks, and natural history collections. Among them are the Rodin Museum and the Franklin Institute Science Museum, named after the scientist and statesman.

Statue of George Washington

Fairmount Waterworks and Interpretive Center
Stately temple-like façades that once housed the nation's first municipal water-pumping station now serve as an interpretive center highlighting the city's water resources ❿

Eakins Oval
Ornate fountains and statues are the centerpieces of this traffic circle named after the 19th-century Philadelphia artist Thomas Eakins ❽

WINTER

★ Franklin Institute Science Museum
A massive statue of Benjamin Franklin sits in the atrium of this interactive science museum with a planetarium and IMAX theater. This is one of the most visited museums in Pennsylvania ❻

RA

STAR SIGHTS

★ **Franklin Institute Science Museum**

★ **Philadelphia Museum of Art**

★ **Rodin Museum**

Academy of Natural Sciences
The oldest continuously operating natural history museum in the Western hemisphere has dinosaur fossils among its more than 17 million specimens ❹

**Moore Colle
Art and Des**

LOCATOR MAP
See Street Finder maps 1 & 2

★ Philadelphia Museum of Art
The country's third largest art museum, sited in a landmark building, has vast collections of paintings, sculptures, and decorative arts **❾**

★ Rodin Museum
This small museum has more than 130 sculptures by Auguste Rodin, including The Thinker. *This is the largest collection of his works outside France* **❼**

Free Library of Philadelphia
Founded in the 1890s, the library moved to its permanent home in the Beaux-Arts Main Library Building in 1927 **❶**

Logan Square
Originally called Northwest Square, today Logan Square is centered by the Swann Fountain and flanked by the Free Library of Philadelphia **❷**

Cathedral of Saints Peter and Paul **❸**

KEY

– – – Suggested route

0 meters	200
0 yards	200

The Beaux-Arts façade of the Free Library of Philadelphia

Free Library of Philadelphia ❶

1901 Vine St. **Map** 2 E2. 🎫 *(215) 686-5322.* 🚇 *Suburban Station.* 🚋 *Race-Vine.* 🚌 *38, Philly Phlash.* ◗ *9am–9pm Mon–Wed, 9am–5pm Thu–Sat, 1–5pm Sun.* ◑ *Sun in summer, public hols.* ☑ *tour starts at Rare Book Dept at 11am.* ♿ Ⓦ *www.library.phila.gov*

Opened in 1894, the Free Library first occupied three rooms in City Hall. It relocated a few times before moving into its current Beaux-Arts building in 1927. Constructed of Indiana limestone with a granite base, it is similar in appearance to the adjacent building that houses the Philadelphia city courts.

Today, the library has up to 1.75 million volumes, and its key collections include maps, children's books, social sciences and history books, and the largest public library chamber music collection in the eastern US. The Rare Book Department is also one of the nation's largest, with holdings that span 4,000 years and include Sumerian cuneiform tablets, medieval manuscripts, incunabula, early American children's books, and letters and manuscripts from authors such as Charles Dickens and Edgar Allen Poe *(see p94).*

Logan Square ❷

19th St at Benjamin Franklin Parkway. **Map** 2 D3. 🚇 *Suburban Station.* 🚋 *Race-Vine.* 🚌 *38, Philly Phlash.*

Part of William Penn's original grid plan, Logan Square (then known as Northwest Square) was initially used as a burial ground, then for pastureland, and later for public executions. It was renamed Logan Square in 1825 in honor of Penn's secretary James Logan. The square changed dramatically during the 1920s, when the construction of the Benjamin Franklin Parkway turned it into a traffic circle, which is why it is today also referred to as Logan Circle.

At its center is the Swann Memorial Fountain, designed by Alexander Stirling Calder in 1924. It features three statues, meant to represent the city's three main waterways – the Delaware and Schuylkill Rivers, and Wissahickon Creek. Today, the shaded area is a popular spot along the Parkway, with children often dipping in the fountain on hot summer days.

Cathedral of Saints Peter and Paul ❸

18th St at Benjamin Franklin Parkway. **Map** 2 E3. 🎫 *(215) 561-1313.* 🚇 *Suburban Station.* 🚋 *Race-Vine.* 🚌 *38, Philly Phlash.* ◗ *7am–4:30pm Mon–Sat.* ✝ *daily.* ♿

Window of the Cathedral of Saints Peter and Paul

This grand cathedral, with a copper dome more than 60 ft (18 m) high, is a prominent city landmark. Designed by architects John Notman and Napoleon LeBrun, the Victorian Italianate basilica with Renaissance features was modeled after the Lombard Church of St. Charles in Rome and completed in 1864. The sanctuary is shaped in the form of a cross with a white marble floor, a marble altar, and six marble columns rising more than 40 ft (12 m) along the curved walls of the apse. Stained-glass windows add a touch of beauty to the main altar area, side altars, and the eight side chapels. Of particular note is the organ, one of the largest in the city, with 75 pipes and four manuals. The cathedral is now the seat of Philadelphia's Roman Catholic Archdiocese.

Logan Square's Swann Memorial Fountain, named after the founder of the Philadelphia Fountain Society

Exhibit at Dinosaur Hall, Academy of Natural Sciences

Academy of Natural Sciences ❹

1900 Benjamin Franklin Parkway.
Map 2 D3. *(215) 299-1000.*
Suburban Station. Race-Vine.
38, Philly Phlash. 10am–4:30pm
Mon–Fri, 10am–5pm Sat & Sun.
Jan 1, Thanksgiving, Dec 25.
www.acnatsci.org

A NATURAL HISTORY museum
and research library, the
Academy of Natural Sciences
was founded in 1812 by seven
naturalists, who pooled their
fossils and specimens to foster
education and research about
the earth's diverse species. Its
collection has since swelled to
17 million specimens. Exhibits
are housed on four levels, and
include mounted animals,
ranging from birds native to
Pennsylvania to bison from
North America and cape
buffalo from Africa. Dinosaur
Hall is a favorite with children,
while the live butterfly exhibit
is a reproduction of a tropical
rainforest. The animals in the
Live Animal Center cannot sur-
vive in the wild and are thus
used for teaching purposes.

Moore College of Art and Design ❺

20th St & Benjamin Franklin Parkway.
Map 2 D3. *(215) 568-4515.*
Suburban Station. Race-Vine.
38, Philly Phlash. galleries:
10am–5pm Tue–Fri, noon–4pm Sat &
Sun. Mon, public hols.
www.moore.edu

T HIS SCHOOL is the first and
only women's art and
design college in the United
States, and one of only two in
the world. It was founded as
the Philadelphia School of
Design for Women in 1848 by
Sarah Worthington Peter
(1800–77). Her aim was to
educate women for careers
that would lead to financial
independence, and in
accordance with that, the
original curriculum
provided training in
the new fields
spawned by the
Industrial
Revolution, such
as textile design.
Today, the college
offers nine under-
graduate degree
programs in fine
arts and design.
Two galleries of
the college are open to the
public. Rotating exhibitions
highlight the works of alum-
nae and women artists. The
Paley Gallery exhibits national
and international artists, while
the Levy Gallery showcases
local artists and provides a
center for exploration and
experimentation for emerging
and established talent. Past
shows have featured work by
Mary Cassatt, Karen Kilimnik,
and Jacqueline Matisse.

Franklin's statue in the museum atrium

Franklin Institute Science Museum ❻

222 N 20th St at Benjamin Franklin
Pkwy. **Map** 2 D3. *(215) 448-1176.*
Suburban Station. Race-Vine.
38, Philly Phlash. museum:
9:30am–5pm; IMAX theater: 9:30am–
5pm Sun–Thu, 9:30am–9pm Fri & Sat.
www.fi.edu

T HE OLDEST science and
technology institution
in continuous use in North
America, this museum was
founded in 1824. Named after
Benjamin Franklin (see p53),
the institute's first location was
in the building that now
houses the Atwater Kent
Museum (see p50). The
current building opened in
the 1930s and contains a
spacious rotunda with a
21-ft (6-m) tall marble
statue of Franklin.
Exhibits highlight
Franklin's accom-
plishments in
medicine,
astronomy,
meteorology, and
optics. Among the
museum's attrac-
tions are Electricity
Hall, which showcases his
discovery of electricity, the
Giant Walk-Through Heart
with interactive devices (see
p26), and the Train Factory,
which has an original
Baldwin steam locomotive.
From February to September
2007 the museum is hosting
the *Tutankhamun and the
Golden Age of the Pharaohs*
exhibition, featuring more
than 130 treasures from the
famous tomb and other sites.

Moore College of Art and Design, housed in a modern building

Rodin's sculpture, *The Thinker*, outside the Rodin Museum

Rodin Museum ❼

22nd St at Benjamin Franklin Parkway.
Map 2 D2. 📞 *(215) 763–8100.* 🚉
Suburban Station. Ⓢ *Spring Garden.*
🚌 *38, Philly Phlash.* ⏰ *10am–5pm
Tue–Sun.* ⬤ *Mon, public hols.* 📷
♿ 📷 Ⓦ *www.rodinmuseum.org*

Frech sculptor Auguste
Rodin's (1840–1917) most
famous artwork, *The Thinker*,
sits outside the columned
façade that leads into the
courtyard of this small, temple-
like museum. With nearly 130
sculptures, it contains the
largest collection of Rodin's
work outside of Paris.
   Opened in 1929, the Rodin
Museum's entrance showcases
the impressive, 20-ft (6-m)
high *The Gates of Hell*, which
Rodin worked on for 37 years
until his death. Inside is the
life-sized sculpture of six
heroes of the Middle Ages,
known as *The Burghers of
Calais*. Other notable works
include *Apotheosis of Victor
Hugo*, a sculpture of the
French writer, and different
sculptures of kissing lovers,
known as *Eternal Springtime*.

Eakins Oval ❽

Benjamin Franklin Parkway. **Map** 1
C1. 🚉 *30th St Station.* Ⓢ *Spring
Garden.* 🚌 *38, Philly Phlash.*

Named after prominent
Philadelphia artist Thomas
Eakins, this oval was part of
the Benjamin Franklin Parkway
project in the 1920s. Located
opposite the entrance to the
Philadelphia Museum of Art,
Eakins Oval has a prominent
equestrian statue of President
George Washington at its
center. The center also
features a fountain, which
has figurines of wild
animals surrounding
four statues that
symbolize four of
the country's major
rivers – the Delaware,
Mississippi, Hudson,
and Potomac. Two
smaller fountains
flank the large
central one – the
Ericsson fountain,
named for the
engineer who
designed the USS
Monitor, a Union
naval vessel of the Civil War,
and another named after
Fairmount Park Commission
chairman Eli Kirk Price
(1797–1884) who led efforts
to build the parkway. Today,
the oval is at the center of a
traffic circle and includes a
shaded green area with park
benches and a parking lot.

**Washington's statue
at Eakins Oval**

Philadelphia Museum of Art ❾

See pp88–9.

Fairmount Waterworks and Interpretive Center ❿

640 Waterworks Dr. **Map** 1 B1.
📞 *(215) 685-4908.* 🚉 *30th St
Station.* Ⓢ *Spring Garden.* 🚌 *38,
Philly Phlash.* ⏰ *10am–5pm Tue–Sat,
1–5pm Sun.* ⬤ *Mon, public hols.*
📷 ♿ Ⓦ *www.
fairmountwaterworks. com*

Situated on the elevated
banks of the Schuylkill
River, these impressive Greek
Revival buildings were constructed between 1812 and
1871 to supply drinking
water to Philadelphia –
the first American city to
take on providing
water as a municipal
service. When it opened in
1822, its cutting-
edge technology of
the time – huge
water wheels, tur-
bines, and pumps –
and the beauty of
the site made it a
destination point for
engineers and visitors from
the US and Europe. Water
pumping ended in 1909, and
today the restored buildings
house old pumping apparatus
and an interpretive center
with interactive exhibits.
Water In Our World chal-
lenges children and adults
alike to learn about water
resources. Other exhibits
include a real-time fish migra-
tion up the river, a virtual
helicopter tour of the watershed, and a computer simula-
tion of historic technology.

Fairmount Waterworks, now a National Historic Landmark

Reconstruction of Al Capone's cell at the Eastern State Penitentiary

Eastern State Penitentiary ⑪

22nd St at Fairmount Ave. **Map** 2 D1.
🅲 (215) 236-3300. 🆂 Spring
Garden. 🚌 38, Philly Phlash. 🔲 Apr–
Nov: 10am–5pm Wed–Sun. ⬤ Easter,
Thanksgiving, Dec–Mar. 🖼 children
under 7 not allowed. 🗲 ♿
🆆 www.easternstate.org

NAMED THE "House" by inmates and guards, the Eastern State Penitentiary was a revolutionary concept in criminal justice. Prior to its opening, convicts lived in despicable conditions and suffered brutal physical punishments. The Philadelphia Quakers proposed an alternative in the form of a facility where a lawbreaker could be alone to ponder and seek penitence for his misdeeds. This led to the opening of the penitentiary in 1829. During incarceration, with sentences seldom less than five years, prisoners were hooded when outside their cells to prevent interaction with others.

The prison, with its imposing, fortress-like Gothic Revival façade, had a single entrance and 30-ft (9-m) high boundary walls. Inside, seven elongated cellblocks extended from a central rotunda, and each solitary cell had a skylight and private outdoor exercise yard. In the early 20th century, the isolation form of imprisonment was abandoned, and more cellblocks were added. Over the years, the prison has housed several infamous personalities, the most prominent being the gangster Al Capone.

Officially closed in 1971, it is now a National Historic Landmark and museum. Today, the structure's chipped walls and aging cellblocks host changing exhibitions from its collections of old artifacts and photographs. The prison also conducts tours, with audio excerpts from former guards and inmates.

Thomas Eakins House ⑫

1729 Mt Vernon St. **Map** 2 E1.
🅲 (215) 685-0750. 🆂 Spring
Garden. 🚌 38, Philly Phlash.
🔲 hours vary. 🆆 www.muralarts.org

THIS BRICK ROW house was home to the artist Thomas Eakins for most of his life, with the exception of the time he spent abroad: first in Paris

studying art at the École des Beaux-Arts from 1866 to 1868, and then traveling to Spain in 1869 before returning home in 1870. One of the country's most renowned Realist painters of the late 19th and early 20th centuries, Eakins' works often reflected life in Philadelphia through portraits and family paintings, as well as through his popular city and nature paintings, which included sculling and sailing scenes on the Schuylkill and Delaware Rivers.

Today, the Thomas Eakins House is home to the city's Mural Arts Program. Changing exhibitions in the building's galleries highlight artwork created by Philadelphia's youth participating in the Mural Arts and other outreach programs.

Façade of Thomas Eakins House, home to the Mural Arts Program

---

MURAL ARTS PROGRAM

Philadelphia has America's largest collection of colorful, outdoor and indoor murals, which are emblazoned on walls all across the city. Through artists' visions and the sheer manpower of inspired local youth, more than 2,500 variegated and vibrant murals have been painted since the Mural Art Program's inception in 1984 as an anti-graffiti initiative. With extensive preparation including scaffolding and under-coating, a typical mural is completed within two months and can cost as much as $15,000. The murals often highlight famous community leaders, role models, artistic cityscapes, and themes of culture, history, diversity, and anti-drug messages.

Murals on city walls, a tradition in the city of Philadelphia

Philadelphia Museum of Art ❾

FOUNDED IN THE country's centennial year of 1876, Philadelphia's most prominent museum attracts major exhibitions to supplement its superlative permanent collections. More than 200 galleries showcase works of art spanning more than 4,000 years, with some Asian exhibits dating from the third millennium BC. The medieval cloister courtyard and fountain on the second floor is very popular, as are the French Gothic chapel and the pillared temple from Madurai, India. In addition to outstanding collections of Old Master, Impressionist, and Postimpressionist paintings, Pennsylvania Dutch and American decorative arts are also featured with American art. Scattered throughout the museum are computerized stations with information on the exhibits.

Beaux-Arts roof detail

Mask of Shiva
A 9th-century copper alloy artifact from India.

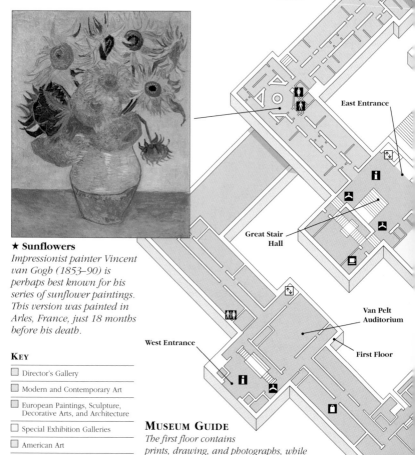

★ Sunflowers
Impressionist painter Vincent van Gogh (1853–90) is perhaps best known for his series of sunflower paintings. This version was painted in Arles, France, just 18 months before his death.

East Entrance

Great Stair Hall

Van Pelt Auditorium

West Entrance

First Floor

KEY

- ☐ Director's Gallery
- ☐ Modern and Contemporary Art
- ☐ European Paintings, Sculpture, Decorative Arts, and Architecture
- ☐ Special Exhibition Galleries
- ☐ American Art
- ☐ Arms and Armor
- ☐ Middle East and Asian Art
- ☐ Non-exhibition space

MUSEUM GUIDE

The first floor contains prints, drawing, and photographs, while galleries on the second floor display Impressionist, Postimpressionist, American, and contemporary art. The third floor has the most extensive collections, including European art, arms and armor, and Asian art.

The West Entrance of the Philadelphia Museum of Art

VISITORS' CHECKLIST

26th St & Benjamin Franklin
Parkway. **Map** 1 C1. *(215)
763-8100.* 30th St Station.
Philly Phlash. 10am–5pm
Tue–Sun; 10am–8:45pm Fri.
Mon, public hols.
www.
philamuseum.org

Ming Dynasty Ceramics
*Delicate ceramics, fine hardwood
furniture, and other objects of the Ming
Dynasty are on display in the Chinese
gallery, including this 15th-century
bowl, the* Three Friends.

Third Floor

**Cloister with Elements from the Abbey
of Saint-Genis-des-Fontaines**
*Surrounded by marble arcaded walkways
and centered by a rare fountain, this cloister is based on medieval French design.*

Second Floor

★ **Renaissance
Paintings**
*The museum has an
extensive collection of
Renaissance art, such
as* The Nativity,
*painted in the 1430s
by Paolo Schiavo
(1397–1478).*

★ **Thomas Eakins
Collection**
Miss Blanche Hurlbert
*(1892) by Thomas Eakins,
acclaimed Philadelphian
artist, forms a part of the
museum's impressive
collection of works by
local artists.*

STAR EXHIBITS

★ **Sunflowers**

★ **Renaissance
Paintings**

★ **Thomas Eakins
Collection**

Exploring the Philadelphia Museum of Art

Stained glass roundel, France (1246–48)

T HE MUSEUM OF ART is home to over 300,000 objects from Europe, Asia, and the Americas, spanning more than 4,000 years. Its key exhibits include European paintings, from medieval and Renaissance to Impressionist and Postimpressionist pieces. Modern art collections feature works by Pablo Picasso and Henri Matisse, while Asian art includes furniture and ceramics. American art sections contain extensive works by Philadelphia artists Thomas Eakins and Charles Willson Peale, and the museum's collections of prints, drawings, and photographs feature works by 19th- and 20th-century US and European artists. It also has one of the oldest and largest collections of costumes and textiles in America.

Ruben's *Prometheus Bound* (1618) is a centerpiece painting combining historical and mythological subjects.

The first floor has some excellent Impressionist and Postimpressionist paintings by artists such as Renoir, Monet, Cezanne, Pissarro, and van Gogh. Works include Renoir's *Great Bathers* (1884–87), van Gogh's *Sunflowers* (1889), Cezanne's *Large Bathers* (1906), and Monet's *Poplars* (1891), to name just a few.

Fra Angelico's *Dormition of the Virgin* (c. 1427)

EUROPEAN PAINTINGS, SCULPTURE, DECORATIVE ARTS, AND ARCHITECTURE

M OST OF THE museum's second floor is devoted to European art from 1500 to 1850. In addition, it has rooms with sculpture, furniture, descriptive interiors, and original façades that highlight periods of European history from 1100 to 1800. The Portal from the Abbey Church of Saint-Laurent dates to 1125. Its imposing stone arched walls were once the main entrance to the Augustinian abbey church of Saint-Laurent in France.

The Cloister with Elements from the Abbey of Saint-Genis-des-Fontaines is based on one in a late 13th-century abbey in Roussillon in

Jester Vase (1894) by Marc-Louis-Emmanuel Solon

southwestern France. Other decorative arts include ceramic vases, stained and painted glass, stone sculptures, and metal and wooden objects ranging from candelabra to mahogany furniture and glass goblets. Key European paintings include masterpieces by Fra Angelico, Sandro Botticelli, Rogier van der Weyden, Peter Paul Rubens, and Nicolas Poussin, as well as classic European views and land- and cityscapes from 18th-century verdute artists Canaletto, his nephew and pupil Bernardo Bellotto, and Francesco Guardi. Renaissance portraits and religious paintings include Jan van Eyck's *Saint Francis of Assisi Receiving the Stigmata* (1428–30), Botticelli's *Stories of Saint Mary Magdalene* (1484–91) and Joos van Cleve's *King Francis I* (1525).

AMERICAN ART

R ECOGNIZED AS ONE of the finest public holdings of American art, the museum's collection is sourced from the Philadelphia area. Decorative arts, paintings, and sculptures include 18th- and 19th-century silver, ceramics, and porcelain, as well as Pennsylvania German items including toys, textiles, furniture, and elaborate illuminated folk art called fraktur. Impressive bookcases, desks, chairs, and chests made in colonial Philadelphia, along with other decorative arts,

The Staircase Group (1795) by Charles Willson Peale

Japanese ceremonial teahouse, surrounded by a bamboo garden

demonstrate the cultural links between European and early American lifestyles and designs. Key paintings include Charles Willson Peale's *Rachel Weeping* (1772) and *The Staircase Group* (1795), in which he painted his sons ascending a staircase. Thomas Eakins' works are the most significant part of the museum's collection of 19th-century paintings, which also includes the renowned artist's sculptures and sketches. Other paintings include Winslow Homer's *A Huntsman and Dogs* (1891) and Edward Hick's *Noah's Ark* (1846).

Bird Tree, Pennsylvania (1800–1830)

furniture. Works by Japanese artists from the 12th to 20th centuries include exquisitely painted scrolls and screens, decorative arts, lacquer, and fine modern designs. A centerpiece exhibit is *Evanescent Joys*, a ceremonial teahouse acquired from Japan in 1928. Korean art includes ceramics, lacquer, and sculpture, of which an example is a rare 15th-century cast-iron tiger. Also on display are outstanding Persian and Turkish carpets, including the showpiece 16th- to 17th-century *Tree Carpet*. The carpets were gifted by collectors Joseph L. Williams and John D. McIlhenny in the 1940s and 50s. The museum's Indian art collection includes *Nandi, the Sacred Bull of Shiva*, a 13th-century schist carving from Mysore, and the impressive Pillared Hall from Madurai. Reconstructed from the ruins of three temples, its granite pillars are the only examples of stone architecture from India in an American museum.

MIDDLE EAST AND ASIAN ART

WITHIN THE second-floor galleries of Asian Art are exquisite carpets, delicate jade carvings, porcelains, ink paintings, and sculptures forming part of the museum's collections of Southeast Asian, Korean, Chinese, Japanese, Persian, and Turkish art.

The Chinese Ming Dynasty (1368–1644) is represented by a room brought from China, the imposing Reception Hall from a Nobleman's Palace, and ceramics and hardwood

MODERN AND CONTEMPORARY ART

THE MUSEUM'S modern art collection began with acquisitions of works by Pablo Picasso and Constantin Brancusi in the 1930s. Today key holdings include Picasso's *Self-Portrait* (1906) and *Three Musicians* (1921), encompassing his decade-long study of Synthetic Cubism. Works by Marcel Duchamp include the *The Large Glass* (1915–23), applied on two planes of glass with lead foil, fuse wire and dust, and the 1912 *Nude Descending a Staircase (No. 2)*, a mechanical portrayal of a subject with Cubist qualities. Salvador Dali's surrealistic 1936 painting *Soft Construction of Boiled Beans (Premonition of Civil War)* and Henri's Matisse's *Mademoiselle Yvonne Landsberg* (1914) also form part of the collection.

COSTUMES AND TEXTILES

ACQUISITIONS FROM the 1876 Centennial Exposition initiated the museum's costume and textile collections. The first textiles showcased designs and techniques used in India, Europe, and the Middle East. The collections grew in the early 20th century with the addition of 18th- and 19th-century French textiles, and today number over 20,000 objects, including fashionable Philadelphia apparel, Pennsylvania Dutch quilts, weaving pattern books, and colonial-era clothing. One of the most famous costumes is the wedding dress worn by Princess Grace of Monaco, a Philadelphian. Other items include African-American quilts, 20th-century hats, 19th-century needlework, church embroideries and vestments, and three-century old Japanese Noh robes, dating from between 1615 and 1867.

Gala Ensemble, Italy (late 19th to early 20th century)

FARTHER AFIELD

THE GROWTH OF neighborhoods away from the city's historic center only began in the 19th century, with the exception of areas such as Germantown and Fairmount Park, which were distinct areas in colonial times. These are home to some of the city's most renowned sights, including the University of Pennsylvania just beyond the Schuylkill River.

Statue at Fairmount Park

Fairmount Park ru leading to the ch of Manayunk a while just western bord the Barnes Foundation with a huge collection of Impressionist paintings. Sights to the south include the Italian Market and the Mummers Museum, while to the east are the varied attractions of the Camden Waterfront.

SIGHTS AT A GLANCE

Historical Buildings and Districts
Boathouse Row and
   Kelly Drive **6**
Camden Waterfront **15**
Chestnut Hill **3**
Edgar Allen Poe National
   Historic Site **1**
Fort Mifflen **14**
Germantown **2**
Italian Market **11**
Main Street Manayunk **4**
University of Pennsylvania
   and University City **8**
Walt Whitman House **16**

Parks, Gardens, and Zoos
Fairmount Park **5**
Philadelphia Zoo **7**

Museums and Galleries
*Barnes Foundation
   pp98–9* **10**
Mario Lanza Institute
   and Museum **12**
Mummers Museum **13**
University of Pennsylvania
   Museum of Archaeology
   and Anthropology **9**

KEY

▢	Main sightseeing area
▢	Urban area
✈	Airport
▬	Highway
▬	Major road
═	Minor road
—	Railway
– –	State border

0 kilometers   4

0 miles   4

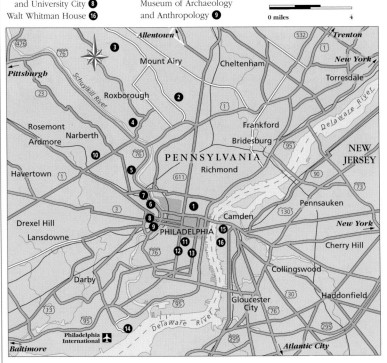

◁ **Turrets punctuate the roofline of Rosemont College, near Philadelphia**

Three-story brick house rented by Edgar Allan Poe in the mid-1840s

Edgar Allan Poe National Historic Site ❶

532 N 7th St. 📞 (215) 597-8780. 🚇 Spring Garden. 🚌 47. 🕐 9am–5pm Wed–Sun. ● Mon, Tue; Jan 1, Veterans Day, Thanksgiving, Dec 25. ♿ limited. 🌐 www.nps.gov/edal

THE GREAT American writer Edgar Allan Poe (1809–49) lived in Philadelphia for six years from 1838 to 1844 in several residences. This three-story brick house was his rented residence for about a year between 1843 and 1844, and his only home that remains today in the city.

The inside, with original walls and creaking wooden floors, is empty as there are no accurate descriptions of what the house looked like during Poe's time, and none of his personal belongings have survived. The visitor area, though, has exhibits and a video highlighting his life and a room decorated as depicted in his essay "The Philosophy of Furniture."

In fact, Poe's years in the city were some of his most productive with the publishing of "The Murders in the Rue Morgue," "The Gold Bug," and "The Tell-Tale Heart." Poe fans seem to think that the house's basement may have inspired him to write "The Black Cat." One wall has brick columns similar to where, in the story, the murderer had entombed his victim. The raven statue outside is a tribute to one of his poems, "The Raven."

Germantown ❷

Centered by Germantown Avenue at Chelten Ave. 🚆 R8 SEPTA regional rail to Chelten Ave station. 🚌 23.

A FEW MILES northwest of Philadelphia, this neighborhood was first inhabited in 1683 by German settlers wooed by Penn's promise of religious freedom. Its most prominent historical period was during and after the American Revolutionary War. It was the site of the Battle of Germantown in 1777, when British troops withstood an attack by the Continental Army, forcing the Americans to retreat to Valley Forge for the winter (see pp20–21). In 1793, President Washington and his family moved here to escape the yellow fever epidemic in the city. Several historic homes in this now urban neighborhood have been preserved and are open to visitors (see pp106–107).

At its center is Market Square, a busy marketplace in colonial times and now a small park dominated by a Civil War memorial. Flanking the square are the Deshler-Morris House, and the **Germantown Historical**

Society and Visitor Center. The center's museum features rotating exhibitions chosen from among its 20,000 historical artifacts and documents, some of which date back to the 1600s. To its north is the **Awbury Arboretum**, a landscaped area with gardens, ponds, and a Victorian estate originally owned by a Quaker family. The neighborhood is best visited during the day as it is less safe at night.

🏛 **Germantown Historical Society and Visitor Center**
5501 Germantown Ave. 📞 (215) 844–1683. 🕐 9am–5pm Tue & Thu, 1–5pm Sun. 🎫 ♿
🌷 **Awbury Arboretum**
1, Awbury Rd. 📞 (215) 849-2855. 🕐 dawn–dusk. ♿ limited access.

Chestnut Hill ❸

Centered by Germantown Ave at Chestnut Hill Ave. 🚆 R7 or R8 SEPTA regional rail to Chestnut Hill stations.

WHAT BEGAN as a settlement of farmhouses and taverns in the mid-1700s is now one of Philadelphia's most upscale neighborhoods. Located on the city's northern border, Chestnut Hill is an urban village bisected by Germantown Avenue. Its shaded, cobblestoned streets

Boutiques and cafés line the sidewalks of Chestnut Hill

are lined with boutiques, fine-food restaurants, cafés, and galleries. Within its hilly terrain are the Wissahickon Gorge greenbelt and the **Morris Arboretum and Gardens**, an immense area that includes thousands of rare plants and "trees-of-record," greenhouses, ponds, and meadows. Some of the other attractions in this area include the **Woodmere Art Museum**, which is housed in a Victorian mansion and features a collection of more than 300 paintings and sculptures. The **Chestnut Hill Historical Society** has a collection of more than 15,000 items that date from the 1680s to the present, including artifacts, documents, and photographs.

🌸 **Morris Arboretum and Gardens**
100 Northwestern Ave.
📞 *(215) 247-5777.*
🕐 *Apr–Oct: 10am–4pm Mon–Fri, 10am–5pm Sat & Sun; Jun–Aug: 10am–8:30pm Thu; Nov–Mar: 10am–4pm.*
📷 ♿

🏛 **Woodmere Art Museum**
9201 Germantown Ave. 📞 *(215) 247-0476.* 🕐 *10am–5pm Tue–Sat, 1–5pm Sun.* 📷 ♿

🏫 **Chestnut Hill Historical Society**
8708 Germantown Ave. 📞 *(215) 247-0417.* 🕐 *9:30am–2:30pm Tue & Fri; appointments preferred.*
🌐 *www.chhist.org*

Main Street Manayunk ❹

Main St, Manayunk. 📞 *(215) 482-9565.* 🚉 *R6 SEPTA regional rail Manayunk Station.* 🚌 *61.*
🌐 *www.manayunk.com*

ONCE AN industrial urban village, this neighborhood has been revitalized in recent years with trendy stores, galleries, restaurants, and cafés lining the fashionable Main Street. In 1824, it changed its name to Manayunk, from the Lenape word *manaiung*, which means, "Where we go to drink." With the completion of the Manayunk Canal, the

Outdoor seating at a café along Manayunk's Main Street

early 19th-century town grew into a thriving mill and industrial town. Today, the old mills are home to upscale apartments and an eclectic mix of store-fronted shops. Main Street comes to life especially on weekends when sidewalk café tables fill up. The pedestrian walk along the canal is also popular with walkers and bikers.

Rose at Morris Arboretum

Fairmount Park ❺

On both sides of the Schuylkill River & along Wissahickon Creek. 📞 *(215) 685-0000.* 🚉 *30th St Station.* Ⓢ *Spring Garden.* 🌐 *www. phila.gov/fairpark*

STRETCHING ALONG the shores of the Schuylkill River and Wissahickon Creek, Fairmount Park forms part of an

extensive greenbelt. Its grassy fields and dense wooded areas are dotted with statues and crisscrossed by miles of hiking paths. The most popular path runs parallel to Kelly and West River drives and stretches 8 miles (13 km) along both sides of the river.

West of the Schuylkill River is the Mann Center for the Performing Arts, an outdoor amphitheater and summer home of the Philadelphia Orchestra *(see p164)*. The nearby **Horticulture Center** has elongated ponds with fountains, while the **Shofuso Japanese House and Garden** is a 17th-century-style Shoin mansion that has a peaceful koi pond stuffed with fish and floating lily pads. The grand **Memorial Hall**, a centerpiece during the country's centennial celebration, was formerly the city's art museum. It was dedicated by President Ulysses S. Grant, but is now closed to the public except for special events.

Other key attractions include 18th- and early 19th-century mansions that were once the rural homes of prominent colonial families *(see pp108–109)*.

🌸 **Horticulture Center**
📞 *(215) 685-0096.* 🕐 *Jul–Sep: 9am–5pm; Oct–Jun 9am–3pm.* 📷 ♿

🌸 **Shofuso Japanese House and Garden**
📞 *(215) 878-5097.* 🕐 *May–Oct: 10am–4pm Tue–Fri, 11am–5pm Sat & Sun.* ⚫ *Nov–Apr.* 📷

🏫 **Memorial Hall**
📞 *(215) 334-3472.* ⚫ *closed to the public.*

Geese at Fairmount Park, part of Philadelphia's greenbelt

Boathouse Row and Kelly Drive **❻**

West of Philadelphia Museum of Art along Kelly Drive. 🚊 *30th St Station.* 🚌 *38, Philly Phlash.*

THIS ROW OF quaint stone and brick boathouses is home to what's affectionately known as the "Schuylkill Navy," namely rowing and sculling clubs patronized by area universities and high schools. Situated on the river's eastern shore, some feature Victorian Gothic architecture and date back to the 19th century. These boathouses, and others farther upstream, host the country's largest intercollegiate sculling contest in May, the annual Dad Vail Regatta *(see p33).*

At one end of Boathouse Row is the Azalea Garden, where people picnic under the magnolias and large oaks. At the other end is the small 1887 lighthouse that once flashed beacons to warn barges and steamboats of the nearby Fairmount dam. Also close to Boathouse Row is Icelandic sculptor Einar Jonsson's 1918 statue of Thorfinn Karlsefni, the Viking explorer who is said to have landed in America a millennium ago. At night, strings of lights illuminating the boathouses reflect

Hummingbird at Philadelphia Zoo

off the river, creating an idyllic scene often highlighted on calendars and postcards. A popular path along Kelly Drive offers miles of walking and biking on both sides of the Schuylkill River.

Philadelphia Zoo **❼**

3400 Girard Ave. 📞 *(215) 243-1100.* 🚊 *30th St Station.* Ⓢ *34th St.* 🚌 *38.* 🕐 *Feb–Nov: 9:30am–5pm; Dec–Jan: 9:30am–4pm.* ⬤ *Jan 1, Jun 9, Thanksgiving, Dec 24, 25, & 31.* ♿ Ⓦ *www.phillyzoo.org*

BOASTING Victorian gardens and historic architecture, including the country home of William Penn's grandson John, the Philadelphia Zoo was opened in 1874. Housed in a large area, the zoo is the country's oldest and is home to more than 1,600 exotic animals from around the world. The zoo houses several rare species such as naked mole rats and blue-eyed lemurs. A walk-through giant otter habitat shows these animals at their playful best. The magnificent big cats – clouded leopards, lions, tigers (including rare white tigers), and jaguars – are kept in near-natural habitats or inside the Carnivora House, in weather-protected cages that provide a close-up view. Other features are an open

birdhouse with uncaged finches and hummingbirds; the Reptile and Amphibian House with venomous king cobras, giant tortoises, and alligators basking in a tropical paradise; and a large reserve area for ten primate species. The Zooballoon takes passengers aloft for panoramic views of the city.

University of Pennsylvania and University City **❽**

Main Campus between Chestnut St & University Ave and between 32nd & 40th Sts. 📞 *(215) 898-5000.* 🚊 *SEPTA R1 regional rail to University City Station.* Ⓢ *34th St.* 🚌 *42.* Ⓦ *www.upenn.edu*

THIS HIGHLY REGARDED Ivy League school has the honor of being America's first university. Founded by Benjamin Franklin in 1749, the University of Pennsylvania started classes two years later, beginning what would become the nation's first liberal arts curriculum. The university is also home to the country's first medical school, student union, and the oldest collegiate football field still in use.

Today, with more than 20,000 students enrolled in undergraduate, graduate, and professional school programs, it is often listed among America's top ten universities. Its vast urban campus features

Scenic Boathouse Row along Schuylkill River, to the west of the city

Shaded walkway at the University of Pennsylvania campus

19th-century buildings along grassy areas and shaded walkways, including Locust Walk, its main pedestrian street. Among the notable sculptures on the campus are two of Franklin along Locust Walk, one with the statesman and inventor seated on a bench.

The Penn campus is located within University City, a revitalized neighborhood with one of the Philadelphia area's most ethnically diverse and educated populations. It has Victorian-era homes, as well as its own brand of galleries, cafés, and restaurants. Within University City are also several medical centers and other institutions of higher learning, including Drexel University.

University of Pennsylvania Museum of Archaeology and Anthropology ❾

3260 South St. ☎ (215) 898-4000.
🚊 R1 University City Station. 🚌 34th St. 🚌 42. ⏰ 10am–4:30pm Tue–Sat, 1pm–5pm Sun. ⬤ Mon, public hols; Sun in summer. 📷 🔲 💷 🍴 🖥 ♿
W www.museum.upenn.edu

A WORLD-CLASS museum with nearly one million artifacts, this institute is one of Philadelphia's best. The museum's expansive 90 ft (27 m) rotunda is the largest unsupported masonry dome in the country, and features Chinese art and early Buddhist sculpture. The museum's collections have been gathered since its founding in 1887 through more than 400 archaeological digs and research expeditions around the world. More than 30 galleries spread over three floors house impressive remnants of civilizations past and present spanning the earth, including a 13-ton (28,650-lb) granite Sphinx of Rameses II from 1200 BC, well-preserved mummies, an Etruscan warrior helmet from the 7th century BC, Zapotec figures from Mexico, African stringed musical instruments, and an Alaskan Umiak, a whaling boat with a skin hull.

Barnes Foundation ❿

See pp98–9.

Italian Market ⓫

Along 9th St between Christian & Wharton Sts. ☎ (215) 922-5557.
🚇 Ellsworth-Federal. 🚌 47.
⏰ 9am–5pm Tue–Sat, 9am–1pm Sun. ⬤ Mon. W www.phillyitalianmarket.com

U NDER NUMEROUS awnings and corrugated tin roofs, this open-air market is the largest and oldest of its kind in the country. The market dates to the late 1800s, when Italian immigrants sold meats and produce, and Jewish merchants sold clothing. Although still predominantly Italian, today it comprises a mix of nationalities. The sights and sounds of the market, however, have not changed much from a century ago. Several stalls offer fresh fruit and vegetables, butcher shops sell prime cuts, poultry and game meats, while seafood vendors stack fish and shellfish on ice. Other specialties include pastas, cheeses from all over the world, spices, coffees, and teas. Bakeries have pastries ranging from ricotta-filled Italian cannolies to Amish baked goods. Food stands and cafés dish up Philly cheesesteaks, pizzas, and traditional Italian dishes.

A flower stall at the Italian Market

Mural depicting the Italian Market and Frank Rizzo, 1970s city mayor

Barnes Foundation ⑩

Floral motif, chest detail

ESTABLISHED IN 1922 by pharmaceutical magnate Albert C. Barnes, the Barnes Foundation has one of the world's best displays of Impressionist, French Modern, and Postimpressionist paintings. There are more than 800 works on view, including 181 by Renoir, 69 by Cezanne, and 60 by Matisse, among others by artists such as Modigliani, Rousseau, van Gogh, and Picasso. Other exhibits include ancient Egyptian and Greek art, American furniture, and African sculpture. Grouped into 96 ensembles, the collection is displayed without labels and with little regard for chronology, so as to highlight artistic affinities between diverse works. The collection is in keeping with the foundation's aim of promoting "the advancement of education and the appreciation of the fine arts." The foundation is currently in the process of being relocated to Center City.

★ The Postman
Painted by Vincent van Gogh in 1889 in Arles, France, this is a portrait of postman Joseph Roulin. The foundation is home to seven van Gogh paintings.

Gardanne
Paul Cezanne, the renowned French artist, painted this scenic landscape of the town of Gardanne in the mid-1880s. 69 of Cezanne's works are at the Barnes, helping to make it one of the finest Impressionist collections in the world.

★ Arboretum and Gardens
The arboretum has a diverse collection of plants and trees, and highlights one of the foundation's aims of imparting education in horticulture.

Lower Level

Entrance

STAR EXHIBITS

- ★ **The Postman**
- ★ **Arboretum and Gardens**
- ★ **After the Concert**
- ★ **Card Players and Girl**

GALLERY GUIDE
Artworks can be viewed on both the first and second floors. Galleries in the foundation display various paintings and sculptures that highlight different themes. An artist's oeuvre is not necessarily displayed together.

KEY

- ☐ Second floor
- ☐ First floor
- ☐ Non-exhibition space

Gallery Building Exterior
Designed by Paul Philippe Cret, the French Renaissance structure is adorned with Doric columns and African motifs.

Second Floor

22
23
19

★ After the Concert
The Barnes has over 180 works by Pierre-Auguste Renoir, including this one, which was completed by the famous French Impressionist in 1877. Renoir painted several thousand works over 60 years, even while suffering from severe arthritis toward the end of his life.

1
14
13
8
12
9
11
10

First Floor

★ Card Players and Girl
Often referred to as the father of modern art, Paul Cezanne completed this painting in 1892. Cezanne's compositions and use of color greatly influenced 20th-century art.

Main Gallery
The expansive Main Gallery has a vaulted ceiling and large windows. Extending across the top of one wall is The Dance, a mural by Matisse that was specially commissioned for this room by Dr. Barnes in 1931.

Art Deco façade of the three-story Mummers Museum

Mario Lanza Institute and Museum ⓬

Columbus House, 712 Montrose St.
 (215) 238-9691. Ⓢ Ellsworth-Federal. 🚌 47. ◯ 10am–3pm Mon–Sat, 11am Thu. ● Sun, public hols.
🏠 Ⓦ www.mario-lanza-institute.org

Housed in a former church rectory, the museum honors the world-famous Philadelphia tenor and movie star, Mario Lanza (1921–59). Lanza developed an interest in opera as he grew up, and his talents were soon recognized. His career flourished with **Mario Lanza bust** best-selling recordings and starring roles in several major films of the 1940s and 50s, such as *The Great Caruso* and *For The First Time.*

Through posters, newspaper clippings, photographs, and other memorabilia, the museum charts his life from his childhood to his death in Rome from a heart attack. The museum shop sells many of the 460 songs Lanza recorded during his career.

Mummers Museum ⓭

1100 S 2nd St. (215) 336-3050.
🚌 57. ◯ Oct–Apr: 9:30am–4:30pm Tue–Sat, noon–4:30pm Sun; May–Sep: 9:30am–9:30pm Tue, 9:30am–4:30pm Wed–Sat, noon–4:30pm Sun; library research by appt. ● Mon, public hols; Jul–Aug: Sun. 🈳 🏠 ♿
Ⓦ www.mummers.com

Opened during the nation's bicentennial year in 1976, this museum celebrates the city's Mummers tradition and annual New Year's day Mummers Parade where thousands of people strut to the rhythm of marching string bands *(see p35)*. Permanent and rotating exhibits showcase the museum's extensive collections. Artifacts from past parades are displayed to recreate the excitement of the event. They include floats, musical instruments used in the parades, and plumed and sequinned costumes. The museum's library has newspaper clippings dating back to the late 19th century, and more than 6,000 manuscripts, photographs, works of art, and films that highlight the parade's history and tradition. In the summer months, string bands perform so that visitors can sample the sounds of the Mummers celebrations.

Fort Mifflin ⓮

Fort Mifflin Rd near Island Ave.
 (215) 685-4167. ◯ Apr–Nov: 10am–4pm Wed–Sun. ● public hols; Dec–Mar, except for groups. 🈳
Ⓦ www.phila.gov/recreation/historical/fortmifflin.html

Historic fort mifflin, with its well-preserved ramparts and soldiers' barracks, is the only fort in Philadelphia. Surrounded by a moat, it overlooks the Delaware River and offers views of the city skyline, and the nearby and often noisy Philadelphia airport.

Construction of the fort began with the installation of sturdy granite walls in 1771 – the only remnants of the original fortification that remain today – and the fort stayed in continuous use through the Korean War in the 1950s.

Its most prominent moment, however, was during the Revolutionary War, when the Continental troops in the fort managed to keep the British at bay for seven weeks. This allowed Washington to retreat to Valley Forge and thwarted British efforts to open a supply route along the Delaware River for their troops who had occupied Philadelphia.

Today, Fort Mifflin is a popular tourist attraction. The

Mummers Tradition and Parade

The Mummers tradition dates to the late 1600s when Swedish and Finnish settlers ushered in the new year with parades and masquerades. Others soon joined in with the use of costumes based on Greek celebrations of King Momus, the Italian feast of Saturnalia, and the British Mummery Play. Today, the parade features the Comics, who dress as hobos and clowns and poke satirical fun at the crowds; the Fancies, who dazzle in sequined, feathered outfits; the Fancy Brigades, who perform themed, choreographed shows; and the String Bands, where marchers play banjos, saxophones, drums, and glockenspiels.

Costumed revelers at a Mummers Day parade

former soldiers' barracks now house a small museum and a diorama depicting the siege of 1777. On display are tools, cannonballs, and grapeshot from the Revolutionary War, as well as items from the American Civil War, when Confederate soldiers, Union deserters, and civilian lawbreakers were imprisoned at the fort.

Moat around 18th-century Fort Mifflin, Philadelphia's lone fort

Camden Waterfront 🕧

Delaware River, NJ. 📞 *(856) 757-9400.* 🚇 *PATCO Speedline from Center City, New Jersey Transit.* 🚌 *New Jersey Transit.* 🚢 *RiverLink Ferry.* 🔳 *www.camdenwaterfront.com*

THIS SPACIOUS riverfront area in New Jersey, opposite Penn's Landing, has gardens, a music venue, an IMAX theater, and attractions for both adults and children.

One of the biggest draws is the **Adventure Aquarium**. With one of the largest tanks in North America, it contains over 5,000 aquatic creatures, such as sharks, seals, and stingrays. Moored nearby is the floating museum, the **Battleship New Jersey**, with nine 16-inch (40-cm) guns in three triple turrets. One of the nation's most decorated battleships, she served in World War II and the Vietnam War. The waterfront

is also home to the 6,500-seat Campbell's Field, which hosts the Camden Riversharks, a minor league baseball team. For concerts, head to the Tweeter Center, an indoor and outdoor amphitheater. The **RiverLink Ferry** *(see p186)* offers a scenic ride across the Delaware River to and from Penn's Landing.

➤ **Adventure Aquarium**
1, Riverside Dr. 📞 *(856) 365-3300.* 🔳 *Apr 16–Sep 15: 9:30am–5:30pm; Sep 16–Apr 15: 9:30am–4:30pm Mon–Fri, 10am–5pm Sat & Sun.* 🈲 🔳 *www.adventureaquarium.com*

🏛 **Battleship New Jersey**
📞 *(866) 877-6262.* 🔳 *Jan–Feb: 9am–3pm Fri–Mon; Mar: 9am–3pm; Apr–Sep: 9am–5pm; Oct–Dec 9am–3pm.* 🈲 🔳 *www.battleshipnewjersey.org*

🚢 **RiverLink Ferry**
📞 *(215) 925-5465.* 🔳 *Apr: 9:20am–6pm Fri–Sun; May–Sep: 9:20am–6pm.* 🈲 ♿ 🔳 *www.riverlinkferry.org*

Adventure Aquarium, exterior detail

Walt Whitman House 🕕

328 Mickle Boulevard, NJ. 📞 *(856) 964-5383.* 🚇 *PATCO Speedline, New Jersey Transit.* 🚌 *New Jersey Transit.* 🚢 *RiverLink Ferry.* 🔳 *only by appointment: 10am–noon, 1–4pm Wed–Sat.*

THIS MODEST, two-story house two blocks east of the Camden Waterfront is the only home that renowned American poet Walt Whitman (1819–92) ever owned. He lived here from 1884 until his death in 1892.

Whitman left Washington DC after suffering a stroke in 1873, coming to live with his brother George in Camden. When his brother decided to move to a nearby rural area, Whitman opted to stay on here. With the surprising success of the 1882 edition of his most famous volume of poetry, *Leaves of Grass*, he was able to purchase this home. Already a prominent poet, Whitman was visited in Camden by famous writers, such as Charles Dickens and Oscar Wilde, and Philadelphia artist and friend Thomas Eakins *(see p87)*, who photographed and painted the aging poet.

Today, the house, a National Historic Landmark, contains some of Whitman's personal belongings, letters, and old photographs, including the earliest known image of the poet from 1848.

USS *New Jersey*, berthed at the dock adjacent to the Tweeter Center at Camden Waterfront

TWO GUIDED WALKS
AND A DRIVE

PHILADELPHIA'S colonial history around Society Hill and Independence Mall, also called "America's most historic square mile," is best explored on foot. However, for those who wish to explore other historical areas, this section introduces some neighborhoods that can be explored through a guided walk or drives.

The first is a walking tour around the Penn's Landing area along the scenic Delaware River. This tour includes stops at Gloria Dei (Old Swedes') Church, the oldest church in Pennsylvania, and the Irish, Korean, and Vietnam memorials. The second

Maritime painting in the Seaport Museum

walk explores colonial-era homes along Germantown, which was settled in 1683. This 90-minute walk includes the "White House," where the first president of the US, George Washington, and his family stayed to escape the city's 1793 yellow fever epidemic. The third is a drive through Fairmount Park, close to the Philadelphia Museum of Art on the banks of the Schuylkill River. This tour also highlights historic homes, many of which were once the summer retreats of the colonial elite. This drive includes splendid panoramic views of the city skyline at Belmont Plateau.

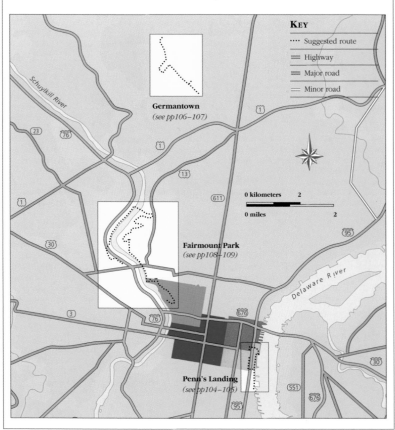

KEY

···· Suggested route
═══ Highway
═══ Major road
─── Minor road

Germantown
(see pp106–107)

Fairmount Park
(see pp108–109)

0 kilometers 2

0 miles 2

Penn's Landing
(see pp104–105)

◁ **One of the rowing teams of the "Schuylkill Navy" brings its boat ashore at Boathouse Row**

A Two-Hour Walk Along Penn's Landing

Penn's statue at Welcome Park ①

PENN'S LANDING'S PLAZA, walkways, marina, and Christopher Columbus Park provide the setting for a scenic walk along the Delaware River, the natural boundary between the states of Pennsylvania and New Jersey. Docked along the riverside are some of Philadelphia's historic ships and popular dinner cruise boats, as this area is now a thriving commercial and entertainment zone. The walk, which starts in the neighborhood of Old City and includes historic sights, stretches south along the river to the Gloria Dei Church and then doubles back to include the city's monuments to the Vietnam War and Korean War.

Independence Seaport Museum ⑥, showcasing US maritime heritage

Corn Exchange National Bank, with a unique domed clock tower ②

Welcome Park to Irish Memorial

The walk begins in Welcome Park ① *(see p55)* at 2nd Street and the Sansom Street alley. Dedicated to William Penn, the park is located where his home, the Slate Roof House, once stood. Pass by the historic Thomas Bond House Bed and Breakfast *(see p134)* along 2nd Street to Chestnut Street, where the Corn Exchange National Bank building ② sits across the street. Designed in Colonial Revival style, the structure dates back to the mid-19th century and now contains a bank, restaurants, and a newspaper office.

Turn right onto Chestnut Street and stop in front of 126 Chestnut ③. A time capsule is buried at the site and a plaque on the sidewalk reads: "From the people of the Bicentennial to the Tricentennial – our mementos to be opened by the Mayor of Philadelphia on July 4, 2076."

Cross Front Street to the Irish Memorial ④, a memorial to those who suffered during the Irish Potato Famine (1845–50).

Detail of Irish Memorial Sculpture ④

Irish Memorial to Christopher Columbus Park

Pass over I-95 and enter Penn's Landing ⑤ *(see p66)*. Head down the curving walkway toward the river for great views of the Franklin Bridge and the Camden Waterfront *(see p101)*, home to the Adventure Aquarium and the *Battleship New Jersey*.

Walk past the RiverLink Ferry port and the Independence Seaport Museum ⑥ *(see pp64–5)*, where the museum's cruiser *Olympia* and submarine *Becuna* are berthed. A dead-end walkway stretches out into the Delaware River offering splendid views of the river and the Walt Whitman Bridge. Continue around the marina to Christopher Columbus Park ⑦, which has as its centerpiece a tribute dedicated in 1992 to the 500th anniversary of the explorer's voyage to America. Across from the *Olympia* and *Becuna* is the Penn's Landing Visitor Center.

Christopher Columbus Park to Korean War Memorial

Continue south along the waterfront to the *Moshulu* ⑧, a 1904 four-masted sailing ship that is now a floating restaurant *(see p148)*. The *Spirit of Philadelphia*, a dinner cruise ship, is also berthed here. Then walk along Columbus

Camden Waterfront, across Penn's Landing and along the scenic Delaware River ⑤

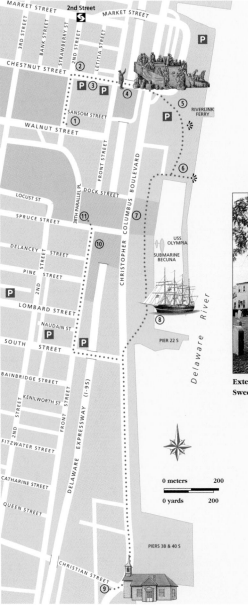

TIPS FOR WALKERS

Starting point: Welcome Park on 2nd St between Chestnut and Walnut Sts.

Length: 2 miles (3 km).

Getting there: Philly Phlash.

Stopping-off points: Stop at the Irish Memorial, take in the views along the river at Penn's Landing, and relax under the trees at Christopher Columbus Park. Take time to explore the Gloria Dei Church and a few moments to reflect at the Vietnam War and Korean War memorials.

Exterior of the restored Gloria Dei (Old Swedes') church, founded in 1677 ⑨

was completed in 1700, with the steeple added in 1703. Now an Episcopal parish, the church still contains the original marble baptismal font and carved wooden cherubim holding a bible, which were brought to the New World by the Swedish colonists. Among those buried in the church cemetery are soldiers of the Revolutionary War.

Head back up Columbus Boulevard and cross back over I-95 using the South Street overpass. Turn right on Front Street and continue to the Vietnam War Memorial ⑩. It pays tribute to the city's 80,000 veterans who served in the Vietnam War (1960–75), and has the names of more than 600 of those killed etched in stone. Cross Spruce Street and enter Foglietta Plaza, whose centerpiece is the Korean War Memorial ⑪ with the names of 603 local veterans killed or declared missing in action during the Korean War (1950–53).

Boulevard past the old Municipal Piers 38 and 40. Cross the boulevard at Christian Street to reach the Gloria Dei (Old Swedes') Church ⑨, the oldest in the state. Swedish Lutherans, who settled here in 1643, founded the church in 1677, before the arrival of William Penn. The brick building standing today

A 90-Minute Walk of Historic Homes in Germantown

ONCE A SMALL country town a few miles northwest of Old City, Germantown *(see p94)* is now one of Philadelphia's oldest neighborhoods. It was settled in 1683 by immigrants from the Rhine Valley in Germany, who were attracted by Penn's promise of religious freedom. Within a century it evolved into a retreat for wealthy Philadelphia families. The homes on this walk, along cobblestoned Germantown Avenue, have been well preserved by the active Germantown Historical Society and are National Historic Landmarks. The stop-offs should be made during the day, as the area is best avoided at night. The route can be easily driven through, and tourism markers make the homes easy to find.

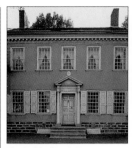

The Deshler-Morris House, now a National Park Service property ③

Germantown Historical Society and Visitor Center ①

Germantown Historical Society and Visitors Center to Deshler-Morris House

The walk starts at the Germantown Historical Society and Visitors Center ①. The center houses a museum that traces Germantown's history, in addition to selling maps of the region. The museum's rotating exhibits are culled from the society's 20,000-artifact collection of paintings, kitchenware, toys, and period clothing. Exit the center, turn left on Germantown Avenue, and walk a few blocks to

Grumblethorpe ②, built in 1744 and home of wine merchant John Wister. Sally, his daughter, lived here during the American Revolution and kept a diary recording her impressions of the turbulent times. British General James Agnew died here after being mortally wounded in the fierce Battle of Germantown in 1777 *(see p21)* and a bloodstain remains on the first floor. The Georgian Grumblethorpe displays items that belonged to the family and the gardens outside still retain their 19th-century appearance.

Head back up Germantown Avenue to one of the community's most famous homes, the Deshler-Morris House ③. The house is situated opposite the Visitor Center and Market Square, which has a Civil War monument as its centerpiece. Built in the mid-1700s by Quaker David Deshler, the home served as the headquarters of British General William Howe during the

Battle of Germantown. After the Revolutionary War, the building became known as the Germantown "White House" when President Washington and his family lived here to escape the 1793 yellow fever epidemic. Today, the house exhibits period furnishings and original paintings by colonial artists Gilbert Stuart and Charles W. Peale.

Grumblethorpe, home to one family for 160 years ②

Back parlor of the Wyck House and Garden ④

Tips for Walkers

Starting point: *Germantown Historical Society and Visitor Center.* ☎ *(215) 844-1683.*
Length: *1.5 miles (2.5 km).*
Getting there: *Take the R8 SEPTA regional rail to Chelten Avenue station.*
Stop-off points: *Visits to all homes are recommended, though these would be dependent on opening hours.*

Deshler-Morris House to Ebenezer Maxwell Mansion
Continue up Germantown Avenue several blocks to the Wyck House and Garden ④, owned for three centuries by nine generations of the same Quaker family. It contains the family's belongings, collected from 1689 until 1973, including antiques, books, and manuscripts that highlight the family's history and its devotion to the Quaker faith.

Turning left on Walnut Lane, walk two blocks to turn right on Greene Street to the Ebenezer Maxwell Mansion ⑤. Built in 1859, it is the city's only authentically restored Victorian residence. It features original 19th-century stenciled designs in the upstairs rooms, Rococo furniture in the dining room and parlor, and various other period items that reflect life in the 1860s.

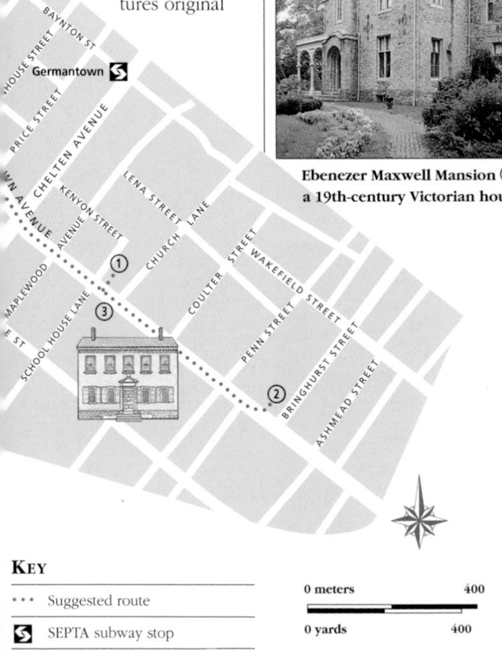
BAYNTON ST
HOUSE STREET
Germantown
PRICE STREET
CHELTEN AVENUE
AVENUE
KENYON STREET
LENA STREET
AVENUE
LANE
CHURCH
MAPLEWOOD
SCHOOL HOUSE LANE
COULTER
STREET
WAKEFIELD STREET
PENN STREET
BRINGHURST STREET
ASHMEAD STREET
E ST
1
2
3
KEY
Suggested route
SEPTA subway stop
0 meters 400
0 yards 400

Ebenezer Maxwell Mansion to Cliveden
Turn right on Tulpehocken Street back to Germantown Avenue and turn left for the Johnson House ⑥, built in 1768. This stone house was owned by three generations of an abolitionist Quaker family, who made it into the city's only stop on the Underground Railroad that led slaves to freedom in Canada and the northern states *(see p60)*.

Ebenezer Maxwell Mansion ⑤, a 19th-century Victorian house

Continuing up Germantown Avenue, the next home on the walk is Upsala ⑦. Built around 1740 and expanded in 1800, the home is an outstanding example of Federal architecture, with wooden and marble mantels inside *(see p28)*. This house is where the Continental Army made its stand during the Battle of Germantown on October 4, 1777. Across the street is Cliveden ⑧. Built in 1767, it is one of the finest surviving colonial homes in the city. During the Battle of Germantown, British troops occupied the Georgian-style Cliveden and repulsed the colonial army. Chipped bricks from rifle shots are still evident on the home's façade, and one room has an original musket ball hole from the battle that raged in the street outside. Reenactments of the battle are held on the grounds on the first Saturday of every October.

The study at Cliveden, an example of a colonial-era house ⑧

A Three-Hour Drive Around Fairmount Park Historic Mansions

One of the many statues in Fairmount Park

Boathouse Row along Kelly Drive

PROMINENT COLONIAL Philadelphia families took note of the trees and rolling hills in the landscape just west of the city along the Schuylkill River, and built mansions in what is today Fairmount Park *(see p95)*. Some of the homes had working farms with grazing lands and orchards, while others were upscale summer retreats. The park was established when the city began purchasing these properties in the mid-19th century, thus preserving scenic land and the homes in their architectural splendor. They are open for tours and are best seen as part of a driving tour. Those without vehicles can take a trolley tour conducted by Fairmount Park.

Lemon Hill to Laurel Hill

Begin the drive from the parking lot at the Philadelphia Museum of Art's West Entrance ①. Turn left at the traffic light onto Kelly Drive, then drive straight on. At the seated statue of President Lincoln ②, take the fork to the right, and then make a sharp left to reach Lemon Hill ③. The house was named after the lemon trees that once grew here when Revolutionary War financier and signer of the Declaration of Independence Robert Morris owned the land. A later owner, Henry Pratt, built the mansion in 1800. The oval rooms, with curved doors, fanlights, and fireplaces on all three levels, are Federal elements, while the Palladian windows are Georgian remnants. Return to the Lincoln statue, and turning right, continue up Kelly Drive past Boathouse Row. At the statue of Ulysses S. Grant turn right onto Fountain Green Drive and then left for Mount Pleasant ④. Once described by President John Adams as "the most elegant seat in Pennsylvania," this Georgian house has ornate woodwork and classical motifs in the entrance hall and stairway. Returning to Fountain Green Drive, which merges with Reservoir Drive, continue to Ormiston ⑤. Built in the 1790s in Georgian style, the house has an original Scottish oven and an open fireplace. Events and rotating exhibits at Ormiston highlight the area's British heritage.

Drive down Reservoir Drive and turn left onto Randolph Drive. Continue to Edgeley Drive for Laurel Hill ⑥, a 1767 Georgian-style country house with a two-story octagonal wing, perched on a prominent bluff overlooking the river.

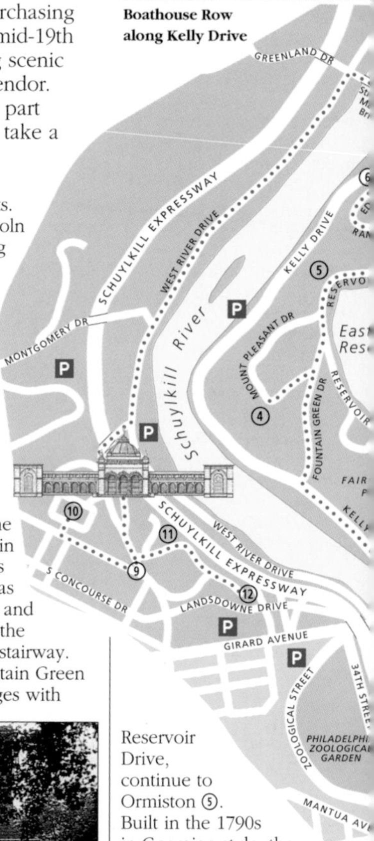

Mount Pleasant, built between 1762 and 1765 ④

Woodford, a National Historic Landmark ⑦

Laurel Hill to Memorial Hall

Continue through an intersection that has an equestrian statue of an American Indian, and onto Dauphin Drive. Turn left before 33rd Street onto Greenland Drive to reach Woodford ⑦, built in 1758 by William Coleman, a merchant and friend of Benjamin Franklin. The Georgian house has an array of exquisite colonial decorative arts and furniture, donated by Naomi Wood, a Philadelphian collector. Continue up Greenland Drive a short distance to Strawberry Mansion ⑧, with its Federal-style center

wing built by Judge William Lewis in 1789. Two large wings, in Greek Revival style, were added later. The house displays Empire and Federal period furnishings. Key exhibits include a doll collection and a well-preserved Victorian dollhouse. Drive down Strawberry Mansion Drive, turn right at Woodford Drive, and cross the Strawberry Mansion Bridge. Make a quick left onto West River Drive, continue for about a mile (1.6 km) and turn right onto Black Road toward the Smith Civil War Memorial ⑨. Turn right at the Memorial onto North Concourse Drive to reach Memorial Hall ⑩. Built in Beaux-Arts style, it was the city's first art museum and is the only surviving major building from the 1876 Centennial Exhibition.

Memorial Hall to Sweetbriar
Returning to the Smith Civil War Memorial, turn left, and then make a quick right onto Cedar Grove Drive and head to Cedar Grove ⑪, a house that was built elsewhere and reassembled in Fairmount Park. This Georgian house has an unusual two-sided wall of closets on the second floor, and much of its original, early Pennsylvania furniture. It is now maintained by the Philadelphia Museum of Art. For the last stop, turn right after Cedar Grove towards the

Sweetbriar, a three-story house built in Federal style ⑫

Federal-style Sweetbriar ⑫, the home of merchant Samuel Breck, built in 1797. The Etruscan Room is decorated in keeping with Breck's interest in classical forms and ancient Etruscan wall painting.

Other historic homes such as Chaminoux, Ridgeland, and the Belmont Mansion are not open for visitors to tour.

| 0 meters | 500 |
| 0 yards | 500 |

KEY

• • • Suggested route

P Parking

Cedar Grove, built as a summer home in 1750 ⑪

BEYOND
PHILADELPHIA

EXPLORING BEYOND PHILADELPHIA 112-113
THE PENNSYLVANIA DUTCH COUNTRY 114-119
GETTYSBURG 120-123
THE TRI-STATE AREA: PENNSYLVANIA,
DELAWARE, AND NEW JERSEY 124-129

Exploring Beyond Philadelphia

Statue, Gettysburg

To the west of Philadelphia, the area encompassing Lancaster County is known as the Pennsylvania Dutch Country, and is made up of bucolic hills and farmland as far as the eye can see. The region is home to the Amish *(see p115)* who wear traditional clothing and are often seen riding in horse-drawn buggies. Farther west is the town of Hershey, home of the chocolates, and Gettysburg, site of the American Civil War's bloodiest battle. To the east, the glitzy casinos of Atlantic City are just over an hour's drive away, and a little farther is the idyllic beach resort of Cape May.

Fountains at Longwood Gardens

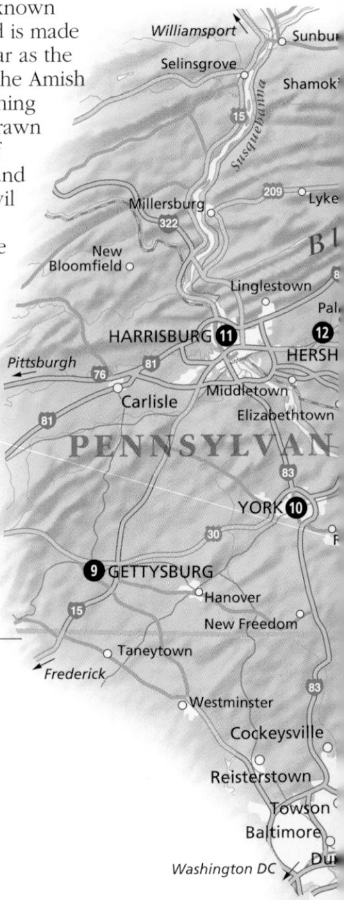

Sights at a Glance

Atlantic City, NJ 19
Bird-in-Hand, PA 6
Brandywine Battlefield State Park 24
Brandywine River Museum 25
Cape May, NJ 20
Ephrata, PA 4
Doylestown, PA 14
Gettysburg, PA 9
Hagley Museum 21
Hershey, PA 12
Harrisburg, PA 11
Intercourse, PA 5
Lancaster, PA 1
Landis Valley Museum pp116–17 2
Lititz, PA 3
Longwood Gardens 23
New Hope, PA 15
Paradise, PA 7
Pennsbury Manor 18
Reading, PA 13
Strasburg, PA 8
Trenton, NJ 17
Valley Forge National Historic Park 26
Washington Crossing Historic Park 16
Winterthur Museum 22
York, PA 10

See Also

- ***Where to Stay*** pp139–41
- ***Restaurants and Cafés*** pp151–3

Boy outside a candy and ice cream store in Strasburg

Key

- Highway
- Major road
- Other roads
- Major rail
- Minor rail
- State boundary

Farmers using horse-drawn wagons and traditional implements in Lancaster County, Pennsylvania

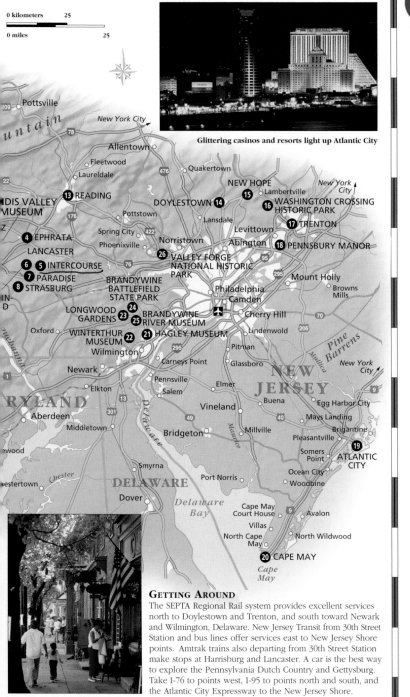

0 kilometers   25

0 miles   25

Glittering casinos and resorts light up Atlantic City

Pottsville

New York City

Allentown

Fleetwood

Laureldale

Quakertown

13 READING

NEW HOPE

Lambertville

New York City

DOYLESTOWN **14**

15

DIS VALLEY MUSEUM

16 WASHINGTON CROSSING HISTORIC PARK

Pottstown

Lansdale

4 EPHRATA

Spring City

Norristown

Levittown

17 TRENTON

LANCASTER

Phoenixville

Abington

18 PENNSBURY MANOR

6 5 INTERCOURSE

VALLEY FORGE NATIONAL HISTORIC PARK

26

7 PARADISE

8 STRASBURG

Philadelphia

Mount Holly

Camden

Browns Mills

BRANDYWINE BATTLEFIELD STATE PARK

Cherry Hill

LONGWOOD GARDENS **23**

24

Oxford

WINTERTHUR MUSEUM **22**

25 BRANDYWINE RIVER MUSEUM

21 HAGLEY MUSEUM

Lindenwold

Wilmington

Pitman

Newark

Carneys Point

Glassboro

NEW

New York City

Elkton

Pennsville

Elmer

JERSEY

RYLAND

Salem

Vineland

Buena

Egg Harbor City

Aberdeen

Mays Landing

Middletown

Bridgeton

Millville

Brigantine

Pleasantville

Somers Point

19 ATLANTIC CITY

ewood

Smyrna

Port Norris

Ocean City

Woodbine

esterown

DELAWARE

Dover

Delaware Bay

Cape May Court House

Avalon

Villas

North Cape May

North Wildwood

20 CAPE MAY

Cape May

Shoppers at Main Street, Lititz

GETTING AROUND

The SEPTA Regional Rail system provides excellent services north to Doylestown and Trenton, and south toward Newark and Wilmington, Delaware. New Jersey Transit from 30th Street Station and bus lines offer services east to New Jersey Shore points. Amtrak trains also departing from 30th Street Station make stops at Harrisburg and Lancaster. A car is the best way to explore the Pennsylvania Dutch Country and Gettysburg. Take I-76 to points west, I-95 to points north and south, and the Atlantic City Expressway to the New Jersey Shore.

Soldiers and Sailors Monument in Penn Square, Lancaster

Lancaster ❶

Lancaster County, PA. 🏠 56,000. 🚉 🚌 🛈 *Pennsylvania Dutch Country Visitor Center: Route 30 at Greenfield Exit; (717) 299-8901.* 🖳 *www. padutchcountry.com*

F OUNDED BY John Wright in 1730 and named after his birthplace in England, today Lancaster is the county seat. Its tree-shaded streets are still lined with 18th- and 19th-century buildings. In the heart of downtown is Penn Square with its centerpiece Soldiers and Sailors Monument, dedicated in 1874 to local men who fought in the American Civil War between 1861 and 1865. On the square's northwest corner, three adjoining buildings dating from the 1790s house the **Lancaster Cultural History Museum**. Its collection includes striking colonial grandfather clocks. A Renaissance-style mural adorns the vaulted ceiling of one of the buildings.

At the **Lancaster Central Market**, next to the museum, vendors and Amish farmers sell cheeses, meats, flowers, fresh produce, and treats such as homemade cider. Nearby, in a Beaux Arts-style building modeled after New York's Penn Station, is the **Lancaster Quilt & Textile Museum** with a collection of 82 Amish and Mennonite quilts.

Located west of downtown is **Wheatland**, the estate of

the 15th president of the US, James Buchanan, who served during the tumultuous years leading up to the Civil War. The house, named for the wheat fields it once overlooked, still features most of Buchanan's original belongings.

🏛 Lancaster Cultural History Museum
13, W King St. 📞 *(717) 299-6440.* 🕐 *10am–5pm Tue–Sat; noon–5pm Sun.* 🖳 *www. lancasterheritage.com*

🏛 Lancaster Quilt & Textile Museum
37 N Market St. 📞 *(717) 397-2970.* 🕐 *10am–5pm Tue–Sat; noon–5pm Sun.* 🖳 *www.quiltandtextilemuseum.com*

🏯 Wheatland
1120 Marietta Ave. 📞 *(717) 392-8721.* 🕐 *Apr–Oct: 10am–3:45pm; Nov: 10am–3:45pm Fri–Mon; Dec: days vary but open from Dec 26–30, 10am–3:45pm.* ⬤ *Thanksgiving, Dec 25, Jan–Mar.* 🖳 *www.wheatland.org*

Landis Valley Museum ❷

See pp116–17.

Lititz ❸

Lancaster County, PA. 🏠 9,000. 🚌 🛈 *Lititz Welcome Center: 18 N Broad St, (717) 626-8981.*

N AMED AFTER a town in Bohemia, Lititz was founded by Moravians in 1756 and remained a closed settlement

for nearly a century. The town, with restored 18th-century buildings and a quaint Main Street shopping district, features the lovely Lititz Springs Park, which has a natural spring-fed creek.

Moravian Church Square today includes the centerpiece church. Nearby is the **Lititz Museum** with its star exhibit, the Johannes Mueller House, a restored 1792 Moravian stone house named for a local tanner and dyer. A room in the museum is dedicated to General John Sutter, founder of Sacramento and a Lititz resident. It was the discovery of gold on his land that led to the 1849 California Gold Rush.

An old-fashioned pretzel

The **Sturgis Pretzel House**, dating from 1861, offers visitors pretzel tours. The **Wilbur Chocolate Candy Store and Museum** displays 19th-century chocolate molds and recipe cards that highlight the company's history since 1884.

🏛 Lititz Museum
137–145 East Main St. 📞 *(717) 627-4636.* 🕐 *Memorial Day–Oct: 10am–4pm Mon–Sat; special weekends in May, Nov, & Dec.* 🖳 🛈

🏯 Sturgis Pretzel House
219 East Main St. 📞 *(717) 626-4354.* 🕐 *9am–5pm Mon–Sat.* 🖳 *www. sturgispretzel.com*

🏛 Wilbur Chocolate Candy Store and Museum
48 N Broad St. 📞 *(717) 626-3249.* 🕐 *10am–5pm Mon–Sat.* 🖳 *www. wilburbuds.com*

Lititz's historic Main Street shopping district

The Amish, Mennonites, and Brethren

THE MENNONITES and the Amish trace their roots to the Swiss Anabaptist ("New Birth") movement of 1525, an offshoot of the Protestant Reformation, whose creed rejected the formality of the established churches. Lured by the promise of religious freedom held out to them by William Penn, the Mennonites were the first to arrive in Germantown in the late 17th century. They were soon followed by the Amish

Detail from an Amish quilt

who settled in what is now Lancaster County in the early 18th century. However, not all Pennsylvania Dutch are Amish or Mennonites; Brethren and other sub-groups are also part of the community. The mostly German heritage of these groups has given rise to a popular myth about the name "Pennsylvania Dutch" – it is thought that it came from other early colonists mispronouncing "Pennsylvania Deutsch."

Amish farms *have changed little since the 17th century. Farming is usually done with horsedrawn equipment with bare metal wheels.*

AMISH

The Amish sect began in the 1690s when Jacob Amman, a Swiss bishop, split from the Mennonites. The conservative Old Order Amish disdain any device that would connect them to the larger world, including electricity, cars, modern farm tools, and telephones.

Amish families *dress in plain, dark attire, with women in white caps and men in straw hats.*

Buggies are used even today

MENNONITES

Taking their name from Menno Simons, a young Dutch priest who advocated adult baptism by faith in the 1530s, Mennonites are pacifists and believe in simple living. However, they do not segregate themselves from society, and in recent years, urbanization has lured many to the cities.

Mennonites in traditional dress

Old Order Brethren at a Pennsylvania Dutch Country covered bridge

BRETHREN

Alexander Mack founded this movement in 1708, breaking away from the established and reformed faiths of the time and following the German Pietists in espousing worship on a more personal level. The pacifist Brethren migrated to America in the late 1720s. They believe in adult baptism and adhere only to the teachings of the New Testament.

The Brethren church *is where the community worships and baptizes adults by "dunking" them thrice in the name of the Holy Trinity.*

Landis Valley Museum ❷

Wares at the Country Store

The descendents of German settlers, brothers George and Henry Landis, started the Landis Valley Museum in the 1920s. At that time, it included more than 75,000 objects from the 18th and 19th centuries, featuring the traditions and farming culture of the Pennsylvania German community. Now supported and run by the state Historical and Museum Commission, Landis Valley is a living history village of Pennsylvania German life and home to nearly 100,000 artifacts such as quilts, rugs, leather goods, carriages, kitchen utensils, baskets, and lace. More than 30 homes, barns, sheds, shops, and other structures highlight the trades and crafts of earlier generations, complemented by regular demonstrations by craftspeople.

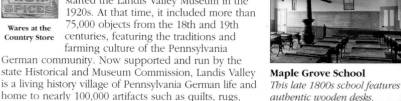

Maple Grove School
This late 1800s school features authentic wooden desks.

★ Landis Collections Gallery
Items like this silver lamp are displayed in the museum's historic collection, which dates from 1740 to 1940.

Country Store
A wide range of items, including farm tools, saddles, phonograph records, and glass-jarred licorice, stock the shelves of this reconstructed store.

Star Sights

★ Landis Collections Gallery

★ Transportation Building

★ Landis Brothers House and Stable

★ Gun Shop

Firehouse and Surveyor Shop
The larger firehouse, which has original pumpers inside, resembles a late 19th-century fire company.

★ Transportation Building

An assortment of late 19th-century sleighs is one of the displays in this building, which also houses horse-drawn buggies, carriages, wagons, and hand-drawn carts once used for light chores.

VISITORS' CHECKLIST

Route 272, 2451 Kissel Hill Road, Lancaster, PA. 📞 (717) 569-0401; Weathervane Museum Store (717) 569-9312. 🚉 Amtrak from 30th St Station to Lancaster. 🕐 9am–5pm Mon–Sat, noon–5pm Sun. ⬤ Jan 1, Thanksgiving, Dec 25. 📷 ♿ call to arrange. 📱 🅆 www.landisvalleymuseum.org

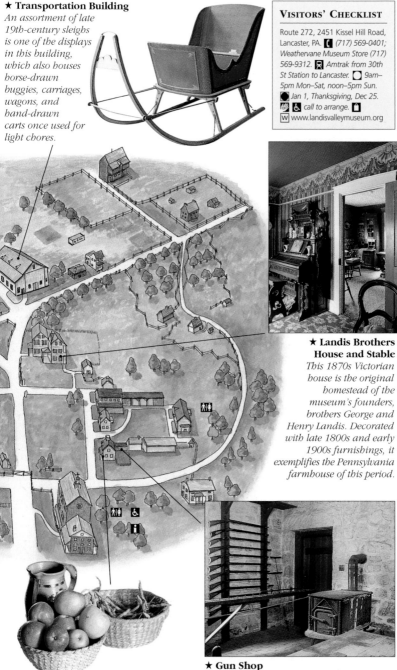

★ Landis Brothers House and Stable

This 1870s Victorian house is the original homestead of the museum's founders, brothers George and Henry Landis. Decorated with late 1800s and early 1900s furnishings, it exemplifies the Pennsylvania farmhouse of this period.

Tavern

The spacious brick-paved kitchen of the inn, with its enormous walk-in fireplace and displays of baskets, utensils, and stoneware jugs, reflects 18th-century cooking methods.

★ Gun Shop

An elaborate exhibit of Pennsylvania long rifles, powder horns, and gunsmithing tools sits within this stone structure. Early settlers used such shops to perfect the accuracy of their weapons.

Austere interior of the Saal, the meetinghouse in Ephrata Cloister

Ephrata ❹

Lancaster County, PA. 🏚 13,000. 🚌
🛈 77 Park Ave, Suite 1; (717) 738-9010. Ⓦ www.ephrata-area.org

THIS NORTHERN Lancaster County community was settled in 1732 by a German religious order led by Conrad Beissel, who founded one of America's earliest communal societies. The order built the medieval-style buildings that make up the **Ephrata Cloister**. Today, nine structures from the mid-1700s remain. The Sisters' House, next to the meetinghouse, has rows of windows for each small chamber where members slept on narrow benches. Other buildings include a schoolhouse, bakery, woodshop, and print shop. The visitor center displays artifacts, such as the Mennonites' 1,500-page *Martyrs' Mirror*. Just north of town, vendors at the Green Dragon Farmers' Market sell antiques, Pennsylvania Dutch treats, and crafts every Friday.

🏛 Ephrata Cloister
632 W Main St. 📞 (717) 733-6600. ◐ 9am–5pm Mon–Sat, noon–5pm Sun. 🖼
Ⓦ www.ephratacloister.org

Intercourse ❺

Lancaster County, PA. 🏚 4,500.
🚌 🛈 3551 Old Philadelphia Pike; (717) 768-3231. Ⓦ www.intercoursevillage.com

THEORIES ABOUND on how the village acquired its interesting name, including it coming from the intersection of the two main roads, from an old racecourse, or even from Intercourse being a center for social interaction. Founded in 1754, the village is one of the main centers for Amish business. Key to its success are the extensive gift shops and stores that lure tourists by the busloads. For instance, Kitchen Kettle Village, a mini-shopping center, has over 30 restaurants and country shops selling everything from quilts and baskets to woodcraft. One store delights customers with homemade jellies and relishes bottled on the spot by Amish women. In the center of town, along Old Philadelphia Pike, is the **People's Place Quilt Museum**. Opened in 1988, the museum displays antique Mennonite and Amish quilts through rotating exhibitions.

West of the town center is the **Amish Experience**, where visitors can learn about local culture by touring a modern Amish home and through the multimedia show, *Jacob's*

Exhibit detail at the People's Place Quilt Museum

Choice, which chronicles an Amish family's efforts to preserve its lifestyle.

🏛 People's Place Quilt Museum
3518 Old Philadelphia Pike. 📞 (800) 828-8218. ◐ 9am–5pm Mon–Sat.
♿ Ⓦ www.ppquiltmuseum.com
🏛 Amish Experience
Route 340 between Bird-In-Hand & Intercourse. 📞 (717) 768-3600.
◐ mid-Mar–Jun: 9:30am–5pm Mon–Sat; Jul–Oct: 8:30am–8pm Mon–Sat; Nov–Dec: 9:30am–5pm Mon–Sat; Jan–mid-Mar: 9:30am–5pm Sat; year-round: 10:30am–5pm Sun.
Ⓦ www.amishexperience.com

Bird-In-Hand ❻

Lancaster County, PA. 🏚 300. 🚌
🛈 2727 Old Philadelphia Pike; (717) 768-8271. Ⓦ www.bird-in-hand.com

THIS VILLAGE IS said to have received its unusual name from a historic 1734 inn *(see p141)* that once dangled a tavern sign depicting a man with a perched bird in his hand. The village contains a cluster of restaurants, stores, hotels, and quaint farmhouses.

The **Farmers' Market** bustles with stalls packed with foods ranging from farm vegetables to fresh bacon and sausage. Across the street, the **Americana Museum** displays antiques from 1890 through 1930, which depict important professions and trades, and include an early 20th-century toy store, apothecary, print shop, wheelwright shop, and milliner's. Set up in 1877, the Weavertown One-Room

Amish boys ride a buggy into the village of Intercourse

School showcases a typical schoolhouse still attended by Amish children today.

🔲 Farmers' Market
Rte 340 & Maple Ave. ⬜ *Apr–Jun & Nov: 8:30am–5:30pm Wed, Fri, & Sat; Jul–Oct: 8:30am–5:30pm Wed–Sat; Dec–Mar: 8:30am–5:30pm Fri & Sat.*

🏛 Americana Museum
2709 Old Philadelphia Pike. 📞 *(717) 391-9780.* ⬜ *Apr–Nov: 10am–5pm Tue–Sat; winter tours by request.* 📷

Paradise ❼

Lancaster County, PA. 👥 *1,000.* 🚌 ℹ️ *Pennsylvania Dutch Country Visitor Center: Route 30 at Greenfield Exit; (717) 299-8901.* 🌐 *www.padutchcountry.com*

T HE ORIGINS OF this small village along Route 30 date from colonial times when the road served as a link between Lancaster and Philadelphia. Paradise grew as the number of inns and taverns increased along Route 30. One of them, the Historic Revere Tavern, was built in 1740 and is still a working restaurant *(see p153).* President James Buchanan purchased it in 1841 as a home for his brother, a reverend, whose wife was the sister of songsmith Stephen Foster, writer of such American favorites as "Oh! Susanna" and "My Olde Kentucky Home".

A short drive east is the one-of-a-kind **National Christmas Center**, where the spirit of Yuletide is always in the air. Spread over 20,000 sq ft (1,860 sq m) are life-sized scenes depicting Christmas feasts and snowy villages, toy train and nativity displays, and several versions of St. Nicholas from around the globe.

🏛 National Christmas Center
3427 Lincoln Hwy. 📞 *(717) 442-7950.* ⬜ *May: 10am–6pm Fri–Sun; Jun–Dec: 10am–6pm.* ⚫ *Jan–Apr, Thanksgiving, Dec 25.* 🌐 *www.nationalchristmascenter.com*

An Amish house and buggy in Strasburg

Strasburg ❽

Lancaster County, PA. 👥 *2,800.* ℹ️ *Pennsylvania Dutch Country Visitor Center: Route 30 at Greenfield Exit; (717) 299-8901.*

I NITIALLY SETTLED BY French Huguenots in the early 1700s, Strasburg is named after the cathedral city of Strasbourg in France. The first structures, built in 1733, are now part of the historical district along with numerous colonial stone and log homes. The town developed as an educational and cultural center as followers of different faiths chose to settle here. But by the mid-19th century, it had become home to the railroads that are today its most popular attraction. Set up in 1832, the **Strasburg Railroad** offers 45-minute rides in refurbished railcars pulled by early 20th-century coal-fired, smoke-belching locomotives. Directly across the highway is the **Railroad Museum of Pennsylvania**, with spacious hangars housing one of the nation's largest collections of classic railroad cars, locomotives, and colorful cabooses. The **National Toy Train Museum** has exhibitions of collector-item locomotives and exquisite

Signage at the National Christmas Center

model train layouts. The **Choo Choo Barn**, meanwhile, has one of the most unique model railroads in the world, with 22 trains running through scenes of Lancaster County.

North of town is the **Amish Village** with an 1840s Amish house, smokehouse, black-smith shop, and operational water wheel. The majestic Millennium Theater nearby is home to inspirational, Biblical-themed stage productions.

🚂 Strasburg Railroad
Rte 741, E of Strasburg. 📞 *(717) 687-7522.* ⬜ *Feb–Dec; check website or call for times.* ⚫ *Jan.* 🌐 *www.strasburgrailroad.com*

🏛 Railroad Museum of Pennsylvania
300 Gap Rd. 📞 *(717) 687-8628.* ⬜ *Apr–Oct: 9am–5pm Mon–Sat, noon–5pm Sun; Nov–Mar: 9am–5pm Tue–Sat, noon–5pm Sun.* ⚫ *Jan 1, Easter, Nov 11, Thanksgiving, Dec 24, 25, & 31.*

🏛 National Toy Train Museum
Off Rte 741, E of Strasburg. 📞 *(717) 687-8976.* ⬜ *Apr & Nov–Dec: 10am–5pm Sat–Sun; May–Oct: 10am–5pm; Dec 26–31: 10am–5pm.*

🏛 Choo Choo Barn
Rte 471, E of Strasburg. 📞 *(717) 687-6529.* ⬜ *Apr–Dec: 10am–4:30pm.* ⚫ *Jan–Mar, Easter, Thanksgiving, Dec 25.*

🚂 Amish Village
Rte 896, N of Strasburg. 📞 *(717) 687-8511.* ⬜ *Apr–Oct: 9am–5pm Mon–Sat, 10am–5pm Sun, until 6pm in summer; Nov: 9am–4pm Mon–Sat, 10am–4pm Sun.*

Gettysburg ❾

Lincoln's chair at Wills House

THIS SOUTH-CENTRAL Pennsylvania town amidst gently sloping hills is home to the greatest military encounter ever fought in North America, the Battle of Gettysburg in 1863, during the Civil War (1861–65). Shaded streets are lined with well-preserved Civil War-era buildings, which served as makeshift hospitals during the conflict. Many of these have today been converted into museums, restaurants, and hotels. Shops sell Civil War souvenirs and artifacts, including authentic rifles and a seemingly unending supply of cannon balls and bullets unearthed from the battleground. Other attractions include museums with dioramas – some with waxwork figures – depicting events of the Gettysburg battle and the Civil War.

The *Gettysburg Cyclorama*, a 360-degree painting of Pickett's Charge

🏛 Gettysburg National Military Park Visitor Center and Cyclorama Center

97 Taneytown Rd. 📞 *(717) 334-1124.* ⭘ *Sep–May: 8am–5pm; Jun–Aug: 8am–6pm; Cyclorama Center: 9am–5pm.* ⬤ *Jan 1, Thanksgiving, Dec 25; Cyclorama Center painting closed until late 2007.* 🏷 Ⓦ *www.nps.gov/gett*

The Gettysburg National Military Park Visitor Center houses a museum with wide-ranging Civil War artifacts, from a corridor with rifles lining the walls to an impressive display of artillery shells and fuses. The narrated Electric Map presentation uses colored lights to explain the three-day battle. First exhibited in Boston in 1883, the *Gettysburg Cyclorama*, a colossal panoramic painting of Pickett's Charge, the conflict's climactic moment *(see pp122–3)*, is displayed at the Cyclorama Center. A larger visitor center and cyclorama are scheduled for completion in late 2007.

🍴 Dobbin House Tavern

89 Steinwehr Ave. 📞 *(717) 334-2100.* ⭘ *11:30am onward.* Ⓦ *www.dobbinhouse.com*

Built in 1776, this stone house is Gettysburg's oldest standing structure. An upstairs museum displays a secret crawl space that once hid runaway slaves as part of the Underground Railroad *(see p60)*. Now a restaurant, the building has original fireplaces, hand-carved woodwork, and a colonial wooden bar in the downstairs tavern *(see p152)*.

🍴 Eisenhower National Historic Site

97 Taneytown Rd. 📞 *(717) 338-9114.* ⭘ *9am–4pm.* ⬤ *Jan 1, Thanksgiving, Dec 25.* 🏷 📷 *mandatory.* Ⓦ *www.nps.gov/eise*

Before being elected president in 1952, Dwight D. Eisenhower had served as Supreme Commander of the Allied Forces during World War II. While president, he and his wife Mamie owned this farm on the outskirts of Gettysburg and used it for weekend retreats. Inside are original furnishings and exhibits highlighting his career as general and president.

🍴 Farnsworth House Inn

401 Baltimore St. 📞 *(717) 334-8838.* ⭘ *hours vary.* Ⓦ *www.farnsworthhousedining.com*

Dating from 1810, this historic home sheltered Confederate sharpshooters, one of whom is thought to have shot Jennie Wade. Most impressive are the more than 100 bullet piercings still evident on the house's brick façade from Union soldiers returning fire. Now an inn *(see p152)*, the house offers ghost tours and an interesting Mourning Theatre in the cellar with Civil War-related ghost tales told around a coffin by candlelight.

🍴 General Lee's Headquarters

401 Buford Ave. 📞 *(717) 334-3141.* ⭘ *mid-Feb–Nov: 9am–5pm.* ⬤ *Dec–mid-Feb.*

Confederate General Robert E. Lee chose to spend the night of July 1, 1863, at this house so he could see the Union line with his fieldglasses. Inside are war artifacts and the original wooden table on which he dined.

General Lee's Headquarters, today a museum

Entrance to the Pennsylvania Memorial in Gettysburg

VISITORS' CHECKLIST

🛈 Gettysburg Convention & Visitors Bureau: 102 Carlisle St, Gettysburg, Adams County, PA; (717) 334-6274, (800) 337-5015. ◗ 8:30am–5pm Mon–Sat, 9:30am–3pm Sun. 🎪 Apple Blossom Festival (May), Gettysburg Anniversary Civil War Battle Reenactments (Jul), Apple Harvest Festival (Oct), Remembrance Day (Nov). W www.gettysburgcvb.org

🏛 Schriver House Museum

309 Baltimore St. 📞 (717) 337-2800. ◗ Apr–Nov: 10am–5pm Mon–Sat, noon–5pm Sun; Dec–Mar: noon–5pm Sat & Sun. 🎫 🎫 mandatory.
This 19th-century home portrays the life of a family under the three-day Confederate occupation. The third-floor attic has original holes in the brick wall where rebel sharpshooters stood poised. A small museum displays artifacts, including three unfired bullets discovered during restoration.

🏛 Wills House and Lincoln Room Museum

12 Lincoln Square. 📞 (717) 334-8188. ◗ 9am–5pm; extended hours on some weekends.
President Abraham Lincoln slept in this corner house on the town's center square the night before he delivered the Gettysburg Address. His bedroom, where he made final revisions to his speech, is part of the Lincoln Room Museum. It houses copies of the letter sent by attorney and home-owner David Wills inviting Lincoln to visit the town.

🏚 Jennie Wade House

758 Baltimore St. 📞 (717) 334-4100. ◗ spring & fall: 9am–5pm; summer: 9am–9pm. 🎫
Twenty-year-old Jennie Wade was the only civilian killed during the Battle of Gettysburg. A sharpshooter's bullet pierced two doors and struck her while she baked bread for Union soldiers. The home contains original furnishings, and a statue of her stands outside.

🏚 Lincoln Railroad Station

35 Carlisle St. ◗ 10am–5pm; extended hours in summer.
This 1858 Italianate-styled railroad depot is where President Lincoln stepped off the train from Washington, a day before delivering the Gettysburg Address. Inside is an interpretive center, with exhibits about the train station and town history, and information on sights, attractions, and tours.

🏛 Soldiers' National Cemetery

Taneytown Rd, across Visitor Center. W www.nps.gov/gett/gncem.htm
This peaceful and shaded cemetery contains the graves of 6,000 US servicemen killed in various conflicts in America's history, from the Civil War to the Vietnam War. More than 3,500 are Union soldiers killed at the three-day Battle of Gettysburg. They are buried in a semi-circle around the Soldiers' National Monument, which marks the spot where President Lincoln delivered his moving Gettysburg Address. The now-famous address is commemorated by the nearby Lincoln Speech Memorial, which contains an inscription of his speech and his bust.

Soldiers' National Monument

LINCOLN'S GETTYSBURG ADDRESS

Four months after the battle, President Abraham Lincoln visited Gettysburg to dedicate a cemetery for Union soldiers. Although not the main speaker, and asked only to make "a few appropriate remarks," Lincoln's 272-words, two-minute speech on November 19, 1863 not only gave new meaning to the war's losses, but was an inspiration to preserve a nation divided. His words conferred significance on the sacrifice of the thousands who died during the battle, urging for the "resolve that these dead shall not have died in vain."

Lincoln's bust at Soldiers' National Cemetery

A Tour of Gettysburg National Military Park

The Battle of Gettysburg was fought on the first three days of July 1863. Not only was it the turning point of the American Civil War between the North and South, it was also the war's largest battle, leaving more than 51,000 Union and Confederate soldiers killed, wounded, captured, or missing. Although the Union army won this critical battle, it took a further two years for them to decisively win the Civil War on April 26, 1865. This self-guided tour traces the course of the three-day battle.

Eternal Light Peace Memorial [2]
From Oak Hill, Confederates attacked Union forces on the first day. This memorial to "Peace Eternal in a Nation United" was built in 1938.

McPherson's Ridge [1]
This quiet farm with McPherson's barn is where the Battle of Gettysburg began early in the morning on July 1, 1863. Confederate infantry advanced eastward and engaged in heavy fire with Union Cavalry.

Oak Ridge [3]
Union troops held this ridge but retreated to Cemetery Hill on July 1 as their defenses collapsed.

North Carolina Memorial [4]
On the second day, the Confederates stood on Seminary Ridge. Union troops held Culp's and Cemetery Hills.

Virginia Memorial [5]
This monument on Seminary Ridge overlooks the field where, on July 3, 12,000 Confederates launched their last major assault, known as "Pickett's Charge." In less than an hour, 10,000 of them were dead or wounded.

Pitzer Woods [6]
Confederates occupied these woods on the second day. An observation tower offers grand views of the "Pickett's Charge" battlefield.

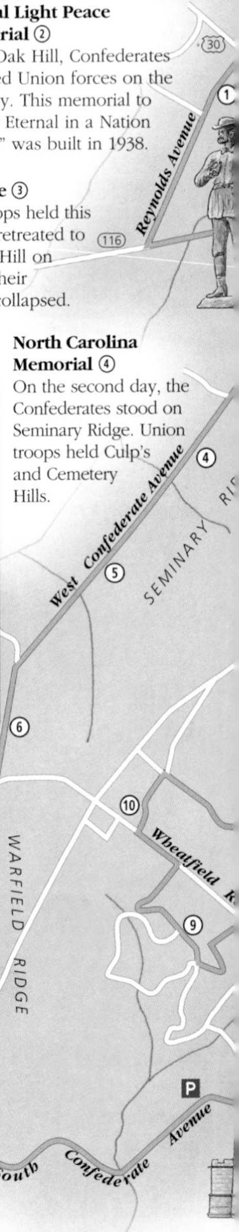
30
1
Reynolds Avenue
116
4
West Confederate Avenue
SEMINARY RI
5
6
EISENHOWER NATIONAL HISTORIC SITE
10
Wheatfield R
9
West Confederate Avenue
WARFIELD RIDGE
BR 15
P
7
South Confederate Avenue
Emmitsburg
0 meters 500
0 yards 500

Warfield Ridge [7]
On the battle's second day, Confederates charged Union troops at Devil's Den and Little and Big Round Tops.

Key

- Suggested route
- Other roads
- [i] Visitor information
- [P] Parking

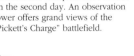

masburg

High Water Mark ⑮
On the last day, Union troops held off "Pickett's Charge" here, forcing the Confederates to retreat. The spot is marked by memorials and old cannon.

National Cemetery ⑯
This is the site of Lincoln's Gettysburg Address. 3,500 Civil War dead are buried here.

GETTYSBURG

York Street
ast Middle Street

East Cemetery Hill ⑭
Confederates unsuccessfully attacked Union forces occupying the hill, ending the battle's second day.

Spangler's Spring ⑬
Confederates attacked the Union army at this spring below Culp's Hill, but were forced to retreat after seven hours of fighting. The spring has since been covered.

Baltimore

Plum Run ⑪
Union forces crossed this area as they retreated from Peach Orchard to Cemetery Ridge.

Pennsylvania Memorial ⑫
An ornate, stately memorial marks the Union position along Cemetery Ridge.

Peach Orchard ⑩
On the second day, Confederate soldiers overran this position despite heavy Union cannon fire.

The Wheatfield ⑨
Charges and countercharges here on the second day left over 4,000 men dead and wounded.

Little Round Top ⑧
At first undefended on the second day, this position was reinforced when an alert Union general called for help. Monuments, such as this one to the 155th Pennsylvania Volunteer Infantry, dot the hill.

TIPS FOR DRIVERS

Tour length: 18 miles (29 km).
Duration of tour: About 3 hours.
Distance from Philadelphia:
118 miles (189 km). This is usually a 2-hour drive.
Starting point: Gettysburg National Military Park Visitor Center.
Stop-off points: The tour has 16 stops, all of which have plaques explaining historical significance. Some stops have a scattering of monuments.
When to go: Mar–Dec.
Tourist information:
Gettysburg National Military Park Visitor Center, 97 Taneytown Road, Gettysburg, PA. ☎ (717) 334-1124. Ⓦ www.nps.gov/gett/

The Golden Plough Tavern, one of York's historic establishments

York ⑩

York County, PA. 👥 40,000. 🚆 🚌
ℹ 1425 Eden Rd, (717) 852-9675.
🌐 www.yorkpa.org

T
HE FIRST Pennsylvania town west of the Susquehanna River, York was laid out in 1741, with inhabitants that were mainly tavern-keepers and craftspeople catering to pioneers heading west. Since then, manufacturing has been the town's economic strength.

East of York is the **Harley-Davidson Final Assembly Plant**, noisy, colorful, and the size of two football fields. Its giant presses mold steel while motorcycles fly overhead. A small museum depicts Harley Davidson's history from its 1903 inception as a motorized bike company to the present.

🏛 Harley-Davidson Final Assembly Plant

1425 Eden Rd. 📞 (877) 883-1450.
🕐 8am–4pm Mon–Fri. 📷 9am–2pm Mon–Fri; some Saturdays in summer; children under 12 not allowed.

Harrisburg ⑪

Dauphin County, PA. 👥 48,000. 🚆
🚌 ℹ Hershey Capital Region Visitors Bureau: (717) 231-7788. 🌐 www. hersheycapitalregion.com

F
IRST SETTLED IN the early 1700s by Englishman John Harris, Harrisburg is situated along the Susquehanna River. The city was not planned until the 1780s and became the capital of Pennsylvania in 1812. Today, the state government is the biggest employer in the city, which has the impressive **State Capitol** as a focal point. The Renaissance-style building was dedicated in 1906 by President Theodore Roosevelt.

The **National Civil War Museum** tells the story of the war through permanent displays of artifacts, photographs, manuscripts, and documents from its 24,000-item collection. City Island, located in the middle of the Susquehanna, offers panoramic views of the city. It includes marinas, parks and nature areas, riverboat rides and dinner cruises, and a replica of John Harris's 18th-century trading post.

🏛 State Capitol

3rd & State Sts. 📞 (800) 868-7672.
🕐 8:30am–4:30pm Mon–Fri. 📷
8:30am–4pm Mon–Fri, 9am, 11am,

1pm, 3pm Sat–Sun & hols. 🌑 Jan 1, Easter, Thanksgiving, Dec 25. ♿

🏛 National Civil War Museum

Lincoln Circle (Reservoir Pk). 📞 (717) 260-1861. 🕐 10am–5pm Mon–Sat, noon–5pm Sun. 🌑 Mon, Jan–Mar. 📷 ♿ 🌐 www. nationalcivilwarmuseum.org

Hershey ⑫

Dauphin County, PA. 👥 12,800.
🚆 🚌 🌐 www.hersheypa.com

T
HIS FACTORY town, now a tourist destination, revolves around chocolate, so much so that even its streetlights are shaped like silver-foil-wrapped Hershey Kisses. The town's main attraction is **Chocolate World**, which features a 15-minute ride through animated tableaux that reveal Hershey's chocolate-making process. A free sample awaits at the end of the tour. Shops at Chocolate World sell souvenirs and all Hershey products. Nearby is Hershey Park, an amusement park that has 80 rides on offer, and one of the finest four-row carousels in existence today.

Hershey's Chocolate World signage

🏛 Chocolate World

SR 743 & US 422. 📞 (717) 534-4900.
🕐 hours vary. 📷 🌐 www.hersheys. com/chocolateworld

State Capitol complex in Harrisburg, the seat of Pennsylvania's government

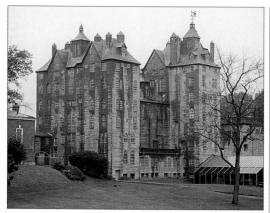

The towers and parapets of Mercer Castle, Doylestown

Reading ⑬

Berks County, PA. 🏙 80,000. 🚉 🚌
ℹ️ 352 Penn St, (800) 443–6610.

ONCE A CENTER of industry, Reading has reinvented itself as a discount-store capital *(see p157)*, with more than 80 name-brand stores, from Brooks Brothers to Mikasa and Wedgewood. The Reading Pagoda, on the outskirts of the town, is the main attraction here. Built in the early 1900s, it is modeled after a Shogun structure.

North of town, the **Mary Merritt Doll Museum** has over 1,500 dolls ranging in origin from 7th-century Egypt to 20th-century America.

🏛 **Mary Merritt Doll Museum**
843 Ben Franklin Hwy, Douglassville, PA. 📞 (610) 385-3809.

Doylestown ⑭

Bucks County, PA. 🏙 9,200. 🚉 🚌
ℹ️ Bucks County Visitors Center: 3207 Street Road, Bensalem, (800) 836-2825.

THE ORIGINS of Doylestown date to 1745, when William Doyle built a tavern here. The town was later developed as a cultural and commercial center, and today it is also the Bucks County seat.

The biggest attractions in town are the castle-like museums that tower over shaded grassy areas close to the town center. The **Mercer Museum**, built by archaeologist Henry Mercer in 1916, displays his collection of folk art, woodwork, textiles, and furnishings. After his death in 1930, his 44-room home, **Fonthill**, was turned into a tile museum.

Named after a famous writer from this area, the **James A. Michener Art Museum**, located in a 19th-century county jail, has a world-class collection of Pennsylvania Impressionist paintings.

🏛 **Mercer Museum**
84 S Pine St. 📞 (215) 345-0210.
🕐 10am–5pm Mon–Sat, noon–5pm Sun, until 9pm Tue.

🏛 **Fonthill Museum**
E Court St and Rt 313. 📞 (215) 348-9461. 🎫 mandatory; reservations advised.

🏛 **James A. Michener Art Museum**
138 S Pine St. 📞 (215) 340-9800.
🕐 10am–4:30pm Tue–Fri, 10am–5pm Sat, noon–5pm Sun, until 9pm on Wed in summer. 🎫

New Hope ⑮

Bucks County, PA. 🏙 2000. ℹ️ Visitor Center: Main & Mechanic Sts, (215) 862-5880. 🌐 www.newhopepa.com

THIS DELIGHTFUL waterfront village and shoppers' paradise teems with upscale boutiques and restaurants. Tracing its roots to the early 1700s, it gained its name when Benjamin Parry's gristmill, which ground grain, burned down in 1790. He rebuilt it and named it "New Hope Mills" with a promise of prosperity for the town.

Today, that prosperity is evident with more than 200 art galleries, boutiques, and craft and antiques shops, including a branch of the **James A. Michener Art Museum**. Train rides aboard restored 1920 passenger cars, horse-drawn carriages, and mule-drawn barge trips down the scenic 19th-century canal add to the town's ambience.

Parry, who also helped finance the first bridge across the Delaware, built a house in 1784 that was occupied by successive generations of his family until 1966. Today, the **Parry Mansion Museum** showcases its separate rooms, decorated according to different periods of its history.

🏛 **Parry Mansion Museum**
45 S Main St. 📞 (215) 862-5652.
🕐 late Apr–early Dec: 1–5pm Sat & Sun. 🎫 by appointment. 🎫

🏛 **James A. Michener Art Museum – New Hope**
500 Union Square Dr, New Hope.
📞 (215) 862-7633. 🎫 🌐 www.michenerartmuseum.org

Storefronts line New Hope's old-world, picturesque streets

Delaware River at Washington Crossing Historic Park

Washington Crossing Historic Park ⓰

Washington Crossing, PA. **C** (215) 493-4076. ⬤ 9am–5pm Tue–Sat, noon–5pm Sun. ⬤ public hols except Jul 4, Memorial Day, Labor Day, Dec 25. ♿

THIS WATERFRONT park, set up in 1917 to commemorate Washington's historic crossing of the Delaware River, is divided into two sections. The McConkey's Ferry section, named after a local 18th-century inn, includes the riverbank from which Washington and his army departed in Durham boats. A monument marks this area outside the visitor center. Nearby is a 19th-century boathouse containing replicas of the boats, which are now used for the annual Christmas Day crossing reenactment.

About 4 miles (6 km) upstream is the Thompson's Mill section, which includes historic buildings, a gristmill, an observation tower, and a cemetery along the peaceful Delaware Canal containing the graves of Revolutionary War soldiers.

On the New Jersey side of the river, Washington Crossing State Park marks the site where Washington landed. This forested area includes historic homes, a visitor center and museum, and miles of hiking, riding, and biking trails.

Trenton ⓱

Mercer County, NJ. ⓲ 85,000. ⊞ ▦ ⓘ Lafayette at Barrack St, (609) 777-1770. ⓦ www.trentonnj.com

The capital of New Jersey, Trenton's origin dates to 1679 when Quaker Mahlon Stacy built a gristmill along the Delaware. In 1714, his son sold land to merchant William Trent who laid out a new city called "Trent's Town" in 1721. Today, a big attraction is the Trenton Battle Monument. It pays tribute to the Battle of Trenton, in which General Washington and 2,400 men crossed the ice-clogged Delaware River on December 25, 1776, to launch an attack on British and Hessian soldiers. The latter were defeated and this battle was the turning point in the Revolutionary War. Prior to this, the Continental Army had suffered many defeats, and a win was badly needed

Plaque marking the river crossing

to boost morale in the fight for independence. The Old Barracks, dating to 1758, were occupied by Hessian soldiers during the encounter, and now house a museum.

🏛 Old Barracks Museum
Barrack St. **C** (609) 396-1776. ⬤ 10am–5pm. ⬤ Jan 1, Easter, Thanksgiving, Dec 24–25. ♿

Pennsbury Manor ⓲

400 Pennsbury Memorial Rd, Morrisville, PA. **C** (215) 946-0400. ⬤ 9am–5pm Tue–Sat, noon–5pm Sun. ⬤ Dec–mid-Mar: Tue–Sat, 2pm Sun; mid-Mar–Nov: 10am, 11:30am, 1:30pm & 3:30pm Tue–Sat, 1:30pm & 3:30pm Sun. ♿

AN ELEGANT brick Georgian house 26 miles (42 km) north of Philadelphia, this manor is a re-creation of William Penn's country home and estate from the 1680s. The plantation sits on the site chosen by Penn, and this manor was built in 1939 on original foundations, where some 17th-century bricks are the only remnants of Penn's initial home. Inside, a hall served as a waiting room between the family's quarters and governor's parlor, while the second floor had three bedrooms and a nursery.

The estate today includes farm animals similar to those owned by Penn. Other recreated structures include a blacksmith shop, brew house, smokehouse, and horse shelter. The visitor center plays a short audio-visual presentation as an introduction to the estate.

Gardens at Pennsbury Manor, Penn's country estate

Atlantic City's glamorous resorts by night – lighting up the Jersey coast

Atlantic City ⑲

Atlantic County, NJ. 🏃 40,000. 🚉 🚌
ℹ️ Greater Atlantic City Convention
& Visitors Bureau: 2314 Pacific Ave.
📞 (609) 449-7130, (888) 288-4748.
🌐 www.atlanticcitynj.com

CALLED THE "Queen of the
Coast" by generations of
beachgoers, Atlantic City has
been a favored vacation spot
since the mid-1800s. The
first casino opened on
the famous
Boardwalk in
1978, and
since then
the town has
become one of
the most popular
destinations on the
eastern seaboard.
All gambling –
euphemistically referred to as
"gaming" – takes place in the
large, ostentatious casino
hotels that lie within a block
of the beach and Boardwalk,
which is lined with shops and
amusement arcades.

While the beaches are still
popular, the casino resorts
draw the biggest crowds
today. More than a dozen –
with their towers shooting up
along the Boardwalk – make
up the dazzling city skyline.
They include Caesars, Bally's,
Harrah's, Showboat, Resorts,
Tropicana, and the properties
owned by billionaire developer Donald Trump, such as
the 51-story Trump Taj Mahal
(see p139). One of the flashiest
hotels to open in the recent
past is the Borgata Hotel
Casino and Spa, a $1-billion,
2,000-room hotel that opened
in 2003. Many of these resorts
also include spas, several

**Playing cards used
in gaming**

restaurants each, convention
facilities, and nightclubs and
concert halls featuring popular comedy and musical acts.

Visitors not enchanted by
the casinos instead head for
the lively local attractions.
Amusement parks with roller
coasters jut out over the ocean
on the Central Pier Arcade and
Speedway, and the famous
Steel Pier. Another attraction
is the Absecon Lighthouse,
the tallest lighthouse
in New Jersey,
which offers
splendid
views of
the city
and water-
front. Atlantic
City also hosts the
prestigious and pop-
ular annual Miss
America Pageant, which has
been held here since 1928.

In nearby Margate City,
Lucy the Elephant stands
tall in celebration of American
marketing ingenuity. Built by
a real estate developer
in 1881 to draw
prospective buyers to
his holdings, "Lucy" has
served as a residence
and a tavern over the
years. Today, guided
tours take visitors into
the structure that has
become instantly
recognizable as part of
the Jersey shoreline.

🐘 **Lucy the Elephant**
3200 Atlantic Ave, Margate.
📞 (609) 823-6473. 🕐 mid-
Jun–Labor Day: 10am–8pm
Mon–Sat, 10am–5pm Sun;
weekends in spring and fall;
Nov–Dec: hours vary. 🦽
🌐 www.lucytheelephant.org

Cape May ⑳

Cape May County, NJ. 🏃 4,000.
ℹ️ Cape May Welcome Center: Elmira
& Lafayette Sts, (609) 884-9562.

FIRST EXPLORED by Cornelius
Mey for the Dutch West
India Company in 1621, Cape
May is one of the oldest resorts
on the Atlantic coast. Popular
with Philadelphia socialites
during the late 1800s, it has,
since then, continued to enjoy
a fine reputation among beach
lovers. The building boom of
the Victorian era characterizes
Cape May today. **Historic
Cold Spring Village** is a
living history museum showcasing 25 restored buildings,
with costumed actors portray-
ing 19th-century lifestyles.

🏛️ **Historic Cold Spring
Village**
720 US 9. 📞 (609) 898-2300. 🕐 mid-
Jun–Labor Day: 10am–4:30pm Tue–
Sun; only weekends Labor Day–mid-
Sep & Memorial Day–mid-Jun. 🦽 &

**Brightly painted façade of a house at Cape
May, America's largest Victorian district**

Hagley Museum ㉑

Rte 141, Wilmington, DE. ☎ *(302) 658-2400.* ◯ *Jan–mid-Mar: 9:30am–4:30pm Sat & Sun, mid-Mar–Dec: 9:30am–4:30pm daily.*
● *Thanksgiving, Dec 25 & 31.* ☑
Jan–mid-Mar: 1:30pm Mon–Fri. ⬚
◪ Ⓦ *www.hagley.org*

N OT A MUSEUM in the conventional sense, this forested site along the rocky Brandywine River is where the DuPont Company was founded. In 1802, French immigrant Eleuthere Irenee du Pont built a factory to manufacture gunpowder and "black powder" used in explosives. The earliest buildings included the first du Pont family home, gardens, and company office. Through its 119-year-history, overseen by five generations of du Ponts, the mill expanded downriver, with waterwheels powering production facilities that sifted, mixed, and crushed raw materials into fine powder.

Today, only the façades of the original buildings remain. Some have working exhibitions, such as a rolling mill using safe charcoal. Staff members demonstrate the workings of a steam engine and the operations in a machine shop, but most impressive is the ignition of a powder sample. Some buildings house artifacts, original furniture, and rare du Pont cars, including a 1911 electric car and a 1928 Phaeton.

View of the Brandywine River at Hagley Museum

Interior of the conservatory at Longwood Gardens

Winterthur Museum ㉒

Rte 52, Winterthur, DE. ☎ *(302) 888-4600.* ◯ *10am–5pm Tue–Sun.*
● *Mon (except hols), Jan 1, Thanksgiving, Dec 25.* ◪ ☑ ⬚
Ⓦ *www.winterthur.org*

O NCE THE home of Henry Francis du Pont, great-grandson of Eleuthere Irenee du Pont, this vast estate contains an extraordinary 175-room mansion. The original home, the core of the current mansion, dates to 1839. It was built by J.A. Bidermann and his wife, Evelina, Eleuthere du Pont's daughter. Henry Francis inherited the estate in 1926, expanding it during the two-decade-long conversion of his home into a museum. Today, it houses 85,000 items from the 17th to the 19th centuries, including paintings, textiles, furniture, ceramics, and Chinese porcelain. The main dining room features original silver tankards crafted by Paul Revere, and works of art by Gilbert Stuart and Benjamin West. The parlor features a unique oval Mont Morency staircase and is elegantly decorated with Chippendale furniture. The estate contains meadows, streams, and woods, including a tulip-poplar tree, which has been around when William Penn was alive.

Longwood Gardens ㉓

Rte 1, Kennett Square, PA. ☎ *(800) 737-5500, (610) 388-1000.* ◯ *Apr–Oct: 9am–6pm; Nov–Mar: 9am–5pm.*
● *Mon (except hols), Jan 1, Thanksgiving, Dec 25.* ◪ ♿
Ⓦ *www.longwoodgardens.org*

T HIS WELL-MANICURED horticultural wonderland consists of colorful gardens, woodlands, lush meadows, greenhouses, and spectacular fountains amid idyllic bucolic scenery. Settler George Pierce acquired the land in 1700, and in 1798, his descendants established an arboretum that, by the mid-19th century was one the nation's finest.

Industrialist Pierre S. du Pont bought it in 1906 and it is his design that remains today. It includes over 11,000 plant varieties in both indoor and outdoor displays, whimsical topiaries, and a children's garden. The massive main greenhouse and conservatory are engineering marvels that shelter an array of exotic plant life. But the most breathtaking sights are the fabulous fountains with choreographed eruptions highlighted at night by colored lights, which create dazzling displays that are often the backdrop of musical events.

Brandywine Battlefield State Park ㉔

Route 1, Chadds Ford, PA. 📞 (610) 459-3342. ⏲ 9am–5pm Tue–Sat, noon–5pm Sun. ● Mon. ♿ 🅿

THE BATTLE OF Brandywine, fought on these rolling hills on September 11, 1777, was the biggest engagement of the American Revolution. General Washington stationed his troops atop this high ground at Chadds Ford along the Brandywine River in an attempt to stop the advancing British. The Americans were outmaneuvered as the British crossed the Brandywine River at an unguarded ford to the north of Washington's troops, forcing them to retreat from Chadds Ford.

Today, the battlefield is a state park with a visitor center and two historic houses, both restored to the way they were in 1777. The Benjamin Ring House was owned by a Quaker farmer and served as Washington's headquarters on the eve of the battle. The French patriot and American Revolution hero, Marquis de LaFayette, stayed in the farmhouse of Quaker Gideon Gilpin. The visitor center includes a small museum.

Brandywine River Museum ㉕

Rte 1, Chadds Ford, PA. 📞 (610) 388-2700. ⏲ 9:30am–4:30pm. ● Dec 25. 🎫 Apr–mid-Nov: timed tours of N.C. Wyeth House & Studio, and Kuerner Farm Wed–Sun. ♿ 🍴 🅿 ⓦ www.brandywinemuseum.org

LOCATED IN a Civil War-era gristmill along Brandywine River, this museum is best known for housing artworks by three generations of the Wyeths – N.C., Andrew, and Jamie. Galleries showcase landscapes inspired by the Brandywine River Valley, and paintings and illustrations by the Wyeths and other artists.

N.C. Wyeth (1882–1945) was a famous illustrator of the early 20th century, completing more than 1,000 illustrations, including some for classics such as *Treasure Island* and *Robin Hood*. N.C.'s son Andrew is known for mastering drybrush watercolor and egg tempura mediums. His son Jamie painted portraits of figures such as President John F. Kennedy and artist Andy Warhol.

Tours are organized to the N.C. Wyeth House and Studio, and the Kuerner Farm, which inspired Andrew for over 70 years. A farmhouse and barn display his works related to the farm.

George Washington's restored headquarters at Valley Forge

Valley Forge National Historic Park ㉖

Rte 23 & North Gulph Rd, Valley Forge, PA. 📞 (610) 783-1077. ⏲ Visitor Center: 9am–5pm. ● Jan 1, Thanksgiving, Dec 25. ♿ & 🅿 ⓦ www.nps.gov/vafo

GEORGE WASHINGTON and his soldiers spent the harsh winter of 1777–78 at Valley Forge, retreating to these hills after losing to British forces at Brandywine and Germantown (*see p107*). No battles were fought here, but nearly 2,000 soldiers died of typhus, typhoid, pneumonia, and dysentery. Today, reconstructed cabins, statues, and cannon are scattered through the park. Key exhibits are the National Memorial Arch, designed by Paul Cret, and built in 1917 in the memory of those who died in the winter of 1777–78, and stone farmhouses that once served as officers' quarters. The park has miles of fields and woods crisscrossed by hiking paths, and a visitor center with artifacts such as muskets and powder horns.

The American Revolution Center is the country's first museum dedicated to that conflict. Built within a quarry bluff, the vast space will showcase the largest collection of Revolutionary artifacts, information, and experiences ever assembled.

National Memorial Arch at Valley Forge

Revolutionary War hero LaFayette's quarters at Brandywine Park

Cloth Angels
Handmade by
an Amish girl
12.00 plus tx.

TRAVELERS' NEEDS

WHERE TO STAY 132–141

RESTAURANTS AND CAFÉS 142–153

SHOPS AND MARKETS 154–161

ENTERTAINMENT IN PHILADELPHIA 162–169

CHILDREN'S PHILADELPHIA 170–171

WHERE TO STAY

T HE PHILADELPHIA area offers a wide selection of hotel rooms to fit every style and budget. More expensive hotels include towers overlooking scenic Center City and riverfront views, boutique hotels, upscale chain hotels, and smaller but luxurious bed-and-breakfasts – some with

Doorman at Westin

colonial themes. The more budget-conscious traveler will find a wide range of comfortable chain hotels, motels, inns, and bed-and-breakfasts within the city and beyond. Hotel rates are quite reasonable, though they tend to be higher in the more popular business district and tourist areas.

LOCATIONS

T HE CENTER CITY district has the highest concentration of hotel rooms in the Philadelphia metropolitan area with over 10,000 rooms available. Business travelers prefer to stay in one of the many Center City properties, which include high-end names, such as the Four Seasons Hotel and the Ritz Carlton. In particular, hotels are clustered near Logan Square and on Market, Chestnut, and Walnut Streets, with an abundance in and around Rittenhouse Square, the convention center, and theater district areas.

A few hotels can be found in Old City and Society Hill, while some are also located along the Delaware River waterfront. Quality hotels are also concentrated in University City, along City Line Avenue on the city's north-western edge, at the airport, and in the suburbs of Valley Forge and King of Prussia.

FACILITIES AND AMENITIES

A LL HOTELS IN Philadelphia have standard air conditioning, cable TV, and other conveniences. Upscale properties and some chain hotels have in-room business services and centers, including computer and fax facilities, though only a few smaller hotels or bed-and-breakfasts offer Internet access to guests.

Chain hotels, in particular, offer fitness facilities and some of the larger hotels have pools. Sometimes, hotels make arrangements with nearby health clubs for the use of their facilities by hotel guests. Additional charges may apply for certain amenities, and some may be costly. It is best to call and clarify when booking accommodation.

RESERVATIONS

M OST LARGER CHAIN hotels have toll-free reservation numbers, or visitors can make reservations through their Internet sites, with some offering discounts for online bookings. Prices quoted are often for double occupancy and do not include taxes or parking charges. Online hotel reservation service companies offer reduced rates for rooms, but often add hidden fees and taxes. A good resource is the website of the **Greater Philadelphia Tourism and Marketing Corporation**, with current hotel packages that may include tours, show performance tickets, and other offers.

HIDDEN COSTS

I F YOU ARE traveling solo, always make sure you are quoted the rate for one person, as hotels usually quote room rates assuming double occupancy. Room taxes in Philadelphia amount to around 14 percent, while parking rates range anywhere from $10 to $30 per day. Rooms with a view can also cost more – the splendid panoramas of the waterfront, skyline, and neighborhoods can be seen from the higher floors of many hotels in the city.

View of the First Bank of the US from a Ritz Carlton room *(see p136)*

◁ Jars of traditional Amish jams, jellies, preserves, and pickles at Reading Terminal Market

Sheraton University City Hotel *(see p138)* on the University of Pennsylvania campus

DISCOUNTS

DISCOUNTS ARE often available when booking packages. The "Philly's More Fun When You Sleep Over" promotion runs at different times in the year and offers free parking, gifts, and other discounts on two weekend hotel nights for two. It is also available through the website of the **Greater Philadelphia Tourism and Marketing Corporation**.

BED-AND-BREAKFASTS

ACCOMMODATIONS at places offering bed-and-breakfast (B&Bs) are found within quiet and shaded neighborhoods, with some housed in quaint 18th- and 19th-century buildings and Victorian homes. Prices vary depending on services, amenities, and location. B&Bs include breakfast, but tend not to have restaurants, business facilities or exercise areas. Most B&Bs in the city are located in the neighborhoods of University City,

Chestnut Hill, Center City, and near City Line Avenue. To find out more and make reservations, contact **A Bed and Breakfast Connection of Philadelphia**.

HOSTELS

YOUNGER TRAVELERS and students often stay in hostels, which offer much cheaper accommodation than hotel rooms. Some good hostels are: the **Bank Street Hostel**, in a renovated 19th-century building, has modern amenities and is located near Independence Mall; and the **Hosteling International Chamounix Mansion**, which is situated in one of Fairmount Park's historic homes.

TRAVELING WITH CHILDREN

WITH PHILADELPHIA'S many historic attractions and science-oriented museums, children are warmly welcomed at most city hotels. Younger children can usually stay for free in their parents' rooms, but it is best to check when making reservations. Ask about family rates and suites that might better accommodate kids. Hotels often supply cots at an additional cost. Family hotel packages are available through the **Greater Philadelphia Tourism and Marketing Corporation** website. These may include accommodations, meals, tickets for different historic tours, or free child meals and free parking.

DISABLED TRAVELERS

MOST OF THE larger hotels accommodate wheelchairs, while smaller establishments, such as B&Bs, may not have full amenities for the disabled as they are housed in 18th- and 19th-century homes. For more information, contact the hotels or call the **Mayor's Commission on People with Disabilities**.

DIRECTORY

ONLINE BOOKING SERVICES

Hotels.com.
W www.hotels.com

Lodging.com
W www.lodging.com

HOTEL PACKAGES AND PROMOTIONS

Greater Philadelphia Tourism and Marketing Corporation
W www.gophila.com

BED-AND-BREAKFAST BOOKING

A Bed and Breakfast Connection of Philadelphia
(*(800) 448-3619, (610) 687-3565.*
W www.bnbphiladelphia.com

HOSTELS

Bank Street Hostel
32 S Bank St. **Map** 4 E3.
(*(215) 922-0222.*
W www.bankstreethostel.com

Hosteling International Chamounix Mansion
3250 Chamounix Drive, W Fairmount Park.
(*(800) 379-0017, (215) 878-3676.*
W www.philahostel.org

DISABLED TRAVELERS

Mayor's Commission on People with Disabilities
1401 JFK Blvd. **Map** 2 F4.
(*(215) 686-2798.*
W www.phila.gov/aco/index.html

Bedroom at Rittenhouse Square Bed & Breakfast *(see p136)*

Choosing a Hotel

Hotels have been selected across a wide price range for facilities, good value, and location. All rooms have private bath, TV, air conditioning, and have disabled access unless otherwise indicated. Most have Internet access, and in some cases, fitness facilities may be offsite. The hotels are listed by area. For map references, *see pp194–97*.

PRICE CATEGORIES
The price ranges are for a standard double room per night, including tax, during the high season. Breakfast is not included, unless specified.
ⓢ $60–$105
ⓢⓢ $106–$145
ⓢⓢⓢ $146–$185
ⓢⓢⓢⓢ $186–$240
ⓢⓢⓢⓢⓢ Over $240

OLD CITY

Comfort Inn of Philadelphia
ⓢⓢ
100 N Columbus Blvd, Philadelphia **Tel** *(215) 627-7900* **Fax** *(215) 238-0809* **Rooms** *185*   **Map** *4 E2*

This budget-priced, high-rise hotel has no frills but is in a great location within walking distance of historic sites. It offers clean, comfortable rooms, as well as a free Continental breakfast. In addition, children under 18 stay free with parents. It offers easy access to the I-95 and good views of the Delaware River. **www.comfortinnphila.com**

Hilton Garden Inn
ⓢⓢ
1100 Arch St, Philadelphia **Tel** *(215) 923-0100* **Fax** *(215) 925-0800* **Rooms** *279*   **Map** *3 C2*

This popular and fashionable chain hotel is located near the Pennsylvania Convention Center and is only a block or two from Chinatown. All rooms are outfitted with modern amenities, such as microwaves and refrigerators. The rooftop restaurant and lounge offer city views. **www.philadelphiacentercity.gardeninn.com**

Society Hill Hotel
ⓢⓢ
301 Chestnut St, Philadelphia **Tel** *(215) 925-1919* **Fax** *(215) 925-3780* **Rooms** *12*   **Map** *4 E3*

Built in 1832, this corner B&B was the city's first such accommodation. Rooms have brass double beds and offer all modern amenities. A complimentary Continental breakfast is included with rooms and the hotel has a popular bar and restaurant on its premises. Parking is available a short distance away. **www.societyhillhotel.com**

The Thomas Bond House
ⓢⓢ
129 S 2nd St, Philadelphia **Tel** *(215) 923-8523* **Fax** *(215) 923-8504* **Rooms** *12*   **Map** *4 E3*

Once the home of prominent colonial physician, Thomas Bond, this historic inn dates back to 1769. Rooms are decorated with period furniture that create an ambience of colonial warmth and quiet luxury. Guests can make use of fitness facilities at an establishment close to the inn. **www.winston-salem-inn.com/philadelphia**

Best Western Independence Park Hotel
ⓢⓢⓢ
235 Chestnut St, Philadelphia **Tel** *(215) 922-4443* **Fax** *(215) 922-4487* **Rooms** *36*   **Map** *4 E3*

Small, historic hotel dating back to 1856 with exquisitely decorated rooms, located within the heart of Old City and just a few blocks from Independence Mall and Penn's Landing. Lavish European breakfast with make-your-own Belgian waffles. Complimentary tea and cookies provided every morning. **www.independenceparkhotel.com**

Holiday Inn Philadelphia Historic District Hotel
ⓢⓢⓢ
400 Arch St, Philadelphia **Tel** *(215) 923-8660* **Fax** *(215) 923-4633* **Rooms** *364*   **Map** *4 E2*

Comfortable chain hotel with reasonably priced rooms. Its excellent and convenient location – one block from Independence Mall and within walking distance of the Market Street shopping area – make it a popular destination for tourists. Children love the rooftop pool during the warmer months. **www.holiday-inn.com/phlhistoric**

Morris House Hotel
ⓢⓢⓢ
225 S 8th St, Philadelphia **Tel** *(215) 922-2446* **Fax** *(215) 922-2466* **Rooms** *15*   **Map** *3 C3*

This 1787 home is now a luxury boutique hotel and is one of the city's best hotels to experience colonial ambience. It has the coziness of a B&B and unique features such as a private garden, colonial-style reading room, two dining rooms with fireplaces, and rooms with hardwood floors. **www.morrishousehotel.com**

Omni Hotel
ⓢⓢⓢⓢ
401 Chestnut St, Philadelphia **Tel** *(215) 925-0000* **Fax** *(215) 925-1263* **Rooms** *150*   **Map** *4 D3*

This four-star, four-diamond hotel has large-sized rooms with marble bathrooms. It is just a few blocks from key restaurants and nightlife spots, and within walking distance of shopping stores and Jewelers' Row. The rooms offer views of the Independence Mall area. **www.omnihotels.com**

Penn's View Hotel
ⓢⓢⓢⓢ
Front & Market Sts, Philadelphia **Tel** *(215) 922-7600* **Fax** *(215) 922-7642* **Rooms** *51*   **Map** *4 E3*

Cozy and family owned, this European-style hotel features murals and marble throughout the property. Its superb Italian restaurant and the unique "il bar" offers over 120 wines by the glass *(see p147)*. Situated across from Penn's Landing, it is just a block away from excellent restaurants and nightlife. **www.pennsviewhotel.com**

Key to Symbols *see back cover flap*

SOCIETY HILL AND PENN'S LANDING

Sheraton Society Hill

$ $ $

1 Dock St, Philadelphia **Tel** *(215) 238-6000* **Fax** *(215) 922-2709* **Rooms** *365* **Map** *4 E4*

The Sheraton Society Hill is another excellent hotel for the business traveler. Situated on cobblestoned Dock Street, it is also ideal for tourists as it is just a block or two from Penn's Landing. The hotel provides a complimentary shuttle service to downtown business areas. **www.sheraton.com/societyhill**

Hyatt Regency Philadelphia

$ $ $ $

201 S Columbus Blvd, Philadelphia **Tel** *(215) 521-6551* **Fax** *(215) 521-6600* **Rooms** *350* **Map** *4 F3*

Opened in 2000, this upscale property on Penn's Landing is Philadelphia's only waterfront hotel. Twenty-two stories overlook the Delaware River, and also offer superb views of Society Hill and Center City. Elegant rooms with a full range of amenities make it ideal for the business traveler. **www.hyattregencyphiladelphia.com**

CENTER CITY

Rodeway Inn

$

1208 Walnut St, Philadelphia **Tel** *(215) 546-7000* **Fax** *(215) 546-7573* **Rooms** *36* **Map** *3 B3*

This small, family-owned Victorian inn offers all the comfort and friendliness of a B&B. Located one block from the Forrest Theatre, it is within walking distance of Market Street and the city's historic sights. Guests can use the pool and fitness facilities at nearby establishments. **www.choicehotels.com**

Alexander Inn

$ $

12th & Spruce Sts, Philadelphia **Tel** *(215) 923-3535* **Fax** *(215) 923-1004* **Rooms** *48* **Map** *3 B3*

This four-star boutique hotel has modern decor that adds a touch of European charm. It has an excellent Center City location, just a couple of blocks from the theater district. The restaurant only serves a breakfast buffet, and the business center allows guests to access emails. **www.alexanderinn.com**

Hampton Inn

$ $

1301 Race St, Philadelphia **Tel** *(215) 665-9100* **Fax** *(215) 665-9200* **Rooms** *250* **Map** *3 B1*

Located right next to the Convention Center, this property is ideal for people attending conventions. It is situated a few blocks from Chinatown and the Market Street shopping area and within walking distance of historic sights. The clean rooms have modern amenities, including high-speed Internet access. **www.hamptoninn.hilton.com**

Holiday Inn Express Midtown

$ $

1305 Walnut St, Philadelphia **Tel** *(215) 735-9300* **Fax** *(215) 732-2682* **Rooms** *168* **Map** *3 B3*

A comfortable budget chain hotel, this Holiday Inn has a convenient location just a few blocks from the theater district and the Market Street shopping area. Complimentary Continental breakfast is served and the hotel gives passes for a nearby fitness center to those guests who wish to keep in shape. **www.himidtown.com**

La Reserve

$ $

1804 Pine St, Philadelphia **Tel** *(215) 735-1137* **Fax** *(215) 735-0582* **Rooms** *6* **Map** *2 D5*

A luxurious and cozy B&B in a refurbished Philadelphia townhouse, La Reserve has elegant rooms with antiques and beautiful lamps. The establishment has an all-you-can-eat gourmet breakfast and free wireless Internet access. Parking is available at nearby lots. **www.lareservebandb.com**

Travelodge

$ $

1227 Race St, Philadelphia **Tel** *(215) 564-2888* **Fax** *(215) 564-2700* **Rooms** *50* **Map** *3 B1*

This budget chain hotel has clean rooms and serves a complimentary Continental breakfast. Located directly across from the Pennsylvania Convention Center and just one block from Chinatown, it is within walking distance of historic sights and the Market Street shopping district. **www.travelodge.com**

Courtyard Philadelphia Downtown

$ $ $

21 N Juniper St, Philadelphia **Tel** *(215) 496-3200* **Fax** *(215) 496-3696* **Rooms** *498* **Map** *2 F4*

This is a comfortable Marriott-brand hotel housed in the historic, former City Hall Annex building. Located across the street from the Masonic Temple and the Pennsylvania Academy of the Fine Arts, it is just a few blocks from the Convention Center. Lobby and lounge areas are expansive and tastefully decorated. **www.courtyard.com**

Doubletree Hotel Philadelphia

$ $ $

237 S Broad St, Philadelphia **Tel** *(215) 893-1600* **Fax** *(215) 893-1664* **Rooms** *434* **Map** *2 F5*

A high-rise hotel in the heart of Philadelphia on the Avenue of the Arts, this property is across from the Kimmel Center, the Academy of Music, and the Merriam Theater. The lobby has a comfortable lounge area and sports bar and bistro, and the roof garden sports a jogging track. **www.philadelphia.doubletree.com**

Latham Hotel ⇅ [P] 🍴 🍸 ♿ $$$

135 S 17th St, Philadelphia ***Tel*** *(215) 563-7474* ***Fax*** *(215) 563-4034* ***Rooms*** *139* ***Map*** *2 D4*

This small, European-style boutique hotel is in the heart of the fashionable Rittenhouse Row shopping district. Rooms are decorated in Victorian style. It offers all modern amenities, including free wireless Internet access in all rooms. It also boasts a hip bar and restaurant *(see p148)*. **www.lathamhotel.com**

Rittenhouse 222 ⇅ [P] 🍸 ♿ $$$

222 W Rittenhouse Sq, Philadelphia ***Tel*** *(215) 222-7275* ***Fax*** *(215) 222-4450* ***Rooms*** *98* ***Map*** *2 D5*

This historic 1926 high-rise tower overlooking Rittenhouse Square has posh corporate suites featuring luxurious mahogany furniture, plush carpeting, and a marble kitchen. The lobby is accented with marble, mosaics, and gilded elevators. The city's best restaurants and shopping lie within a couple of blocks. **www.kormancommunities.com**

Crowne Plaza Philadelphia Hotel Center City ⇅ [P] 🍴 ≋ 🍸 ♿ $$$$

1800 Market St, Philadelphia ***Tel*** *(215) 561-7500* ***Fax*** *(215) 561-4484* ***Rooms*** *445* ***Map*** *2 E4*

Located within the city's cluster of skyscrapers, this chain hotel is ideal for business travelers. It offers modern, comfortable rooms. Just a few blocks from Rittenhouse Square with its many fine restaurants and boutiques, it is within walking distance of the theater and museum districts. **www.ichotelsgroup.com**

Loews Philadelphia ⇅ [P] 🍴 ≋ 🏋 🍸 ♿ $$$$

1200 Market St, Philadelphia ***Tel*** *(215) 231-7356* ***Fax*** *(215) 231-7305* ***Rooms*** *583* ***Map*** *3 B2*

This high-rise luxury hotel is housed in the landmark PSFS building, a 1932 former bank office. It has been renovated with elegant decor and Art Deco accents, including exotic woods and carved glass. Rooms offer astounding views. A spa and fitness center encompass the entire fifth floor of the hotel. **www.loewshotels.com**

Park Hyatt Philadelphia at the Bellevue ⇅ [P] 🍴 🍸 ♿ $$$$

Broad & Walnut Sts, Philadelphia ***Tel*** *(215) 893-1234* ***Fax*** *(215) 732-8518* ***Rooms*** *172* ***Map*** *2 E5*

A residential-style hotel with international flair, the Hyatt is perched on the upper floors of the 100-year-old Bellevue Building, which was once nicknamed the "Grand Dame of Broad Street." Marble staircases and chandeliers highlight the old world elegance. The property has upscale shops on its premises. **www.parkhyatt.com**

Philadelphia Marriott ⇅ [P] 🍴 ≋ 🏋 🍸 ♿ $$$$

1201 Market St, Philadelphia ***Tel*** *(215) 625-2900* ***Fax*** *(215) 625-6000* ***Rooms*** *1,410* ***Map*** *3 B2*

A world-class convention hotel connected to the Convention Center and Reading Terminal Market, the Philadelphia Marriott offers upgraded amenities on concierge-level floors. It is located in the heart of the Market Street shopping area and is within walking distance of historic sights and the theater district. **www.marriott.com/phldt**

Radisson Plaza-Warwick Hotel Philadelphia ⇅ [P] 🍴 🏋 🍸 ♿ $$$$

1701 Locust St, Philadelphia ***Tel*** *(215) 735-6000* ***Fax*** *(215) 789-6105* ***Rooms*** *545* ***Map*** *2 E5*

One block from fashionable Rittenhouse Square, this is a prestigious hotel whose guests have included celebrities and presidents. Built in 1926 in English Renaissance style, it has a majestic two-story lobby with a sweeping staircase, and an upscale steakhouse, The Prime Rib *(see p149)*. Pets are allowed on a dedicated pet floor. **www.radisson.com**

Sofitel Philadelphia ⇅ [P] 🍴 🍸 ♿ $$$$

120 S 17th St, Philadelphia ***Tel*** *(215) 569-8300* ***Fax*** *(215) 564-7436* ***Rooms*** *306* ***Map*** *2 E4*

An elegant, four-diamond hotel with a distinctive French flair in design and embellishments, the Sofitel houses a chic French restaurant, and the lobby has a bar with dramatic floor-to-ceiling windows. The spacious rooms have elegant and modern decor. Rittenhouse Row shopping areas and restaurants are only a block away. **www.sofitel.com**

The Westin Philadelphia ⇅ [P] 🍴 🏋 🍸 ♿ $$$$

99 S 17th St, Philadelphia ***Tel*** *(215) 563-1600* ***Fax*** *(215) 564-9559* ***Rooms*** *290* ***Map*** *2 E4*

This is an elegant chain hotel with luxuriously decorated lobby, lounge areas, and restaurants. The hotel is connected to Liberty Place, which has trendy shops and boutiques. It has a great location just a few blocks from the Rittenhouse Row shopping hub, and the theater and museum districts. **www.westin.com/philadelphia**

The Rittenhouse Hotel ⇅ [P] 🍴 ≋ 🏋 🍸 ♿ $$$$$

210 W Rittenhouse Sq, Philadelphia ***Tel*** *(215) 546-9000* ***Fax*** *(215) 732-3364* ***Rooms*** *98* ***Map*** *2 D5*

This top-of-the-line luxury hotel is one of the city's finest and boasts two award-winning restaurants, the Lacroix and the Smith & Wollensky steakhouse *(see p149)*. A five-diamond property with lavishly decorated rooms and marble bathrooms, the hotel also has an upscale spa and salon. **www.rittenhousehotel.com**

Rittenhouse Square Bed & Breakfast ⇅ ♿ $$$$$

1715 Rittenhouse Sq, Philadelphia ***Tel*** *(215) 546-6500* ***Fax*** *(215) 546-8787* ***Rooms*** *10* ***Map*** *2 D5*

This 10-room B&B offers posh accommodations in a refurbished 1900s Philadelphia carriage house. It boasts a private, elegant, and luxurious lobby, and serves a complimentary Continental breakfast in a Parisian-like breakfast room. Parking is available at nearby lots. **www.rittenhousebb.com**

The Ritz Carlton ⇅ [P] 🍴 🏋 🍸 ♿ $$$$$

10 S Broad St, Philadelphia ***Tel*** *(215) 523-8000* ***Fax*** *(215) 568-6445* ***Rooms*** *330* ***Map*** *2 F4*

This exquisite, five-diamond luxury hotel sits directly across from City Hall in the former Girard/Mellon Bank Building. It has an impressive columned façade entrance and the lobby is situated in the expansive rotunda. The rooms are lavishly decorated and have superb city views. **www.ritzcarlton.com/hotels/philadelphia**

Key to Price Guide *see p134* **Key to Symbols** *see back cover flap*

LOGAN SQUARE AND THE MUSEUM DISTRICT

Best Western Center City Hotel
501 N 22nd St, Philadelphia **Tel** *(215) 568-8300* **Fax** *(215) 557-0259* **Rooms** *183*
$$ $
Map 2 D1

A four-story budget hotel, this Best Western has the advantage of a good location within walking distance of the museum district. Some rooms offer excellent views of the Philadelphia skyline. Children who are 18 and younger can stay for free with a paying adult. **www.bestwestern.com/centercityhotel**

Embassy Suites Hotel Philadelphia Center City
1776 Benjamin Franklin Pkwy, Philadelphia **Tel** *(215) 561-1776* **Fax** *(215) 561-5930* **Rooms** *288*
$$ $ $
Map 2 E3

Popular hotel in a landmark cylindrical building opposite Logan Square. This chain features only suites – every room has an adjacent living room and a balcony. Situated in the museum district and close to the Museum of Art and Rittenhouse Square. The fitness room has a jogging track. **www.philadelphiacentercity.embsuites.com**

Wyndham Philadelphia at Franklin Plaza
17th & Race Sts, Philadelphia **Tel** *(215) 448-2000* **Fax** *(215) 448-2864* **Rooms** *758*
$$ $ $
Map 2 E3

This upscale, high-rise hotel is ideal for both the business and vacation traveler. Located four blocks from the Convention Center, it has a fabulous steakhouse *(see p150)* and an impressive modern design with a four-story high lobby atrium. The comfortable and gracious rooms have all the modern amenities. **www.wyndham.com**

Hotel Windsor
1700 Benjamin Franklin Pkwy, Philadelphia **Tel** *(215) 981-5678* **Fax** *(215) 981-5609* **Rooms** *267*
$$ $ $ $
Map 2 E3

Specialty hotel that offers furnished suites and unfurnished apartments. All rooms have complimentary high-speed Internet access. Some suites have fully-equipped kitchens, living rooms, separate sleeping areas, and private balconies. The hotel has two restaurants on its premises. **www.windsorhotel.com**

Four Seasons Hotel
1 Logan Sq, Philadelphia **Tel** *(215) 963-1500* **Fax** *(215) 963-9506* **Rooms** *364*
$$ $ $ $ $
Map 2 E3

One of Philadelphia's most elegant hotels, the Four Seasons is luxuriously decorated with Federal-style furnishings. It features one of the city's best restaurants *(see p150)*, as well as a courtyard café with decorative water fountains. It is located close to the financial, commercial, and museum districts. **www.fourseasons.com**

FARTHER AFIELD

Best Western Hotel Philadelphia
11580 Roosevelt Blvd, Philadelphia, PA, 19116 **Tel** *(215) 464-9500* **Fax** *(215) 464-8511* **Rooms** *100*
$

This reliable and comfortable chain hotel has well-decorated rooms with modern amenities. The hotel is within walking distance of several restaurants, while the Franklin Mills Outlet Mall and the Philadelphia Park Race Track are a short drive away. Convenient access to major interstates and turnpikes. **www.bestwesternhotelphiladelphia.com**

Holiday Inn Philadelphia – Cherry Hill
Rt 70 and Sayer Ave, Cherry Hill, NJ, 08002 **Tel** *(856) 663-5300* **Fax** *(856) 662-2913* **Rooms** *186*
$

In the heart of southern New Jersey, this Holiday Inn is a popular, mid-range chain hotel that caters to both business and leisure travelers. The in-house restaurant is the Red Hot & Blue, a Memphis-style barbecue restaurant. Close to attractions along the Camden Waterfront. **www.holidaycherryhill.com**

Howard Johnson Express Inn
2389 W Marlton Pike, Cherry Hill, NJ, 08002 **Tel** *(856) 317-1900* **Fax** *(856) 317-0800* **Rooms** *100*
$

This budget hotel is located within 5 miles (8 km) of Center City in Philadelphia. It is also well-placed to visit other sights, such as the Adventure Aquarium and the Camden Waterfront. The hotel offers a complimentary Continental breakfast and there is an Indian restaurant on the premises.

Radisson Hotel Mount Laurel
915 Rt 73, Mount Laurel, NJ, 08054 **Tel** *(856) 234-7300* **Fax** *(856) 802-3912* **Rooms** *283*
$

A pleasant suburban hotel, the Radisson in Mount Laurel is excellent for both business travelers and tourists. The hotel has a garden courtyard with a heated pool. Concierge-level rooms have upgraded amenities and balconies. There is also a game room for children, as well as basketball and tennis courts. **www.radisson.com/mtlaurelnj**

Ramada Inn Philadelphia
76 Industrial Hwy, Essington, PA, 19029 **Tel** *(610) 521-9600* **Fax** *(610) 521-9388* **Rooms** *292*
$

Located 3 miles (5 km) south of Philadelphia Airport, this comfortable hotel has a complimentary, 24-hour shuttle service to the airport. Each room has its own balcony. Special discounts are available for groups of ten or more people. **www.phillyramadainn.com**

Chestnut Hill Hotel

    📶 P $$

8229 Germantown Ave, Philadelphia, PA, 19118 **Tel** *(215) 242-5905* **Fax** *(215) 242-8778* **Rooms** *28*

Built in 1891, this historic hotel is situated along the cobblestoned streets of Germantown Avenue. Although furnished with 18th-century decor, it offers all modern amenities. Within walking distance of Fairmount Park's Wissahickon Gorge and a short drive from historic Germantown. **www.chestnuthillhotel.com**

Clarion Hotel & Conference Center

    📶 P 🍴 ≋ 📺 🛁 $$

1450 Rt 70 E and I-295, Cherry Hill, NJ, 08034 **Tel** *(856) 428-2300* **Fax** *(856) 354-7662* **Rooms** *196*

Across the Delaware River, this hotel and conference center is ideal for both the business and leisure traveler. An in-house café serves breakfast, entrées, and pastries, and a neighborhood-like pub and restaurant is next door. The hotel is a short drive from the Camden Waterfront and central Philadelphia. **www.clarionofcherryhill.com**

Conwell Inn at Temple University

    📶 P 🍴 ≋ 📺 🛁 $$

1331 W Berks St, Philadelphia, PA, 19122 **Tel** *(215) 235-6200* **Fax** *(215) 235-6235* **Rooms** *22*

A small hotel, Conwell Inn lies within the heart of the Temple University campus. A deluxe historic landmark hotel, it has cozy and comfortable rooms and suites that have been decorated very tastefully. The hotel provides a complimentary European breakfast and has a beauty salon on its premises. **www.conwellinn.com**

Hampton Inn Philadelphia Airport

    📶 P 🍴 ≋ 📺 🛁 $$

8600 Bartram Ave, Philadelphia, PA, 19153 **Tel** *(215) 966-1300* **Fax** *(215) 966-1313* **Rooms** *152*

The Hampton Inn is a quality budget hotel with clean and comfortable rooms. The hotel offers a shuttle service to the airport, which is about 2 miles (3 km) away. A short drive away are professional sports stadiums and south Philadelphia sights, including the Italian Market. **www.hamptoninn.com/hi/philadelphia-airport**

Philadelphia Fairfield Inn

    📶 P ≋ 📺 🛁 $$

8800 Bartram Ave, Philadelphia, PA, 19153 **Tel** *(215) 365-2254* **Fax** *(215) 365-2254* **Rooms** *109*

Located just half a mile away from the airport, this comfortable, high-end budget property by Marriott offers full amenities and conveniences at superior value for the dollar. Complimentary Continental breakfast. 3 miles (5 km) from professional sports venues in south Philadelphia. **www.marriott.com**

Quality Inn & Conference Center

    📶 P 🍴 ≋ 📺 🛁 $$

531 Rt 38 W, Maple Shade, NJ, 08052 **Tel** *(856) 235-6400* **Fax** *(856) 727-1027* **Rooms** *111*

This three-diamond hotel and conference center is ideal for both the business and leisure traveler. The bar by the poolside is open only on the weekends. About 10 miles (16 km) from central Philadelphia, it is also close to a number of entertainment areas. **www.choicehotels.com**

Sheraton University City Hotel

    📶 P 🍴 ≋ 🎴 📺 🛁 $$

3549 Chestnut St, Philadelphia, PA, 19104 **Tel** *(215) 387-8000* **Fax** *(215) 387-7920* **Rooms** *316*

This is a large and efficient full-service chain hotel on the University of Pennsylvania campus. Rooms have modern decor with plush beds and oversized chairs. Ideal for visiting Philadelphia Zoo and the Museum of Archaeology and Anthropology. The lobby features complimentary, wireless Internet access. **www.sheraton.com/universitycity**

Cornerstone Bed & Breakfast

    P $$$

3300 Baring St, Philadelphia, PA, 19104 **Tel** *(215) 387-6065* **Fax** *(215) 387-0590* **Rooms** *6*   **Map** *1 A2*

This intimate urban inn sits in a restored 1870s church-stone mansion, and has a wrap-around porch and stained glass windows. Its lavishly decorated rooms and lounge areas have original wood floors and high ceilings. The inn is situated close to the Philadelphia Zoo and the Museum of Art. **www.cornerstonebandb.com**

Embassy Suites Philadelphia

    📶 P 🍴 ≋ 🎴 📺 🛁 $$$

9000 Bartram Ave, Philadelphia, PA, 19153 **Tel** *(215) 365-4500* **Fax** *(215) 365-4803* **Rooms** *263*

This three-diamond, modern chain hotel is an all-suites establishment. It has a unique tropical atrium lobby, which is filled with ducks and fishponds. The hotel offers a complimentary cook-to-order breakfast. Just one mile (1.6 km) from the Philadelphia Airport. Free airport shuttle. **www.embassysuites.com**

Hilton Philadelphia Airport

    📶 P 🍴 ≋ 🎴 📺 🛁 $$$

4509 Island Ave, Philadelphia, PA, 19153 **Tel** *(215) 365-4150* **Fax** *(215) 937-6382* **Rooms** *331*

The Hilton chain offers comfort and a touch of elegance with this full-service hotel, located just one mile (1.6 km) from the airport. The Landing Restaurant and Grill is highly recommended, as are its bar and indoor pool. A complimentary 24-hour airport shuttle service is offered. Close to the city's sports stadiums. **www.hilton.com**

Hilton Philadelphia – Cherry Hill

    📶 P 🍴 ≋ 🎴 📺 🛁 $$$

2349 W Marlton Pike, Cherry Hill, NJ, 08002 **Tel** *(856) 665-6666* **Fax** *(856) 662-3676* **Rooms** *408*

Located in suburban Cherry Hill, this upscale and full-service Hilton property features modern rooms with full amenities, dark oak furniture, and marble countertops. It is convenient for visiting the Adventure Aquarium and the Camden Waterfront, while the Atlantic City beaches and casinos are just an hour away. **www.hilton.com**

Hilton Philadelphia City Avenue

    📶 P 🍴 ≋ 🎴 📺 🛁 $$$

4200 City Ave, Philadelphia, PA, 19131 **Tel** *(215) 879-4000* **Fax** *(215) 879-9020* **Rooms** *209*

An upscale chain hotel on the outskirts of the city, this Hilton hotel is a short drive from Fairmount Park and the Barnes Foundation. It has comfortable and elegantly furnished rooms. Guests can indulge in plenty of shopping and culinary delights in the shops and restaurants on City Avenue. **www.philadelphiacityavenue.hilton.com**

Key to Price Guide *see p134* **Key to Symbols** *see back cover flap*

Holiday Inn Philadelphia Stadium $$$

900 Packer Ave, Philadelphia, PA, 19148 **Tel** *(215) 755-9500* **Fax** *(215) 462-6947* **Rooms** *238*

This modern and efficient chain hotel is ideal for fans taking in a game at one of nearby professional sports venues in south Philadelphia. Comfortable rooms with a full range of amenities for leisure and business travelers as well. There is a sports bar and restaurant on the premises. **www.holiday-inn.com**

The Inn at Penn $$$

3600 Sansom St, Philadelphia, PA, 19104 **Tel** *(215) 222-0200* **Fax** *(215) 222-4600* **Rooms** *238*

Just across the Schuylkill River from Center City, this upscale Hilton hotel sits in the heart of the University of Pennsylvania campus. Also close to the Drexel University, Philadelphia Zoo, 30th Street Amtrak Station, and the University of Pennsylvania's Museum of Archaeology and Anthropology. **www.theinnatpenn.com**

Renaissance Philadelphia Hotel Airport $$$$

500 Stevens Dr, Philadelphia, PA, 19113 **Tel** *(610) 521-5900* **Fax** *(610) 521-4362* **Rooms** *350*

This four-diamond, modern, and upscale chain hotel is on I-95, close to the airport. It is tastefully decorated with the Renaissance's signature European flair. There is an expansive lobby atrium and the rooms have high-speed Internet access. It is in a convenient location for a quick drive into the city on the interstate. **www.marriott.com**

Philadelphia Airport Marriott $$$$$

Arrivals Rd, Philadelphia, PA, 19153 **Tel** *(215) 492-9000* **Fax** *(215) 492-6799* **Rooms** *419*

This upscale and full-service Marriott Hotel is the only one in Philadelphia connected to the airport via a skybridge to Terminal B. Nearby is the convenient R1 commuter train linking the airport with Center City. Terrific in-hotel dining and lounge at Riverbend Bar and Grille. **www.marriott.com**

BEYOND PHILADELPHIA

ATLANTIC CITY Holiday Inn Boardwalk $$$

Chelsea Ave & Boardwalk, Atlantic City, NJ, 08401 **Tel** *(609) 348-2200* **Fax** *(609) 348-0168* **Rooms** *220*

This modern chain hotel sits along the popular Boardwalk amidst casino properties, shopping destinations, and plenty of beach. It offers good value for the dollar. Kids eat free and stay free. The Historic Boardwalk Hall, an indoor venue for entertainment and sports events, is nearby. **www.atlanticcity.holiday-inn.com**

ATLANTIC CITY Bally's Atlantic City $$$$

Boardwalk & Park Place, Atlantic City, NJ, 08401 **Tel** *(609) 340-2000* **Fax** *(609) 340-4713* **Rooms** *1,270*

One of the few remnants of historic Atlantic City, the 1860s Dennis Hotel has been restored as part of this mega-resort complex, which also includes a modern 45-story tower. Fans of the board game Monopoly will know that the hotel stands on the city's most valuable corner. The hotel's casino features a Wild West theme. **www.ballys.com**

ATLANTIC CITY Caesars Atlantic City Hotel Casino $$$$

Arkansas Ave & Boardwalk, Atlantic City, NJ, 08401 **Tel** *(609) 348-4411* **Rooms** *1,140*

A premier destination on the New Jersey shore, Caesars is a luxurious hotel and casino on the Boardwalk with an "Ancient Rome" theme. The hotel's lobby is done up to look like a Roman temple, and the restaurant offers fine Italian dining *(see p152)*. The 1,100-seat Circus Maximus Theater offers the best in entertainment. **www.caesars.com**

ATLANTIC CITY Trump Taj Mahal Hotel Casino and Resort $$$$$

1000 Boardwalk at Virginia Ave, Atlantic City, NJ, 08401 **Tel** *(609) 449-1000* **Rooms** *1,250*

One of Atlantic City's landmark casinos, this luxury five-diamond resort has all the opulence that lives up to the Trump name. A 51-story tower hovers over the Boardwalk, and the themed hotel and casino has nine in-house restaurants *(see p152)* and a 5,000-seat arena for concerts and sports events. **www.trumptaj.com**

BRANDYWINE VALLEY Brandywine River Hotel $$

Rts 1 & 100, Chadds Ford, PA, 19317 **Tel** *(610) 388-1200* **Fax** *(610) 388-1200* **Rooms** *39*

A Victorian-style country B&B, the Brandywine River Hotel has elegantly decorated rooms with fireplaces and Jacuzzis. It is a short drive from Longwood Gardens, Brandywine Battlefield, Brandywine River Museum, Chadds Ford, and Winterthur. The hotel is surrounded by several award-winning restaurants. **www.brandywineriverhotel.com**

BRANDYWINE VALLEY Hotel du Pont $$$$$

11th & Market Sts, Wilmington, DE, 19801 **Tel** *(302) 594-3100* **Fax** *(302) 594-3108* **Rooms** *216*

Dating back to 1913, this four-diamond, four-star hotel is the ultimate in luxury in Delaware. Each room is lavishly furnished with mahogany furniture and brass bathroom fixtures. Close to most of the region's attractions, including the Brandywine River Museum, Winterthur, Hagley Museum, and Longwood Gardens. **www.hoteldupont.com**

CAPE MAY Chalfonte Hotel $$

301 Howard St, Cape May, NJ, 08204 **Tel** *(609) 884-8409* **Fax** *(609) 884-4588* **Rooms** *66*

This whitewashed Victorian-era hotel offers old-fashioned charm with rocking chairs on the wrap-around front porch. Chalfonte has always been unconventional – rooms have no televisions or phones, and the hotel is just two blocks from the beach. **www.chalfonte.com**

CAPE MAY Queen's Hotel   🅿 $$$$

601 Columbia Ave, Cape May, NJ, 08204 **Tel** *(609) 884-1613* **Rooms** *11*

Built in the 1870s and fully restored in 1995, this mansard-roofed Victorian inn is located in the heart of Cape May, just a block from the beach, antiques shops, gourmet dining, and historic tours. Bicycles to tour the area are available for free, and the hotel provides a complimentary European breakfast buffet. **www.queenshotel.com**

DOYLESTOWN 1814 House Inn Bed & Breakfast   🅿🛏 $$$

50 S Main St, Doylestown, PA, 18901 **Tel** *(215) 340-1814* **Fax** *(215) 340-2234* **Rooms** *7*

This historic inn is within walking distance of the Mercer Museum and the James A. Michener Art Museum. Many rooms overlook Doylestown Historical Society Park. The rooms are decorated with 19th-century furnishings, but have all modern conveniences. A full country breakfast is offered on weekends. **www.1814houseinn.com**

GETTYSBURG Quality Inn at General Lee's Headquarters   🅿🍴≋🖙🛏 $

401 Buford Ave, Gettysburg, PA, 17325 **Tel** *(717) 334-3141* **Fax** *(717) 334-1813* **Rooms** *45*

Quaint inn with renovated rooms next to Confederate General Robert E. Lee's former headquarters. The three-diamond inn has spacious, bright, and clean rooms with antique furniture. Two-story suites are also available. Free Continental breakfast and admission to General Lee's Headquarters Museum. **www.gettysburgusa.com**

GETTYSBURG Farnsworth House Inn   🅿🍴 $$

401 Baltimore St, Gettysburg, PA, 17325 **Tel** *(717) 334-8838* **Fax** *(717) 334-5862* **Rooms** *11*

This B&B is housed in one of Gettysburg's most historic buildings, with walls that still have bullet holes from the Civil War, and a small open-air garden. The lavish rooms have period decor, and the B&B conducts ghost tours of some of the "haunted" rooms. It also has quaint dining rooms *(see p152)*. **www.farnsworthhouseinn.com**

GETTYSBURG Gettystown Inn   🅿🍴🛏 $$

89 Steinwehr Ave, Gettysburg, PA, 17325 **Tel** *(717) 334-2100* **Fax** *(717) 334-6905* **Rooms** *9*

Victorian B&B consisting of three separate Civil War-era houses near where President Lincoln delivered his famous Gettysburg Address *(see p121)*. Rooms are lavishly decorated with 19th-century antiques and furnishings. A complimentary breakfast is served at the adjacent Dobbin House Tavern *(see p152)*. **www.dobbinhouse.com**

GETTYSBURG The Brafferton Inn   🅿 $$$

44 York St, Gettysburg, PA, 17325 **Tel** *(717) 337-3423, (866) 337-3423* **Rooms** *14*

This elegant and lovely B&B is located in a 1786 fieldstone house – the oldest residence in Gettysburg. All rooms are furnished with 18th- and 19th-century family antiques, elaborate stencils, and family portraits. A two-night stay is the minimum on weekends from April to November. **www.brafferton.com**

GETTYSBURG Hilton Garden Inn Gettysburg   📶🅿🍴≋🖙🖳🛏 $$$

1061 York St, Gettysburg, PA, 17325 **Tel** *(717) 334-2040* **Fax** *(717) 334-2073* **Rooms** *88*

A newly opened, full-service chain hotel, the Hilton Garden Inn is located a short distance away from the historic battlefield, museums, and the town center. It has a bright and spacious lobby, and an upscale café that serves breakfast. **www.hiltongardeninn.com**

HARRISBURG Hilton Harrisburg & Towers   📶🅿🍴≋🖳🛏 $$$

1 N 2nd St, Harrisburg, PA, 17101 **Tel** *(717) 233-6000* **Fax** *(717) 233-6830* **Rooms** *341*

This upscale, full-service Hilton hotel is just three blocks from the State Capitol. It has elegant rooms; "Tower Level" guest rooms are accorded enhanced amenities, including a complimentary Continental breakfast and evening hors d'ouevres. The hotel has four restaurants on its premises. **www.harrisburg.hilton.com**

HERSHEY Hampton Inn & Suites   📶🅿≋🖳🛏 $$$$

East Chocolate Ave, Hershey, PA, 17033 **Tel** *(717) 533-8400* **Fax** *(717) 520-1892* **Rooms** *110*

A comfortable chain hotel in downtown Hershey, the Hampton Inn & Suites is only 1 mile (1.6 km) from the renowned attractions of the area, including Hershey Chocolate World and Hershey Park. The hotel offers a complimentary Continental breakfast and high-speed Internet access. **www.hamptoninn.com**

HERSHEY The Hotel Hershey   📶🅿🍴≋🖙🖳🛏 $$$$$

Hotel Rd, Hershey, PA, 17033 **Tel** *(717) 533-2171* **Fax** *(717) 534-8887* **Rooms** *232*

This grand hotel with its majestic gardens and fountains sits atop a hill overlooking the town. Luxurious and lavishly decorated rooms and common areas have old-world charm, and historic photographs and original artworks line the walls. Turndown service at night with Hershey's "Kisses" chocolates. **www.hersheypa.com**

PENNSYLVANIA DUTCH COUNTRY General Sutter Inn   🅿🍴 $

14 E Main St, Lititz, PA, 17543 **Tel** *(717) 626-2115* **Fax** *(717) 626-0992* **Rooms** *16*

The General Sutter Inn is one of the oldest in Pennsylvania, dating back to 1764. Spacious rooms and suites are decorated with antiques in Victorian style. It is home to two fine restaurants and a lively bar, and has a delightful courtyard that is used for outdoor dining and cocktails. **www.generalsutterinn.com**

PENNSYLVANIA DUTCH COUNTRY Revere Inn & Suites   📶🅿🍴≋🖳🛏 $

3063 Lincoln Hwy, Paradise, PA, 17562 **Tel** *(717) 687-8601* **Fax** *(717) 687-6141* **Rooms** *95*

This unique hotel has comfortable and tastefully decorated rooms and suites in three different buildings, including the 18th-century Revere House. All rooms have modern amenities and the historic Revere Tavern restaurant is situated on the property. Located on Route 30 in the heart of the Pennsylvania Dutch Country. **www.revereinn.com**

Key to Price Guide *see p134* **Key to Symbols** *see back cover flap*

PENNSYLVANIA DUTCH COUNTRY Bird-In-Hand Family Inn

2740 Old Philadelphia Pike, Bird-In-Hand, PA, 17505 **Tel** *(717) 768-8271* **Fax** *(717) 768-1117* **Rooms** *125*

This large, three-diamond property is an ideal getaway for a family holiday. Facilities such as tennis courts, mini-golf, a playground, game room, and even a petting zoo keep the kids busy. It has a family restaurant with an all-you-can-eat buffet. **www.bird-in-hand.com/familyinn**

PENNSYLVANIA DUTCH COUNTRY Bird-In-Hand Village Inn & Suites

2695 Old Philadelphia Pike, Bird-In-Hand, PA, 17505 **Tel** *(717) 293-8369* **Fax** *(717) 768-1117* **Rooms** *24*

This 1734 inn is responsible for the unique naming of this small town. Four well-preserved historic buildings house rooms and suites. The complimentary Continental breakfast includes local freshly-baked treats. Guests can take a 2-hour complimentary bus tour of the area. **www.bird-in-hand.com/villageinn**

PENNSYLVANIA DUTCH COUNTRY Fulton Steamboat Inn

Rt 30 at Rt 896, Strasburg, PA, 17579 **Tel** *(717) 299-9999* **Fax** *(717) 299-9992* **Rooms** *97*

This unique hotel is shaped like a 19th-century steamboat in honor of inventor Robert Fulton, who was born nearby in 1765. Family-oriented, with three "decks" of spacious guest rooms and "cabins" with bunk beds for kids, the inn is not far from the Strasburg Railroad and the Amish Village. Two-night minimum stay. **www.fultonsteamboatinn.com**

PENNSYLVANIA DUTCH COUNTRY Lodging at Kitchen Kettle Village

Rt 340, Intercourse, PA, 17534 **Tel** *(800) 732-3538* **Rooms** *11*

Located among Pennsylvania Dutch Country farms, 11 tastefully decorated rooms and suites are tucked amidst the specialty shops at Kitchen Kettle Village, which comprises 32 shops, restaurants, and lodging. The rooms are comfortable and offer all modern amenities. **www.kitchenkettle.com**

PENNSYLVANIA DUTCH COUNTRY Strasburg Village Inn

1 W Main St, Strasburg, PA, 17579 **Tel** *(717) 687-0900* **Fax** *(717) 687-3650* **Rooms** *10*

Dating back to the late 1780s, this historic inn is situated on one corner of Strasburg's center square. Ten rooms in "Williamsburg" style are warmly furnished in Victorian-style decor with canopy beds and antiques. The inn sits next door to the old-style Strasburg Creamery, an ice cream and sandwich shop. **www.strasburg.com**

PENNSYLVANIA DUTCH COUNTRY Amishview Inns & Suites

Rt 340, 3125 Old Philadelphia Pike, Bird-In-Hand, PA, 17505 **Tel** *(717) 768-1162* **Rooms** *50*

This newly constructed country inn has scenic views of cornfields and silos. It is located halfway between Intercourse and Bird-In-Hand on the Plain and Fancy Farm, which is also home to Lancaster's first family-style restaurant *(see p153)*. Adjacent to the Amish Experience Theater and the Amish Homestead. **www.amishviewinn.com**

PENNSYLVANIA DUTCH COUNTRY Intercourse Village Bed & Breakfast Suites

Rt 340, Main Street, Intercourse, PA, 17534 **Tel** *(717) 768-2626* **Rooms** *12*

This 1909, Victorian-style B&B is a four-diamond facility with traditional fireplaces in suites with beamed ceilings and private baths with Jacuzzis. Enjoy candlelit gourmet breakfasts in the ornate dining room. The B&B is located close to antiques and craft shops in the heart of Intercourse's main shopping street. **www.amishcountryinns.com**

PENNSYLVANIA DUTCH COUNTRY Netherlands Inn and Spa

One Historic Dr, Strasburg, PA, 17579 **Tel** *(717) 687-7691* **Fax** *(717) 687-5290* **Rooms** *102*

Rooms in this upscale inn and spa include a full breakfast for two. The spa offers body wraps and complete facial and skin rejuvenation therapies. For children, the establishment has a game room and a playground on the premises. Bicycles can be rented to tour the surrounding area. **www.netherlandsinn.com**

TRENTON Trenton Marriott at Lafayette Yard

1 W Lafayette St, Trenton, NJ, 08608 **Tel** *(609) 421-4000* **Fax** *(609) 421-4002* **Rooms** *197*

An upscale and modern three-diamond hotel in downtown Trenton, the hotel has elegant guest rooms. It is adjacent to the Trenton War Memorial, and is just one block from the tourist information center and Old Barracks Museum. A short drive away is Washington Crossing State Park and New Hope. **www.marriott.com**

VALLEY FORGE Crowne Plaza Valley Forge

260 Mall Blvd, King of Prussia, PA, 19406 **Tel** *(610) 265-7500* **Fax** *(610) 265-4076* **Rooms** *225*

Opened in 2004, this upscale hotel is walking distance from the colossal King of Prussia Mall. The property has tastefully decorated rooms with many amenities, including Jacuzzis. It also offers complete business facilities. The hotel is 2 miles (3 km) from the Valley Forge National Historic Park. **www.crowneplazavalleyforge.com**

VALLEY FORGE Hilton Valley Forge

251 W DeKalb Pike, King of Prussia, PA, 19406 **Tel** *(610) 337-1200* **Fax** *(610) 337-2224* **Rooms** *300*

This stylish Hilton property, located in the heart of the Valley Forge business district, sits atop a small hill overlooking a busy thoroughfare. Shoppers will be pleased as this hotel offers a complimentary shuttle service to the King of Prussia Mall. It has oversized rooms decorated with traditional-style furniture. **www.valleyforge.hilton.com**

VALLEY FORGE Wayne Hotel

139 E Lancaster Ave, Wayne, PA, 19087 **Tel** *(610) 687-5000* **Fax** *(610) 687-8387* **Rooms** *40*

Dating back to 1906, this century-old hotel along Philadelphia's fashionable Main Line has been restored to its former Victorian elegance. Tudor Revival-style architecture adds to the old-world charm. It is a just a few miles from the King of Prussia Mall. Fitness facilities and pool can be used at nearby establishments. **www.waynehotel.com**

RESTAURANTS AND CAFÉS

Typical Dutch Country pretzel

THOUGH THE CITY is perhaps traditionally best known for the Philadelphia cheesesteak, its culinary repertoire has expanded recently and is today home to some of the country's top-rated restaurants. In addition to superb American fare, some of the city's best dining rooms specialize in international cuisine, including French, Italian, Thai, Moroccan, Chinese, and more. Excellent bistros, seafood restaurants, and steakhouses that feature cooking styles from Southern home cooking and colonial fare to Pennsylvania Dutch can be found in Center City. Modest restaurants and eateries, many serving traditional cheesesteak sandwiches, can be found in every city neighborhood and beyond.

Park-side alfresco dining at Rouge in Rittenhouse Square *(see p149)*

PHILLY FARE

FOR BREAKFAST, the locals love to order grilled pork rolls along with their eggs and hash brown potatoes. At noon, cheesesteaks and lunchmeat-filled "hoagies" or "grinders" are favorites, and these can be found at food courts, pizzerias, and sandwich shops around the city. Hoagies are the "official sandwiches of Philadelphia," and are Italian rolls filled with fresh meats and cheeses, as well as lettuce, tomatoes, and onions, topped off with a dash of oregano. Philly cheesesteaks have finely-sliced grilled beef along with onions, which are topped off with thick cheese sauce served up in a foot-long roll.

In Pennsylvania Dutch Country, meals are influenced by the traditional cooking of the Amish and Mennonites *(see p115)*. Family-style restaurants usually offer a good selection of this distinctive food, while staple and favorite treats are readily available at local farmers' markets scattered throughout the area *(see p144)*.

RESTAURANTS, BISTROS, AND CAFÉS

MANY OF Philadelphia's best restaurants are in Center City. Fine dining rooms can also be found in Center City hotels and near the theater district, home to the Kimmel Center and other performing arts venues. In Old City, head to the area around Market and Chestnut Streets, between Front and 4th Streets, where some popular establishments can be found. Chinatown is home to several excellent restaurants, while some of the best family-owned trattorias are located in the Italian Market in south Philadelphia.

Numerous restaurants in the city's popular outdoor areas, such as Rittenhouse Square and Manayunk, are stylish with upscale bistros and cafés. These offer outdoor tables along the sidewalks, weather permitting. Many are small, cozy establishments serving cocktails and trendsetting dishes in an ambience reminiscent of a Parisian café. Several restaurants and comfortable neighborhood bars are also located along Fairmount Avenue, close to the Museum of Art.

Cuba Libre in Old City recreates 1940s Havana *(see p146)*

Geno's Steaks on Philadelphia's 9th Street *(see p150)*

HOURS AND PRICES

LUNCHEONETTES AND coffee shops open early for breakfast and may stay open through lunch only, catering to office workers. Finer restaurants open for lunch and dinner, with lunch served from 11:30am to 2:30pm or 3pm, and dinner from 5:30pm until 10pm or 10:30pm, and often later on weekends. Late-night restaurants that are also nightclubs stay open until 2am, but may stop serving food earlier.

Breakfast at diners and eateries can cost anywhere from $5 to $10 with a tip, while hotel buffet breakfasts can cost from $10 to $20. Full Sunday brunches at upscale restaurants and hotels range from around $20 to $30 or more per person.

A typical lunch ranges from on-the-go sandwiches and sodas, from $5 to $7, to sit-down meals at restaurants that will cost $8 to $15 with a tip. Dinner is usually the big meal of the day. Starters and salads cost $5 to $10. Entrées can run $10 to $25, and up to $30 or more at high-end steakhouses and restaurants. Desserts and wine by the glass usually cost $5 to $10.

Some ethnic restaurants offer great quality food at less expensive costs. Greek, Chinese, Indian, Mexican, and Middle Eastern restaurants serve very generous portions at reasonable prices, with meals costing up to $15 or more per person.

EATERIES AND FAST FOOD

GOOD PIZZA, salads, hoagies, and Italian hot sandwiches are an inexpensive alternative found in the city's many pizzerias. Eateries in food courts serve balanced and tasty meals for $5 or more. Similar prices are charged at fast food restaurants that serve hamburgers, tacos, and fried chicken.

ALCOHOL AND SMOKING

MANY RESTAURANTS serve wine by the glass or bottle. Eateries and fast food restaurants do not serve alcohol, while patrons of some establishments have the option to "bring your own bottle" (of wine). Restaurants and bars stop serving alcohol by 2am. The legal drinking age in Pennsylvania is 21, and restaurant staff may ask to see proof of age. Restaurants in Philadelphia have no-smoking sections, but many allow smoking at or near the bar area, if the restaurant has one. Smoking may be permitted at outdoor café-style eating places.

RESERVATIONS AND DRESS

RESERVATIONS FOR dining at upscale restaurants are recommended, and are often required on weekend nights. Nonetheless, some popular spots may not reserve tables, and use waiting lists. Even if you have reservations, you might have to wait for up to an hour on busy days.

Casual wear is accepted at most city restaurants, although there are some trendy and fine-dining establishments that expect patrons to wear smart-casual styles or business attire, so it is best to check when making reservations.

TIPPING

AT MOST RESTAURANTS, your waitperson will bring you your bill, which can be paid through cash, credit cards, or traveler's checks. A 15 percent tip is standard, with up to 20 percent or more for excellent service.

CHILDREN

WELL-BEHAVED children are usually welcome in restaurants. It is not recommended, however, to bring young children to establishments that have late-night crowds and a large bar area, as patrons aged 21 or younger may not be allowed inside.

Le Bec-Fin, a celebrated French restaurant *(see p149)*

Flavors of the Pennsylvania Dutch Country

PHILADELPHIANS SAVOR the broad range of American and ethnic tastes from the many cultures that call the city home. Nearby Pennsylvania Dutch Country has its own unique flavors, comprising basic, hearty foods prepared from simple recipes. Amish and Mennonite cooks take advantage of the plentiful harvests to prepare dishes often characterized as good home cooking. To preserve the excess from the harvests, fresh country produce is both canned and jarred in homes and small shops, with much of it turned into tangy relishes and sweet jams. Such treats are available at various farmers' markets.

Corn-on-the-cob

Fresh produce at a farmer's market in Lancaster County

fields through traditional methods with horse-drawn farming equipment. They grow all manner of fresh vegetables including corn, string beans, carrots, beets, onions, tomatoes, peppers, lettuce, potatoes, sweet potatoes, cauliflower, and more. Fruits include apples, cherries, plums, peaches, and sweet watermelon, with many used as ingredients for the delicious desserts that have made the Pennsylvania Dutch Country famous.

MEATS AND DELIS

AMISH DELIS and restaurants feature a wide variety of cheeses, meats, and poultry, including fresh country sausages, sweet bologna, bacon, ham, dried beef and jerky, and smoked turkey. Cuts of fresh beef, pork, and chicken are favorites among the locals, who serve them up as part of tasty recipes such as scrapple, a dish that is made of pork, onions, cornmeal, and spices.

BOUNTIFUL HARVESTS

AMISH AND Mennonite food stems from the cultural tastes that the settlers brought from their home countries of Germany and Switzerland – recipes later adapted to the available crops that could be cultivated in the New World. Throughout the generations, the Amish have continued to nurture their gardens and

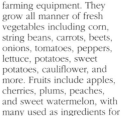

Molasses cookies   **Whoopie pie**   **Mincemeat cookies**   **Apple pie**   **Shoofly pie**

A selection of Pennsylvania Dutch Country cakes and desserts

LOCAL DISHES AND SPECIALITIES

Pennsylvania Dutch restaurants are known for their family-style buffets with meat dishes such as golden fried chicken, roast beef, chicken pot pie, and spicy sausage. Staples include mashed potatoes, home-made noodles and breads, and a choice of vegetables. Popular jellies and relishes include smooth apple butter, and Chow Chow, a mixture of sweet pickled vegetables. Amish recipes are handed down from mother to daughter to granddaughter, making for unique tastes. Dishes include Amish bean soup, corn fritters, spare ribs and sauerkraut, baking powder biscuits, cornmeal mush, and "Schnitz and Knepp," made with dried apples and ham. Popular desserts include Whoopie pie – chocolate cake surrounding white icing – and Shoofly pie, which has a coffeecake-like topping with a thick molasses bottom.

Fresh green apples

Chicken pot pie *comprises tender chicken pieces with vegetables and noodles, cooked in a pot of broth*

Choosing a Restaurant

The restaurants have been selected for value, quality of food, atmosphere, and location. They are listed by area, starting with Philadelphia's Old City and moving on to restaurants farther away and beyond the city. Unless specified, all offer non-smoking sections. For map references, *see pp194–97.*

PRICE CATEGORIES
The price ranges represent a three-course evening meal for one, a glass of house wine, tax, and service charges.

$ $25
$$ $26–$35
$$$ $36–$50
$$$$ $51–$70
$$$$$ Over $70

OLD CITY

Ariana Restaurant
$

134 Chestnut St, Philadelphia, PA, 19106 **Tel** *(215) 922-1535*   **Map** *4 E3*

This small and cozy restaurant serves authentic Afghan cuisine featuring Kabuli *pulao* (rice with vegetables and meat), marinated lamb kebabs, and dishes scented with spices such as cinnamon and cumin. The decor includes ethnic photographs, creating a unique atmosphere. There is bay window seating for groups in traditional Afghan style.

Aromatic House of Kebob
$

113 Chestnut St, Philadelphia, PA, 19106 **Tel** *(215) 923-4510*   **Map** *4 E3*

A family-owned eatery in historic Old City, this restaurant features a comfortable café-like setting. It specializes in traditional Persian cooking, but also offers other popular fare such as *souvlaki* and *gyros* (Greek meat dishes) and kebabs. The restaurant usually stays open for patrons visiting the Old City in the late hours.

The Bourse
$

111 S Independence Mall East, Philadelphia, PA, 19106 **Tel** *(215) 625-0300*   **Map** *4 D3*

The lobby of the Bourse, a historic 19th-century commodities exchange building *(see p156)*, is home to a food court and several souvenir shops. Its many eateries offer Chinese food, pizzas, cheesesteaks, sandwiches, burgers, and more. The food court is an ideal lunch venue for sightseers in Independence Mall.

Mexican Post Restaurant and Bar
$

104 Chestnut St, Philadelphia, PA, 19106 **Tel** *(215) 923-5233*   **Map** *4 E3*

This informal and friendly restaurant serves a wide range of popular Mexican dishes. It features an extensive menu of taco salads, sizzling fajitas, burritos, salads, soups, and chicken and fish specialties, in addition to combination meals. The lively bar serves eight flavors of margaritas.

Continental Restaurant and Martini Bar
$$

138 Market St, Philadelphia, PA, 19106 **Tel** *(215) 923-6069*   **Map** *4 E3*

With its imaginative interior, the Continental is one of the hippest and most popular after-dark spots in the Old City's lively nightlife district. It serves contemporary cuisine with a pan-Asian flair, and has extensive martini, champagne, and wine lists. Latin and lounge music is played. Weekday lunch, weekend brunch, and daily dinner service.

Kabul Afghan Cuisine Restaurant
$$

106 Chestnut St, Philadelphia, PA, 19106 **Tel** *(215) 922-3676*   **Map** *4 E3*

This popular ethnic restaurant near the heart of Old City has traditional Afghan decor and a warm and welcoming atmosphere. The menu is replete with meat kebab and vegetarian specialties cooked with exotic Afghan spices. Call in advance to dine in traditional Afghan style on a platform with rugs and pillows. No lunch service.

Karma Restaurant and Bar
$$

114 Chestnut St, Philadelphia, PA, 19106 **Tel** *(215) 925-1444*   **Map** *4 E3*

An upscale and cheerful Indian restaurant decorated with contemporary art. It serves up traditional dishes from all over India, with baked salmon and chicken tikka masala among other specialties. The lunch buffet provides a taste of the chef's award-winning dishes. The restaurant also has banquet facilities and a full bar.

Brasil's Restaurant and Night Spot
$$$

112 Chestnut St, Philadelphia, PA, 19106 **Tel** *(215) 413-1700*   **Map** *4 E3*

Try out this restaurant and nightclub in Old City for Brazilian cuisine and Latin-style dancing. The food includes hearty meat and seafood dishes with exciting South American and tropical accents. The nightclub offers dancing lessons and bands playing Brazilian, South American, and Caribbean music. Closed Sunday–Tuesday.

Café Spice
$$$

35 S 2nd St, Philadelphia, PA, 19106 **Tel** *(215) 627-6273*   **Map** *4 E3*

A trendy, vibrant bistro which gives a contemporary edge to traditional fare from all over India, such as kebabs and chicken tikka. Spacious interiors with modern decor and warm colors add to the chic and elegant atmosphere. The bar offers an extensive martini list. A DJ spins on weekends.

Key to Symbols *see back cover flap*

City Tavern 👪♿🍸 $$$
138 S 2nd St, Philadelphia, PA, 19106 ***Tel*** *(215) 413-1443* ***Map*** *4 E3*

Authentic colonial-style cuisine, such as West Indies pepperpot soup, is served at this historically accurate reconstruction of the original 1773 tavern. Colonial ales brewed according to George Washington's and Thomas Jefferson's original recipes are also served. Three floors with colonial decor and staff in period costume.

Cuba Libre Restaurant and Rum Bar 👪♿◗🍸 $$$
10 S 2nd St, Philadelphia, PA, 19106 ***Tel*** *(215) 627-0666* ***Map*** *4 E3*

Trendy and happening, this restaurant's spacious atrium reaches out onto the sidewalk for alfresco dining in warmer months. Bright colors and balconies evoke memories of 1940s Havana. Two bars and four dining rooms serve up contemporary Cuban and inventive Latin cuisine. Brunch is on offer on the weekend.

DiNardo's Famous Crabs 👪♿🍸 $$$
312 Race St, Philadelphia, PA, 19106 ***Tel*** *(215) 925-5115* ***Map*** *4 E2*

A favorite since 1976, this seafood restaurant serves up excellent crabs in a casual and friendly atmosphere. Specialties include steamed Louisiana crabs served "hot and dirty" Baltimore-style, jumbo shrimp, stuffed flounder, and more. Located one block from St. George's Church and Fireman's Hall. No lunch service on Sunday.

Eulogy Belgian Tavern 👪♿◗🍸 $$$
136 Chestnut St, Philadelphia, PA, 19106 ***Tel*** *(215) 413-1918* ***Map*** *4 E3*

This cozy pub and restaurant features an enormous selection of 185 international and Belgian beers. Traditional Belgian fare, including fish, meatballs, fries, and mussels, is prepared in five different sauces. The restaurant has limited wheelchair access and does not allow children after 8pm.

Philadelphia Fish & Company 👪♿🍸 $$$
207 Chestnut St, Philadelphia, PA, 19106 ***Tel*** *(215) 625-8605* ***Map*** *4 E3*

This popular restaurant has an outdoor deck, and has a continually evolving menu that showcases fish, meat, and fowl dishes in dazzling sauces. The eatery has upbeat, modern interiors with rich mahogany trim and furnishings in a Zinfandel red and pale meadow green color scheme. Children allowed only on request.

The Plough & The Stars 👪♿🎵🍸 $$$
207 Chestnut St, Philadelphia, PA, 19106 ***Tel*** *(215) 733-0300* ***Map*** *4 E3*

This trendy Irish pub is housed in the Corn Exchange Building. The restaurant plays traditional Irish music on Sundays and has plenty of Guinness on tap. The fare, however, is not necessarily traditional but instead gourmet and creative. The pub has some outdoor seating in the warmer months.

Serrano ♿🎵◗🍸 $$$
20 S 2nd St, Philadelphia, PA, 19106 ***Tel*** *(215) 928-0770* ***Map*** *4 E3*

This stylish restaurant sits in a 1820s townhouse-like building with the popular folk music café, Tin Angel, on the second level. It offers international cooking, with specialties such as Malaysian pork chop, vegetable *kung pao*, and calamari. No lunch service.

Spasso Italian Grill 👪◗🍸 $$$
34 S Front St, Philadelphia, PA, 19106 ***Tel*** *(215) 592-7661* ***Map*** *4 E3*

This old world-style trattoria is located across from Penn's Landing and features traditional Italian cuisine with dishes from both southern and northern Italy. Popular dishes include home-made pastas, fresh seafood, veal, and chicken. The restaurant sports a warm and casual atmosphere. No lunch service on the weekend.

Warmdaddy's 👪🎵◗🍸 $$$
4 S Front St, Philadelphia, PA, 19106 ***Tel*** *(215) 627-8400* ***Map*** *4 E3*

Southern cuisine can be enjoyed at this Old City nightclub and restaurant with live jazz, zydeco, and blues by renowned R&B and soul artists. Opened in 1995, it has red-themed decor. Specialties include cornbread catfish, ribs, chicken, and Southern-style collard greens. No lunch service.

Bluezette 👪♿◗🍸 $$$$
246 Market St, Philadelphia, PA, 19106 ***Tel*** *(215) 627-3866* ***Map*** *4 E3*

The menu of this upbeat restaurant has an array of dishes from down-home Southern and soul food to Caribbean, Cajun, and Creole, including crawfish *remoulade* and grouper Creole. Do not leave without trying the fried green tomatoes or the mac-and-cheese. Children not allowed after 10pm. Closed Monday.

Fork 👪♿◗🍸 $$$$
306 Market St, Philadelphia, PA, 19106 ***Tel*** *(215) 625-9425* ***Map*** *4 E3*

Located in the heart of the Old City nightlife district, Fork offers a mix of casual sophistication and an urban, upscale style. It serves new American, bistro-style cuisine with an international flavor. Decor includes delicately painted velvet curtains and chandeliers. It also has a unique center bar. No lunch service on Saturday.

Patou 👪♿◗🍸 $$$$
312 Market St, Philadelphia, PA, 19106 ***Tel*** *(215) 928-2987* ***Map*** *4 E3*

Cool Mediterranean colors add to the ambience of this spacious, modern French bar and restaurant that features an open-air kitchen. Côte d'Azur-influenced seafood dishes dominate the menu, with a mix of traditional French cooking accented with a contemporary flair. No lunch service on the weekend. Closed Sunday–Monday.

Key to Price Guide *see p145* **Key to Symbols** *see back cover flap*

Ristorante Panorama and il bar
🧒 ♿ 🍸 [$][$][$][$]

Front and Market Sts, Philadelphia, PA, 19106 ***Tel*** *(215) 922-7800* ***Map*** *4 E3*

This is an exquisite family-owned hotel *(see p134)* and restaurant near Penn's Landing. The bustling trattoria decorated with Florentine tiles and hand-painted murals features Italian food – home-made pastas and the finest cuts of veal. The unique "il bar" features the world's largest wine dispensing system and offers 120 wines by the glass.

Swanky Bubbles
🧒 ♿ 🎵 ☂ 🍸 [$][$][$][$]

10 S Front St, Philadelphia, PA, 19106 ***Tel*** *(215) 928-1200* ***Map*** *4 E3*

An eclectic and premier champagne bar and restaurant serving sushi and pan-Asian cuisine with French and Spanish influences. Located opposite Penn's Landing, it features an extensive selection of champagnes and sparkling wines, some of which are sold by the glass. Dinner is served from 5pm until 1am. No lunch service.

Buddakan
🧒 ♿ ☂ 🍸 [$][$][$][$][$]

325 Chestnut St, Philadelphia, PA, 19106 ***Tel*** *(215) 574-9440* ***Map*** *4 E3*

Tables are set amidst a gilded Buddha in one of the city's most happening and elegant restaurants. Modern Asian cuisine is served in a lively atmosphere. Most popular are communal tables where guests participate in a family-style, pass-the-plate dining experience. Wear smart casual to dressy clothes.

Morimoto
🧒 ♿ ☂ 🍸 [$][$][$][$][$]

723 Chestnut St, Philadelphia, PA, 19106 ***Tel*** *(215) 413-9070* ***Map*** *4 D3*

This renowned restaurant's dining room is elegant and upscale with modern decor. One of the best fusion restaurants in Philadelphia, it brings contemporary Japanese cuisine to the table through Chef Morimoto's blending of traditional Japanese cooking with Western flair.

SOCIETY HILL AND PENN'S LANDING

Jim's Steaks
🧒 ♿ ☂ [$]

400 South St, Philadelphia, PA, 19147 ***Tel*** *(215) 928-1911* ***Map*** *4 D4*

With its distinctive Art Deco storefront, Jim's is undoubtedly one of Philadelphia's busiest and most popular eateries. Long lines often stretch onto hip South Street as visitors and locals alike flock here for authentic Philly cheesesteaks with mounds of onions and dripping hot cheese. It also serves excellent hoagies.

South Street Souvlaki
🧒 ♿ 🍸 [$]

509 S St, Philadelphia, PA, 19147 ***Tel*** *(215) 925-3026* ***Map*** *4 D4*

One of the town's oldest and most popular Greek restaurants, this South Street icon recently celebrated its 25th anniversary. Specialties include classic Greek and Mediterranean cuisine, including lamb, seafood, and vegetarian dishes. Pleasant dining room and streetfront takeout window as well.

Jon's Bar and Grille
🧒 ♿ ☂ 🍸 [$][$]

606 S 3rd St, Philadelphia, PA, 19147 ***Tel*** *(215) 592-1390* ***Map*** *4 D4*

A hip restaurant with an upstairs deck and patio seating along busy South Street. The building that houses this eatery was the birthplace of actor Larry Fine of *Three Stooges* fame. Though most popular for burgers and Philly cheesesteaks, the menu also offers a wide range of home-made soups, steaks, and fish.

Bistro Romano
🧒 ♿ 🍸 [$][$][$]

120 Lombard St, Philadelphia, PA, 19147 ***Tel*** *(215) 925-8880* ***Map*** *4 E4*

Once an 18th-century granary, the main dining room of this classic Italian restaurant was part of the Underground Railroad *(see p60)*. Authentic, regional Italian dishes and the popular Caesar salad are prepared tableside. It has a piano bar and displays include 18th-century artifacts. Children allowed on request. No lunch service.

Bridget Foy's
🧒 ♿ ☂ 🍸 [$][$][$]

200 South St, Philadelphia, PA, 19147 ***Tel*** *(215) 922-1813* ***Map*** *4 E5*

An American grill in the South Street district, it faces New Market and Head House Square. The menu offers American cuisine, with old standards such as steaks, fresh fish, burgers, and sandwiches. An outdoor café makes this great spot to break for lunch on bustling South Street.

Dark Horse Pub
🧒 ♿ ☂ 🍸 [$][$][$]

421 S 2nd St, Philadelphia, PA, 19147 ***Tel*** *(215) 928-9307* ***Map*** *4 E4*

A popular watering hole that doubles up as a restaurant. This colonial inn-style restaurant serves hearty pub fare, including steak and mushroom pie, as well as gourmet cuisine. It has five bars with a range of beers and wines. No lunch service on Monday.

Downey's
🧒 ♿ 🎵 ☂ 🍸 [$][$][$]

526 S Front St, Philadelphia, PA, 19147 ***Tel*** *(215) 625-9500* ***Map*** *4 E5*

Blessed with its great location at South and Front Streets, Downey's – a "drinking house and dining saloon" – has been a neighborhood mainstay since 1976. Pub decor includes antiques and Irish memorabilia, while the menu features hearty Irish stews and American fare. It is also a vibrant night spot.

Sfizzio Restaurant

$$$

237 St. James Place, Philadelphia, PA, 19106 **Tel** (215) 925-1802   **Map** 4 E4

This trendy restaurant sits nestled under the Society Hill Towers and serves fresh Italian fare with an accent on Naples and southern Italy. Specialties include Pasta Positano and *langostino* pastas. Features a mosaic decor with postmodernist touches. Some tables have views of the landmark Merchants' Exchange Building.

Chart House

$$$$

555 S Columbus Blvd at Penn's Landing, Philadelphia, PA, 19147 **Tel** (215) 625-8383   **Map** 4 E5

Seafood appetizers, entrées, and chowders dominate the menu of this contemporary restaurant and Philadelphia institution. Opened in 1961 on a prime waterfront location on the Delaware, it offers stunning river views. This is a great place for a Sunday brunch of shrimp, crab, tuna, and mussels.

Mallorca Restaurant

$$$$

119 South St, Philadelphia, PA, 19147 **Tel** (215) 351-6652   **Map** 4 E5

Authentic Iberian cuisine with a dash of flamenco dancing and entertainment. The menu, prepared by Spanish chefs using original ingredients, includes such specialties as garlic shrimp, *mariscada* (seafood stew), lobster, goat, paella, and more. Also serves tapas. Situated on bustling South Street, it often attracts a lively crowd.

Moshulu

$$$$$

401 S Columbus Blvd, Philadelphia, PA, 19106 **Tel** (215) 923-2500   **Map** 4 F4

Lovely fine-dining restaurant aboard a restored, century-old sailing ship moored off Penn's Landing. The four-masted vessel is ablaze with lights at night, and offers excellent river and skyline views from indoor dining rooms and from atop the deck in warmer months. Bar and deck menu also available.

CENTER CITY

Cosi

$

1128 Walnut St, Philadelphia, PA, 19107 **Tel** (215) 413-1608   **Map** 3 B3

Comfortable and casual, this café-style restaurant has heart-warming soups, tangy salads, baked breads and sandwiches, pasta dishes, pizzas, and more. There are several Cosis, and this branch is situated a few blocks from the theater district and across from the Forrest Theatre.

Penang

$

117 N 10th St, Philadelphia, PA, 19107 **Tel** (215) 413-2531, (215) 413-2532   **Map** 3 C2

This trendy, storefront restaurant in the heart of Chinatown is always buzzing with activity. It has a predominantly Malaysian cuisine featuring spicy curry and seafood dishes, along with some Thai, Indian, and Indonesian specialties as well.

Imperial Inn

$$

142 N 10th St, Philadelphia, PA, 19107 **Tel** (215) 627-2299, (215) 627-5588   **Map** 3 C2

Despite its modest decor, the locals will tell you the Imperial Inn is one of Chinatown's best. Opened in 1973, this casual dining restaurant has consistently been serving traditional, quality Chinese food, including dim sum dishes, as well as wines and liquors. An excellent option for those looking for great Chinese food at good prices.

Jolly's American Restaurant & Bar

$$

135 S 17th St, Philadelphia, PA, 19103 **Tel** (215) 563-8200   **Map** 2 E4

With fashionable black leather chairs and funky lighting, this hip bar and restaurant nestles in a comfortable subterranean spot inside the Latham Hotel (see p136). A great destination for some excellent prime rib, thick steaks, fresh seafood, Maryland crab cakes, and sandwiches. Children allowed only on request.

Joseph Poon Asian Fusion Restaurant

$$

1002 Arch St, Philadelphia, PA, 19107 **Tel** (215) 928-9333   **Map** 3 C2

Both the menu and decor of this Chinatown restaurant are bright and contemporary, with a dash of adventure. Renowned chef Joe Poon creates Asian-fusion cuisine using the flavors and textures of Italy, Mexico, France, Singapore, Malaysia, Korea, and Vietnam. The house specialties are Peking Duck and fresh seafood.

The Black Sheep Pub and Restaurant

$$$

17th & Latimer Sts, Philadelphia, PA, 19103 **Tel** (215) 545-9473   **Map** 2 E5

Dine on hearty Irish stews and other favorites, including shepherd's pie, sandwiches, crab cakes, and more. Just one block from Rittenhouse Square, this pub and restaurant offers a relaxed atmosphere and has friendly staff. There are three floors with antique bars, and a drink selection from around the world. Wheelchair access limited to first level.

Brasserie Perrier

$$$

1619 Walnut St, Philadelphia, PA, 19102 **Tel** (215) 568-3000   **Map** 2 E4

Chef Georges Perrier's second venture in Philadelphia after Le Bec-Fin, this is a trendy restaurant along Rittenhouse Row. Its menu features modern French cuisine with Italian and Asian influences. Art Deco interiors with silver leaf ceilings and light cherry wood. Definitely more affordable than Le Bec-Fin. No lunch service on Sunday.

Key to Price Guide see p145 **Key to Symbols** see back cover flap

McCormick and Schmick's Seafood Restaurant $$$

1 S Broad St, Philadelphia, PA, 19102 **Tel** *(215) 568-6888*   **Map** *2 F4*

This upbeat and lively restaurant is an upscale fish house, located just across from historic City Hall. Features over 40 varieties of fresh fish that are flown in daily from both the Atlantic and Pacific Oceans. The two-story restaurant has a dark wood-paneled dining room accented by stained glass ceilings and mosaic floor.

Pietro's Coal Oven Pizzeria $$$

1714 Walnut St, Philadelphia, PA, 19103 **Tel** *(215) 735-8090*   **Map** *2 E5*

This lively restaurant offers thin-crust pizzas baked in a coal oven, served with a choice of 17 gourmet toppings, and other Italian specialties such as home-made pasta entrées in family-sized portions. There is outdoor seating along Walnut Street in warmer months.

Rouge $$$

205 S 18th St, Philadelphia, PA, 19103 **Tel** *(215) 732-6622*   **Map** *2 D5*

A hip bistro and popular late night spot in the swanky Rittenhouse Square area. They have wines of exquisite vintage and a trendsetting menu that is a cross between Continental, American, and French fare with contemporary seafood, poultry, and beef dishes. The biggest draw is the location, with outdoor seating facing the square.

Roy's $$$

124 S 15th St, Philadelphia, PA, 19102 **Tel** *(215) 988-1814*   **Map** *2 E4*

This restaurant features unique Hawaiian fusion cuisine. Chef-owner Roy Yamaguchi's specialties are created with local ingredients accented with European sauces and bold Asian spices. Just one block from Rittenhouse Row, the restaurant is housed in a refurbished bank building. No lunch service.

Devon Seafood Grill $$$$

225 S 18th St, Philadelphia, PA, 19103 **Tel** *(215) 546-5940*   **Map** *2 D5*

A much-visited and comfortable restaurant, the Devon Seafood Grill serves fresh fish specialties, including Maryland crab cakes, pan-roasted Alaskan halibut, live Maine lobsters, Block Island swordfish, and more. The dining room is elegant. It is particularly popular in the warmer months with sidewalk seating facing Rittenhouse Square.

Susanna Foo Chinese Cuisine $$$$

1512 Walnut St, Philadelphia, PA, 19102 **Tel** *(215) 545-2666*   **Map** *2 E5*

Not traditional Chinese by any means, this is one of the city's most popular fine-dining restaurants along ritzy Rittenhouse Row. Owner and chef Susanna Foo adds a French influence to classical Chinese dishes, creating more flavorful sauces. No lunch service on the weekend. Reservations are advised.

The Prime Rib $$$$

1701 Locust St, Philadelphia, PA, 19103 **Tel** *(215) 772-1701*   **Map** *2 E5*

This upscale steakhouse is one of Philadelphia's best. Housed in the prestigious Radisson-brand Warwick Hotel *(see p136)*, its decor is reminiscent of a 1940s Manhattan supper club. Its specialties include aged prime rib, blue-ribbon steaks, extra thick chops, and fresh seafood. Children are allowed only on request. Formal dress required. No lunch service.

Zanzibar Blue $$$$

200 S Broad St, Philadelphia, PA, 19102 **Tel** *(215) 732-4500*   **Map** *2 F5*

A popular destination for music lovers, this fine-dining nightclub combines the very best in international jazz and global cuisine. Located in the century-old Bellevue Building *(see p156)*, it features a world-class menu that includes the likes of Parisian salad and Creole roasted salmon. Offers brunch on Sunday.

Lacroix at the Rittenhouse $$$$$

210 W Rittenhouse Square, Philadelphia, PA, 19103 **Tel** *(215) 790-2533*   **Map** *2 D5*

Elegant restaurant on the second floor of the Rittenhouse Hotel *(see p136)* with stunning views of Rittenhouse Square. Decorated with minimalist and Asian theme, it serves French-American cuisine with options of three, four, or five courses, and diners can also create their own menus. Dessert complimentary as a gift from the chef.

Le Bec-Fin $$$$$

1523 Walnut St, Philadelphia, PA, 19102 **Tel** *(215) 567-1000*   **Map** *2 E5*

Philadelphia's best and one of the country's top French restaurants run by chef-owner Georges Perrier. Mirrored walls and silk panels add to the elegant dining experience with exquisite dishes like *escargot* in champagne and hazelnut garlic butter sauce, served by an army of waiting staff. There is an extensive wine cellar with 700 wines. Formal dress required.

Smith & Wollensky $$$$$

210 W Rittenhouse Square, Philadelphia, PA, 19103 **Tel** *(215) 545-1700*   **Map** *2 D5*

One of the top steakhouses Philadelphia has to offer. *The New York Times* referred to this high-end restaurant chain as "a steakhouse to end all arguments." Patrons are treated to up to 18 and 28-ounce cuts, good chops, salads, seafood, and an excellent wine list too. Located in the posh Rittenhouse Hotel *(see p136)*.

Striped Bass $$$$$

1500 Walnut St, Philadelphia, PA, 19102 **Tel** *(215) 732-4444*   **Map** *2 E5*

The original marble columns and high ceiling of this former brokerage building add to the grandeur of one of the city's most noted seafood houses. Known for tower-like food arrangements, its menu is dominated by often pricey and carefully prepared fish specialties, including, of course, striped bass. The dress code is casual to dressy.

LOGAN SQUARE AND THE MUSEUM DISTRICT

Illuminare 🧒 ♿ 🍸 $$

2321 Fairmount Ave, Philadelphia, PA, 19130 ***Tel*** *(215) 765-0202* ***Map*** *2 D1*

From brick oven pizza to veal chops and filet mignon, this upscale restaurant serves wide-ranging Italian cuisine, which also includes fresh pastas and seafood. Housed in a renovated rowhouse, it has elegant decor that showcases stunning handcrafted woodwork, tile-work, and stained glass.

The Bishop's Collar 🧒 ♿ ☀ 🍸 $$$

2349 Fairmount Ave, Philadelphia, PA, 19130 ***Tel*** *(215) 765-1616* ***Map*** *2 D1*

This friendly corner watering hole and restaurant serves creative pub fare, along with a wide-ranging selection of beers and ales. Tables are set up outdoors in the warmer months. Situated a couple of blocks from the Philadelphia Museum of Art and the Kelly Drive walking path along Boathouse Row.

Gloria's Gourmet Seafood 🧒 ♿ ♫ ☀ 🍸 $$$

2120 Fairmount Ave, Philadelphia, PA, 19130 ***Tel*** *(215) 235-3082* ***Map*** *2 D1*

An elegant seafood restaurant and upbeat nightclub with some of Philadelphia's best jazz music. Menu features fresh fish, crab, and lobster specialties, as well as Southern-style and soul food dishes. A few blocks from the Philadelphia Museum of Art and across from the Eastern State Penitentiary. Children are not allowed after 7pm.

Jack's Firehouse 🧒 ♿ ♫ ☀ 🍸 $$$

2130 Fairmount Ave, Philadelphia, PA, 19130 ***Tel*** *(215) 232-9000* ***Map*** *2 D1*

This unique restaurant sits within a former firehouse building that still retains its original interiors – complete with a firemen's sliding pole and an expansive arched doorway. Popular chef-owner Jack McDavid uses fresh local ingredients for "down home" American fare, often accenting Southern cooking styles.

London Grill 🧒 ♫ ☀ 🍸 $$$

2301 Fairmount Ave, Philadelphia, PA, 19130 ***Tel*** *(215) 978-4545* ***Map*** *2 D1*

Trendy and comfortable, this corner restaurant combines the coziness of a neighborhood pub with the elegance of fine dining. The menu changes daily, and dishes such as roasted chicken with garlic mashed potato cake, broccoli rosemary jus, and honey glazed grilled salmon are on offer. No lunch service on Saturday.

Rembrandt's 🧒 ♿ ♫ ☀ 🍸 $$$

741 N 23rd St, Philadelphia, PA, 19130 ***Tel*** *(215) 763-2228, (800) 736-2726* ***Map*** *2 D1*

Located near the Philadelphia Museum of Art, this elegant restaurant is known for its fine dining, accented by fabulous views of the city skyline. Specialties include creative seafood, meat, pasta, and vegetarian dishes. It also has a full tavern menu and eight draught beers on tap.

Zorba's Tavern 🧒 🍸 $$$

2230 Fairmount Ave, Philadelphia, PA, 19130 ***Tel*** *(215) 978-5990* ***Map*** *2 D1*

Discover sumptuous Greek food at this family-owned restaurant. Paintings depicting old-world Greece add a special ambience to the authentic cuisine. It offers a full menu with lamb and seafood specialties, and all the traditional dishes. Located within walking distance of the Philadelphia Museum of Art and Boathouse Row. Closed Monday.

Fountain Restaurant 🧒 ♿ 🍸 $$$$$

1 Logan Square, Philadelphia, PA, 19103 ***Tel*** *(215) 963-1500* ***Map*** *2 E2*

Living up to the reputation of the posh Four Seasons Hotel *(see p137)*, this restaurant has been repeatedly rated as one of the city's best restaurants, serving Continental cuisine with delicate international influences. Elegant dining room with rich fabrics and warm woods. The restaurant offers splendid views of the Swann Fountain. Formal dress required.

Shula's Steak House 🧒 ♿ 🍸 $$$$$

17th & Race Sts, Philadelphia, PA, 19103 ***Tel*** *(215) 448-2700* ***Map*** *2 E2*

Another fabulous steakhouse in Philadelphia, this was founded by former pro-football coach Don Shula. Sited in the Wyndham Philadelphia *(see p137)* and ranked among America's top five steakhouses, it serves Certified Angus Beef® cuts, including a 48-ounce porterhouse, and lamb, seafood, and live Maine lobsters. No lunch service on weekends.

FARTHER AFIELD

Geno's Steaks 🧒 ♿ ☀ $

1219 S 9th St, Philadelphia, PA, 19147 ***Tel*** *(215) 389-0659*

Geno's is one of Philadelphia's cheesesteak giants on the outskirts of the Italian Market. Founded in 1966 opposite Pat's King of Steaks, it serves delicious, piping hot cheesesteak sandwiches 24 hours a day, seven days a week from a bright, neon-lit corner storefront.

Key to Price Guide *see p145* **Key to Symbols** *see back cover flap*

Pat's King of Steaks
1237 E Passyunk Ave at 9th St, Philadelphia, PA, 19147 ***Tel*** *(215) 468-1546*

Founded in and family-owned since 1930, Pat's is known as the originator of the Philly che eye steak, onions, cheese, and fresh Italian bread. In fact, locals will tell you it makes the cit windows and outside seating only. It is located at the Italian Market. Open 24 hours a day.

Chickie's and Pete's Café 🚸
1526 Packer Ave, Philadelphia, PA, 19145 ***Tel*** *(215) 218-0500*

This casual, south Philadelphia hotspot near the city's sports venues is always busy when the home teams play. Sightings of local personalities is common. The menu features crab fries, sandwiches, and cheesesteaks. Children have to be accompanied by adults after 10pm. A DJ plays recorded music.

Manayunk Brewery and Restaurant 🚸♿🎵🌙🍸 $$
4120 Main St, Manayunk, Philadelphia, PA, 19127 ***Tel*** *(215) 482-8220*

Housed in a former Manayunk textile mill, this upbeat restaurant with an in-house brewery serves classic American and Continental fare – grilled meats and seafood, pastas, and pizza. It has a rotisserie and sushi bar too, and a range of beverages. There is a large outdoor dining area that overlooks the Schuylkill River.

Zocalo Restaurant 🚸♿🍸 $$
3604 Lancaster Ave, Philadelphia, PA, 19104 ***Tel*** *(215) 895-0139*

Located in University City, this hip, bistro-like restaurant serves traditional, mouthwatering Mexican favorites enhanced by contemporary tastes. The drinks menu features margaritas, beers, and wine, which is sold by the glass. Outdoor dining is an option in the warmer months.

Ralph's Italian Restaurant 🚸♿ $$$
760 S 9th St, Philadelphia, PA, 19147 ***Tel*** *(215) 627-6011*

Cozy, comfortable, and classy restaurant at the Italian Market. Owned and operated by four generations of the same family since 1900, this neighborhood restaurant is one of the city's most popular Italian eateries. It serves up classic red sauce and pastas, veal, poultry, seafood, and meat dishes, including the likes of Pork Chops Pizzaiola.

Sonoma 🚸♿🌙🍸 $$$
4411 Main St, Manayunk, Philadelphia, PA, 19127 ***Tel*** *(215) 483-9400*

Located on Manayunk's lively Main Street, the restaurant features an eclectic menu – shrimp ravioli, baked goat cheese salad, and BBQ chicken pizza. Modern decor with a grand staircase to the second floor. Café-style seating and a private courtyard. The greenhouse bar features martinis, and also has over 200 vodkas to choose from.

White Dog Café 🚸♿🎵🌙🍸 $$$
3420 Sansom St, Philadelphia, PA, 19104 ***Tel*** *(215) 386-9224*

An eclectic University City café housed in three adjacent Victorian brownstones. On the menu is an unusual blend of contemporary American cuisine that uses fresh ingredients from local, self-reliant farmers. Music is played in the smoke-free piano parlor. The bar offers happy hours from 10pm to midnight Sunday through Thursday.

Zesty's 🚸♿🎵🍸 $$$
4382 Main St, Manayunk, Philadelphia, PA, 19127 ***Tel*** *(215) 483-6226, (800) 816-3463*

This upbeat restaurant offers a unique Greek and Roman menu prepared the old-fashioned way. Serves regional Mediterranean fish not found elsewhere in the city, such as pageot, sargo, and royal dorado from Greece. Calamari, lamb, veal, and lots of traditional dishes too. The wine list includes Greek wines.

General Lafayette Inn and Brewery 🚸♿🎵🌙🍸 $$$$
646 Germantown Pike, Lafayette Hill, PA, 19444 ***Tel*** *(610) 941-0600, (800) 251-0181*

A short drive from Chestnut Hill, this fine-dining American-fare restaurant is housed in a well-preserved 1732 country inn. Six working fireplaces and Baroque music add to the colonial ambience. An added attraction is the upstairs "haunted" dining room. Expect generous portions of delicious Southern and Native American dishes.

Hikaru 🚸♿ $$$$
4348 Main St, Manayunk, Philadelphia, PA, 19127 ***Tel*** *(215) 487-3500*

A sushi bar is the highlight of this classy restaurant with a view of the Manayunk Bridge. Teppanyaki (tableside cooking) offers a host of specialties in addition to sashimi, sukiyaki, teriyaki, tempura, and more. Has one of the most extensive sushi menus in the Delaware Valley. Hikaru has another restaurant on South Street.

BEYOND PHILADELPHIA

ATLANTIC CITY Atlantic City Bar and Grill 🚸♿🌙🍸 $$
1219 Pacific Ave, Atlantic City, NJ, 08401 ***Tel*** *(609) 348-8080, (609) 449-1991*

This family-owned restaurant opened more than 25 years ago and has become a favorite among locals, tourists, and even visiting celebrities and sports figures. Steaks, crabs, shrimp cocktail, lobsters, mussels, home-made pastas, pizzas, and sandwiches all feature on the menu. The dining room is spacious and lively, with sports programming.

CITY Hard Rock Café   🏃‍♂️ ♿ ➤ 🍸 $$

Boardwalk at Virginia Ave, Atlantic City, NJ, 08401 **Tel** *(609) 441-0007*

...ght on the Boardwalk, this chain restaurant is known for its rock 'n' roll memorabilia, signed guitars, and an all-American cuisine. Pastas, steaks, burgers, and smokehouse dishes are the most popular. Housed within the colossal Trump Taj Mahal Hotel Casino and Resort *(see p139)*, it offers seating on the Boardwalk in the warmer months.

ATLANTIC CITY Primavera   🏃‍♂️ ♿ ➤ 🍸 $$$$$

Arkansas and the Boardwalk, Atlantic City, NJ, 08401 **Tel** *(609) 348-4411, (800) 223-7272*

Fine dining with a range of northern Italian specialties and an extensive wine list in one of Atlantic City's best-known casino hotels, Caesars *(see p139)*. Try out the appetizer of oversized prawns with lemon-caper sauce. Intimate tables amidst artworks and murals of Venice enhance the ambience. Service is formal and reservations are required.

ATLANTIC CITY Suilan by Susanna Foo   🏃‍♂️ ♿ 🍸 $$$$$

One Borgata Way, Atlantic City, NJ, 08401 **Tel** *(609) 317-1000*

Prominent Philadelphia restauranteur Susanna Foo has brought her signature Chinese-fusion cooking style to Atlantic City's newest casino, The Borgata's. Elegant decor creates a modern and bold ambience. Traditional Chinese dishes are prepared with French accents and a European flair. Closed Tuesday and Wednesday.

BRANDYWINE VALLEY Buckley's Tavern   🏃‍♂️ ♿ 🍸 $$

5812 Kennett Pike, Centreville, DE, 19807 **Tel** *(302) 656-9776*

A favorite meeting place for locals in the Brandywine Valley, this tavern serves a variety of fine food, from the likes of Maryland crab cakes to Vietnamese shrimp salad. There is a popular outdoor dining patio. It is close to Longwood Gardens, Winterthur, and other attractions such as the Brandywine River Museum and Brandywine Battlefield.

BRANDYWINE VALLEY Chadds Ford Tavern and Restaurant   🏃‍♂️ ♿ 🍸 $$$

US Rt 1 (1 mile south of Rt 202), Chadds Ford, PA, 19317 **Tel** *(610) 459-8453*

Family-owned and operated since 1968, this quaint country restaurant offers a menu ranging from home-made pub fare to fine food dishes. Housed in an 1830s tavern, the dining room is lit with hurricane candles and Tiffany lamps. Sample the crab cakes, a best-selling entrée. Reservations are recommended.

CAPE MAY Cabanas on the Beach   🏃‍♂️ ♿ 🎵 ➤ 🍸 $$

Beach & Decatur Aves, Cape May, NJ, 08204 **Tel** *(609) 884-4800*

Enjoy great sandwiches, seafood, and more at this casual and easy-going beach bar that serves good food. Other attractions include a children's menu, open-air dining, and live blues and reggae entertainment acts. Oysters, shrimps, lots of shellfish specialties, crab, chicken, and prime ribs, are all on the menu.

CAPE MAY The Water's Edge Restaurant   🏃‍♂️ ♿ 🍸 $$$$

Beach & Pittsburgh Aves, Cape May, NJ, 08204 **Tel** *(609) 884-1717*

Gourmet and creative American cuisine served, yes, next to the beach. Sit in the open air, oceanfront patio or in the elegant inside dining room to enjoy carefully prepared meat and seafood specialties. A superb selection of wines by the glass, single malt scotches, single barrel bourbons, and sipping tequilas are served.

DOYLESTOWN Paganini Ristorante   🏃‍♂️ ♿ 🍸 $$$

81 West State St, Doylestown, PA, 18901 **Tel** *(215) 348-5922*

A local favorite for fine Italian cuisine, this restaurant is in the heart of downtown Doylestown. It has several small dining rooms where patrons can ask for custom cooking such as fresh pastas and a variety of sauces. No dinner service on Saturday and no lunch service on Sunday.

GETTYSBURG Dobbin House Tavern   🏃‍♂️ ♿ 🍸 $$$

89 Steinwehr Ave, Gettysburg, PA, 17325 **Tel** *(717) 334-2100*

This cozy and quaint colonial tavern and restaurant *(see p140)* date to 1776. Full of antiques, it has costumed servers and a historic ambience. The menu consists of old-fashioned hearty dishes such as charbroiled meats and fowl. It is located across from where Abraham Lincoln delivered the Gettysburg Address *(see p121)*.

GETTYSBURG Farnsworth House Inn   🏃‍♂️ ♿ 🎵 🍸 $$$

401 Baltimore Ave, Gettysburg, PA, 17325 **Tel** *(717) 334-8838*

Quaint dining rooms housed in a historic 1810 Gettysburg inn *(see p140)*, where over 100 bullet holes from the Civil War can still be seen. Period specialties include game pie, pumpkin fritters, peanut soup, and sweet potato pudding. It features dinner theater every Friday and Saturday evening from December through February.

GETTYSBURG Herr Tavern and Public House   🏃‍♂️ ♿ 🍸 $$$$

900 Chambersburg Rd, Gettysburg, PA, 17325 **Tel** *(717) 334-4332*

Once used as the first Confederate hospital during the Battle of Gettysburg, this 1815 country inn is now a B&B with five elegantly decorated dining rooms. The menu offers carefully prepared meat and seafood entrées served with tasteful garnishes and sauces. Reservations are required on weekends. No lunch service on Sunday.

HARRISBURG Parev Restaurant   ♿ 🎵 ➤ 🍸 $$$$

215 Pine St, Harrisburg, PA, 17101 **Tel** *(717) 920-1800, (866) 257-2738*

Parev is an upscale restaurant with an exclusive business club that features fine dining. An eclectic menu of carefully prepared seafood and meat specialties with rich sauces and creative garnishes is served in the 110-seat dining room. A few blocks from the State Capitol and near the Susquehanna River. No lunch service. Closed Sunday.

Key to Price Guide *see p145* **Key to Symbols** *see back cover flap*

HERSHEY Lebbie Lebkicher's

West Chocolate Ave and University Dr, Hershey, PA, 17033 **Tel** *(717) 533-3311, (800) 437-7439*

This casual and friendly restaurant, located in the Hershey Lodge, offers full hot and cold buffets ranging from salads and soups to seafood and prime rib selections. A special buffet is set up for children with pizzas, chicken nuggets, macaroni and cheese, and other kid favorites. Near Hershey Park and other attractions.

KING OF PRUSSIA California Café

The Plaza at King of Prussia Mall, 160 N Gulph Road, King of Prussia, PA, 19406 **Tel** *(610) 354-8686*

Buttercup yellow walls and funky sea-green architectural details set the tone for this cool California-style restaurant, part of a countrywide dining chain. Eclectic and themed menu offering "savory" American fare, all of which is prepared with fresh, regional foods of the season. An upbeat dining experience while at the King of Prussia Mall.

NEW HOPE Logan Inn Restaurant

10 W Ferry St, New Hope, PA, 18938 **Tel** *(215) 862-2300*

A fine-dining restaurant in a historic inn dating back to 1727, Logan Inn is one of the five oldest in the US. Located in the heart of New Hope, it features a lovely dining room and a porch that offers views of the bustling town center. Carefully prepared duck, seafood, beef, and pasta specialties available.

NEW HOPE Odette's Restaurant

South River Road, New Hope, PA, 18938 **Tel** *(215) 862-2432*

Just a few steps south of quaint New Hope center, Odette's is housed in a 200 year-old inn and features fine dining. Creative Continental cuisine, featuring a variety of beef, veal, fowl, seafood, and pasta specialties, is served in elegantly decorated dining rooms with views of the Delaware River. The piano bar is open late. Closed Tuesday.

PENNSYLVANIA DUTCH COUNTRY Plain and Fancy Farm Restaurant

3121 Old Philadelphia Pike, Bird-In-Hand, PA, 17505 **Tel** *(717) 768-4400*

Everyday is like grandmother's home cooking at this popular family-style restaurant near the Amishview Inns *(see p141)* in the Pennsylvania Dutch Country. Friendly pass-the-platter dining features roast beef, golden fried chicken, baked Lancaster County sausage, mashed potatoes, shoofly pie, apple dumplings, and more.

PENNSYLVANIA DUTCH COUNTRY The Family Cupboard Restaurant

3370 Harvest Dr, Intercourse, PA, 17534 **Tel** *(717) 768-4510*

Amish and Mennonite home cooking does not get much better than this. Daily specials and full lunch and dinner buffets feature made-from-scratch pies and dishes from fresh farm vegetables such as green beans and carrots, mashed potatoes, and ham, chicken, and beef. Great for family dining.

PENNSYLVANIA DUTCH COUNTRY Kling House Restaurant

Rt 340, Intercourse, PA, 17534 **Tel** *(717) 768-2746, (800) 732-3538*

This popular restaurant offers unique Pennsylvania Dutch Country and American fare with home-made jellies and relishes made at the adjoining Kitchen Kettle Village. House specials include portabella mushroom focaccia and grilled pita pizza, among others. Closed Sunday.

PENNSYLVANIA DUTCH COUNTRY Miller's Smorgasbord

2811 Lincoln Hwy East (Rt 30), Ronks, PA, 17572 **Tel** *(717) 687-6621*

Sample a wide range of Pennsylvania Dutch treats and eat as much as you want at this buffet-style eatery – a tradition since 1929. Chilled steamed shrimp and carved top sirloin, turkey, chicken pot pie, and fresh bakery desserts are favorites. No lunch service. Breakfast is served only on Sunday mornings starting at 8am. Located on busy Route 30.

PENNSYLVANIA DUTCH COUNTRY 1764 Restaurant

14 E Main St, Lititz, PA, 17543 **Tel** *(717) 626-2115*

An elegant dining room with colonial decor adds to the charm of this restaurant within the landmark 18th-century General Sutter Inn. Black Angus beef, oversized chops, seafood, fowl, and pasta highlight the menu's fine food selections. Breakfast specialties include farm fresh eggs and grilled cinnamon buns.

PENNSYLVANIA DUTCH COUNTRY Historic Revere Tavern

3063 Lincoln Hwy E, Paradise, PA, 17562 **Tel** *(717) 687-8601*

Built in 1740, this tavern was once owned by the 15th US president, James Buchanan. Casual dining in a colonial atmosphere with fireplaces. Seafood, steaks, and unique snapper turtle soup highlight the menu. Along busy Route 30 in the Pennsylvania Dutch Country. No lunch service on Sunday and Monday.

PENNSYLVANIA DUTCH COUNTRY Doneckers Restaurant

333 N State St, Ephrata, PA, 17522 **Tel** *(717) 738-9501*

This elegant French restaurant is housed within a community of fine fashion and art stores in the Pennsylvania Dutch Country. Exceptional nouveau French-American cuisine made from farm fresh ingredients and an excellent wine list with more than 500 international wines. Closed Sunday and Wednesday.

WASHINGTON CROSSING Washington Crossing Inn

1295 Washington Memorial Rd, Washington Crossing, PA, 18977 **Tel** *(215) 493-3634*

Dating to 1817, this restaurant sits near where General Washington crossed the Delaware River in 1776. New-style American cuisine is served in a colonial ambience. Chops, steaks, and seafood are very well prepared. Lunch menu includes radicchio and arugala salad, grilled rib-eye steak, and smoked turkey breast arugala.

SHOPS AND MARKETS

THE PHILADELPHIA area is a stronghold for shopping with stores and outlets ranging from specialty boutiques, grand shopping centers, and malls to discount retailers and factory stores. Key shopping areas mentioned on the following pages include Center City's boutiques and shops on Market and Walnut Streets, and the shops and galleries in Old City and in the chic district

Precious gems at Jewelers' Row

of South Street. Situated in downtown Philadelphia are Antique Row and Jewelers' Row, while a variety of upscale and trendy shops are the highlights on the main streets of Manayunk and Chestnut Hill. The King of Prussia Mall is one of the nation's largest retail shopping complexes, while the city of Reading has perhaps the largest number of factory outlet stores in the country.

SHOPPING HOURS

MOST RETAILERS in central Philadelphia are open seven days a week, from 10am to 6pm on Mondays through Saturdays with some varying hours, and from noon until 5pm or 6pm on Sundays. Many Center City stores are open for an extra hour or two on Wednesday nights and sometimes on Friday nights.

Outside the city, individual retail stores usually have similar hours from 10am to 6pm. Malls, however, are often open until 9pm or 9:30pm Monday through Saturday, and noon until 6pm or 7pm on Sundays. Some specialty stores have reduced hours on weekends, or may close one or two days during the week.

The popular VF Outlet Village in Reading, Pennsylvania

Storefronts on a street in Chestnut Hill, Philadelphia

TAXES

THERE IS NO sales tax on clothing and shoes in Pennsylvania. For all other items, there is a 6 percent state sales tax and an additional 1 percent tax within Philadelphia, adding up to a 7 percent sales tax when shopping in the city. However, no sales tax is levied if your purchases are shipped to an address outside Pennsylvania, but additional shipping fees may apply. Foreign visitors may have to pay duties on larger purchases they wish to take home.

SALES

FINDING A SALE in the US is as easy as picking up a local newspaper – especially on weekends. Most large retailers compete on a daily basis, with many regularly slashing prices. Smaller stores may have clearance racks with reduced items, while sales are often more limited in trendy

shops and high-end boutiques. The nation's "biggest shopping day of the year" occurs on the day after Thanksgiving and is called "Black Friday," when prices are cut by 70 percent or more. Similar sales take place after Christmas.

PAYMENT

EXCEPT FOR THE smallest stores, major credit cards are accepted at most shops, boutiques, and retail outlets. In fact, department stores usually issue their own credit cards for return shoppers, though these are often issued at higher interest rates. In the US, the major credit cards accepted are Visa, MasterCard, American Express, Discover Card, and Diners Club.

Cash is always accepted, and identification is necessary when using traveler's checks. Personal checks are discouraged, unless drawn from a local or well-known US bank. Stores do not accept foreign currency.

RETURNING MERCHANDISE

MOST SHOPS AND stores will willingly issue refunds and credits for returns, providing the merchandise is in good condition and not used or damaged. Sales receipts must accompany goods. Time limits for returns vary from store to store, with most allowing between ten to 30 days. Be aware, however, that certain items purchased during special sales or promotions are nonreturnable, and that some stores will issue in-store-credit returns only and not cash.

A couple enjoying shopping

DEPARTMENT STORES

THERE IS NO shortage of world-class department stores in the Philadelphia area, with most concentrated in the **King of Prussia Mall** *(see p156)*, Center City, and a few other area malls. **Lord and Taylor**, one of America's oldest specialty department stores, is located in Center City's historic Wanamaker Building *(see p70)*. The store's Grand Court houses an organ that is played for shoppers twice a day from Monday to Saturday, at noon and 5pm (7pm on Wednesdays). Another Lord and Taylor store is in the King of Prussia Mall. **Strawbridge's**, the last of the large family-owned department stores in Philadelphia, also has outlets in both locations. It offers an assortment of household items, as well as women's and men's fashions. In the King of Prussia Mall, the high-end department store **Neiman Marcus** offers the ultimate shopping experience with some of the best names in fashion in women's apparel, accessories, shoes, and jewelry. The same is true for children's and men's clothing. The store also offers quality bed and bath items, novelty rugs, and furniture.

Nordstrom, another leading fashion specialty store, offers high-quality gifts, apparel, shoes, and beauty products from several hundred brand names. High fashion, stylish accessories, and the latest fragrances can be found at **Bloomingdale's**, which also stocks a wide range of house gifts, luggage, and more. **Macy's** is one of America's most popular department stores that offers good value when shopping for clothing, shoes, house wares, home decor, and jewelry. The same is true for **JCPenney** with its broad range of apparel, shoes, and gifts for men, women, and children. **Sears** is also one of the nation's best-known department stores, known for its large appliances, tools, lawn and garden gear, automobile repair services, and household services.

DIRECTORY

CENTER CITY

Lord and Taylor
13th & Market Sts. **Map** 3 B2.
(215) 241-9000.
www.lordandtaylor.com

Strawbridge's
The Gallery at Market East, Market St. **Map** 3 C2.
(215) 629-6000.

KING OF PRUSSIA MALL

Bloomingdale's
(610) 337-6300.
www.bloomingdales.com

JCPenney
(610) 992-1096.
www.jcpenney.com

Lord and Taylor
(610) 992-0333.
www.lordandtaylor.com

Macy's
(610) 337-9350.
www.macys.com

Neiman Marcus
(610) 354-0500.
www.neimanmarcus.com

Nordstrom
(610) 265-6111.
www.nordstrom.com

Sears
(610) 962-6489.
www.sears.com

Strawbridge's
(610) 265-5100.

Interior of King of Prussia Mall, a retail shopping complex

Interior of Shops at Liberty Place, a shopping mall in Center City

MALLS

There are several indoor malls in and around Philadelphia, allowing people to enjoy and indulge in year-round shopping, dining, and entertainment.

The Gallery at Market East, the city's largest mall, is located in Center City along Market Street between 8th and 12th Streets. The four-level mall connects with both the Pennsylvania Convention Center and Market East Station. One of its biggest stores is Strawbridge's (see p155). It houses another 130 shops and eateries, and more than 30 pushcarts stocked with merchandise ranging from sunglasses and artworks to household wares and all manner of eclectic items.

The **King of Prussia Mall**, located in a suburb to the northwest of the city, is accessible via the Schulykill Expressway and is a 30-minute drive from Center City. With eight department stores (see p155) and vast parking lots and garages, it is one of the nation's largest retail shopping complexes comprising two separate sections: The Plaza and The Court. Expansive buildings with elaborate glass-ceiling atriums house more than

360 specialty shops, and an array of 40 restaurants and eateries. Nearby, Mall Boulevard hosts retail and wholesale stores, and a multi-screen movie complex. North of the city, along Route 1 in Bensalem, is the **Neshaminy Mall**, which includes 125 stores, restaurants, and a colossal 24-screen cinema complex.

SPECIALTY SHOPPING CENTERS

Groups of specialty shops are housed in large central Philadelphia buildings, offering visitors and office workers easy access to shopping – especially during the lunch hour or after work.

With offices and the luxury Park Hyatt hotel above it, the century-old **Bellevue Building** in Center City has a host of upscale boutiques, world-class restaurants, a spa, a food court, the prominent jazz club, Zanzibar Blue (see p166), and more to offer. Also in Center City, the **Shops at Liberty Place** features 60 shops that sell fine apparel, shoes, jewelry, specialty foods, and beauty products.

Shop sign at Manayunk

An impressive glass dome sits atop a circular rotunda – all part of the complex that makes up Liberty Place (see p79).

The Bourse Food Court and Specialty Shops is in the heart of Independence Mall, directly across from the Liberty Bell Center. The Bourse offers tourists in Old City a break from sightseeing itineraries with gift and souvenir shops and a food court.

SHOPPING DISTRICTS

Clusters of shops and restaurants in popular neighborhoods are known as shopping districts. One of Center City's most chic areas, **Rittenhouse Row**, includes upscale establishments along Walnut Street leading up to Rittenhouse Square (see p78). Several restaurants have storefronts facing the square, with outdoor seating in summer.

Anchored by New Market and Head House Square, **South Street** (see p67) offers a diversity of stores, shops, restaurants, eateries, and bars. Many of these cater to the avant-garde and eclectic trends of the younger crowds that often cram the area along South Street from Front to 11th Streets. **Main Street Manayunk** (see p95) is very popular on weekends for its many restaurants, pubs, and nightlife. Clothes and shoe shops, salons, antique shops, and a host of

Shops and boutique windows at Main Street Manayunk

boutiques and galleries also line Main Street. In **Chestnut Hill** *(see p94)*, over 200 boutiques, galleries, antiques stores, restaurants, and cafés take up nearly a dozen blocks along Germantown Avenue. **Jewelers' Row** and **Antique Row** span several blocks in Center City.

MARKETS

THE CITY's central farmers' market is the popular **Reading Terminal Market** *(see p73)*, where vendors sell farm-fresh produce, meats, poultry and seafood, flowers, pastries, and baked goods. Amish specialties and ethnic dishes representing the city's diverse population are particularly popular.

The nation's oldest and largest outdoor market, the **Italian Market** *(see p97)*, features several blocks of vendors who sell seafood, fresh produce, meats, Italian specialties, and desserts. The area is home to some of the city's best Italian restaurants.

To savor some delicious, home-style cooking of the Pennsylvania Dutch Country,

Vendors at the Italian Market, one of the city's oldest outdoor markets

take some time to drive out to the small villages of Bird-In-Hand and Intercourse. **The Amish Barn Restaurant and Gift Shop**, for instance, offers authentic local food as well as handicrafts and souvenirs.

DISCOUNT AND OUTLET MALLS

LOCATED IN an area northeast of Philadelphia is the **Franklin Mills Mall**, home to more than 200 retail and factory stores such as Last Call, Neiman Marcus, Ann Taylor, and Factory Store. Its outlets include those for Casual Corner, Saks Fifth

Avenue, Polo Ralph Lauren, JCPenney, and many others.

A complex of restored old factory buildings, **VF Outlet Village** in Reading is one of the county's largest groupings of factory store outlets. Several multistory buildings house discounted clothing, shoes, and household wares from Vanity Fair, Wrangler, Lee, Liz Claiborne, London Fog, Tommy Hilfiger, and Reebok.

Atlantic City Outlets, The Walk, in New Jersey, has merchandise from manufacturers, including Van Heusen, Guess, Geoffrey Beene, Casual Corner, and Brooks Brothers, at reduced prices.

DIRECTORY			
MALLS	**Shops at the Bellevue** 200 S Broad St. **Map** 2 F5. (*(215) 875-8350.*	**Main Street Manayunk** Main Street, Manayunk. (*(215) 482-9565.*	**Reading Terminal Market** 12th & Arch Sts. **Map** 3 B2. (*(215) 922-2317.*
The Gallery at Market East Market St between 9th & 11th Sts. **Map** 3 C2. (*(215) 625-4962.*	**Shops at Liberty Place** 16th & Chestnut Sts. **Map** 2 E4. (*(215) 851-9055.*	**Rittenhouse Row** Area around Rittenhouse Square. **Map** 2 D5. (*(215) 735-4899.*	**DISCOUNT AND OUTLET MALLS**
King of Prussia Mall Rt 202 & Mall Blvd, King of Prussia. (*(610) 265-5727.*	**SHOPPING DISTRICTS**	**South Street** South St from Front to 11th Sts. **Map** 3 B4. (*(215) 413-3713.*	**Atlantic City Outlets, The Walk** Michigan Ave between Pacific & Baltic Aves, Atlantic City, NJ. (*(609) 343-0387.*
Neshaminy Mall 1 & Bristol Rd, Bensalem. (*(215) 357-6100.*	**Antique Row** Pine St between 9th & 17th Sts. **Map** 3 B4.	**MARKETS**	**Franklin Mills Mall** 1455 Franklin Mills Circle, PA.
SPECIALTY SHOPPING CENTERS	**Chestnut Hill** 7600–8700 Germantown Ave, Chestnut Hill. (*(215) 247-6696.*	**The Amish Barn Restaurant and Gift Shop** 3029, Old Philadelphia Pike, Rte 340, Bird-in-Hand, PA. (*(717) 768-8886.*	(*(800) 336-6255,* *(215) 632-1500.*
The Bourse Food Court and Specialty Shops 111 S. Independence Mall East. **Map** 4 D3. (*(215) 625-0300.*	**Jewelers' Row** Sansom St between 7th & 8th Sts; and 8th St from Chestnut to Walnut Sts. **Map** 3 C3. (*(215) 627-1834.*	**Italian Market** 9th St between Christian & Wharton Sts. **Map** 3 C5. (*(215) 922-5557.*	**VF Outlet Village** 801 Hill Avenue, Reading, PA. (*(800) 772-8336,* *(610) 378-0408.*

Fashion and Accessories

CENTER CITY IS Philadelphia's main shopping district with more than 2,100 retail stores. Many offer the finest in clothes, shoes, accessories, and jewelry. Key fashion shops and boutiques are located along Walnut Street on Rittenhouse Row. Designer clothing stores are also found at the Gallery at Market East mall, as well as within the small shopping centers at the Bellevue Building and Liberty Place. When looking for the latest in high fashion, do not forget the department stores and specialty stores at the King of Prussia Mall.

Entrance to the upmarket shops in Liberty Place

WOMEN'S FASHION

WITH SO MANY stores and boutiques to choose from, women will be delighted with a shopping spree in Center City. Located just one block from Rittenhouse Square on Walnut Street, **Jones New York** offers a range of fine apparel. Nearby, the **Knit Wit and Danielle Scott** boutique carries a variety of elegant black cocktail dresses as well as cruise-wear. **Ann Taylor**, on the same block, has upbeat and high-fashion designs for both business and pleasure. Their Liberty Place store is called the **Ann Taylor Loft**. **Casual Corner** and lingerie store **Victoria's Secret** are also at Liberty Place.

The number of women's apparel stores in the King of Prussia Mall is extensive. In addition to Victoria's Secret and Ann Taylor, there are the latest classic and trendy fashions from **New York and Company** and **Lane Bryant**, and the risqué designs of **Frederick's of Hollywood**.

Main Street Manayunk features several women's clothing boutiques. **Best Friends** offers a unique line of clothing and accessories. **Chico's** specializes in casual wear, while **Paula Hian Designs** has a fashion designer studio and store.

MEN'S FASHION

MEN LOOKING FOR the perfect suit or designer clothing will not leave the city empty handed. **Boyds Philadelphia** has been around for over 60 years and is one of Center City's premier stores, while **Paris Europa** has a range varying from beachwear to office attire. One of the most elegant shops at the Bellevue, **Polo Ralph Lauren** has a full line of clothing from the world-renowned designer. Men will also find a variety of stores at the Shops at Liberty Place, including **Jos. A. Bank, Christopher's Mens' Store**, and **Kuhlman's**. In the King of Prussia Mall, **Boss Hugo Boss Shop** features a clothing, sportswear, and accessories. Other popular men's stores include **Bachrach**, one of the nation's largest privately-owned retailers, and **Talbots Mens** with its line of casual wear and outerwear.

Casual sneakers

MEN'S AND WOMEN'S FASHION

WITH SHOPS IN the Bellevue Building and Manayunk, **Nicole Miller** features men's and women's formalwear, as well as accessories. A line of both casual and dressy apparel can be found at **J. Crew** and **Express** at the Shops at Liberty Place, while casual wear is the highlight of **Old Navy** and **Gap** at the Gallery at Market East. **Guess** features more trendsetting clothing at the same mall. At King of Prussia, **Brooks Brothers** sells traditional, fine-quality apparel. **Eddie Bauer** features winter clothes, while **Banana Republic** offers casual jeans and dressy jackets. Other popular outlets include **Abercrombie & Fitch**, and the glamorous styles of **DKNY**.

SHOES AND ACCESSORIES

FEATURING A line of fur, shearling, leather, and cloth, **Jacques Ferber** on Walnut Street offers unique outerwear. **Touches**, in Center City, has many one-of-a-kind varieties of jewelry, picture frames, and scarves.

For men's shoes, **Sherman Brothers** offers a wide selection of top brands and hard-to-find sizes. Both men's and women's choices for shoes abound in the King of Prussia Mall, with stores including **Bakers**, **Kenneth Cole**, **Rockport**, **Timberland**, **Bostonian**, and **Jarman**.

Window shopping at one of Center City's numerous upscale boutiques

JEWELRY

Philadelphia's Jewelers' Row was established in 1851, and is the nation's oldest and one of the largest diamond districts. Stores on the row include a seemingly unlimited selection of diamonds, rubies, sapphires, and emeralds. Owned by the same family for four generations, **Barsky Diamonds** specializes in diamonds. **Safian and Rudolph Jewelers**, in business for over 50 years, deals in precious stones, while **Tiffany and Company**, in Center City, has offered the finest in jewelry, crystal, and accessories for more than 150 years. Other prominent Center City jewelers include **Govberg Jewelers** and **LAGOS The Store**.

DIRECTORY

WOMEN'S FASHION

Ann Taylor
1713 Walnut St.
Map 2 E5.
((215) 977-9336.
King of Prussia Mall.
((610) 354-9380,
(610) 354-0770.

Ann Taylor Loft
Liberty Place. **Map** 2 E4.
((215) 557-9181.

Best Friends
4329 Main Street,
Manayunk.
((215) 487-1250.

Casual Corner
Liberty Place.
Map 2 E4.
((215) 563-3057.

Chico's
4367 Main Street,
Manayunk.
((215) 482-3536.

Frederick's of Hollywood
King of Prussia Mall.
((610) 265-1499.

Jones New York
1711 Walnut St.
Map 2 E5.
((215) 864–0110.

Knit Wit and Danielle Scott
1718 Walnut St.
Map 2 E5.
((215) 564-4760.

Lane Bryant
King of Prussia Mall.
((610) 265-6106.

New York and Company
King of Prussia Mall.
((610) 354-0560.

Paula Hian Designs
106 Gay St, Manayunk.
((215) 487-3067.

Victoria's Secret
Liberty Place. **Map** 2 E4.
((215) 569-1058.

MEN'S FASHION

Bachrach
King of Prussia Mall.
((610) 265-8830.

Boss Hugo Boss Shop
King of Prussia Mall.
((610) 992-1400.

Boyds Philadelphia
1818 Chestnut St.
Map 2 D4.
((215) 564-9000.

Christopher's Mens' Store
Liberty Place. **Map** 2 E4.

Jos. A. Bank
Liberty Place. **Map** 2 E4.
((215) 563-5990.

Kuhlman's
Liberty Place. **Map** 2 E4.
((215) 561-5638.

Paris Europa
1315 Walnut St.
Map 2 F5.
((215) 893-1115.

Polo Ralph Lauren
200 S Broad St. **Map** 2 F5.
((215) 985-2800.

Talbots Mens
King of Prussia Mall.
((610) 962-0881.

MEN'S AND WOMEN'S FASHION

Abercrombie & Fitch
King of Prussia Mall.
((610) 265-5650.

Banana Republic
King of Prussia Mall.
((610) 768-9007.

Brooks Brothers
King of Prussia Mall.
((610) 337-9888.

DKNY
King of Prussia Mall.
((610) 337-4020.

Eddie Bauer
King of Prussia Mall.
((610) 337-4633.

Express
Liberty Place. **Map** 2 E4.
((215) 563-3057.
King of Prussia Mall.
((610) 337-8912.

Gap
The Gallery at Market East,
Market St between 9th &
11th Sts. **Map** 3 C2.
((215) 925-9770.

Guess
The Gallery at Market East,
Market St between 9th &
11th Sts. **Map** 3 C2.
((215) 627-3573.

J. Crew
Liberty Place. **Map** 2 E4.
((215) 977-7335.

Nicole Miller
200 S Broad St. **Map** 2 F5.
((215) 546-5007.
4249 Main Street,
Manayunk.
((215) 930-0307.

Old Navy
The Gallery at Market East,
Market St between 9th &
11th Sts. **Map** 3 C2.
((215) 413-7012.

SHOES AND ACCESSORIES

Bakers
King of Prussia Mall.
((610) 265-8948.

Bostonian
King of Prussia Mall.
((610) 265-4323.

Jacques Ferber
1708 Walnut St.
Map 2 E5.
((215) 735-4173.

Jarman
King of Prussia Mall.
((610) 265-5336.

Kenneth Cole
King of Prussia Mall.
((610) 337-2650.

Rockport
King of Prussia Mall.
((610) 337-3310.

Sherman Brothers Shoes
1520 Sansom St.
Map 2 E4.
((215) 561-4550.

Timberland
King of Prussia.
((610) 768-0988.

Touches
225 S 15th St. **Map** 2 E5.

JEWELRY

Barsky Diamonds
724 Sansom St.
Map 4 D3.

Govberg Jewelers
1428 Walnut St.
Map 2 E5.

LAGOS The Store
1735 Walnut St.
Map 2 E4.

Safian & Rudolph Jewelers
701 Sansom St.
Map 4 D3.

Tiffany and Company
1414 Walnut St.
Map 2 E5.

Specialty Shops

W ITH SHOPPING DISTRICTS, upscale shops, and one-of-a-kind stores, central Philadelphia has a wide range of merchandise that would satisfy even the hard-to-please shopper. Many specialty shops and gift stores specialize in finding the perfect gift or souvenir. Antique Row has numerous stores along an eight-block stretch in Center City, while in Old City sits a large cluster of art galleries. Other key shopping areas with unique crafts, books, and flower stores include Manayunk and Chestnut Hill. The colossal King of Prussia Mall has a seemingly unending choice of everything, from home furnishings and electronics to sporting goods.

Shops located in the Chestnut Hill market area

ANTIQUES

S PREAD OVER eight blocks on Pine Street between 7th and 11th Streets, Antique Row *(see p157)* features boutiques and shops offering a selection of fine furniture, period antiques, collectibles, estate jewelry, and vintage clothing. One such store is **M. Finkel & Daughter**, which sells period furniture, 17th- to 19th-century needlework, and decorative accessories. The nearby **Classic Antiques** offers a large selection of country French furniture, mirrors, and accessories as well as 18th- and 19th-century European antiques. The **South Street Antiques Market** is the city's only indoor antiques market with 25 dealers selling pieces from vintage Victorian to modern, including estate jewelry, furniture, pottery, and accessories.

ART GALLERIES

T HE OLD CITY Arts Association has 50 members, including art galleries, which are open until 9pm on the first Friday of every month – an event

appropriately called "First Friday." The **Berman Gallery** and the **Moderne Gallery** feature contemporary furniture, pottery, fine arts, and metalwork. The **Pringle Gallery** displays the works of emerging and established contemporary artists from the United States and Europe, while the **Artists' House Gallery** offers works rendered by local artists at affordable prices.

Located on Antique Row, **Seraphin Gallery** has art from international contemporary painters, sculptors, and photographers, including 18th- through 20th-century works by artists from America and Europe. In Center City, **Newman Galleries** specializes in 19th-century American and European paintings, and early 20th-century American art from the New Hope School. **Artforms Gallery** in Manayunk has paintings, sculptures, and photography produced by local artists.

BOOKS

A N EXCELLENT choice for mainstream books and magazines is **Barnes & Noble** at Rittenhouse Square. Similar in scope are **Borders** in Chestnut Hill, and at the King of Prussia Mall, and **B. Dalton Bookseller**, which has a store in Gallery at Market East mall.

For hard-to-find books, the **Philadelphia Rare Books and Manuscript Company** features early printed books dating from the 16th century, and manuscripts, old bibles, and other books from around the world that cover a wide realm of topics. Opened in 1936, **Robin's Bookstore** is the oldest independent bookstore in the city with a vast collection of African-American books, literature, poetry, New Age, and children's books.

FOOD AND COOKERY

W ITHIN THE Italian Market are specialty food stores. Family owned for more than 50 years, **DiBruno Bros. House of Cheese** sells more than 400 types of cheese and gourmet foods. **Termini Brothers Gold Medal Pastry Bakery** is a local favorite with handmade Italian confections made from recipes that date to the 1800s. Serving chefs and home cooks since 1906, **Fante's Kitchen Wares Shop** offers an extensive selection of cooking wares and utensils.

Gourmet cheese

GIFTS, CRAFTS, AND SOUVENIRS

A S A RESULT OF its varied traditions and its status as one of America's oldest cities, Philadelphia offers a range of gifts and mementos. **Xenos Candy'n Gifts** has classic souvenirs showcasing Old City sights, including replicas of Liberty Bell, flags, and other collectables. Similar items are found in **The Bourse** nearby, while the **Pennsylvania General Store** has locally-made foods and crafts. **Scarlett Alley** offers art, furnishings, jewelry, leather goods, books, and children's items. **Moon Over Manayunk** and **Sweet Violet** feature fine gifts for personal care as well as for homes. Fine-rolled, handmade cigars can be bought at the **Black Cat Cigar Company** and **Holt's Cigar Company** in Center City.

FLORISTS

A WIDE-RANGING choice of flowers is available from Philadelphia's florists. Some, such as **Nature's Gallery Florist** in Center City, also

assist with party planning, while **Magnifique Balloons & Flowers** provides decorations in the form of balloons, flowers, and custom artwork for private and commercial events.

Music CDs

MUSIC

F OR THE LATEST in music CDs and recordings, Borders and **Sam Goody** in Center City have extensive music selections featuring rock, pop, hip-hop, jazz, folk, classical, and more. Visit **Repo Records**

on South Street to thumb through a wide range of import singles, and rows of used records and CDs.

SPORTING GOODS

T HE NATION'S largest family-owned sports goods chain, **Modell's Sporting Goods**, has stores in Center City and King of Prussia Mall, and also sells home-team apparel and footwear. For camping gear, kayaks, and other outdoor items, shop at **Eastern Mountain Sports**, also at King of Prussia Mall.

DIRECTORY

ANTIQUES

Classic Antiques
922 Pine St. **Map** 3 C4.
((215) 629-0211.

M. Finkel & Daughter
936 Pine St. **Map** 3 C4.
((215) 627-7797.

South Street Antiques Market
615 S 6th St. **Map** 3 D5.
((215) 592-0256.

ART GALLERIES

Artforms Gallery
106 Levering St,
Manayunk.
((215) 483-3030.

Artists' House Gallery
57 N 2nd St. **Map** 4 E2.
((215) 923-8440.

Berman Gallery
136 N 2nd St. **Map** 4 E2.
((215) 733-0707.

Moderne Gallery
111 N 3rd St. **Map** 4 E2.
((215) 923-8536.

Newman Galleries
Map 2 E5.
((215) 563-1779.

Pringle Gallery
323 Arch St. **Map** 4 E2.
((215) 592-7746.

Seraphin Gallery
1108 Pine St. **Map** 3 B4.
((215) 923-7000.

BOOKS

B. Dalton Bookseller
The Gallery at Market East,
Market St. **Map** 3 C2.
((215) 592-8700.

Barnes & Noble
Map 2 D4.
((215) 665-0716.

Borders
1 S Broad St. **Map** 3 B2.
((215) 568-7400.
8701 Germantown Ave,
Chestnut Hill.
((215) 248-1213.
King of Prussia Mall.
((610) 337-9009.

Philadelphia Rare Books and Manuscript Company
((215) 744-6734.

Robin's Bookstore
108 S 13th St. **Map** 3 B3.
((215) 735-9600.

FOOD AND COOKERY

DiBruno Bros. House of Cheese
Italian Market, 930 S
9th St. **Map** 3 C5.
((215) 922-2876.
109 S 18th St. **Map** 2 E4.
((215) 665-9220.

Fante's Kitchen Wares Shop
Italian Market, 1006 S
9th St. **Map** 3 C5.
((215) 922-5557.

Termini Brothers Gold Medal Pastry Bakery
1523 S 8th St.
((215) 334-1816.

GIFTS, CRAFTS, AND SOUVENIRS

Black Cat Cigar Company
1518 Sansom Street.
Map 2 E4.
((800) 220-9850.

The Bourse
5th between Market &
Chestnut Sts. **Map** 4 D3.
((215) 625-0300.

Holt's Cigar Company
1522 Walnut St. **Map** 2 E5.
((215) 732-8500.

Moon Over Manayunk
4327 Main St, Manayunk.
((215) 483-7255.

Pennsylvania General Store
Reading Terminal Market.
Map 3 C2
((215) 592-0455.

Scarlett Alley
241 Race St. **Map** 4E2.
((215) 592-7898.

Sweet Violet
4361 Main St, Manayunk.
((215) 483-2826.

Xenos Candy'n Gifts
Map 4 E3.
((215) 922-1445.

FLORISTS

Magnifique Balloons & Flowers
4134 Manayunk Ave,
Manayunk
((215) 483-6880.

Nature's Gallery Florist
Map 2 D4.
((215) 563-5554.

MUSIC

Repo Records
538 South St. **Map** 4 D4.

Sam Goody
The Gallery at Market East,
Market St. **Map** 3 C2.
((215) 627-2066.

SPORTING GOODS

Eastern Mountain Sports
King of Prussia Mall.
((610) 337-4210.

Modell's Sporting Goods
934 Market St. **Map** 3 C2.
((215) 629-0900.
King of Prussia Mall.
((610) 337-4522.

ENTERTAINMENT IN PHILADELPHIA

STRETCHING ALONG the "Avenue of the Arts," Broad Street is home to a plethora of renowned performing arts facilities. Heading the list are the Kimmel Center for the Performing Arts and the Academy of Music, home to the world-class Philly POPS, Philadelphia Orchestra, Opera Company of Philadelphia, and the Pennsylvania Ballet. Numerous other venues feature

Detail of façade at the Forrest Theater

live chamber music, theater productions and musicals, rock, hip hop and jazz-fusion concerts, and varied programs of gospel. Universities also put on several music, theater, and dance shows. Nightclubs hosting live bands abound in Old City and South Street, while a drive or train ride of an hour or so brings you to Atlantic City's glittering casinos on the New Jersey shoreline.

Visitors wait for a show at Kimmel Center for the Performing Arts

INFORMATION

THERE ARE several websites and newspapers that carry the latest information on musical concerts, theatrical performances, nightlife, and other entertainment options in and around the city.

The *Weekend* section of the **Philadelphia Inquirer**, published every Friday, details the goings-on in town, from the latest movies to gallery exhibitions to extensive listings of live performances, including ballet, chamber and classical music, opera, theater, and jazz. The art district has its own website, Avenue of the Arts.

The **Philadelphia City Paper** and **Philadelphia Weekly** also showcase arts, music, and cinema listings. They also have extended information on daily nightclub acts and performances. These two publications are weeklies and are available free at many cafés, pubs, and bookstores throughout the city. They also have websites with up-to-date listings.

TICKETS

SEATS FOR MOST of the major symphony, opera, chamber music, ballet, and pop performances in Philadelphia can be booked through **Ticket Philadelphia**. The main box office is in the **Kimmel Center for the Performing Arts**. Tickets can be bought in person, on the phone or online. Tickets for various

events and theatrical performances can also be bought at the box office of each venue, or over the phone, online or in person via **Ticketmaster**. Be aware, however, that ticketing services often add a fee to the total cost. Outlets of Ticketmaster in and around Philadelphia include Tower Records and Strawbridge's *(see p155)*. Ticketmaster is one of the world's largest e-commerce sites, in addition to having more than 3,300 retail outlets and 19 worldwide telephone call centers. It serves more than 8,000 clients worldwide and acts as the exclusive ticketing service for various performing arts venues and theaters.

Some hotels may also sell show tickets – especially those in Center City or near the theater district. Check with the concierge in your hotel for the best options of purchasing tickets.

The Philadelphia Orchestra at Verizon Hall in the Kimmel Center

"Avenue of the Arts" lights up for a night of theater and culture

ENTERTAINMENT DISTRICTS

THE HUB OF Philadelphia's performing arts and the-ater district extends south of City Hall on South Broad Street, called the **Avenue of the Arts**. This two-block area is anchored by the Kimmel Center for the Performing Arts and the world-renowned **Academy of Music** *(see p76)*. Also located in this area is the Merriam Theater, hosting professional touring produc-tions, as well as the 300-seat Wilma Theater *(see p164)*, whose productions address current political and social issues. Three blocks east of the area is the Forrest Theatre *(see p164)*, while the Prince Music Theater is on Chestnut Street. Inside the Bellevue Building at the corner of South Broad Street and Walnut Street is the city's prominent jazz club, Zanzibar Blue *(see p166)*.

Besides theater and cultural activities, Philadelphia has a thriving nightlife with scores of restaurants, nightclubs, smaller theater venues, and comedy clubs concentrated along South Street. A vibrant nightlife scene also abounds in the Old City area around Chestnut, Market, Front, and 2nd Streets with restaurants, cozy pubs, and martini bars.

Along the Delaware River, Columbus Avenue is home to some of Philadelphia's up-and-coming nightspots north and south of Penn's Landing – some on piers stretching into the river, while others are seasonal outdoor clubs.

Much of the city's lesbian and gay nightlife centers on the neighborhood between Pine and Chestnut Streets north to south and Broad and 11th Streets west to east.

Across the Delaware, mean-while, the Tweeter Center at the Camden Waterfront *(see p101)* hosts concerts through the year, drawing big-name musical acts, as does the Wachovia Complex in south Philadelphia *(see p166)*.

Going beyond Philadelphia, Atlantic City *(see p127)* is an entertainment destination in itself with more than a dozen sprawling casino hotels and resorts, most of which have popular nightclubs, concert venues, and pulsing and glitzy discos.

South Street – an entertainment hub for the younger crowd

DISABLED ACCESS

MOST OF THE major concert halls and theaters in Philadelphia accommodate disabled patrons and wheelchairs. The Kimmel Center for the Performing Arts and the Academy of Music have accessible wheelchair seating locations for perfor-mances, captioning for the hearing impaired, and assisted listening devices available on a first-come, first-served basis. Call ahead for details.

Some smaller venues and clubs may be less than adequate in accommodating disabled patrons. Check with the venue or the **Mayor's Commission on People with Disabilities** for more information. The commission provides a forum for the disabled to express opinions on programs and services in Philadelphia.

DIRECTORY

TICKETING

Ticketmaster
Various Outlets.
(*(215) 336-2000.*
w www.ticketmaster.com

Ticket Philadelphia
(*(215) 893-1999.*
w www.ticketphiladelphia.org

DISABLED ACCESS

Kimmel Center & Academy of Music
Department of Audience & Visitor Services. **Map** 2 E5.
(*(215) 670-2327.*
w www.kimmelcenter.org

Mayor's Commission on People with Disabilities
1401 JFK Blvd. **Map** 2 F4.
(*(215) 686-2798.*
w www.phila.gov/aco/ index.html

USEFUL WEBSITES

Avenue of the Arts
w www.avenueofthearts.org

Philadelphia Citypaper.net
w www.citypaper.net

Philadelphia Weekly Online
w www.philadelphiaweekly.com

Philly.com (Philadelphia Inquirer)
w www.philly.com

The Arts in Philadelphia

A CULTURAL MECCA for the performing arts, Philadelphia has world-class venues that host excellent chamber and symphony music, and some of the finest performances in opera, ballet, and theater. Topping the list are concerts by the renowned Philadelphia Orchestra and Philly POPS, which are performed in the city's premier venue, the multitheater Kimmel Center for the Performing Arts. Chamber music ensembles play before smaller crowds, while grand opera and ballet productions take the stage in the Victorian-era Academy of Music. Several theaters in and around Center City host performances that range from Broadway productions and musicals to African-American theater. Entertainment is also provided by choral groups and the area's top music schools, which hold classical concerts and dance performances by students.

Forrest Theater, host to touring dance and theater companies

CLASSICAL MUSIC AND SYMPHONY

ONE OF THE city's best, the **Philadelphia Orchestra** has shared the stage with some of the world's most influential classical musicians for more than 100 years. The orchestra's home was the **Academy of Music**, but it now performs at the Verizon Hall in the **Kimmel Center for the Performing Arts**.

Also performing at Verizon Hall is one of the nation's most-renowned POPS orchestras playing big band, classics, Broadway hits, and rock'n roll tunes. Grammy Award-winning pianist and band leader Peter Nero has been leading the **Philly POPS** since 1979. In summer, both orchestras

perform at an outdoor venue, the **Mann Center for the Performing Arts**, also home to jazz, dance, opera, and musical theater programs.

Chamber music can be enjoyed on Sunday afternoons and Monday evenings at the Kimmel Center's Perelman Theater. The **Chamber Orchestra of Philadelphia** performs here, playing a musical repertoire from the 18th century to the present day. The **Philadelphia Chamber Music Society** presents more than 60 chamber music, piano, vocal, and choral concerts a year, which are performed by internationally-known groups as

Pennsylvania Ballet dancer performing *Swan Lake*

well as emerging artists. Presenting a unique classical experience is the **Philomel Baroque Orchestra** – a small ensemble of accomplished musicians who play early classical and Baroque music on period instruments.

THEATERS AND THEATER COMPANIES

STAGE PRODUCTIONS run the gamut from national touring shows to politically inspired acts produced locally. The

Academy of Music, oldest opera house in the US still used for its original purpose

Philadelphia Theatre Company is the city's leading producer of contemporary American theater, while the **Arden Theatre Company** brings to life dramatic and theatrical stories by the greatest storytellers of all time.

The **Forrest Theatre** hosts Broadway shows and is the city's premier theatrical arts venue. The **Walnut Street Theatre** – America's oldest – is home to musicals and plays.

The **Wilma Theater** has productions with contemporary themes, while the smaller **Society Hill Playhouse** features offbeat and "off-Broad Street" productions. The **Freedom Theatre**, located on the northern stretch of the Avenue of the Arts, is one of the country's leading venues for African-American performances.

OPERA AND BALLET

LOCAL LOVERS OF grand opera have been enjoying performances by the **Opera Company of Philadelphia** for more than 30 years. The **Pennsylvania Ballet**, which has been thrilling audiences for over 40 years, performs at the Academy of Music and the Merriam Theater. Its season has six productions, including the old Yuletide favorite, *The Nutcracker (see p35)*, which has become an annual Philadelphia tradition.

VOCAL ARTS AND CHOIRS

THERE ARE SEVERAL choral groups in the city such as the renowned **Philadelphia Boys Choir and Chorale**. The 100-member choir performs patriotic music and Broadway show tunes. The group holds more than 40 performances each year, and travels on international tours.

The **Philadelphia Singers**, an ensemble of 24 professional vocalists, performs with leading national and local orchestras and other performing arts organizations such as the Philadelphia Orchestra, the Pennsylvania Ballet, and the Curtis Institute of Music. A 100-voice symphonic chorus, the **Choral Arts Society of Philadelphia** also appears often with the Philadelphia Orchestra. The **Academy of Vocal Arts**, around since 1934, produces operas with the **Chamber Orchestra of Philadelphia**. The academy's resident artists also hold recitals and concerts.

MUSIC SCHOOLS' PERFORMANCES

OFTEN CONSIDERED one of the most prestigious conservatories, the **Curtis Institute of Music** trains some of the best young musicians from around the world. The students hold free public recitals and concerts in the institute's Field Concert Hall located opposite Rittenhouse Square, and play in various venues around the city when they are not touring.

Local musicians and students training in classical, jazz, dance, and theater arts also hold recitals and concerts at the **University of the Arts**, Temple University's **Esther Boyer College of Music and Dance**, and through **PENN Presents** at the University of Pennsylvania's Annenberg Center for the Performing Arts.

DIRECTORY

CLASSICAL MUSIC AND SYMPHONY

Academy of Music
Broad & Locust Sts.
Map 2 E5.
(215) 790-5800;
box office: (215) 893-1999.

Chamber Orchestra of Philadelphia
Perelman Theater,
Kimmel Center.
Map 2 E5.
(215) 545-5451;
box office: (215) 893-1999.

Kimmel Center for the Performing Arts
Broad & Spruce Sts.
Map 2 E5.
(215) 790-5800;
box office: (215) 893-1999.

Mann Center for the Performing Arts
52nd St & Parkside Ave.
(215) 546-7900.

Peter Nero & the Philly POPS
Verizon Hall,
Kimmel Center.
Map 2 E5.
(215) 546-6400;
box office: (215) 893-1999.

Philadelphia Chamber Music Society
Various venues.
(215) 569-8587; box office: (215) 569-8080.

Philadelphia Orchestra
Verizon Hall, Kimmel Center. **Map** 2 E5.
(215) 893-1900; box office: (215) 893-1999.

Philomel Baroque Orchestra
Various venues.
(215) 487-2344;
box office: (215) 569-9700.

THEATERS AND THEATER COMPANIES

Arden Theatre Company
40 N 2nd St.
Map 4 E2.
(215) 922-1122.

Forrest Theatre
1114 Walnut St.
Map 3 B3.
(215) 923-1515.

Freedom Theatre
1346 N Broad St.
(215) 765-2793.

Philadelphia Theatre Company
1714 DeLancy St.
Map 2 D5.
(215) 985-1400.

Society Hill Playhouse
507 S 8th St. **Map** 3 C4.
(215) 923-0210.

Walnut Street Theatre
825 Walnut St. **Map** 3 C3.
(215) 574-3550.

Wilma Theater
265 S Broad St. **Map** 2 F5.
box office: (215) 546-7824.

OPERA AND BALLET

Opera Company of Philadelphia
Academy of Music.
Map 2 E5.
(215) 893-3600; box office: (215) 732-8400.

Pennsylvania Ballet
Merriam Theater,
Academy of Music.
Map 2 E5.
(215) 551-7000.

VOCAL ARTS AND CHOIRS

Academy of Vocal Arts
Various venues.
(215) 735-1685.

Choral Arts Society of Philadelphia
Various venues.
box office: (215) 545-8634.

Philadelphia Boys Choir and Chorale
225 N 32nd St.
Map 1 B2.
(215) 222-3500.

Philadelphia Singers
Kimmel Center
& various venues.
Map 2 E5.
(215) 751-9494.

MUSIC SCHOOLS' PERFORMANCES

Curtis Institute of Music
Field Concert Hall
& various venues.
1726 Locust St.
Map 2 E5.
(215) 893-7902; box office: (215) 893-1999

Esther Boyer College of Music and Dance
Temple University,
1715 N Broad St.
(215) 204-8307.

PENN Presents
Annenberg Center for the Performing Arts,
University of Pennsylvania.
(215) 898-6701;
box office: (215) 898-3900.

University of the Arts
Broad & Pine Sts.
Map 2 E5.
(215) 875-4800.

Music and Nightlife

PHILADELPHIA FILLS ITS after-dark hours with the latest sounds in rock, folk, pop, jazz-fusion, hip-hop, and salsa. These rhythms can be heard at venues offering live music, sometimes seven days a week. Many are clustered within the prominent entertainment districts of South Street, Old City, Main Street Manayunk, and the areas along the Delaware Avenue waterfront. Philadelphia is often a regular stop for major bands and musical acts on world tours, including top rock, jazz, hip-hop, and country and pop musicians. Those opting for a less energized night out can enjoy conversation and cocktails at friendly neighborhood taverns and bars located throughout the city.

ROCK AND FOLK MUSIC

FOR THE TOP touring rock bands, check listings in local newspapers *(see p162)* for concerts at the **Wachovia Complex** and other major venues, including the **Tower Theater**, **Keswick Theatre**, and the **Tweeter Center**. Also check listings for concerts held in Atlantic City.

For a taste of local rock music, **Khyber** in Old City has shows several nights a week and is a mainstay for Philadelphia's rock scene. Live performances by local rock groups also take place at the **Pontiac Grille** on South Street and the **Grape Street Pub** in Manayunk.

Folk musicians and fans frequent the **Tin Angel** in Old City. One of the region's most-renowned venues that attracts folk artists and other acts is **Point** in suburban Bryn Mawr, where guitarists strum in a comfortable, living room-like atmosphere.

BLUES, JAZZ, AND WORLD MUSIC

BLUES AND JAZZ clubs range from upbeat nightspots and restaurants, where top artists perform, to smaller and cozier lounges. **Zanzibar**

Alma de Cuba, famous for its Cuban cuisine and live music

Blue is Philadelphia's most high-profile jazz club. Opened in 1990, this venue books renowned jazz musicians who have topped the charts for decades. **Ortlieb's Jazzhaus** is another hot venue that offers world-class jazz music six nights a week. **Warmdaddy's** on Front Street is a popular nightspot with a touch of southern hospitality. The establishment puts up shows that feature zydeco, blues, rhythm and blues, and soul music artists. Some clubs offer a range of international

music, such as salsa, flamenco, and more. For instance, musicians at **Alma de Cuba** belt out live Cuban music performances every week.

NIGHTCLUBS AND DISCOS

THE YOUNGER crowd parties late into the night with clubs churning out music until 2am. The cutting-edge dance club **Shampoo** features dance halls and lounges with multiple bars and DJs. Along Delaware Avenue, **Egypt Nightclub** features concerts, in-club radio broadcasts and DJs, and an Oldies Night on Sundays. **Poly Esther's and the Culture Club** is the city's only 1970s disco and has a *Saturday Night Fever* theme dance floor. A trendy nightspot for the city's chic elite is the **32° Luxe Lounge** in Old City. It includes two premium bars and a lush VIP lounge with European bottle service. The Polynesian-themed **Tiki Bob's Cantina** has a signature drink, the Tiki Nut. For classic funk to old-school hip-hop and reggae, **Tribecca** is an after-hours club with a lounge, two DJ stands, pool tables, and fashionable decor.

BARS AND TAVERNS

MANY CENTER CITY hotels and restaurants have comfortable bars that are ideal for relaxing and for conversation. Philadelphia also has a number of neighborhood bars and pubs that play live music. The **Red Head Piano Bar and Lounge**, in Latham Hotel off Rittenhouse Square, plays some jazz and rock music, while **Monk's Café** in the same neighborhood is a bistro with more than 200 beer brands and 20 Belgian draught ales.

Irish pubs with great food and Guinness beer on tap include **Fergie's Pub**, which has live music and a traditional Irish menu, and the **Irish Pub** that serves Irish-American food in a casual dining

Draught Guinness

ZANZIBAR BLUE

international jazz + cuisine

Sign outside Zanzibar Blue, a landmark jazz club

ambience. The **Bishop's Collar** has a friendly atmosphere with a selection of microbrews, and creative but inexpensive pub fare. It is a great place to unwind after visiting the Museum of Art or Boathouse Row.

GAY CLUBS AND BARS

SEVERAL NIGHTCLUBS and bars are centered in the city's main gay and lesbian district, located between Broad and 11th Streets, and Chestnut to Pine Streets. The **Bump Lounge** is the city's premier gay lounge serving food and cocktails seven days a week. With three floors of energizing house music, disco, and hip-hop, **Pure** has been the city's prominent gay nightspot for more than 30 years. Nearby is **Sisters**, the city's largest lesbian bar with dining

and dancing. For more information, visit the Greater Philadelphia Tourism and Marketing Corporation's website *(see p133)* or look at the Philadelphia Convention and Visitors Bureau's *Gay and Lesbian Travel Guide*, available at the Independence Visitors Center.

COMEDY CLUBS

MANY CLUBS in town and across the river in New Jersey feature stand-up comedy acts. The city's "Original Comedy Club," the **Laff House** on South Street, brings in comedians from all over the country, with open mike

Pure, a prominent gay nightspot in Philadelphia

nights, and main acts on Friday and Saturday nights. The **Rascals** comedy club is located just over the Benjamin Franklin Bridge in the Hilton Philadelphia in Cherry Hill. Luring national headliner acts Thursdays through Sundays, the club has been entertaining audiences for more than 20 years. Special packages include dinner, a show, and guest room accommodations.

DIRECTORY

ROCK AND FOLK MUSIC

Grape Street Pub
4100 Main St,
Manayunk.
☎ (215) 483-7084.
ⓦ www.grapestreet.com

Keswick Theatre
Easton Rd & Keswick Ave,
Glenside, PA.
☎ (215) 572-7650.

Khyber
56 S 2nd St. **Map** 4 E3.
☎ (215) 238-5888.

Point
880 W Lancaster Ave,
Bryn Mawr, PA.
☎ (610) 527-0988.

Pontiac Grille
304 South St. **Map** 4 D5.
☎ (215) 925-4053.

Tin Angel
20 S 2nd St. **Map** 4 E3.
☎ (215) 928-0770.

Tower Theater
69th & Ludlow Sts,
Upper Darby, PA
☎ (215) 568-3222.
ⓦ www.cc.com/tower

Tweeter Center
1 Harbour Blvd,
Camden Waterfront,
New Jersey.
☎ (856) 365-1300.
ⓦ www.tweetercenter.
com/philadelphia

Wachovia Complex
Broad St & Pattison Ave.
☎ (215) 336-3600.
ⓦ www.comcast-
spectator.com

BLUES, JAZZ, AND WORLD MUSIC

Alma de Cuba
1623 Walnut St.
Map 2 E4.
☎ (215) 988-1799.

Ortlieb's Jazzhaus
847 N 3rd St.
☎ (215) 922-1035.

Warmdaddy's
4 S Front St. **Map** 4 E3.
☎ (215) 627-8400.
ⓦ www.warmdaddys.com

Zanzibar Blue
Broad & Walnut Sts.
Map 2 F5.
☎ (215) 732-4500.
ⓦ www.zanzibarblue.com

NIGHTCLUBS AND DISCOS

32° Luxe Lounge
416 S 2nd St. **Map** 4 E4.
☎ (215) 627-3132.

Egypt Nightclub
Map 4 F1.
☎ (215) 922-6500.

Poly Esther's and the Culture Club
1201 Race St. **Map** 3 B1.
☎ (215) 851-0776.

Shampoo
417 N 8th St. **Map** 4 D1.
☎ (215) 922-7500.

Tiki Bob's Cantina
461 N 3rd St. **Map** 4 E1.
☎ (215) 928-9200.

Tribecca
Richmond &
Cumberland Sts.
☎ (215) 423-7990.

BARS AND TAVERNS

Bishop's Collar
Map 2 D1.
☎ (215) 765-1616.

Fergie's Pub
Map 2 F5.
☎ (215) 928-8118.

Irish Pub
Map 2 D4.
☎ (215) 925-1588.

Monk's Café
264 S 16th St. **Map** 2 E5.
☎ (215) 545-7005.

Red Head Lounge and Piano Bar
135 S 17th St. **Map** 2 E4.
☎ (215) 563-8200.

GAY CLUBS AND BARS

Bump Lounge
Map 2 F5.
☎ (215) 732-1800.

Pure
Map 2 F5.
☎ (215) 735-8485.

Sisters
Map 3 B3.
☎ (215) 735-0735.

COMEDY CLUBS

Laff House
221 South St. **Map** 4 E5.
☎ (215) 440-4242.

Rascals
2349 W Marlton Pike,
Cherry Hill, NJ.
☎ (856) 662-9200.

Outdoor Activities and Sports

WHETHER YOU ARE AN active participant or simply a spectator, there is no shortage of sporting activities in Philadelphia all year round. In the warmer months, the region's many recreational areas and parks are packed with hikers, bicyclists, joggers, and golfers. In the winter months, outdoor enthusiasts opt for ice-skating or head for the nearby ski slopes in the Pocono Mountains. Local sports fans are passionate about their many professional home teams that play throughout the year. They flock to the city's stadiums and arenas to watch baseball, football, basketball, and hockey. The area's colleges and universities compete in the above sports and others such as volleyball, swimming, and gymnastics.

Inline skater

BICYCLING, JOGGING, AND SKATING

PHILADELPHIA HAS an extensive greenbelt running through it with miles of walking and biking trails, most of which are found in Fairmount Park (*see p95*). On warmer days, hundreds of enthusiasts take to the city's most popular trail, the 8.4-mile (13.5-km) paved inline skating, walking, and biking path that runs parallel to Kelly and West River Drives (*see p96*) along both sides of the Schuylkill River. **Drive Sports** rents out bicycles, inline skates, and running equipment along the

path on Boathouse Row. The **Bicycle Club of Philadelphia** has information about the various bike paths within the area, and schedules bike rides each weekend for cyclists of all experience levels.

Other popular hiking and biking trails can be found along Wissahickon Gorge in Fairmount Park. There are also 6 miles (9.6 km) of trails within **Valley Forge National Historic Park** (*see p129*). Valley Forge is a starting point for the 22-mile (35-km) bike path ending in Fairmount Park. The path runs on a former railroad track route along the Schuylkill River.

GOLF AND TENNIS

THE PHILADELPHIA area has numerous 18-hole golf courses that challenge players at all levels. Courses situated in the city include the **Cobbs Creek Golf Club** and the **Walnut Lane Golf Club**, located within Wissahickon Valley Park. The **Valley Forge Golf Club** is near the rolling hills of the suburban National Historic Park, while the **Tattersall Golf Club** sits in scenic West Chester countryside.

Public tennis courts in many parks are free on a first-come, first-served basis. Local tennis clubs that charge a fee include **Friends of Chamounix Tennis** in Fairmount Park and **Riverside Indoor Tennis** in nearby Bala Cynwyd.

WINTER ACTIVITIES

AS CHRISTMAS approaches, many outdoor enthusiasts bundle up and trade their inline blades for ice skates. Philadelphia and its surrounding areas have several ice-skating rinks, but the most popular is the **Blue Cross RiverRink** at Penn's Landing, where skaters enjoy an Olympic-sized rink with views of the Ben Franklin Bridge and the Delaware River.

Skiers head to the Pocono Mountains. This usually involves a day trip, and most ski slopes are within a two-hour drive. The **Pocono Mountains Vacation Bureau, Inc.** has information about ski slopes and snow conditions.

PROFESSIONAL SPECTATOR SPORTS

SOUTH PHILADELPHIA'S modern stadiums are the venue for most professional sports competitions held in the city. The **Philadelphia Phillies** play throughout the summer season at the new Citizens Bank Park. Opened in 2004, the 43,000-seat stadium is one of the most fan-friendly ballparks to host major league baseball games. Rough-and-tumble football action kicks off in August as the

Paved walking and biking path in Fairmount Park

Philadelphia Eagles start their season with games at Lincoln Financial Field, a 68,000-seat stadium.

During the cold winter months, sports fans head back indoors to watch basketball played by the **Philadelphia 76ers** at the Wachovia Center, which seats 21,000. Hockey fans flock to the Wachovia Center as well for spirited games on ice with the **Philadelphia Flyers**. The area's minor league baseball team, the **Camden Riversharks**, plays ball at Campbell's Field at the Camden Waterfront. Other popular home teams play soccer and lacrosse.

For horse racing fans, the **Philadelphia Park Racetrack** has live thoroughbred racing all year round every Saturday through Tuesday. The racetrack is home to the GII Pennsylvania Derby on Labor Day.

Camden Riversharks in baseball action at Campbell's Field

COLLEGE SPORTS

O
VER A dozen colleges and universities in the Philadelphia area take part in intercollegiate sports programs and competitions, a tradition that dates back more than 200 years. Some of the nation's best college basketball is played by what is called the Big Five – **St. Joseph's**
University, University of Pennsylvania, Temple University, Villanova University, and LaSalle University. Schools in the area have both men's and women's activities in a full range of other sports, and competitions in football, soccer, field hockey, volleyball, swimming, gymnastics, and more are held regularly.

DIRECTORY

BICYCLING, JOGGING, AND SKATING

Bicycle Club of Philadelphia
[(215) 735-2453.

Drive Sports
2601 Pennsylvania Ave.
Map 1 C1.
[(215) 232-7368.
W www.drivesports.com

Valley Forge National Historic Park
Rt 23 & N Gulph Rd.
[(610) 783-1077.
W www.nps.gov/vafo

GOLF AND TENNIS

Cobbs Creek Golf Club
72nd & Lansdowne Aves.
[(215) 877-8707.

Friends of Chamounix Tennis
Chamounix Dr,
Fairmount Park.
[(215) 877-6845.

Riverside Indoor Tennis
600 Righters Ferry Rd,
Bala Cynwyd, PA.
[(610) 664-6475.

Tattersall Golf Club
1520 Tattersall Way, West Chester, PA.
[(610) 738-4410.

Valley Forge Golf Club
401 N Gulph Rd.
[(610) 337-1776.

Walnut Lane Golf Club
800 Walnut Lane.
[(215) 482-3370.

WINTER ACTIVITIES

Blue Cross RiverRink
Penn's Landing. **Map** 4 F3.
[(215) 925-7465.
W www.riverrink.com

Pocono Mountains Vacation Bureau, Inc.
1004 Main St,
Stroudsburg, PA 18360.
[(800) 762-6667.

PROFESSIONAL SPECTATOR SPORTS

Camden Riversharks
Campbell's Field, Camden.
[(856) 963-2600.
W www.riversharks.com

Philadelphia 76ers
Wachovia Center.
[(215) 339-7600.
W www.nba.com/sixers

Philadelphia Eagles
Lincoln Financial Field.
[(267) 570-4510.
W www.philadelphiaeagles.com

Philadelphia Flyers
Wachovia Center.
[(215) 465-4500.
W www.philadelphiaflyers.com

Philadelphia Park Racetrack
3001 Street Rd,
Bensalem.
[(215) 639-9000,
(800) 523-6886.
W www.philadelphiapark.com

Philadelphia Phillies
Citizens Bank Park.
[(215) 463-1000.
W www.phillies.com

COLLEGE SPORTS

LaSalle University
1900 W Olney Ave.
[(215) 951-1999.
W www.lasalle.edu

St. Joseph's University
5600 City Ave.
[(610) 660-1712.
W www.sju.edu

Temple University
801 N Broad St. **Map** 2 F1.
[(215) 204-8499.
W www.temple.edu

University of Pennsylvania
3451 Walnut St.
Map 1 A4.
[(215) 898-6151.
W www.upenn.edu

Villanova University
[(610) 519-4500.
W www.villanova.edu

CHILDREN'S PHILADELPHIA

Parents will find a plethora of activities that will keep their children amused when in Philadelphia and the surrounding area. Museums, such as the Franklin Institute and the Academy of Natural Sciences, thrill kids with hands-on exhibits and workshops, while the Adventure Aquarium and the

Actor dressed as a colonial figure

Philadelphia Zoo entertain with an array of sea creatures and animals. Educational tours can be taken at historic buildings, where actors dress up as colonial figures and perform skits. In the Dutch Country, kids can enjoy Amish-style buggy rides and more at the Dutch Wonderland Family Amusement Park in Lancaster.

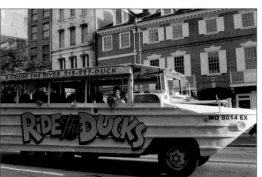
Ride the Ducks pleasure craft going around Philadelphia

HISTORIC SIGHTS AND TOURS

Tour guides at key historic buildings provide informative tours to young and old alike; however, some sights will interest children more than others. The **National Constitution Center** *(see pp48–9)* features interactive exhibits explaining the US Constitution, where children, for example, might try on a judge's robe at a replica of the Supreme Court bench, or cast their ballot for their all-time favorite president. Many tours

Historic Lights of Liberty show at Independence Hall

cater to families, such as the popular **Ride the Ducks** *(see p175)*. Using amphibious vehicles, the tour whisks visitors through Old City and Society Hill and Penn's Landing before taking a dip in the Delaware River for an exhilarating cruise. Children and parents show their enthusiasm by raucously blowing colorful "duck whistles."

Kids also enjoy the multimedia **Lights of Liberty Show** *(see p175)*, a brisk walking tour through Old Town at dusk. Participants don headphones and watch images – which tell the story of the American Revolution – projected on historic buildings. For younger children, ask for a special version for ages six to 12.

MUSEUMS

Philadelphia's premier museum for children is the **Please Touch Museum**. Designed for kids aged seven

and younger, it has several exhibits that enhance a child's ability to learn discovery and play. For instance, the Alice's Adventures in Wonderland exhibit is based on the popular classic story and includes many settings from the book to encourage problem solving and language skills. The SuperMarket has checkouts, shopping carts, and toy food items, while Barnyard Babies teaches about life on a farm. Other activities include interactive theater performances with musicians, dancers, and storytellers.

The **Franklin Institute Science Museum** *(see p85)* has hands-on exhibits, with some such as Electricity Hall reflecting Benjamin Franklin's inventions. Children learn about the human heart and bioscience at the Giant Walk-Through Heart. Other exhibits include the Train Factory, which has an actual 350-ton (770,000-lb) locomotive, and the Franklin Air Show, which has a flight simulator. The Fels Planetarium features virtual tours through space. At the **Academy of Natural Sciences** *(see p85)*, children can see the fossils of a Tyrannosaurus rex and other species in Dinosaur Hall. Youngsters can also check out the Live Animal Center, which houses over 100 animals, and live butterflies stored in a tropical rainforest habitat that has been replicated at the museum. In addition to

Banner at the Academy of Natural Sciences

model boats and deep-sea diving apparatus, kids enjoy squeezing through the small hatches and passageways of the submarine *Becuna* at the **Independence Seaport Museum** *(see pp64–5)*. Boys, in particular, enjoy the old fire engines and pumpers at **Fireman's Hall** *(see p51)*. At the **Fairmount Water Works and Interpretive Center** *(see p86)*, interactive exhibits challenge children to learn about city water resources. The center also has a virtual helicopter tour of the watershed.

The **National Liberty Museum** *(see p53)* takes a more serious approach to entertaining children by helping combat violence and bigotry through interactive exhibits, glass artworks, and more. One display is Kids Vote, which asks youngsters to take a stand on such issues as handgun law and the death penalty. Another exhibit, Jellybean People, features two life-sized models made of multicolored jelly-beans to show that people are the same inside, regardless of skin color.

For children with an artistic flair, the **Philadelphia Museum of Art** *(see pp88–91)* offers drawing classes and gallery tours on Sundays. The **Pennsylvania Academy of the Fine Arts** *(see pp74–5)* has workshops on most Saturday mornings.

Beyond Philadelphia, in the Pennsylvania Dutch Country, Strasburg offers kids train

Philadelphia Zoo, home to many animal species

displays, a train museum, and rides on the **Strasburg Railroad** *(see p119)*. In Hershey, children will love the simulated chocolate factory at **Chocolate World** *(see p124)*, and the roller coaster rides and attractions at Hershey Park.

GARDENS, ZOOS, AND WATERFRONT ACTIVITIES

An INSTANT HIT with children is the **Philadelphia Zoo** *(see p96)*. While close-up views of wild animals such as lions and rare white tigers at the Carnivora House are a big draw, kids also enjoy the Tastykake Children's Zoo, where they can pet docile sheep, rabbits, and newly hatched chicks.

Tarantulas at the Insectarium

At the **Philadelphia Insectarium**, youngsters can safely observe the workings of a beehive from behind a glass partition, touch the likes of tarantulas and giant

beetles, and see thousands of other live and mounted insects. Kids can also play in a man-made spider web. The **Adventure Aquarium** at the Camden Waterfront *(see p101)* has a huge tank with hundreds of aquatic species, including sharks, sea turtles, and more than 1,000 kinds of fish. Kids can touch harmless species in the Touch-a-Shark exhibit and see seals frolic in outdoor pools. Also at the waterfront, the **Camden Children's Garden** is an interactive park with different areas, including the Butterfly Garden, Railroad Garden, Dinosaur Garden, and the Storybook Gardens. The latter has themes from classic children's books such as Frances Hodgson Burnett's *The Secret Garden* and Lewis Carroll's *Alice in Wonderland*.

DIRECTORY

MUSEUMS

Please Touch Museum
210 North 21st Street. **Map** 2 D3.
☎ *(215) 963-0667*.
W www.pleasetouchmuseum.org

GARDENS, ZOOS, AND WATERFRONT ACTIVITIES

Adventure Aquarium
1 Riverside Dr, Camden, NJ.
☎ *(856) 365-0352*.
W www.adventurequarium.com

Camden Children's Garden
3 Riverside Drive, Camden, NJ.
☎ *(856) 365-8733*.
W www.camdenchildrensgarden.org

Philadelphia Insectarium
8046 Frankford Ave.
☎ *(215) 338-3000*.
W www.insectarium.com

Interactive exhibits inside Fairmount Waterworks

SURVIVAL
GUIDE

PRACTICAL INFORMATION 174–181
TRAVEL INFORMATION 182–189
PHILADELPHIA STREET FINDER 190–197

PRACTICAL INFORMATION

PHILADELPHIA THRIVES ON tourism thanks to its rich colonial history and culture, and its world-class museums and restaurants. Efficient infrastructure – such as clearly marked signs, a state-of-the-art visitor center, and a well-planned city transit system – has been created by the city authorities and the National Park Service to give visitors a memorable holiday. Although an abundance of

Independence Visitor Center sign

local operators provide tours and sightseeing packages, most of Philadelphia's central neighborhoods can be easily explored on foot. Most areas in the city are safe, but visitors should always take sensible precautions as they would in any major city. The following pages include tips on a wide range of practical matters to help ensure a trouble-free stay in Philadelphia and its surrounding areas.

Tour guide in colonial attire leads tourists in Old City

VISITOR INFORMATION

THE MODERN **Independence Visitor Center** (see p45) is located in the heart of Independence Mall and is within walking distance of many sights in Philadelphia's central historic core. Brochure racks are full of information and discount passes for shopping, attractions, restaurants, and hotels in the city and its surrounding areas.

The **Philadelphia Convention & Visitors Bureau** provides information for tour groups, conventions, and international visitors on their website. Staff are always at hand to answer questions and help plan sightseeing itineraries. Most hotels also provide tourism information and help with planning.

OPENING HOURS

MOST HISTORIC buildings and museums are open from 9am or 10am until 5pm. Some of the smaller colonial

houses and attractions in Independence National Historic Park have varying hours and touring schedules. For the most part, businesses and banks maintain standard 9am–5pm hours, with a few banks closing earlier or staying open later. Stores in central Philadelphia open around 10am and stay open till 6pm, with many extending hours on Wednesday evenings. Malls around the city do not close until 9pm or 9:30pm.

ETIQUETTE

SMOKING IS prohibited in most buildings and stores, except in designated areas. While smoking is usually acceptable in taverns and pubs, restaurants often have smoking sections. Check for signs before lighting up. Waiters and waitresses expect tips of a minimum of 15 percent of the bill, and up to 20 percent or

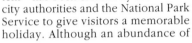

No smoking sign

more for excellent service. At the bar, $1 per drink is usually a good rule of thumb. At hotels, tip $1 per bag and at least that much for the room maid ($2 at upscale properties). Up to $10 or more would be appreciated by a helpful hotel concierge, while airport porters also expect $1 per bag. Tip $1–$2 for valet parking attendants and 10–15 percent of the fare for cab drivers.

TAXES

THE STATE SALES tax levied in Pennsylvania is 6 percent, but the city imposes an additional 1 percent, making it 7 percent in Philadelphia. However, there is no sales tax on clothing and shoes and footwear. Hotel taxes in the city are 14 percent, while car rental taxes and fees can add up to 20 percent or more.

FOREIGN VISITORS AND CUSTOMS

SECURITY measures in the US now require that visitors who plan to stay in the US for up to 90 days, and are from countries that do not need visas for entry, must have machine-readable passports. These countries include the UK, most Western European nations, Japan, New Zealand, and Australia. Canadian citizens require only proof of residence. Visitors from other countries must have valid

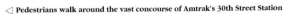

passports and visas for entry, and should check with their national passport-issuing agency for more information.

LIQUOR LAWS

THE LEGAL drinking age in Pennsylvania is 21. Young people need to show photo identification as proof of age when ordering alcohol in pubs and restaurants. Liquor and wine can be bought only at state-run stores, while beer is sold at special distribution centers or by the six-pack over-the-counter in bars.

The ISIC card provides a range of student discounts

STUDENTS AND SENIORS

THE PHILADELPHIA AREA has numerous colleges and universities, so an International Student Identification Card (ISIC) or Student Advantage Card for American students are recommended and are widely accepted to receive discounts. Senior citizens also receive wide-ranging discounts, including reduced movie prices and admission to many events and attractions.

DISABLED TRAVELERS

MOST CITY BUILDINGS and sidewalks accommodate disabled persons as required by US law, but some historic colonial structures do not have the required provisions. Two companies, **SEPTA CCT** and **ADA Paratransit**, offer transportation for the disabled with lift-equipped vehicles. The **Mayor's Commission on People with Disabilities** provides information for disabled visitors to Philadelphia.

ELECTRICITY

ELECTRICITY IN THE US is discharged at 110–120 volts using a standard two flat-pronged plug. Adapters may be needed for 220-volt appliances with different plugs, but keep in mind that most hotel rooms have hair dryers, irons, and dedicated sockets for electric shavers.

GUIDED TOURS

MOST CITY TOURS, ranging from walking tours to horse-drawn carriage tours, are centered around the historic Independence Mall district. The **Big Bus Company** offers tours on double-decker, open-roof buses with unlimited hop-ons and hop-offs at the 20 sights included in its loop. **Walk Philadelphia** has more than

Historic Lights of Liberty Show at Independence Hall

40 walking tours covering different neighborhoods. The popular **Ride the Ducks** is a driving tour in an amphibious vehicle that finally takes a dip in the Delaware River for a cruise near Penn's Landing, with passengers blowing loud "duck whistles". **Ghost Tours of Philadelphia** includes a candlelit walk with haunting tales through Old City and Society Hill. The **Lights of Liberty Show** is a nighttime walking tour through Old City, with participants wearing headsets and watching projections on historic buildings that tell the story of America's struggle for independence.

Personal Security and Health

Philadelphia police insignia

FOR THE MOST part, central Philadelphia is generally safe and the majority of visitors touring the sights do not have any problems with crime. Nonetheless, like in any big American city, taking common sense precautions will ensure a trouble-free visit. Although major crime is rare in high-density tourist areas, it is advisable to always be aware of your surroundings. Public transportation and walking much of the central area is usually safe during the day, but visitors should opt for a taxi at night or for staying in prominent nightlife areas such as those in Old City, Center City, and Society Hill and Penn's Landing.

Philadelphia police officers on bicycles

LAW ENFORCEMENT

WITH INCREASED security in recent years, there is often a heavy, 24-hour presence of police and National Park Service rangers around key sights at Independence Mall. The Philadelphia Police Department provides round-the-clock car patrols as well as bicycle, horseback, and foot patrols. Traffic and parking enforcement officers also make rounds on foot. Most are friendly when approached, but visitors should not take them to be tour guides. Instead, park rangers are usually helpful with answering questions about city sights and attractions.

PERSONAL SAFETY GUIDELINES

MOST MAJOR crimes in Philadelphia occur in particular neighborhoods to the north and west of Center City, so plan on avoiding those areas unless you are familiar with them or visiting friends and family. In safe areas, it is still wise to watch out for petty criminals such as purse-snatchers and pickpockets. When possible, stay in heavily frequented tourist spots that have park rangers and regular police patrols, and avoid wandering into deserted streets and dark alleys. Parks are best avoided at night.

Do not leave personal items such as purses or handbags unattended, and do not carry lots of cash or wear excessive jewelry. A good idea is to carry only one credit card and enough cash for the day's activities. Other credit cards, traveler's checks, cash, and your passport should be securely locked in the hotel room safe or a safe deposit box. Passports should be carried only when exchanging currency or traveler's checks. Remember to keep the passport separate from your money or wallet. Another option is to carry valuables in a money belt or in a secure inside pocket. In addition, it is wise to make copies of your passport and keep a record of your credit card numbers in case of theft.

Visitors should try and avoid looking like tourists as they are often targets of petty crime. Carry cameras and camcorders securely and close to your body, obscuring them when possible, and study maps and itineraries beforehand to avoid being approached by criminals looking for an opportunity. Avoid making eye contact with the homeless, as some may be aggressive and will insist on a cash handout.

MEDICAL CONCERNS AND PHARMACIES

Hospital sign

PHILADELPHIA HAS excellent medical facilities should you become ill during your visit. As in any metropolis in the world, there are a number of walk-in clinics that will treat minor ailments, while all main hospitals in the city offer accident and emergency care.

Visitors should be advised, however, that medical care can be expensive. Even if carrying medical insurance, you may still have to pay upfront and claim reimbursement from your insurance company later, so do not forget to ask for all necessary forms and receipts. Most medical facilities in the city accept credit cards.

A 24-hour CVS pharmacy in a Philadelphia neighborhood

Police car

Police SUV

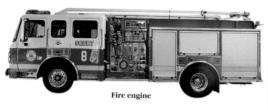

Fire engine

Pack enough prescription drugs, and it is advisable to keep two sets of the same medicines in different travel bags, in the unlikely event that one is lost or stolen.

Central Philadelphia as well as areas in the outer reaches of the city have several 24-hour pharmacies, if needed. Visitors can ask hotel personnel to pinpoint the one nearest to them.

EMERGENCIES

As IN OTHER parts of the United States, call 911 to report life-or-death emergency situations or matters requiring an immediate response from medical, police or fire department personnel. Most hospital emergency rooms in and around the city are open 24 hours a day, seven days a week and take walk-in patients or those delivered by ambulance. Hotel personnel can help you locate the nearest one, or arrange a doctor's appointment for non-life threatening medical conditions. The city also has a number of separate agencies assisting in dental emergencies and accidental poisonings. It is best to ask your hotel staff for assistance.

TRAVEL INSURANCE

Purchasing travel insurance is strongly urged when visiting the US, mostly because of the high cost of medical care. Packages should include medical and dental coverage, along with other options such as trip cancellation, flight delay, lost or stolen baggage, and even death and dismemberment insurance. Visitors should check the details with a travel agency or travel insurance provider in their home countries.

LOST PROPERTY

If YOUR PROPERTY is lost or stolen, bear in mind that chances of recovery are slim. Nonetheless, contact local police through the non-emergency line to file a report and keep a copy of the same for insurance purposes. At times, it is helpful to contact the Lost and Found Department in department stores or airports. Similarly, visitors can try contacting a taxi company or public transit system in the event missing items turn up when in transit.

Call your credit card company to report a lost or stolen credit card, and contact your currency exchange provider for lost traveler's checks. If your passport is lost or stolen, contact your country's consulate or embassy immediately.

DIRECTORY

CRISIS PHONE NUMBERS

All Emergencies
911 for police, fire, and emergency medical attention.

Accidental Poisoning
(215) 386-2100, (800) 222-1222 (outside Philadelphia).

Airport Medical Emergencies
(215) 937-3111.

Dental Emergencies
(215) 925-6050.

Finding a Doctor (Non-emergency)
(215) 563-5343.

Philadelphia Police (Non-emergency)
(215) 686-3103.

Special Assistance (Relay Services)
(800) 654-5984.

US Customs
(215) 596-1972.

24-HOUR PHARMACIES

CVS
1826 Chestnut St. **Map** 2 D4.
(215) 972-0909.

Rite Aid
2301 Walnut St. **Map** 1 C4.
(215) 636-9634.
5040 City Line Ave.
(215) 877-2116.

LOST OR STOLEN CREDIT CARDS

American Express
(800) 528-4800.

MasterCard
(800) 307-7309.

Visa
(800) 847-2911.

Banking and Currency

THERE IS NO shortage of prominent banks in Philadelphia, and most banks' headquarters and some branches are located in Center City. Cash can be easily withdrawn through the numerous automated teller machines (ATMs) placed throughout the city. Foreign notes can be exchanged for American dollars in hotels and at currency exchange offices. However, be advised that most currency exchange offices and banks are closed on Sundays, and it is prudent not to carry all your money and credit cards on you at the same time.

Façade of PNC Bank in Philadelphia

BANKS

MOST PHILADELPHIA banks are open on weekdays from 9am until 5pm. However, some bank branches have varying hours – a few close earlier than 5pm, while others remain open later on Fridays. Most banks also open on Saturdays from 9am until noon. An exception is the New Jersey-based **Commerce Bank**, with branches in Philadelphia, that has lobby hours seven days a week, and extended hours on some days. Other prominent area banks include **PNC Bank** and **Wachovia Bank**.

ATMs

CASH IS easily accessible through the numerous ATMs in the Philadelphia area. They are found at bank entrances, in office complexes, at shopping malls, grocery stores and restaurants, and even in convenience stores. Cash is distributed in $10 and $20 bills, and can be withdrawn with an ATM card or credit card, including VISA or **MasterCard**.

ATMs often charge a fee for withdrawals by non-bank members, while the user's bank might also charge a fee. Check with your bank which transaction fees apply. Use ATMs during the day when more people are nearby to avoid being robbed.

CREDIT CARDS

MAJOR CREDIT cards are accepted at most locations throughout the area. Visa, MasterCard, American Express, Discover Card, and Diners Club are the most prominent and are accepted in restaurants, stores, kiosks at malls, and even some fast food restaurants. It is essential to have a credit card to rent a car, and most hotels ask for a credit card number to make a room reservation.

Besides being safer than carrying lots of cash, some credit cards also offer insurance benefits on retail goods while providing reward points or airline miles. For travelers, credit cards are essential in the event of a medical emergency, as they are honored as payment at most US hospitals.

Automated Teller Machines (ATM) dispense cash and accept deposits

CURRENCY EXCHANGE

UNLIKE EUROPEAN countries, there are few currency exchange stands in America and they are not always easily accessible. Also, the commissions charged can be high. Banks and hotels do accept foreign currency, but it is advisable to first check the fees, which are often higher at hotels. Currency exchanges in Philadelphia are located in Center City, and are usually open from 9am to 5pm. They include the **American Express Travel Services Office** and Thomas Cook Currency Services, which also has kiosks at the airport. It is a good idea to bring in $100 when entering the US in case exchange services are not readily available.

CASHING TRAVELER'S CHECKS

MOST RESTAURANTS, shops, and hotels accept traveler's checks in US dollars as payment without charging a fee. These can also be cashed at local banks, though proper identification is required in the form of a passport, driver's license or student identification card to do so.

Checks in foreign currency can be cashed at a bank branch offering foreign currency exchange, usually at the bank's main locations. Personal checks in foreign currency are rarely accepted in the US.

Coins

American coins (actual size shown) come in 1-, 5-, 10- and 25-cent, as well as $1 denominations; 50-cent pieces are minted but rarely used. Each coin has its own name: 1-cent coins are known as pennies; 5-cent coins as nickels; 10-cent coins as dimes; and 1-dollar coins (and bills) are sometimes called "bucks."

**25-cent coin
(a quarter)**

**10-cent coin
(a dime)**

**5-cent coin
(a nickel)**

**1-cent coin
(a penny)**

Bank Notes

The units of currency in the US are dollars and cents, with 100-cents to the dollar. Notes, or "bills," come in $1, $5, $10, $20, $50, and $100 denominations. There is also a $2 bill, but it is rarely used and is more of a collector's item. In recent years, new versions of the $5 bill and higher denominations have been produced to thwart counterfeiters. The new bills have slight variations of color, and portraits of the presidents and other notable figures in US history are larger and positioned off center.

1-dollar bill ($1)

5-dollar bill ($5)

10-dollar bill ($10)

20-dollar bill ($20)

50-dollar bill ($50)

100-dollar bill ($100)

Communications and Media

A colorful US postage stamp

PHILADELPHIA HAS A wide spectrum of the latest communications systems. Card- or coin-operated pay phones abound in hotels, malls, restaurants, and on many street corners. The US Postal Service is reliable and efficient, with regular pickups at mailboxes placed throughout the city. Media outlets include numerous local television and radio stations, as well as two major daily newspapers. Internet, e-mail, and fax services are readily available, and cell phone signals are strong throughout the city.

PAY TELEPHONES

THE MAIN LOCAL telephone companies providing phone services throughout the greater Philadelphia area are Verizon and AT&T. Numerous coin-operated and credit card pay phones are located in hotel and office lobbies, shopping areas and malls, restaurants, gas stations, bars, and along city streets.

Local calls usually require only a few coins, but prices can vary for calls outside the local area and abroad as different telephone companies set their own rates. It is best to check with an operator first, but note that operator-assisted calls are usually more costly than calling direct. Make sure you have lots of dimes, nickels, and quarters when using a coin-operated phone.

For more information about calling in Philadelphia, check the local *Yellow Pages* directory, which also lists country codes for international calls.

CELL PHONES

SEVERAL COMPANIES provide cell phone services in Philadelphia, such as Sprint, Verizon, AT&T, and Nextel, among others. Signals are strong throughout the region, but can drop off in heavily wooded areas and in valleys that run through some of the densely-forested suburbs. American cell services are often not compatible with those in other countries other than Canada and Mexico, so check with your own carrier if you plan on using one. Cell phones can be rented locally through **AllCell Rental** in Center City.

USING A COIN-OPERATED PHONE

1 Lift the receiver and listen for the dial tone.

3 Dial or press the number.

Coins
Make sure you have the correct coins before you dial.

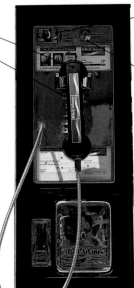

5 cents

10 cents

25 cents

2 Insert the necessary coin or coins. The coin drops as soon as you insert it.

4 If you do not want to complete your call or it does not get through, retrieve the coin(s) by pressing the coin return.

5 If the call is answered and you talk longer than the allotted three minutes, the operator will interrupt and ask you to deposit more coins. Pay phones do not give change.

USEFUL DIALING CODES

- Area code for central Philadelphia is **215**, which is also used in areas north of the city along with **267** and **445**. Western suburbs and surrounding areas use **610**, **484**, and **835**. The area code for the Pennsylvania Dutch Country and Gettysburg is **717**.
- For calls outside the local area but within the US and Canada, dial **1** followed by the area code and phone number.
- For local operator assistance, dial **0**.
- For local directory inquiries, dial **411**. Directory assistance for toll-free numbers is **1–800–555–1212**, and **411** for other numbers.
- For emergency police, fire, or ambulance services, dial **911**.
- **1–800** indicates a toll-free number, as do numbers with the area codes **888**, **877**, and **866**.
- For international direct-dial calls, dial **011** followed by the country code, city or area code, and number.
- To make an international call via the operator, dial **01** and then follow the same procedure as detailed above.
- For international directory inquiries, dial **00**.

INTERNET, E-MAIL AND FAXES

INTERNET ACCESS is available to visitors throughout the city at Internet cafés, public libraries, and at some office-supply and photocopy centers such as FedEx Kinko's, which may also have fax services. Philadelphia is a destination for a large number of business travelers, and many of the larger hotels have business centers for guests to check their e-mails or to send and receive faxes. These business center services are usually charged by the minute or by 15-minute blocks, which can add up quickly. It is therefore a good idea to check the business facilities offered by a hotel before making reservations. Library Internet services are often free but may have time limits.

POSTAL SERVICES

POST OFFICES ARE located throughout the city, catering to separate neighborhoods. Philadelphia's **Main Post Office** is at Market and 30th Streets, directly across from the 30th Street Station, and has window service 18 hours a day, seven days a week. All other area post offices, including those outside the city, are open from 9am to 5pm Monday through Friday, with most also open on Saturday from 9am to noon. Post offices in the US are closed on Sundays and on all federal holidays.

Letters and parcels that weigh under 16 ounces require only stamps and can be mailed in standard blue mailboxes on street corners, or in letter slots in all hotels and office buildings. Many hotels sell stamps and will mail letters for their guests. Larger packages often require a trip to a post office to ensure proper postage and prompt delivery. The US Postal Service offers different delivery services including standard first-class mail for most letters, Priority Mail for guaranteed delivery in two to three days, and Express Mail for overnight deliveries on business days. Courier companies offer both domestic and international delivery services. **FedEx** and **DHL** offer a variety of overnight letter and parcel services, while **UPS** delivers large boxes and packages. Letters or packages must be inserted into proper courier envelops or boxes and the paperwork should be filled out accurately. Smaller parcels can be deposited in the many courier mailboxes scattered around town for pickup at the end of the business day. Alternatively, the courier can be asked to pick up the parcel.

Standard blue mailbox, found on most streets

TV AND RADIO

PHILADELPHIA'S television stations represent the major US broadcast networks. They include CBS on channel 3, ABC on channel 6, NBC on channel 10, PBS on channel 12, WB on channel 17, FOX on channel 29, and UPN on channel 57. Cable companies carry a host of popular sports, news, and entertainment and movie networks, such as ESPN, HBO, and CNN. Radio stations, on both the AM and FM frequencies, include a variety of music, talk, and news shows. The city's most popular 24-hour news and talk radio programming can be heard on KYW 1060(Hz) AM.

NEWSPAPERS

THE CITY HAS two major daily newspapers, the *Philadelphia Inquirer* (see p162) and the *Philadelphia Daily News*, both of which provide a gamut of information. Other news and current affairs publications include the *Philadelphia Tribune* that caters to and targets the African-American community, and the *Philadelphia Business Journal* that covers financial stories. For those interested in entertainment and political news, refer to the *Philadelphia City Paper* and the *Philadelphia Weekly*.

DIRECTORY

POST OFFICES

Center City
1234 Market St. **Map** 2 F4.

Main Post Office
2970 Market St. **Map** 1 B4.
◯ *6am–midnight.*
📞 *(800) 275-8777,*
(215) 895-8980.

Old City
316 Market St. **Map** 4 E3.

OVERNIGHT COURIERS

DHL
📞 *(800) 225-5345.*

FedEx
📞 *(800) 463-3339.*

UPS
📞 *(800) 742-5877.*

CELL PHONE RENTAL

AllCell Rental
1528 Walnut St, Suite 1904.
Map 2 E5.
📞 *(215) 985-2355.*

Selection of local Philadelphia newspapers at a newsstand

GETTING TO PHILADELPHIA

WHETHER TRAVELING from within or outside the country, Philadelphia is easily accessible by air, train, bus, and car. The city is served by Philadelphia International Airport. Amtrak's 30th Street Station is a busy rail hub on the Northeast Corridor line that runs between Washington DC and Boston. The station is also a

US Airways plane

stop for trains arriving from other regions of the country. A number of interstate highways, which crisscross most of the Philadelphia metropolitan area, cater to motorists and long-distance bus services. The city also has a cruise ship terminal along the Delaware River, which serves as a stop on some liners' itineraries.

View of Terminal A at Philadelphia International Airport

ARRIVING BY AIR

WHILE DRIVING may be the most comfortable mode of transportation, the easiest way to get to Philadelphia is by air. The city is about five hours flying time from US destinations on the West Coast, between one to three hours from the Midwest, three to five hours from the Caribbean, and seven to ten hours from

cities in Europe. Philadelphia is a hub for **US Airways**, and is also served by airlines such as **Air Canada**, **Air France**, **British Airways**, **American Airlines**, **Continental Airlines**, and **Delta Airlines**.

PHILADELPHIA INTERNATIONAL AIRPORT

PHILADELPHIA'S only major airport, this modern facility is located 8 miles (5 km) south of Center City. Its six terminals accommodate more than 1,000 arrival and departure flights daily to and from more than 100 cities, including 30 international destinations. Services include non-stop flights to Europe, Canada, and the Caribbean, and also connecting flights to Asia.

Opened in May 2003, the International Terminal (with concourses A-West and A-East) is a four-level facility with 13 gates and 60 ticket counters for international flights. The spacious terminal also has two-dozen retail

shops and restaurants. Its Arrivals Hall welcomes foreign visitors with large inscriptions and signatures from the Declaration of Independence emblazoned on the walls. The terminal is served by US Airways' international flights as well as British Airways, **Lufthansa**, American Airlines, and others.

Terminals B and C are dominated by departures and arrivals for US Airways' domestic flights. Terminal D has Air Canada, AirTran Airways, **America West Airlines**, Continental Airlines, and **United Airlines**. Terminal E includes Air France, Delta Airlines, **Northwest Airlines**, Southwest Airlines, and Midwest Express, while Terminal F serves US Airways Express commuter flights.

The airport also features more than 100 shops, restaurants, eateries, and fast food stands scattered throughout the terminals, with more than 30 contained in the Philadelphia MarketPlace

Arrivals Hall at Philadelphia International Airport features words from the Declaration of Independence

between terminals B and C. Shops sell items ranging from sunglasses to office supplies and souvenirs. Businesses also provide other services and specialty carts that function as currency exchanges, newsstands, and airport information desks.

AIR FARES

W HEN SEARCHING for reasonable airfares, it is worth taking the time to look around. It is best to book departing flights at least 14 to 21 days in advance to get the lowest fares, and at least seven days in advance to secure a reasonably-priced ticket. However, be aware that these tickets carry penalties if you change your reservation, so ask about those before purchasing the ticket.

Checking directly with airlines and with travel agents can often land you a good fare, but it is certainly worth examining popular travel Internet sites as well, such as **Expedia Travels**, **Priceline**, and **Lowestfare.com** to name a few. These websites often sell consolidated tickets, which are also available through travel agents.

SEPTA bus, ferrying passengers to Philadelphia

Other options include ticket bookings with smaller airline carriers and flying during the off-season. Philadelphia's high season peaks in the summer months, around Thanksgiving (late November), and in the week before Christmas until after New Year. Also, keep in mind that airline tickets are priced lower when flying on Tuesdays, Wednesdays, and Thursdays.

TRANSPORT INTO THE CITY

S EPTA'S AIRPORT Rail Line, the R1 train, operates every half hour and connects all terminals with Center City and Amtrak's 30th Street Station, which has rail connections to other points in the city and beyond. The train stations for each terminal lie between the ticketing areas and the baggage claim areas, and visitors should look for the relevant signs. SEPTA buses 37 and 108 also ferry passengers into the city.

For shuttle van services, search for **Centralized Ground Transportation** counters in all baggage claim areas. Taxis are plentiful at each terminal, and they charge about $20 for a trip into the city. Rental car companies also operate at airports and most have information phones at all baggage claim areas.

DIRECTORY

AIRPORTS

Philadelphia International Airport
((215) 937-6937,
(800) 745-4283.
W www.phl.org

AIRLINE NUMBERS

Air Canada
((800) 776-3000.

Air France
((800) 237-2747.

American Airlines
((800) 433-7300.

America West Airlines
((800) 235-9292.

British Airways
((800) 247-9297.

Continental Airlines
((800) 525-0280.

Delta Airlines
((800) 451-6000.

Lufthansa
((800) 645–3880.

Northwest Airlines
((800) 225-2525.

United Airlines
((800) 241-6522.

US Airways
((800) 428-4322.

AIR FARES

Expedia Travels
W www.expedia.com

Lowestfare.com
W www.lowestfare.com

Priceline
W www.priceline.com

AIRPORT SHUTTLES

Centralized Ground Transportation
((215) 937-6958.

Philadelphia Airport Shuttle
((215) 969-1818.

AIRPORT HOTELS

Embassy Suites Philadelphia
9000 Bartram Ave.
((215) 365-4500,
(800) 362-2779
W www.embassysuites.com

Hilton Philadelphia Airport
4509 Island Ave.
((215) 365-4150,
(800) 445-8667
W www.hilton.com

Philadelphia Airport Marriott
Arrivals Rd.
((215) 482-9000,
(800) 682-4087.
W www.marriott.com

Philadelphia Fairfield Inn
8800 Bartram Ave.
((215) 365-2254.

Renaissance Philadelphia Hotel Airport
500 Stevens Dr.
((610) 521-5900,
(800) 468-3571.

Philadelphia's 30th Street Station on Amtrak's Northeast Corridor, the second busiest of the Amtrak system

ARRIVING BY TRAIN

Philadelphia is served by Amtrak, the country's passenger rail service, which links the city to the entire nation and to Canada. Most trains serving the city operate along the Northeast Corridor from Boston to Washington DC, with stops in Baltimore, New York and a number of locations in New Jersey, Delaware, Connecticut, and Rhode Island. Amtrak's lines also provide express services such as the premium, high-speed Metroliner Service and the Acela Express.

Tickets can be booked online or by calling Amtrak. When booking, it is best to reserve well in advance and be as flexible as possible to ensure good seating and prices. Note that certain discounts may apply, including those for students and senior citizens. If reserved in advance, tickets can be picked up on the day of travel at either the Amtrak service window or through kiosks at stations. Due to increased security measures, passengers from the US, Canada, and Mexico require photo identification, which may be a driver's license or passport, while other foreign visitors need a passport.

Passenger cars are comfortable and have snack bar services as well as dining cars on longer routes. Seats in coach class for most routes are reserved, but they can be unreserved for shorter trips. Quarters for sleeping are considered first class and are available on trains with longer routes, and some of the first class sleeping accommodations have showers and toilets in the compartment.

Philadelphia's main train hub is Amtrak's 30th Street Station – an impressive Beaux-Arts building with a columned front façade and large atrium. Inside are ticket booths to both Amtrak and SEPTA regional rail lines, restaurants, fast food eateries, gift shops, and newsstands. "Red cap" porters are available to help with luggage. Taxis are also plentiful outside, and if you are carrying baggage, they are recommended for the short hop to a central Philadelphia hotel.

ARRIVING BY CAR

Several major roadways and interstate highways lead to Philadelphia from surrounding states and major cities in the northeast. Driving times to Philadelphia from some of these cities are as follows: six hours from Boston, two hours from Baltimore and New York, and three hours from Washington.

The major north-south highway is I-95, which leads into the city center as it parallels the Delaware River. From the east, motorists driving on the New Jersey Turnpike should take Exit 4 and then follow signs to the Ben Franklin Bridge into Philadelphia. An alternative from the New Jersey Turnpike is taking Exit 6 to connect with the Pennsylvania Turnpike that runs north of the city. This turnpike is the major highway leading into Philadelphia from the west. Take the Valley Forge exit and then proceed east on I-76, the Schuylkill Expressway. It is recommended that visitors carry a road atlas map and a city street map for all trips by car.

An Amtrak train – backbone of America's passenger rail system

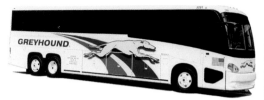

Greyhound buses, such as these, serve destinations across America

ARRIVING BY BUS

SERVING ALL REGIONS of the United States, **Greyhound Lines** has a bus terminal in Center City, between 10th and 11th Streets on Filbert Street, just one block north of Market Street. The terminal handles arrivals daily, including buses from New England, New York, and points south and southwest of Philadelphia and transcontinental buses on routes through St. Louis and Chicago. Stops in the city include Amtrak's 30th Street Station, and in north and south Philadelphia.

In comparison to other modes of transportation such as taking a train or a flight, Greyhound's fares are the most economical. The company offers wide-ranging fare reductions, including discounts for students, senior citizens, children, military personnel, and veterans, as well as cheaper fares if tickets are purchased online. While advance purchases might save you money, walk-up tickets are available at reasonable costs.

Greyhound's buses are modern and efficient. Much of its fleet is either equipped with lifts or has other equipment to accommodate those passengers that have disabilities or need help. Under certain conditions, personal care attendants may ride with disabled passengers at a reduced rate. For more information, visitors should call the **Greyhound Customers with Disabilities Travel Assistance Line** at least 48 hours before departure.

CRUISE SHIP TERMINAL

LOCATED IN THE former Philadelphia Navy Yard, the city's cruise ship berth along the Delaware River is the **Philadelphia Cruise Terminal at Pier 1**. Visitors entering the city this way have access to major tourist sights in central Philadelphia through either their cruise line's shuttle service or public transportation. SEPTA bus 17 from Broad and Flagship Streets, one block north of Pier 1, takes about 30 minutes

to reach the Independence Visitor Center and Independence Mall. Among other services, Pier 1 also has ATM machines and cafés nearby. Cruise lines making port calls or departing from the city include Norwegian Cruise Line, Celebrity Cruises, Holland America Line, Radisson Seven Seas Cruises, and Silversea Cruises.

DIRECTORY

TRAIN SERVICES

Amtrak
(800) 872-7245.
www.amtrak.com

LONG-DISTANCE BUS SERVICES

Greyhound Customers with Disabilities Travel Assistance Line
(800) 752-4841.

Greyhound Lines
(800) 231-2222.
www.greyhound.com

Greyhound Lines (Purchase Tickets)
(800) 229-9424.

Greyhound Bus Terminal
1001 Filbert St. Map 3 C2.
(215) 931-4075.

STATE INTERSTATES & HIGHWAYS

Pennsylvania Department of Transportation
Travel information & interstate road conditions.
(888) 783-6783,
(717) 783-5186 (outside Pennsylvania).
www.dot.state.pa.us

Pennsylvania Turnpike Commission
(717) 939-9551.
www.paturnpike.com

CRUISE SHIP TERMINAL

Philadelphia Cruise Terminal at Pier 1
5100 S Broad St.
(215) 462-6790.

RiverLink Ferry sets sail across the Delaware River

Getting Around Philadelphia

Taxi sign

MOST OF PHILADELPHIA'S famous sights are on Independence Mall, also known as "America's most historic square mile." These sights, including Independence Hall and the Liberty Bell, are within walking distance of each other in Old City, and just a short walk from attractions in Society Hill and Penn's Landing. A quick ride from the historic area brings visitors to Center City and the Museum District. The inexpensive Philly Phlash bus service runs through the heart of the city during the warmer months. Buses and subways operated by the Southeastern Pennsylvania Transit Authority (SEPTA) run year-round. Taxis are also an easy and generally affordable option.

WALKING

WITHOUT A DOUBT, the best way to explore Independence Mall and other historic sights in the surrounding areas is on foot. Key sights in and around Independence Mall and Society Hill are all contained within several blocks and can take up a whole day or more of sightseeing. When traveling up to ten blocks or more, a taxi or public transportation may be the better alternative.

Although almost all city streets are flanked by sidewalks, be careful while crossing. Pedestrians should use the electronic "Walk" signs, which indicate when it is safe to proceed. These are located at many of the larger intersections. Some even have a button that pedestrians can press to activate them.

Many areas are particularly safe for walking, as they have pedestrian walkways, especially within Indepedence Mall, Old City, and Society Hill and Penn's Landing.

STREET GRID

CENTRAL PHILADELPHIA'S city grid is simple, with a crisscross of streets and five squares, as originally laid out by city founder William Penn and surveyor Thomas Holmes (see p18).

Numbered streets run north and south in an ascending westward order – starting with Front Street near the Delaware River to 30th Street just beyond the Schuylkill River. Many streets running east and west are named after trees, once again according to Penn's original city plan.

PHILLY PHLASH TOURIST BUS

THESE COLORFUL purple buses run along Market Street and the Benjamin Franklin Parkway, with round trips from Penn's Landing to the Philadelphia Museum of Art. The buses are in operation seven months a year, from May to November, with a service that runs every 12 minutes from 10am to 6pm. Rides are inexpensive and allow unlimited hop-ons and hop-offs. In most cases, children under five and seniors ride free.

PUBLIC TRANSPORTATION

THE MAIN agency for public transportation in the city is **SEPTA** (see transport map at back). Its key subway routes run through districts in central Philadelphia, making connections to regional rail lines at the Market East, Suburban, and 30th Street Stations.

The Market Frankford Line runs east and west along Market Street with stops at 2nd, 5th, 8th, 11th, 13th, 15th, and 30th Streets. The Broad Street Line runs north and south with stops at Race and Vine Streets, City Hall, Walnut and Locust Streets, and Lombard and South Streets.

SEPTA's bus 38 starts from Independence Mall and runs along Market Street and the Benjamin Franklin Parkway to the Philadelphia Museum of Art and beyond. Bus 21 travels along Chestnut and Walnut Streets from Penn's Landing to the University of Pennsylvania. Bus 42 circles neighborhoods and areas in Society Hill along Spruce Street, and then heads west along Walnut Street to the University of Pennsylvania campus, returning via Chestnut Street.

Most bus fares are $2 and exact change is usually needed. Tokens, discount passes, and day passes can be obtained at SEPTA sales offices or at the Independence Visitor Center (see p45). Visitors should call SEPTA for the locations of these sales offices.

RIVERLINK FERRY

THIS FERRY offers splendid views of the Delaware River as it runs between Penn's Landing and the Camden Waterfront from April through mid-November. **RiverLink Ferry** is the ideal mode of transportation to get to the Adventure Aquarium and the battleship *New Jersey*.

SEPTA bus system, covering the entire city

The RiverLink Ferry at Penn's Landing

The ferry departs every 40 minutes from both Camden and Philadelphia, and visitors can purchase tickets at dockside terminals outside the Independence Seaport Museum for the outbound trip from Philadelphia.

BICYCLES

ONLY A FEW streets in central Philadelphia are bicycle-friendly. For example, a designated cycle path runs along the Benjamin Franklin Parkway up to the Philadelphia Museum of Art. This leads to the city's most popular biking route that runs along Kelly Drive and West River Drive. Bicycles can be rented here during the warmer months *(see p168)*. It is advisable to wear a safety helmet when bicycling in the city.

TAXIS

TAXIS ROAM the streets freely looking for fares, though the best place to find one is at a hotel. Several cab companies serve the city, and if you must reserve a taxi for a specific time, do so at least 30 minutes to an hour in advance. Fares vary for different companies, with at least a $2 base fare and up to another $2 per mile.

DELAWARE RIVER PORT AUTHORITY
of Pennsylvania & New Jersey

Delaware River Port Authority logo

DRIVING IN CENTRAL PHILADELPHIA

EXCEPT FOR RUSH hour traffic, driving in town is not particularly difficult. The main Center City thoroughfares, Broad and Market Streets, have two-way traffic, while most other streets have one-way traffic patterns. Vehicles are driven on the right side in the US, and turns to the right can be made at a red light after a full stop, unless a sign prohibits it. Left turns are also prohibited at some intersections, especially at peak traffic hours. US law dictates you must wear a seatbelt, and violators can incur a fine. With some exceptions, overseas visitors can drive with a valid driver's license issued by their home country. If the license is not in English, an international driving permit is required.

PARKING

STREET PARKING IS usually hard to find and costly, though parking meters in some locations around Center City and Independence Mall are in operation seven days a week until 8pm. Most meters provide up to a 2-hour time limit, with the average rate ranging from 15 to 30 minutes

DIRECTORY

PUBLIC TRANSPORTATION

Philly Phlash
W www.phillyphlash.com

RiverLink Ferry
Penn's Landing.
((215) 925-5465.
W www.riverlinkferry.org

Southeastern Pennsylvania Transportation Authority (SEPTA)
((215) 580-7800.
W www.septa.org

TAXI CAB COMPANIES

City Cab Company
((215) 492-6500.

Olde City Cab Company
((215) 338-0838.

Quaker City Cab
((215) 728-8000.

LIMOUSINES/PRIVATE CARS

Carey Limousine
((610) 595-2800.

King Limousine
((800) 245-5460.

PARKING MATTERS

Philadelphia Parking Authority
((215) 683-9600.

per 25 cents. Make sure you keep the meter fed, as traffic enforcement officers make regular rounds and will write a ticket for an expired meter. Do not park at hydrants or other illegal parking zones. Violators will be ticketed and towed. Retrieving a towed vehicle can cost over $100.

Parking on residential streets is often permitted during the day for non-permit holders, but is restricted at night. Read the signs carefully and abide by them. Parking at the city's many lots is a safe but often expensive alternative, with rates from $15 to $30 and higher charged per day.

Philadelphia taxi

Traveling Outside Philadelphia

P HILADELPHIA HAS AN excellent regional rail service with SEPTA trains running from Center City to far western suburbs, parts of nearby New Jersey, and northern Delaware. Amtrak provides a daily train service to Lancaster, Harrisburg, and towns west of Philadelphia. New Jersey Transit takes passengers to Atlantic City and other areas along the Jersey shore. However, it is advisable and more practical to rent a car when traveling to remote sights in the Pennsylvania Dutch Country and Gettysburg.

SEPTA train – an ideal way to go beyond Philadelphia

REGIONAL RAIL SERVICE

O UTSTANDING RAIL services by **SEPTA** are offered to many of Philadelphia's outermost suburbs to the north, south, and west of the city, with trips to the outermost stops sometimes taking over an hour. Most trains can be boarded at the main train stations in Center City, including **Amtrak**'s 30th Street Station, Market East Station, and Suburban Station.

SEPTA's R1 commuter line provides services to the Philadelphia International Airport (see p183). The R2 travels south with a stop in Wilmington, Delaware. The R5 travels from Center City to points west, including Merion Station for the Barnes Foundation (see pp98–9), and points north with Doylestown (see p125) as the last stop. The R6 runs through Manayunk (see p95), while the R7 and R8 end their routes in Chestnut Hill with stops along the way in Germantown (see pp94–5). Train cars are comfortable

and air-conditioned, with plenty of seating. However, cars fill up quickly during the morning and afternoon rush hour. Tickets can be purchased at the three Center City stations, on trains, and at suburban stations.

SERVICES TO NEW JERSEY

S EVERAL TRAIN AND bus lines run from Philadelphia to New Jersey locations. The quickest way to Trenton,

Interior of 30th Street Station, one of the biggest in Pennsylvania

the capital of New Jersey, is via SEPTA's R7 commuter train, with services from Center City.

New Jersey's state-wide transportation agency, **New Jersey Transit**, provides bus and rail services to points south and north in the state. Buses 313 and 315 provide daily service from the Greyhound Bus Terminal at 10th and Filbert Streets in Philadelphia to Cape May, with traveling times up to three-and-a-half hours. For commuting to the resort town of Atlantic City, visitors can take the **Atlantic City Rail Line** from Amtrak's 30th Street Station.

The Port Authority Transit Corporation (PATCO) Speedline has a number of train stops in Center City. These are at Market and 8th Streets, and Locust and 10th, 12th, and 15th Streets. Speedline takes passengers over the Benjamin Franklin Bridge to the Camden Waterfront.

PENNSYLVANIA DUTCH COUNTRY AND GETTYSBURG

R ENTING A CAR is the best way to explore most of the towns and villages that lie beyond Philadelphia. If driving is not possible, then other options include taking organized bus tours and public transportation.

A train service is provided by Amtrak from Philadelphia's bustling 30th Street Station to towns that are located to the west of Philadelphia, including Lancaster and Harrisburg. In Lancaster, the **Red Rose Transit Authority** (RRTA) operates bus services in the city and to surrounding towns in the county, including Pennsylvania Dutch communities. These buses have busy schedules and tend to have limited services to the outlying smaller communities, including Paradise, Lititz, Intercourse, Bird-In-Hand, and Ephrata. Most of the bus services to these areas usually end after the afternoon rush

Traffic on Interstate 76, Philadelphia

hour. On weekends, service to these towns is scaled back, with limited runs on Saturdays and none on Sundays for certain routes.

Renting a car is essential for visitors who plan to travel to Gettysburg, as the town has no public transportation system or bus services catering to it.

INTERSTATES, TURNPIKES, AND TOLL ROADS

Turnpikes are sometimes interstate highways, but they are always toll roads. In particular, the Pennsylvania Turnpike and the New Jersey Turnpike both require motorists to pick up a toll ticket before entering the highway, and then pay the toll when exiting. The Pennsylvania Turnpike (I-76/276) is the fastest route from Philadelphia to Harrisburg, and a one-way toll can cost in the neighborhood of $5. Although not an interstate, the Atlantic City Expressway is also a toll road. Note that some expressways have both numbers and names, such as the Vine Street Expressway (I-676/30) or the Pennsylvania Turnpike.

When passing through toll booths, be aware there are different types. While some booths take cash or exact change, others operate on an electronic system known as "E-ZPass." This system scans participating vehicles, allowing them to go through while deducting the toll amount from their owners' accounts.

CAR RENTALS AND GASOLINE

To rent a car in the United States, US and Canadian residents must have a valid driver's license, while foreign visitors need an international driver's license and valid passport. The minimum rental age is usually 25, and it is necessary to have a major credit card in your name.

While personal auto insurance often covers rental cars, it is best to check the limitations of coverage with your insurance company. If not, it is always a good idea to purchase liability and collision insurance. Most gas stations in Philadelphia have self-service pumps. However, in New Jersey, state law mandates that attendants must pump gas. Rented cars should be returned to the rental agency with a full tank or additional charges will apply.

Sign for Hertz Rent a Car

SPEED LIMITS, FINES, AND DRIVING SAFELY

The speed limit on interstates is usually 65 miles per hour (105 km/h), and 55 miles per hour (88 km/h) on highways in and around Philadelphia. City streets usually have 25 to 35 miles per hour (40 to 56 km/h) limits. It is advisable to heed speed limits whenever possible, as a ticket can result in hefty fines.

Drive carefully during bad weather, as 18-wheeler trucks often spew mist during heavy rainstorms, resulting in poor visibility. Also, bridges and overpasses can become ice-slicked during winter. Safe driving tips include wearing seatbelts, which is required by law, keeping all doors locked, staying on main roads, avoiding unfamiliar neighborhoods, and not drinking alcohol. Be aware that offenses for drinking and driving are vigorously prosecuted in the US.

PHILADELPHIA STREET FINDER

MAP REFERENCES given in this guide for sights, hotels, restaurants, shops, and entertainment venues refer to the Street Finder maps on the following pages (*see* How the Map References Work). Map references are also given for Philadelphia's hotels *(see pp134–41)* and restaurants *(see pp145–53)*. A complete index of the street names and places of interest marked on the maps can be found on the following pages. The map below shows the area of Philadelphia covered by the four Street Finder maps. This includes the sightseeing areas (which are color-coded) as well as the rest of central Philadelphia. The symbols used to represent sights and useful information on the Street Finder maps are listed in the key below.

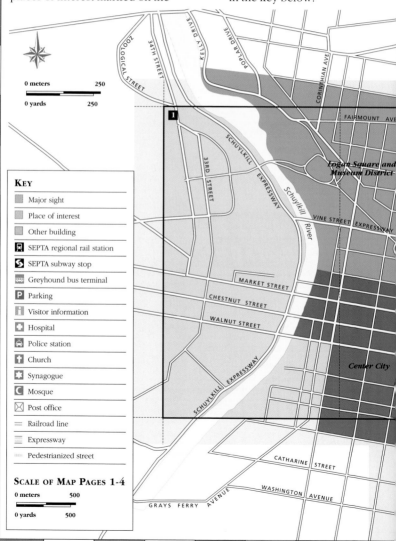

KEY

- ▨ Major sight
- ▨ Place of interest
- ▨ Other building
- 🚆 SEPTA regional rail station
- Ⓢ SEPTA subway stop
- 🚌 Greyhound bus terminal
- 🅿 Parking
- ℹ Visitor information
- ✚ Hospital
- 👮 Police station
- ✝ Church
- ✡ Synagogue
- Ⓒ Mosque
- ⊠ Post office
- = Railroad line
- ▤ Expressway
- ░ Pedestrianized street

SCALE OF MAP PAGES 1-4

| 0 meters | 500 |
| 0 yards | 500 |

HOW THE MAP REFERENCES WORK

The first figure tells you which Street Finder map to turn to.

Eakins Oval 8

Benjamin Franklin Parkway. **Map** 1 C1.
30th St Station. Spring Garden. 38, Philly Phlash.

The letters and numbers form the map coordinates. Letters are along the top of the map, while numbers are along the sides.

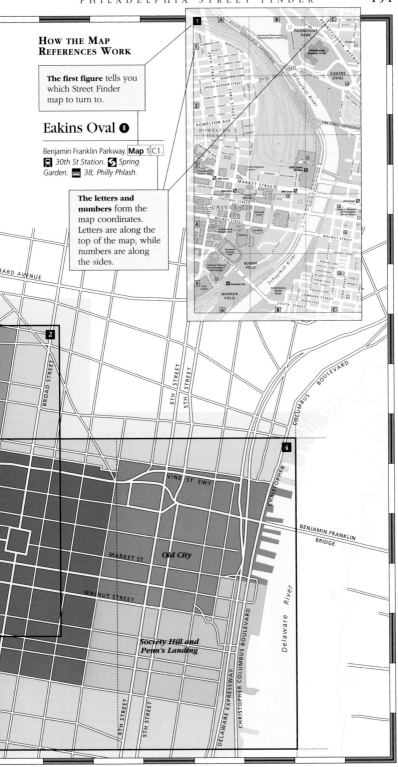

Street Finder Index

2nd Street 4 E5
3rd Street 4 D5
4th Street 4 D5
5th Street 4 D2
6th Street 4 D2
7th Street 4 D2
8th Street 3 C5
9th Street 3 C2
10th Street 3 B5
11th Street 2 F5
continues 3 B5
12th Street 3 C1
13th Street 2 F3
continues 3 B1
15th Street 2 F2
continues 3 A3
16th Street 2 E3
continues 3 A1
17th Street 2 E1
continues 3 A1
18th Street 2 D5
19th Street 2 D4
20th Street 2 D1
21st Street 1 C5
22nd Street 1 C5
23rd Street 1 C3
24th Street 1 C1
25th Street 1 C1
26th Street 1 B5
27th Street 1 B5
30th Street 1 B3
30th Street Station 1 B3
31st Street 1 B2
32nd Street 1 A2
33rd Street 1 A2
34th Street 1 A1
35th Street 1 A2
103rd Engineers
   Armory 1 A3

A

Academy of
   Music 2 E5
Academy of Natural
   Sciences 2 D3
African American
   Museum in
   Philadelphia 4 D2
Alder Street 3 B5
Alter Street 3 A5
American Street 4 E5
Appletree Street 2 D3
Arch Street 1 A3
continues 3 A2
Arch Street
   Friends Meeting
   House 4 E2
Arch Street
   United Methodist
   Church 2 F4
Art Museum
   Drive 1 B1
Atwater Kent
   Museum 4 D3

B

B. Free Franklin
   Post Office 4 E3
Bach Place 3 A3
Bainbridge Street 3 C4
Bank Street 4 E3
Baring Street 1 A2
Beechwood
   Street 2 D3
Benjamin Franklin
   Bridge 4 E2
Benjamin Franklin
   Field 1 A4
Benjamin Franklin
   Parkway 2 D2
continues 3 A1
Betsy Ross House 4 E2
Bishop White
   House 4 E3
Brandywine Street 1 A2
Bread Street 4 E2
Broad Street 2 F2
continues 3 B1
Brown Street 2 F1
Burns Street 2 F3
continues 3 B1
Buttonwood Street 2 E2

C

Callowhill Street 2 D2
continues 4 D1
Camac Street 2 F3
continues 3 B1
Capital Street 2 D1
Carlisle Street 2 F3
continues 3 B1
Carlton Street 2 E2
continues 3 B1
Carpenter Street 3 A5
Carpenters' Hall 4 D3
Catharine Street 4 D5
Cathedral of Saints
   Peter and Paul 2 E3
Chadwick Street 2 E5
Chancellor Street 1 A4
continues 3 A3
Cherry Street 3 A1
continues 1 A3
Chestnut Street 1 A4
continues 3 A2
Christ Church 4 E2
Christ Church
   Burial Ground 4 D2
Christian Street 3 A5
Christopher Columbus
   Boulevard 4 E4
City Hall 3 B2
City Tavern 4 E3
Civic Center 1 A5
Civil War & Underground
   Railroad Museum of
   Philadelphia 2 D5
Clarion Street 2 F3
continues 3 B1

Clifton Street 3 B5
Clinton Street 3 B4
Clover Street 2 F4
continues 3 B2
Clymer Street 3 C5
College of Physicians
   of Philadelphia/
   Mütter Museum 1 C4
Commerce Street 2 F4
continues 3 B2
Community College
   of Philadelphia 2 E2
Convention Avenue 1 A5
Corinthian Avenue 2 D1
Corn Exchange
   National Bank 4 E3
Croskey Street 1 C3
Curtis Center 4 D3
Cuthbert Street 2 D3
continues 3 A2
Cypress Street 1 C5
continues 3 B3

D

Darien Street 3 C3
Declaration House 4 D2
Delancey Place 1 C5
continues 3 A3
Delancey Street 4 E4
Delaware
   Expressway 4 E5
Delhi Street 3 C4
Dock Street 4 E3
Drexel University 1 A4

E

Eakins Oval 1 C1
Eastern State
   Penitentiary 2 D1
Elfreth's Alley 4 E2
Ellsworth Street 3 A5

F

Fairmount Avenue 1 B1
Fairmount Park 2 D5
Fairmount Waterworks
   and Interpretive
   Center 1 B1
Filbert Street 1 A3
continues 3 B2
Fireman's Hall
   Museum 4 E2
First Bank of
   the US 4 E3
Fitzwater Street 3 C5
Franklin Court 4 D3
Franklin Institute
   Science Museum 2 D3
Franklin Square 4 D1
Franklin Street 4 D2
Franklin Town
   Boulevard 2 E2
Free Library of
   Philadelphia 2 E2

Free Quaker
   Meeting House 4 D2
Front Street 4 E5
Fulton Street 4 D5

G

Gaskill Street 4 D4
Green Street 2 D1
Greyhound Bus
   Terminal 3 C2

H

Hahnemann University
   and Hospital 3 A1
Hall Street 3 B5
Hamilton Street 1 A2
Haverford Avenue 1 A1
Hicks Street 3 A5
Hutchinson Street 3 C3

I

Ice Rink 1 B4
Independence Hall 4 D3
Independence Seaport
   Museum 4 F4
Independence
   Square 4 D3
Independence
   Visitor Center 4 D2

J

Jessup Street 3 B5
John F. Kennedy
   Boulevard 1 B3
continues 3 A2
John F. Kennedy
   Plaza 2 E4
Juniper Street 2 F3
continues 3 B2

K

Kater Street 3 A4
Kelly Drive 1 B1
Kenilworth Street 4 D5
Kimball Street 3 A5
Kimmel Center for the
   Performing Arts 3 A3

L

Lambert Street 2 D3
Lancaster Avenue 1 A3
Latimer Street 2 E5
continues 3 A3
Lawrence Street 4 D4
Leithgow Street 4 D5
Lemon Street 2 F1
Letitia Street 4 E3
Liberty Bell
   Center 4 D3
Liberty Place 2 E4
continues 3 A2
Library Company of
   Philadelphia 3 B3
Library Hall 4 D3

Locust Street 1 C4
continues 3 B3
Logan Circle 2 D3
Lombard Street 1 B5
continues 3 A4
Ludlow Street 1 A3
continues 3 A2

M

Magee Rehabilitation
Hospital 3 B1
Manning Street 1 C5
continues 3 C3
Mantua Avenue 1 A1
Market East Station 3 B2
Market Street 2 D4
continues 3 A2
Marshall Street 4 D5
Marvine Street 3 B5
Masonic Temple 3 B2
Melon Street 1 A1
Mikveh Israel 4 E2
Mikveh Israel
Cemetery 3 C3
Mildred Street 3 C5
Mole Street 3 A1
Monroe Street 4 D5
Montrose Street 3 A5
Moore College of
Art and Design 2 D3
Mother Bethel AME
Church 4 D4
Mount Vernon Street 1 A1

N

Napa Street 1 A2
National Constitution
Center 4 D2
National Liberty
Museum 4 E3
National Museum of
American Jewish
History 4 D2
Natrona Street 1 A2
Naudain Street 1 B5
continues 3 A4
Nectarine Street 2 D2
New Market and Head
House Square 4 E4
New Street 4 E2
Noble Street 3 C1
North Street 2 E1

O

Old Pine Street
Church 4 D4
Old St. Joseph's
Church 4 D3
Old St. Mary's
Church 4 D4
Olive Street 1 C1

P

Palestra 1 A4
Panama Street 1 C5
continues 4 D4

Park Towne Place 1 C2
Passyunk Avenue 3 C5
Pearl Street 1 A2
Pemberton Street 3 C5
Penn's Landing 4 F3
Pennsylvania
Academy of the
Fine Arts 3 A2
Pennsylvania
Avenue 1 C1
Pennsylvania Convention
Center 3 B2
Pennsylvania
Hospital 3 C4
Percy Street 3 C4
Perot Street 1 C1
Philadelphia Arts
Bank 3 A4
Philadelphia Museum
of Art 1 C1
Philadephia Merchants'
Exchange 4 E3
Philosophical Hall 4 D3
Physick House 4 D4
Pier 3N 4 F3
Pier 5N 4 F2
Pier 9N 4 F2
Pier 11N 4 F2
Pier 12N 4 F2
Pier 17N 4 F2
Pier 19N 4 F1
Pier 24N 4 F1
Pine Street 1 C5
continues 3 A4
Please Touch
Museum 2 D3
Police
Headquarters 4 D2
Polish American
Cultural Center
Museum 4 E3
Powel House 4 E4
Powelton Ave 1 A2

Q

Quarry Street 4 E2
Queen Street 4 D5
Quince Street 2 F5
continues 3 B4

R

Race Street 1 A3
continues 3 A1
Ranstead Street 2 D4
continues 3 A2
Reading Terminal
Market 3 B2
Reese Street 4 D4
Ridge Avenue 2 F1
continues 3 C1
Rittenhouse Square
West 2 D5
Rittenhouse
Square 2 D5
Rodin Museum 2 D2
Rodman Street 3 A4

Rosenbach Museum and
Library 2 D5
Rosewood Street 3 A5

S

Sansom Street 1 A4
continues 3 A3
Sartain Street 3 B5
Schell Street 3 C5
Schuykill Avenue 1 C4
Schuylkill
Expressway 1 A1
Second Bank of
the US 4 D3
Shedwick Street 1 A1
Smedley Street 2 E5
continues 3 A3
Society Hill
Synagogue 4 D4
South Street 1 B5
continues 3 A4
Spring Garden
Street 1 A2
Spring Street 2 D3
continues 3 C1
Spruce Street 1 C5
continues 3 B3
St. Francis Church 1 C1
St. George's
Church 4 E1
St. James Street 4 D3
St. Joseph's Way 4 D4
St. Mark's Episcopal
Church 3 A3
St. Peter's Episcopal
Church 4 D4
Stampers Street 4 E4
Strawberry Street 4 E3
Suburban Station 2 E4
Summer Street 1 A2
continues 3 A1
Swain Street 2 F1
Sydenham Street 2 E5
continues 3 A3

T

Thaddeus Kosciuszko
National
Memorial 4 E4
Thomas Eakins
House 2 E1
Thomas Jefferson
University 3 B3
Thomas Jefferson
University
Hospital 3 C3
Todd House 4 D3
Tomb of the
Unknown
Soldier 4 D3

U

Uber Street 2 D5
University Center 1 B4
University City Science
Center 1 A3

University Museum of
Archaeology and
Anthropology 1 A5
University of
Pennsylvania 1 A4
University of the
Arts 3 A4
US Mint 4 D2

V

Van Pelt Street 1 C5
Vine Street 2 D3
continues 3 A1
Vine Street
Expressway 1 C2
continues 3 A1

W

Wallace Street 1 A1
Walnut Street 1 A4
continues 3 A3
Warnock Street 3 B5
Warren Street 1 A3
Washington
Avenue 3 A5
Washington Square 4 D3
Washington Square
South 4 D3
Waterworks Drive 1 B1
Watts Street 2 F1
continues 3 B1
Waverly Street 1 C5
continues 3 A4
Webster Street 3 A5
Welcome Park 4 E3
West River Drive 1 A1
Willow Street 3 C1
Winter Street 1 A2
continues 3 C1
Wood Stock Street 2 D3
Wood Street 2 D2
continues 3 A1

4

D
E
F

CHRISTOPHER COLUMBUS BLVD

NOBLE ST

1

WILLOW STREET
CALLOWHILL STREET

FRONT STREET

Pier 24N

VINE STREET EXPRESSWAY

5TH STREET

3RD STREET

WILLOW ST

Pier 19N

WOOD STREET

atown

FRANKLIN
SQUARE

6TH STREET

FRANKLIN STREET

VINE STREET

Pier 17N

St. George's
Church

NEW STREET

VINE ST

Pier 12N

BENJAMIN FRANKLIN BRIDGE

Police
Headquarters

National Constitution
Center

RACE STREET

Fireman's
Hall Museum

DELAWARE EXPRESSWAY

Pier 11N

2

The African
American Museum
in Philadelphia

5TH STREET

US Mint

4TH STREET

CHERRY ST

3RD STREET

QUARRY ST

CHRIST
CHURCH
BURIAL
GROUND

BREAD ST

Betsy Ross
House

Elfreth's
Alley

Pier 9N

Free Quaker
Meeting House

7TH STREET

ARCH STREET

2ND STREET

Pier 5N

Independence
Visitor Center

Arch Street Friends
Meeting House

National Museum of
American Jewish History

OLD
CITY

Declaration
House

Mikveh Israel

Christ Church

Pier 3N

🚩 5th Street

COMMERCE STREET

MARKET ST

er
nt
m

RANSTEAD ST

Liberty Bell
Center

B. Free Franklin
Post Office

🚩 2nd Street

MARKET ST

3

Independence
Hall

Franklin
Court

RANSTEAD ST

National Liberty
Museum

STRAWBERRY ST

LETITIA ST

CHRISTOPHER COLUMBUS BOULEVARD

Penn's

Second Bank
of the US

First Bank
of the US

BANK ST

Corn Exchange
National Bank

Curtis
Center

Philosophical
Hall

INDEPENDENCE
SQUARE

Library
Hall

Carpenters'
Hall

Todd House

Philadelphia
Merchants' Exchange

Landing

NGTON
SQUARE

Bishop
White
House

FRONT STREET

WELCOME
PARK

mb of the
nknown
oldier

ST. JAMES ST

Old St. Joseph's
Church

City Tavern

GTON SQ
OUTH

LOCUST STREET

ROSE
GARDEN

Polish American
Cultural Center
Museum

Independence
Seaport Museum

MAGNOLIA
GARDEN

Powel House

DOCK ST

S ST

Old St. Mary's
Church

ST. JOSEPH'S WAY

LOCUST ST

38TH PARALLEL PLACE

CITY
PARK

4

EY ST
ST

Society Hill
Synagogue

SPRUCE STREET

PANAMA ST

LAWRENCE ST

CYPRESS ST

DELANCEY

SOCIETY
HILL

VIETNAM VETERANS
MEMORIAL PARK

PINE STREET

Physick House

STREET

Old Pine
Street Church

St. Peter's
Episcopal Church

Thaddeus Kosciuszko
National Memorial

2ND STREET

other Bethel
AME Church

LOMBARD STREET

STAMPERS ST

New Market &
Head House
Square

GASKILL STREET

REESE ST

SOUTH STREET

NAUDAIN ST

DELAWARE EXPRESSWAY

Delaware River

5

KENILWORTH ST

5TH STREET

LEITHGOW ST

3RD STREET

4TH STREET

AMERICAN STREET

BAINBRIDGE ST

MONROE STREET

KENILWORTH ST

FITZWATER STREET

FULTON ST

2ND STREET

FRONT STREET

N ST

CATHARINE STREET

QUEEN STREET

D
E
F

General Index

Page numbers in **bold type** refer to
main entries.

155th Pennsylvania Volunteer Infantry
Memorial (Gettysburg National
Military Park) 123
24-hour pharmacies 177
30th Street Station 29, 182, 183,
184, 188

A

Absecon Lighthouse (Atlantic City) 127
Academy of Music 29, **76**, 162,
163, 164
   The Nutcracker 35
Academy of Natural Sciences 11,
26, 82, **85**
   children's section 170
Academy of Vocal Arts 165
Adams, John 42, 60
ADA Paratransit 175
Adventure Aquarium (Camden
Waterfront) 11, 101, 171
African American History Month 35
The African American Museum in
Philadelphia 27, **51**
African Americans 51, 58, 60
African Methodist Episcopal Church 60
After the Concert (Renoir) 99
Agnew, James 106
Air Canada 182
Air France 182
Air travel 182–3
Alcohol 143
Alice in Wonderland (Carroll) 171
All Cell Rental 180
Allen, Richard 58, 60
American Airlines 182
Americana Museum (Bird-In-Hand) 118
American art (Philadelphia Museum
of Art) 88–91
American Automobile Association 189
American Express
   credit card 177
   Travel Services Office 178
American Home (publication) 50
American Jews 41, 46, 47
American National Tree (National
Constitution Center) 49
American Philosophical Society 47
American Revolution **20–21**, 39, 55
   Battle of Brandywine 129
   Battle of Germantown 21, 94, 106
   Battle of Trenton 126
   Fort Mifflin **100–1**
   US Constitution 21, **48**
   Valley Forge 21, 94, 129
   Washington's crossing of the
   Delaware River 126
   Washington Square cemetery 60
   see also Independence National
   Historical Park
American Revolution Center (Valley
Forge National Historic Park) 129
America West Airlines 182
Amish 18, 112, 114, **115**, 118
   Amish Experience (Intercourse) 118
   Amish Village (Strasburg) 119
   food 142, **144**
   quilts 118
   shopping 118, 157
Amman, Jacob 115
Amtrak 184
   30th Street Station 29, 182, 183,
   184, 188
   Amtrak Passenger Stations 189

Angelico, Fra 90
   Dormition of the Virgin 90
Annenberg Center for the Performing
Arts 32, 165
Annual Student Exhibition 33
Antique Row 157, 160
Antiques 160
Apotheosis of Victor Hugo (Rodin) 86
Arboretum and Gardens (Barnes
Foundation) 98
Architecture **28–9**
Arch Street Friends Meeting House **46**
Arch Street United Methodist
Church 71, **72**
Arden Theatre Company 164
Art
   American art 88–91
   costumes and textiles 91
   European paintings, sculpture,
   decorative arts, and architecture
   88–90
   galleries 160
   Impressionist and Postimpressionist
   art 74–5, 88, 90, 98–9, 125
   Middle East and Asian art 88, 91
   Modern and Contemporary art
   88, 91
   Renaissance paintings 89, 91
   see also Monuments, Museums, &
   Statues
Asbury, Francis 51
Assembly Room (Independence Hall)
43
Atlantic City 112, **127**, 163
   getting to 188
   hotels 139
   restaurants 151–2
Atlantic City Outlets, The Walk 157
Atlantic City Rail Line 188
ATMs 178
Atwater Kent Museum 27, 29, **50**
The Aurora (newspaper) 53
Avenue of the Arts 163
Awbury Arboretum (Germantown) 94
Azalea Garden (Boathouse Row) 96

B

Bache, Benjamin Franklin 53
Bache, Richard 46
Banking **178–9**
Barnes, Dr. Albert C. 98, 99
Barnes Foundation 25, 26, 93, **98–9**
Barry, Commodore John 62
Bars and taverns 166–7
Baseball 32, 168, 169
Basketball 34, 169
Battles
   Brandywine 129
   Civil War 22, 77, 120–23
   Germantown 21, **94**, 106, 107
   Gettysburg **120–23**
   Trenton 126
Battleship New Jersey 66, 67, 101, 104
Beaux-Arts architecture **29**
   30th Street Station 29, 184
   Curtis Center **50**
   Free Library of Philadelphia 29,
   83, **84**
   Memorial Hall 22, 29, 109
   Philadelphia Museum of Art 29,
   88–91
   Rodin Museum 26, 29, 83, **86**
USS *Becuna* 15, 27, **64**, 104
Bed-and-breakfasts 133
   A Bed and Breakfast Connection of
   Philadelphia 133

Beissel, Conrad 118
Bell Atlantic Tower 29, 72
Bellevue Building (Center City) 10
   specialty shops and boutiques 156
Bellotto, Bernardo 90
Belmont Mansion (Fairmount Park)
109
Benjamin Franklin Parkway 26, 28,
81, 82
   Philadelphia College Festival 34
   Thanksgiving Day Parade 34
Benjamin Ring House (Brandywine
Battlefield State Park) 129
Betsy Ross House 10, 28, **52**
Beyond Philadelphia **110–29**
   area map 112–13
   hotels 139–41
   Landis Valley Museum **116–17**
   restaurants 151–3
   Tour of Gettysburg National
   Military Park **122–3**
Bicycling 168, 187
   Bicycle Club of Philadelphia 168
Bidermann, J.A. 128
Big Bus Company 175
Birch, William Russell 22, 45
   The City & Port of Philadelphia 22
Bird-In-Hand **118**, 157
Bishop White House **54**
The Black Cat (Poe) 94
Blodgett, Samuel 53
Bloomsday 33
Blue Cross RiverRink 11, 168
Blues 166
The Boardwalk (Atlantic City) 127
Boathouse Row and Kelly Drive **96**
Bond, Thomas 19, 55, 67
The Book and the Cook Festival 32
Books 160
Botticelli, Sandro 90
   Stories of Saint Mary Magdalene 90
The Bourse 10, 160
   Food court and specialty shops 156
Bouvier, Michael 62
Brancusi, Constantin 91
Brandywine Battlefield State Park **129**
Brandywine River 128, 129
Brandywine River Museum **129**
Brandywine Valley
   hotels 139
   restaurants 152
Breck, Samuel 109
Brethren **115**
British Airways 182
Broad Street Run 33
Buchanan, James 114, 119
The Burghers of Calais (Rodin) 86
Burnett, Frances Hodgson 171
   The Secret Garden 171
Buses 175, 185, 186, 188
   for disabled passengers 185

C

Calder, Alexander Milne 72–3
Calder, Alexander Stirling 31, 84
Camden Children's Garden 171
Camden Riversharks 169
Camden Waterfront 11, 66, 93, **101**
Campbell's Field 101
Canaletto 90
Cape May 112, **127**
   hotels 139–40
   restaurants 152
Capone, Al 87
Card Players and Girl (Cezanne) 99
Carey, Mathew 62

Carpenters' Company 19, 54
Carpenters' Hall **54**
Carroll, Lewis 171
   Alice in Wonderland 171
Cars 184, 187, 189
   see also Driving
Casinos 113, 127, 163
Cassatt, Mary 27, 74, 85
Cathedral of Saints Peter and
   Paul 81, 83, **84**
Cedar Grove (Fairmount Park) 109
The Cello Player (Eakins) 74
Cell phones 180
Center City 14, **68–79**
   antiques 160, 161
   area map 69
   Fourth of July Parade 33
   Greyhound bus terminal 185
   hotels 135–6
   Mummer's Day Parade 35
   Pennsylvania Academy of the
   Fine Arts **74–5**
   Puerto Rican Day Parade 34
   Pulaski Day Parade, 34
   restaurants 142, 148–9
   shopping 156, 157, 158, 159, 160
   St. Patrick's Day Parade 32
   street-by-street map 70–71
   Von Steuben Day Gala and
   Parade 34
Centralized Ground Transportation 183
Central Philadelphia **14**
   area map 14–15
   driving in 187
Cezanne, Paul 90, 98, 99
   Card Players and Girl 99
   Gardanne 98
Chamber music 164
Chamber Orchestra of
   Philadelphia 164
Chaminoux (Fairmount Park) 109
Charles II, King 18
Charter for Pennsylvania (1681) 18
Charter of Privileges (1701) 19, 63
Chestnut Hill 93, **94–5**
   shopping 154, 157
Chestnut Hill Historical Society 95
Chihuly, Dale 53
   Flame of Liberty 53
Children's facilities
   hotels 133
   restaurants 143
Children's Philadelphia **170–71**
   family day in Philadelphia 11
   International Children's Festival 32
Chinatown 69, **76**
   Chinese New Year celebrations 35
   restaurants 142
Chocolate World (Hershey) 124, 171
Choo Choo Barn (Strasburg) 119
Chopin, Frederic 63
Choral Arts Society of Philadelphia 165
Christ Church **52**
Christ Church Burial Ground 10,
   40, **46**
*Christ Healing the Sick in the
   Temple* (West) 67
Christmas Day (public holiday) 35
Christmas Tree Lighting 35
Christopher Columbus Park (Penn's
   Landing) 104
Churches and cathedrals
   Arch Street United Methodist
   Church 71, **72**
   Cathedral of Saints Peter and
   Paul 81, 83, **84**

Churches and cathedrals (cont.)
   Christ Church **52**
   Church of the Patriots *see* Old Pine
   Street Church
   Gloria Dei Church *see* Old Swedes'
   Church
   Lady Chapel 78
   Mother Bethel AME Church 58, **60**
   Old Pine Street Church 58, **60**
   Old St. Joseph's Church 59, **63**
   Old St. Mary's Church 59, **62**, 63
   Old Swedes' Church 103, 105
   St. Augustine's Church 22, 51
   St. George's Church **51**, 60
   St. Mark's Episcopal Church **78**
   St. Peter's Episcopal Church 58, **61**
Cigars 161
Citizens Bank Park 32, 168
The City & Port of Philadelphia
   (Birch) 22
City Hall 18, 29, 69, 70, **72–3**
   Christmas Tree Lighting 35
   Penn's statue 72
City Island (Harrisburg) 124
City Tavern 10, **55**
Civil War (1861–65) 22, 77
   Battle of Gettysburg **120–23**
   The Civil War and Underground
   Railroad Museum of Philadelphia **77**
   Civil War Memorial
   (Germantown) 94
   National Civil War Museum
   (Harrisburg) 124
Classical music and symphony 164
Climate *see* Weather
Cliveden (Germantown) 21, 28, 107
Cloister with Elements from the
   Abbey of Saint Genis-des-Fontaines
   89, 90
Clothing 158, 159
Cobbs Creek Golf Club 168
Coin-operated phones 180
Coins 179
Coleman, William 109
College of Physicians of Philadelphia
   79
College sports 169
Columbus, Christopher 34
Columbus Day Parade 34
   public holiday 35
Comedy clubs 167
Commerce Bank 178
Communications **180–81**
Concert halls and venues 162–7
Congress Hall 28, 42
Constitutional Convention (1787) 48, 55
Continental Airlines 182
Copernicus, Nicholas 63
Corn Exchange National Bank 104
Costaggini, Filippo 63
   *The Exaltation of Saint Joseph into
   Heaven* 63
Costumes and textiles (Philadelphia
   Museum of Art) 91
Country Gentleman (publication) 50
Courier services 181
Crafts and Fine Arts Fair 66
Credit cards 154, 178
   lost or stolen 177
Cret, Paul Philippe 78, 99, 129
Crossing the Delaware River (Leutze) 21
Cruise ships 185
Currency exchange 178
Currency notes 179
Curtis Center and Dream Garden
   Mosaic **50**

Curtis, Cyrus H.K. 50
Curtis Institute of Music 165
CVS Pharmacy 177

D

Dad Vail Regatta 33, 96
Dali, Salvadore 91
   *Soft Construction of Boiled Beans
   (Premonition of Civil War)* 91
Dallas, George Mifflin 61
The Dance (Matisse) 99
Daughters of the American
   Revolution 62
Day tours **10–11**
Decatur, Stephen 61
Declaration House **50**
Declaration of Independence 20, **42**
   Independence Hall **42–3**
   Old St. Mary's Church **62**
   Thomas Jefferson 42, 47, 50
De LaFayette, Marquis 47, 129
Delaware River 12, 13, 17
   Crossing the Delaware River
   (Leutze) 21
   Independence Seaport
   Museum **64–5**
   Penn's Landing *see* Penn's Landing
   RiverLink Ferry 101, 186
   Washington's crossing of 126
Delta Airlines 182
Department stores 155
Deshler, David 106
Deshler-Morris House (Germantown)
   28, 103, 106
Desiderio, Vincent 75
   Pantocrator 75
Devon Horse Show and Country
   Fair 33
Dewey, Admiral George 64
DHL 181
Dialing codes 180
Diebenkorn, Richard 74
Disabled travelers 175
   buses 185
   Greyhound Customers with
   Disabilities Travel Assistance
   Line 185
   hotels 133
   Mayor's Commission on People
   with Disabilities 133, 163, 175
   theaters and venues 163
Discos 166, 167
Discount and outlet malls 125, 157
Divers of the Deep (Independence
   Seaport Museum) 65
Dobbin House Tavern (Gettysburg)
   120
Dormition of the Virgin (Angelico) 90
Doylestown **125**
   hotels 140
   restaurants 152
Dream Garden Mosaic (Parrish) 50
Drexel University 97
Drive Sports 168
Driving 184
   Central Philadelphia 187
   safety and toll roads 189
   see also Cars
Duchamp, Marcel 91
   The Large Glass 91
   *Nude Descending a Staircase
   (No.2)* 91
Duffield, George 60
Du Pont, Eleuthere Irenee 128
Du Pont, Henry Francis 128
Du Pont, Pierre S. 30, 128

E

Eakins Oval 82, **86**
Eakins, Thomas 74, 86, 87, 89, 90, 91
  The Cello Player 74
  collection (Philadelphia Museum
    of Art) 89
  Miss Blanche Hurlbert 89
East Cemetery Hill (Gettysburg
  National Military Park) 123
Eastern State Penitentiary 81, **87**
Ebenezer Maxwell Mansion
  (Germantown) 29, 107
Edgar Allan Poe National Historic
  Site **94**
Eisenhower, Dwight D. 120
Eisenhower National Historic Site
  (Gettysburg) 120
Electricity 175
Elfreth, Jeremiah 52
Elfreth's Alley 36–7, **52**
Emergencies **177**
Entertainment **162–9**
  children's Philadelphia 170–71
  classical music 164
  comedy clubs 167
  disabled access 163
  gay clubs and bars 167
  music 166
  nightclubs and bars 166–7
  opera and ballet 164
  outdoor activities and sports 168–9
  theater 164, 165
  tickets 162, 163
Ephrata **118**
Ephrata Cloister 118
Equality Forum 32
Ericsson, John 86
Esther Boyer College of Music and
  Dance 165
Eternal Light Peace Memorial
  (Gettysburg National Military
  Park 122)
Eternal Springtime (Rodin) 86
Etiquette 174
European paintings, sculpture,
  decorative arts, and architecture
  (Philadelphia Museum of Art) 88–90
Evanescent Joys (Philadelphia
  Museum of Art) 91
*The Exaltation of Saint Joseph into
  Heaven* (Costaggini) 63
Expedia Travels 183
Express mail 181
Ezekiel, Sir Moses Jacob 47
  Religious Liberty 47

F

Fairmount Park 30, 93, **95**, **108–109**
  driving tour 103, 108–109
  historic mansions 108–109
  walking and biking trails 168
Fairmount Waterworks and
  Interpretive Center 82, **86**
  children's activities 171
Fall in Philadelphia 34
Family day in Philadelphia **11**
Farmers' Market (Bird-In-Hand) 118
Farnsworth House Inn (Gettysburg)
  120
Fast food 143
Fax services 181
Federal architecture **28**
  Bishop White House **54**
  Congress Hall 28, 42
  Independence Hall, wings 28, **42–3**
  Lemon Hill (Fairmount Park) 108

Federal architecture (cont.)
  Old City Hall 28
  Pennsylvania Hospital, center **67**
  Philosophical Hall and Library
    Hall **47**
  Physick House **61**
  Strawberry Mansion (Fairmount
    Park) 109
  Sweetbriar (Fairmount Park) 109
  Upsala (Germantown) 107
FedEx 181
Ferries 186–7
Festivals and events **32–5**
Field Concert Hall (Curtis Institute of
  Music) 165
Fireman's Hall Museum **51**
  children's activities 171
First Bank of the US 10, **53**
First Continental Congress 54, 55
Fisher Brooks Gallery (Pennsylvania
  Academy of the Fine Arts) 75
Fitzsimons, Thomas 62
Flame of Liberty (Chihuly) 53
Florists 161
F.M. Kirby Auditorium and Theater
  (National Constitution Center) 48
Folk music 166
Fonthill Museum (Doylestown) 125
Food
  Amish food 144
  food and cookery shops 160
  Philly fare 142
  see also Restaurants and Cafés
Football 33, 34, 168, 169
Foreign visitors 174
Forrest Theatre 163, 164
Fort Mifflin **100–1**
Foster, Stephen 119
  My Olde Kentucky Home 119
  Oh! Susanna 119
Fourth of July Parade 33
The Fox Hunt (Homer) 74
Franklin, Benjamin 19, **53**
  American Philosophical Society 47
  burial at Christ Church 46
  Franklin Court **52–3**
  Pennsylvania Hospital 67
  statues 49, 82, 85
  University of Pennsylvania **96–7**
Franklin Bridge 66, 104
Franklin Court and B. Free Franklin
  Post Office **52–3**
Franklin, Deborah 46
Franklin Institute Science Museum 11,
  26, 50, 82, **85**
  children's section 170
Franklin Mills Mall 157
Franklin, Sarah 46
Franklin Square 18
Freedom Rising (National Constitution
  Center) 49
Freedom Theatre 164
Free Library of Philadelphia 29, 83, **84**
Free Quaker Meeting House 40, **45**
Free Quakers 45
Free Society of Traders 58
French and Indian War (1754–63) 19
French Second Empire architecture 29
  City Hall 29, **72**
Friends of Chamounix Tennis 168
Furness and Hewitt 74

G

GII Pennsylvania Derby 169
The Gallery at Market East 11, 156, 158
Gardanne (Cezanne) 98

Gardens *see* Parks and Gardens
The Gates of Hell (Rodin) 86
Gay and Lesbian Travel Guide 167
Gays and lesbians
  clubs and bars 167
  Equality Forum 32
  night life 163
  Philadelphia International Gay and
    Lesbian Film Festival 33
Gazela (fishing boat) 66
General Lee's Headquarters
  (Gettysburg) 120
Georgian architecture **28**
  Betsy Ross House 28, **52**
  Carpenters' Hall **54**
  Cedar Grove (Fairmount Park) 109
  Christ Church 28, **52**
  Cliveden (Germantown) 28, 107
  Declaration House **50**
  Deshler-Morris House
    (Germantown) 28, 106
  Free Quaker Meeting House **45**
  Grumblethorpe (Germantown) 106
  Independence Hall, center 28, **42–3**
  Laurel Hill (Fairmount Park) 108
  Mount Pleasant (Fairmount
    Park) 108
  Ormiston (Fairmount Park) 108
  Pennsbury Manor **126**
  Pennsylvania Hospital, wings **67**
  Powel House 59, **63**
  St. Peter's Episcopal Church 58, **61**
  The Thomas Bond House 55
  Todd House **54**
  Woodford (Fairmount Park) 109
Germantown 93, **94**, **106–107**
  historic homes 103, 106–107
  walking tour 103, 106–107
Germantown Historical Society and
  Visitor Center 94, 106
Gettysburg **120–23**
  battle of 120, 121, 122–23
  hotels 140
  Lincoln's Gettysburg address **121**
  restaurants 152
Gettysburg Cyclorama 120
Gettysburg National Military Park
  122–3
  area map 122–3
  Cyclorama Center 120
Ghost Tours of Philadelphia 11, 175
Gifts and souvenirs 160–61
Gilpin, Gideon 129
Gloria Dei Church *see* Old Swedes'
  Church
The Gold Bug (Poe) 94
Golfing 168
Goode, W. Wilson 23
Gothic Revival architecture 29
  Arch Street United Methodist
    Church **72**
  Eastern State Penitentiary **87**
  St. Mark's Episcopal Church **78**
Graff, Jacob 50
Gratz, Rebecca 47, 67
Great Bathers (Renoir) 90
Greater Philadelphia, map 13
Greater Philadelphia Tourism and
  Marketing Corporation 132, 133
Great Essentials Exhibit
  (Independence Hall) 42–3
Greaton, Reverend Joseph 63
Greek Revival architecture **28–9**
  Atwater Kent Museum 29, **50**
  Fairmount Waterworks and
    Interpretive Center 82, **86**

Greek Revival architecture (cont.)
First Bank of the United States **53**
Philadelphia Merchants' Exchange 28, **54–5**
Second Bank of the US 29, **47**
Green Dragon Farmers' Market (Ephrata) 118
Greyhound Lines 185
bus terminal 185
Customers with Disabilities Travel Assistance Line 185
Grumblethorpe (Germantown) 106
Guardi, Francesco 90
Guided tours 175 *see also* Tours

H

Hagley Museum **128**
Hamilton, Alexander 53
Hamilton, Andrew 42
Harley-Davidson Assembly Plant (York) 124
Harrisburg **124**
hotels 140
restaurants 152
Harris, John 124
Haviland, John 29, 50
Health **176–7**
Hendricksen, Cornelius 17
Hershey 112, **124**
hotels 140
restaurants 153
Hewes, Joseph 46
Hicks, Edward
Noah's Ark 91
Peaceable Kingdom 18
Penn's Treaty with the Indians 16
High Water Mark (Gettysburg National Military Park) 123
Hill, Henry 61
Historical and Museum Commission 116
Historical Society of Pennsylvania 76
Historic Cold Spring Village (Cape May) 127
Historic homes and mansions
Fairmount Park **95**, **108–109**
Germantown **94**, **106–107**
Historic Philadelphia day **10**
History **16–23**
Holiday (publication) 50
Holmes, Thomas 18
Homer, Winslow 74, 91
The Fox Hunt 74
A Huntsman and Dogs 91
Hopkinson, Francis 46
Horse racing 169
Horticulture Center (Fairmount Park) 95
Hostels 133
Bank Street Hostel 133
Hosteling International Chamounix Mansion 133
Hotels 132–41
bed-and-breakfasts 133
Beyond Philadelphia 139–41
Center City 135–6
children 133
disabled travelers 133
discounts 133
Farther Afield 137–9
hidden costs 132
hostels 133
Logan Square and the Museum District 137
Old City 134
reservations and online booking 132

Hotels (cont.)
Society Hill and Penn's Landing 135
taxes 174
Howe, William 106
Hudson, Henry 17
A Huntsman and Dogs (Homer) 91
Huston, John 45
Independence 45
Hutton, Addison 72

I

Ice hockey 34, 169
Ice-skating 168
Impressionist and Postimpressionist art
Barnes Foundation **98–9**
James A. Michener Art Museum (Doylestown) 125
Pennsylvania Academy of the Fine Arts **74–5**
Philadelphia Museum of Art **88–91**
Independence (Huston) 45
Independence Day (public holiday) 35
Independence, Declaration of 20, 40, **42**, 53
Independence Hall 10, 20, 25, 41, **42–3**
Independence Mall **40–9**
Independence National Historical Park **40–9**
opening hours 174
street-by-street map 40–41
walking around 186
Independence Seaport Museum 11, 15, 27, 57, **64–5**, 104
children's activities 171
Independence Visitor Center 10, 40, **45**, 174
Indiana, Robert 70
LOVE artwork 70
Insurance, travel 177
Intercourse 11, **118**, 157
International Children's Festival 32
International Student Identification Card 175
Internet cafés 181
Irish Memorial 66, 104
Italian Market 11, 93, **97**, 157
specialty food stores 160, 161

J

Jack and Jill (publication) 50
Jackson, Andrew 61
Jacob's Choice 11, 118
Jacobsen, Cornelius 17
James A. Michener Art Museum (Doylestown) 125
James A. Michener Art Museum (New Hope) 125
Jam on the River 33
Jazz clubs 166, 167
Jean-Pierre, Ulrick 51
L'Ouverture 51
Jefferson, Thomas 19, 42, 47
Declaration of Independence 42, 50
Jennie Wade House (Gettysburg) 121
Jester Vase (Solon) 90
Jewelers' Row (Center City) 157, 159
Jewelry 159
Jogging 168
Johannes Mueller House (Lititz) 114
John Paul II, Pope 63
Johnson House (Germantown) 107
Jonsson, Einar 96
Thorfinn Karlsefni 96
Joyce, James 33, 77
Ulysses 77

K

Kelly Drive **96**
Keswick Theatre 166
Kilimnik, Karen 85
Kimmel Center for the Performing Arts **77**, 163, 164
Kimmel, Sidney 77
Kimmel Theater (National Constitution Center) 49
King Francis I (van Cleave) 90
King of Prussia Mall 11, 155, 156, 158
Kitchen Kettle Village (Intercourse) 118
Korean War Memorial 105
Kosciuszko, General Thaddeus 61, 63

L

L'Ouverture (Jean-Pierre) 51
Labor Day (public holiday) 35
Ladies Home Journal 50
Lady Chapel (St. Mark's Episcopal Church) 78
Lancaster 112, **114**, 115
Central Market 11, 114
Lancaster Cultural History Museum 11, 114
Lancaster Quilt and Textile Museum 11, 114
Landis, George 116
Landis, Henry 116
Landis Valley Museum 11, **116–17**
Lanza, Mario 100
Large Bathers (Monet) 90
The Large Glass (Duchamp) 91
Laurel Hill (Fairmount Park) 108
Law enforcement 176
USS *Lawrence* 64
Leaves of Grass (Whitman) 101
LeBrun, Napoleon 29, 51, 76, 84
Lee, General Robert E. 120
Lemon Hill (Fairmount Park) 108
Lenni-Lenape Native Americans 17, 50
Let Freedom Ring 33
Leutze, Emmanuel 21
Crossing the Delaware River 21
Levy, Aaron 67
Levy, Nathan 47, 67
Lewis, Judge William 109
Liberty Bell 25, 41, **44**, 61
Liberty Bell Center 10, 41, **44**
Let Freedom Ring 33
Liberty Belle (paddleboat charter) 66
Liberty Place 25, 72, **79**
architecture 29
boutiques and specialty shops 156, 157, 158–9
One Liberty Place 72, 79
Two Liberty Place 72, 79
Library Company of Philadelphia **76**
Library Hall 41, **47**
Lights of Liberty Show 10, 170, 175
Lincoln, Abraham 121
Gettysburg Address **121**
Lincoln Financial Field 169
Lincoln Railroad Station (Gettysburg) 121
Lincoln Speech Memorial (Gettysburg) 121
Liquor laws 175
Lititz **114**
Lititz Museum 114
Little Round Top (Gettysburg National Military Park) 123
Logan, James 84
Logan Square 18, 30, 31, 83, **84**
see also Logan Square and the Museum District

Logan Square and the Museum
District 18, **80–91**
  area map 81
  hotels 137
  museums 26–7
  Philadelphia Museum of Art **88–91**
  restaurants 150
  street-by-street map 82–3
Longwood Gardens 30, **128–9**
  Welcome Spring 35
Lost property 177
LOVE artwork (Indiana) 70
Lowestfare.com 183
Lucy the Elephant (Margate City) 127
Lufthansa 182

M

MacArthur, General Douglas 64
Mack, Alexander 115
Mademoiselle Yvonne Landsberg
  (Matisse) 91
Madison, Dolley 61
Madison, James 54
Magnolia Garden 59, **62**
Main Post Office 181
Main Street Manayunk **95**, 154, 156
Malls and discount malls 125, 156,
  157
Manayunk Arts Festival, 33
Mann Center for the Performing Arts
  (Fairmount Park) 33, 95, 164
Maps
  Beyond Philadelphia 112–13
  Center City 69
  Center City street-by-street 70–71
  Central Philadelphia 14–15
  Fairmount Park drive 108–109
  Farther Afield 93
  Germantown walk 106–107
  Gettysburg 122–3
  Greater Philadelphia 13
  Logan Square and the Museum
    District 81
  Logan Square and the Museum
    District street-by-street 82–3
  North America 12
  Old City 39
  Old City (Independence National
    Historical Park) street-by-street 40–41
  Penn's Landing walk 104–105
  Philadelphia, orientation 12–13
  Philadelphia's Best: Museums 26–7
  Philadelphia's Best: Parks and
    Gardens 30–31
  Society Hill and Penn's Landing 57
  Society Hill and Penn's Landing
    street-by-street 58–9
Mardi Gras 35
Mario Lanza Institute and Museum
  100
Markets 157
  Farmers' Market (Bird-In-Hand) 118
  Green Dragon Farmers Market
    (Ephrata) 118
  Italian Market 11, 93, **97**, 157
  Lancaster Central Market 11, 114
  New Market **66**
  Reading Terminal Market 11, 25,
    71, **73**, 157
Martin Luther King Day (public
  holiday) 35
Martyrs' Mirror (Mennonite book)
  118
Mary Merritt Doll Museum (Reading)
  125
Masonic Temple 69, 70, 71, **72**

MasterCard
  ATMs 178
  credit card 177, 178
Matisse, Henri 90, 91, 98
  The Dance 99
  Mademoiselle Yvonne Landsberg 91
Matisse, Jacqueline 85
Mayor's Commission on People with
  Disabilities 133, 163, 175
McPherson's Ridge (Gettysburg
  National Military Park) 122
Meade, General George 77
Medical facilities 176–7
Medical insurance 176
Mellon Bank Center 29, 72
Memorial Day (public holiday) 35
Memorial Hall (Fairmount Park), 29,
  95, 109
Mennonites 19, **115**, 142
Men's fashion 158
Mercer, Henry 125
Mercer Museum (Doylestown) 125
Merriam Theater 163
Methodist movement 51
Mey, Cornelius 127
Middle East and Asian art
  (Philadelphia Museum of Art) 88, 91
Mikveh Israel 41, **47**
Mikveh Israel Cemetery **67**
Miss Blanche Hurlbert (Eakins) 89
Modern and Contemporary art
  (Philadelphia Museum of Art) 88, 91
Modigliani 98
Monet, Claude 90
  Large Bathers 90
  Poplars 90
Money in Motion (Federal Reserve
  Bank of Philadelphia) 46
USS *Monitor* 86
Monuments
  155th Pennsylvania Volunteer
    Infantry Memorial (Gettysburg
    National Military Park) 123
  Eternal Light Peace Memorial
    (Gettysburg National Military
    Park) 122
  Irish Memorial 66, 104
  Korean War Memorial 105
  National Memorial Arch (Valley
    Forge National Historic Park) 129
  North Carolina Memorial
    (Gettysburg National Military
    Park) 122
  Pennsylvania Memorial (Gettysburg
    National Military Park) 123
  Smith Civil War Memorial
    (Fairmount Park) 109
  Soldiers and Sailors Monument
    (Lancaster) 114
  Soldiers' National Monument
    (Gettysburg) 121
  Thaddeus Kosciuszko National
    Memorial 59, 61
  Trenton Battle Monument
    (Trenton) 126
  Vietnam War Memorial 105
  Virginia Memorial (Gettysburg
    National Military Park) 122
  see also Art, Museums, & Statues
Moore College of Art and Design **85**
Morris Arboretum and Gardens 30, 95
Morris, Robert 108
Moshulu (ship restaurant) 66, 104, 148
Mother Bethel AME Church 58, **60**
Mount Pleasant (Fairmount Park) 108
Mourning Theater (Gettysburg) 120

MOVE 23
Mummers Day Parade 35, **100**
Mummers Museum **100**
Mural Arts Program **87**
The Murders in the Rue Morgue
  (Poe) 94
Museum District *see* Logan Square
  and the Museum District
Museums
  Academy of Natural Sciences 26,
    82, **85**
  The African American Museum in
    Philadelphia 27, **51**
  Americana Museum (Bird-In-Hand)
    118
  Atwater Kent Museum 27, **50**
  Brandywine River Museum **129**
  children 170–71
  The Civil War and Underground
    Railroad Museum of Philadelphia **77**
  Fireman's Hall Museum **51**
  Fonthill Museum (Doylestown) 125
  Franklin Institute Science Museum
    11, 26, 82, **85**
  Hagley Museum (Wilmington) **128**
  Historic Cold Spring Village (Cape
    May) 127
  Independence Seaport Museum 11,
    15, 27, **64–5**
  James A. Michener Art Museum,
    (Doylestown) 125
  James A. Michener Art Museum
    (New Hope) 125
  Lancaster Cultural History Museum
    (Lancaster) 114
  Lancaster Quilt and Textile
    Museum (Lancaster) 11, 114
  Landis Valley Museum 11, **116–17**
  Lititz Museum 114
  Mario Lanza Institute and
    Museum **100**
  Mary Merritt Doll Museum
    (Reading) 125
  Mercer Museum (Doylestown) 125
  Mummers Museum 93, **100**
  Mütter Museum **79**
  National Civil War Museum,
    (Harrisburg) 124
  National Constitution Center 40,
    48–9
  National Liberty Museum **53**
  National Museum of American
    Jewish History 27, 41, **46–7**
  National Toy Train Museum
    (Strasburg) 119
  New Hall Military Museum 54
  Old Barracks Museum (Trenton) 126
  opening hours 174
  Parry Mansion Museum (New
    Hope) 125
  Pennsylvania Academy of the Fine
    Arts 25, 27, 69, 70, 71, **74–5**
  People's Place Quilt Museum
    (Intercourse) 118
  Philadelphia Museum of Art 25, 26,
    29, **88–91**, 171
  Philadelphia's best **26–7**
  Please Touch Museum 11, 170
  Polish American Cultural Center
    Museum 59, **63**
  Railroad Museum of Pennsylvania
    (Strasburg) 119
  Rodin Museum 26, 29, 83, **86**
  Rosenbach Museum and Library **77**
  Schriver House Museum
    (Gettysburg) 121

Museums (cont.)
  University of Pennsylvania
    Museum of Archaeology and
    Anthropology 26, **97**
  Wilbur Chocolate Candy Store and
    Museum (Lititz) 114
  Wills House and Lincoln Room
    Museum (Gettysburg) 121
  Winterthur Museum **128**
  Woodmere Art Museum (Chestnut
    Hill) 95
  see also Art, Monuments, & Statues
Music **166**
  schools 165
  shops 161
Mütter Museum **79**
Mütter, Thomas Dent 79

N

Nandi, the Sacred Bull of Shiva
  (Philadelphia Museum of Art) 91
National Cemetery (Gettysburg
  National Military Park) 123
National Christmas Center (Paradise)
  119
National Civil War Museum
  (Harrisburg) 124
National Constitution Center 10, 25,
  40, **48–9**
  children's tour 170
National Historic Landmark Building
  74
National Liberty Museum **53**
  children's activities 171
National Memorial Arch (Valley
  Forge National Historic Park) 129
National Museum of American
  Jewish History 27, 41, **46–7**
National Park Service 45, 53, 55, 176
National Toy Train Museum
  (Strasburg) 119
The Nativity (Schiavo) 89
Nero, Peter 164
Neshaminy Mall 156, 157
New Hall Military Museum 54
New Hope **125**
  restaurants 153
USS *New Jersey* (Camden Waterfront)
  66, 67, 101, 104
New Jersey Transit 188
New Jersey Turnpike 189
New Market and Head House
  Square **66**
Newspapers 181
New Year's Day (public holiday) 35
New Year's Eve 35
Nightclubs and bars 166–7
Noah's Ark (Edward Hicks) 91
North America, map 12
North Carolina Memorial (Gettysburg
  National Military Park) 122
Northwest Airlines 182
Notman, John 78, 84
Nude Descending a Staircase (No.2)
  (Duchamp) 91
The Nutcracker 35, 164

O

Oak Ridge (Gettysburg National
  Military Park) 122
Odunde Afrikan American Street
  Festival 33
Old Barracks Museum (Trenton) 126
Old City 14, 25, **39–55**
  America's most historic square
    mile 25

Old City (cont.)
  area map 39
  art galleries 160, 161
  hotels 134
  Independence Hall **42–3**
  Liberty Bell Center **44**
  National Constitution Center **48–9**
  restaurants 142, 145–7
  street-by-street map 40–41
  see also Independence National
    Historical Park
Old City Arts Association 160
Old City Hall 15, 28, 43
Old Pine Street Church 58, **60**
Old St. Joseph's Church 59, **63**
Old St. Mary's Church 59, **62**, 63
Old Swedes' Church 103, 105
USS *Olympia* 15, 27, 64, **65**, 104
One Liberty Place see Liberty Place
On the Rivers, On the Shores
  (Independence Seaport Museum) 65
Opening hours 174
  banks 174, 178
  museums 174
  post offices 181
  restaurants 143
Opera and ballet 164, 165
Opera Company of Philadelphia 76,
  162, 164
Ormandy, Eugene 58, 60
Ormiston (Fairmount Park) 108
Outdoor activities and sports **168–9**

P

Pantocrator (Vincent Desiderio) 75
Paradise **119**
Parking 187
Parks and Gardens **30–31**
  Arboretum and Gardens (Barnes
    Foundation) 98
  Azalea Garden (Boathouse Row) 96
  Camden Children's Garden 171
  Christopher Columbus Park 104
  Fairmount Park see Fairmount Park
  Franklin Square 18
  Logan Square 18, 30, 31, 83, **84**
  Longwood Gardens 30, **128–9**
  Magnolia Garden 59, **62**
  Morris Arboretum and Gardens
    30, 95
  Rittenhouse Square see Rittenhouse
    Square
  Rose Garden 59, **62**
  Shofuso Japanese House and
    Garden (Fairmount Park) 95
  Washington Square see Washington
    Square
  Welcome Park 31, **55**, 104
  Wissahickon Gorge 31
Parrish, Maxfield 50
  Dream Garden Mosaic 50
Parry, Benjamin 125
Parry Mansion Museum (New
  Hope) 125
Passports and visas 174–5, 176, 177
PATCO (Port Authority Transit
  Corporation) 188
Payne, Dolley 54
Pay phones 180
Peaceable Kingdom (Hicks) 18
Peach Orchard (Gettysburg National
  Military Park) 123
Peale, Charles Willson 47, 61, 106
  Philadelphia Museum of Art 90–91
  Pennsylvania Academy of the Fine
    Arts 71, 74–75

Peale, Charles Willson (cont.)
  Rachel Weeping 91
  The Staircase Group 90, 91
Peale, James 47
Pemberton House 54
Penn, John 96
PENN Presents 165
Penn Relays 32
Pennsbury Manor **126**
Penn's Landing 15, 25, **66**, **104–105**
  Jam on the River 33
  New Year's Eve 35
  Penn's Landing Festivals 33
  RiverLink Ferry 186
  walking tour 103, **104–105**
  see also Society Hill and Penn's
    Landing
Penn's Landing Festivals 33
Penn's Treaty with the Indians
  (Hicks) 16
Pennsylvania Academy of the Fine
  Arts 23, 25, 27, 69, 70, 71, **74–5**
  Annual Student Exhibition 33
  children's activities 171
Pennsylvania Ballet 76, 162, 164
Pennsylvania Convention Center 69,
  71, **73**
  Philadelphia International Auto
    Show 35
  Philadelphia Flower Show 32
  Philadelphia Furniture and
    Furnishings Show 32
  Philadelphia Museum of Art Craft
    Show 34
Pennsylvania Department of
  Transportation 185
Pennsylvania Dutch 115
Pennsylvania Dutch Country 18, 114,
  118, 119
  cuisine 142, **144**
  day tour 11
  hotels 140–41
  Landis Valley Museum, 116–17
  restaurants 153
  traveling to 188–9
Pennsylvania, founding of 17
Pennsylvania Hospital 19, 56, **67**
Pennsylvania Memorial (Gettysburg
  National Military Park) 123
Pennsylvania Turnpike Commission
  185
Penn, Thomas 67
Penn, William 12, 17–19, 39, 58, 115
  Charter for Pennsylvania (1681) 18
  Charter of Privileges (1701) 19, 63
  grid plan for Philadelphia 14, 18,
    30, 60, 78, 84, 186
  Pennsbury Manor **126**
  Quakerism 18
  Slate Roof House 55, 104
  statue at City Hall 70, **72**, 79
  Welcome Park **55**
People's Place Quilt Museum
  (Intercourse) 118
Perelman Theater (Kimmel Center for
  the Performing Arts) 164
Performing arts **164–5**
Personal security **176–7**
Peter, Sarah Worthington 85
Pharmacies 176, 177
Philadelphia 76ers basketball 34, 169
Philadelphia Airport Shuttle 183
Philadelphia Antiques Show 32
Philadelphia Boys Choir and
  Chorale 165
Philadelphia Business Journal 181

Philadelphia Chamber Music Society 164
Philadelphia City Paper 162, 181
Philadelphia College Festival 34
Philadelphia Convention and Visitors Bureau 174
Philadelphia Cruise Terminal at Pier 1 185
Philadelphia Daily News 181
Philadelphia Eagles football 33, 34, 169
Philadelphia Film Festival 32
Philadelphia Flower Show 32
Philadelphia Flyers hockey 34, 169
Philadelphia Folk Festival 33
Philadelphia Fringe Festival 34
Philadelphia Furniture and Furnishings Show 32
Philadelphia Holiday Festival 35
Philadelphia Inquirer 162, 181
Philadelphia Insectarium 171
Philadelphia International Airport 182
Philadelphia International Auto Show 35
Philadelphia International Gay & Lesbian Film Festival 33
Philadelphia Marathon 34
Philadelphia Merchants' Exchange 10, 28, **54–5**
Philadelphia Museum of Art 25, 26, 29, **88–91**, 171
Philadelphia Museum of Art Craft Show 34
Philadelphia Open Studio Tours 34
Philadelphia Orchestra 77, 162, 164
Philadelphia, orientation map 12–13
Philadelphia Parking Authority 187
Philadelphia Park Racetrack 169
Philadelphia Phillies baseball 32, 168
Philadelphia police 176
Philadelphia Redevelopment Authority 58
Philadelphia Singers 165
Philadelphia street grid 186
Philadelphia Theatre Company 164
Philadelphia, top ten sights 25
Philadelphia Tribune 181
Philadelphia Weekly 162, 181
Philadelphia Zoo **96**, 171
Philly Phlash 186
Philly POPS 162, 164
Philomel Baroque Orchestra 164
Philosophical Hall 41, 43, **47**
The Philosophy of Furniture (Poe) 94
Phones 180
coin-operated 180
dialing codes 180
emergency numbers 177
Physick, Dr. Philip Syng 42, 61, 67
Physick House 59, **61**
Picasso, Pablo 90, 91
Self-Portrait 91
Three Musicians 91
Pickett's Charge 120, 122–3
Pierce, George 128
Pillared Hall (Philadelphia Museum of Art) 91
Pilmoor, Joseph 51
Pissarro, Camille 90
Pitzer Woods (Gettysburg National Military Park) 122
Please Touch Museum 11, 170
Plum Run (Gettysburg National Military Park) 123
PNC Bank 178, 179

Pocono Mountains 168
Pocono Mountains Vacation Bureau, Inc. 168, 169
Poe, Edgar Allen 84, **94**
The Black Cat 94
The Gold Bug 94
The Philosophy of Furniture 94
The Raven 94
The Tell-Tale Heart 94
Polish American Cultural Center Museum 59, **63**
Poplars (Monet) 90
Portal from the Abbey Church of Saint Laurent (Philadelphia Museum of Art) 90
The Postman (van Gogh) 98
Postmodernist architecture **29**
Bell Atlantic Tower 29
Liberty Place 29, **79**
Mellon Bank Center 29
Post offices 181
Poussin, Nicolas 90
Powel House 59, **63**
Powel, Samuel 59, 63
Pratt, Henry 108
Presidents' Day (public holiday) 35
Price, Eli Kirk 86
Priceline 183
Prince Music Theater 163
Priority mail 181
Professional spectator sports 168–9
Prometheus Bound (Rubens) 90
Public holidays 35
Public transportation 186, 189
Pubs 166, 167
Puerto Rican Day Parade 34
Pulaski Day Parade 34, 63
Pulaski, General Casimir 34, 63

Q
Quakerism 17–18
Quakers 17, 18, 45, 46, 54, 55
Arch Street Friends Meeting House 41, **46**
Betsy Ross House **52**
Free Quakers 45
Free Quaker Meeting House 40, **45**

R
Rachel Weeping (Peale) 91
Radio stations 181
Railroad Museum of Pennsylvania (Strasburg) 119
Rare books 84
The Raven (Poe) 94
Reading **125**
factory outlets 154
Pagoda 125
Reading Railroad 73
Reading Terminal Market 11, 71, **73**, 157
Reception Hall from a Nobleman's Palace (Philadelphia Museum of Art) 91
Red Rose Transit Authority 188
Regional rail service 188
Religous Liberty (Ezekiel) 47
Renaissance paintings 89
Renoir, Pierre-Auguste 90, 98, 99
After the Concert 99
Great Bathers 90
Republican National Convention 23
Restaurants and Cafés **142–53**
alcohol 143
Beyond Philadelphia 151–3
Center City 142, 148–9

Restaurants and Cafés (cont.)
children 143
dress code 143
eateries and fast food 143
ethnic 143
Farther Afield 150–51
hours 143
Logan Square and the Museum District 150
Old City 142, 145–7
Pennsylvania Dutch Country 144, 153
Philly fare 142
prices 143
reservations 143
smoking 143, 174
Society Hill and Penn's Landing 147–8
tipping 143, 174
Revere Tavern 119
Ride the Ducks 170, 175
Ridgeland (Fairmount Park) 109
Rising Sun Chair (Independence Hall) 42–3
Rite Aid 177
Rittenhouse, David 67, 78
Rittenhouse Row 10, 156, 157, 158
Rittenhouse Square 14, 18, 30, 31, 69, **78**
hotels 136
restaurants 149
Rittenhouse, Wilhelm 78
RiverLink Ferry 101, 104, 185, 186, 187
Riverside Indoor Tennis 168
Rizzo, Frank 23, 97
Rock music 166, 167
Rockwell, Norman 50
Rodin, Auguste 26, 83, 86
Apotheosis of Victor Hugo 86
The Burghers of Calais 86
Eternal Springtime 86
The Gates of Hell 86
The Shade 26
The Thinker 83, 86
Rodin Museum 26, 29, 83, **86**
Roosevelt, Franklin Delano 48
Rose Garden 59, **62**
Rosenbach, Dr. Abraham Simon Wolf 77
Rosenbach Museum and Library **77**
Bloomsday 33
Ross, Betsy 45, 52
Ross, George 46
Rubens, Peter Paul 90
Prometheus Bound 90
Runge, Gustavus 76
Rush, Dr. Benjamin 46, 60, 67
Rush, William 74

S
Safety *see* Personal security
Sales 154
Salomon, Haym 47, 67
Samuel M.V. Hamilton Building (Pennsylvania Academy of the Fine Arts) 75
Saturday Evening Post 50
Norman Rockwell 27, 50
Schiavo, Paolo 89
The Nativity 89
Schriver House Museum (Gettysburg) 121
Schuylkill Navy 96
Schuylkill River 14, 17, 81, 96
Dad Vail Regatta 33

Second Bank of the US 10, 29, 41, **47**
The Secret Garden (Burnett) 171
Self-Portrait (Picasso) 91
Semiramis (Story) 74
Seniors 175
SEPTA
　Airport Rail Line 183
　bus system 186
　CCT 175
　disabled travelers 175
　subway system 186
　train system 188
The Shade (Rodin) 26
Shofuso Japanese House and Garden
　(Fairmount Park) 95
Shopping **154–61**
　credit cards 154
　department stores 155
　fashion and accessories 158–9
　hours 154
　malls and discount malls 125, 156,
　157
　markets *see* Markets
　payment 154
　returning merchandise 155
　sales 154
　shopping day in Philadelphia 10–11
　shopping districts 156–7
　specialty shops 156, 160–61
　taxes 154
Signers' Hall (National Constitution
　Center) 48, 49
Simons, Menno 115
Skating 168
Skiing 168
Slate Roof House (Welcome Park) 55,
　104
Smith Civil War Memorial (Fairmount
　Park) 109
Smith, Robert 54, 60, 61
Smoking 143, 174
Society Hill 14, 57
Society Hill and Penn's Landing **57–67**
　area map 57
　hotels 135
　Independence Seaport
　　Museum **64–5**
　restaurants 147–8
　street-by-street map 58–9
　see also Society Hill, Penn's Landing
Society Hill Playhouse 164
Society Hill Synagogue 59, **62**
*Soft Construction of Boiled Beans
　(Premonition of Civil War)* (Dali) 91
Soldiers and Sailors Monument
　(Lancaster) 114
Soldiers' National Cemetery
　(Gettysburg) 121
Soldiers' National Monument
　(Gettysburg) 121
Solon, Marc-Louis-Emmanuel 90
　Jester Vase 90
South Street and Walkway 57, **66–7**
　entertainment 163
　Mardi Gras 35
　Odunde Afrikan American Street
　　Festival 33
　shopping 156
South Street Antiques Market 160, 161
South Street Head House District 67
Spangler's Spring (Gettysburg
　National Military Park) 123
Specialty shops 156, 160–61
Speed limit and fines 189
Spirit of Philadelphia (dinner cruise
　ship) 66, 104

Sporting goods 161
Sports **168–9**
Spring in Philadelphia 32–3
The Staircase Group (Peale) 90, 91
State Capitol (Harrisburg) 124
Statues
　Benjamin Franklin (Franklin
　　Institute Museum) 82, 85
　Benjamin Franklin (Signers' Hall)
　　49
　George Washington (Eakins Oval)
　　14, 86
　George Washington (Washington
　　Square) 59, 60
　George Washington (Signers'
　　Hall) 48
　Semiramis (Pennsylvania Academy
　　of the Fine Arts) 74
　The Shade (Rodin Museum) 26
　Signers' Hall 49
　The Thinker (Rodin Museum) 86
　Thorfinn Karlsefni (Boathouse
　　Row) 96
　William Penn (City Hall) 70, 72
　William Penn (Welcome Park) 55,
　　104
　see also Art, Monuments, &
　　Museums
St. Augustine's Church 22, 51
*St. Francis of Assisi Receiving the
　Stigmata* (van Eyck) 90
St. George's Church **51**, 60
St. Mark's Episcopal Church **78**
Stories of Saint Mary Magdalene
　(Botticelli) 90
Story, William Wetmore 74
St. Patrick's Day Parade 32
St. Peter's Episcopal Church 58, **61**
　Semiramis 74
Strasburg **119**
　children's activities 171
Strasburg Railroad 11, 119, 171
Strawberry Mansion (Fairmount
　Park) 28, 109
Street grid 186
Strickland, William 28, 55, 61
Stuart, Gilbert 106, 128
Students 175
Sturgis Pretzel House (Lititz) 114
Sully, Thomas 77
Summer in Philadelphia 33
Sunflowers (van Gogh) 88, 90
Sunoco Welcome America 33
Susquehanna River 124
Sutter, General John 114
Swann Fountain 81, 83, 84
Swedish Lutherans 17, 105
Sweetbriar (Fairmount Park) 109
Swiss Anabaptist Movement 115
Synagogues
　Mikveh Israel 41, **47**
　Society Hill Synagogue 59, **62**

T
Tastykake Children's Zoo 171
Tattersall Golf Club 168, 169
Taverns
　City Tavern 10, **55**
　Dobbin House Tavern (Gettysburg)
　　120
　Revere Tavern (Paradise) 119
Taxes 174
Taxis 187
Television stations 181
The Tell-Tale Heart (Poe) 94
Tennis 168

Terror Behind the Walls (Eastern
　State Penitentiary) 34
Thaddeus Kosciuszko National
　Memorial 59, **61**
Thanksgiving Day Parade (public
　holiday) 34
Theaters and venues
　Academy of Music 164
　Annenberg Center for the
　　Performing Arts 32, 165
　Arden Theatre Company 164
　Esther Boyer College of Music and
　　Dance 165
　Field Concert Hall 165
　F.M. Kirby Auditorium and
　　Theater 48
　Forrest Theatre 163, 164
　Freedom Theatre 164
　Keswick Theatre 166
　Kimmel Theater 49
　Mann Center for the Performing
　　Arts 33, 95, 164
　Merriam Theater 163
　Mourning Theater 120
　Perelman Theater 164
　Philadelphia Theatre Company 164
　Prince Music Theater 163
　Tower Theater 166
　Tweeter Center 101, 163, 166
　University of the Arts 165
　Van Pelt Auditorium 88
　Verizon Hall 164
　Wachovia Complex 163, 166
　Walnut Street Theatre 164
　Wilma Theater 163, 164
The Thinker (Rodin) 83, 86
The Thomas Bond House 55, 104, 134
Thomas Cook Currency Services 178
Thomas Eakins House **87**
Thorfinn Karlsefni (Jonsson) 96
Three Musicians (Picasso) 91
Ticketmaster 162
Ticket Philadelphia 162
Tiffany, Louis Comfort 50
Time capsule (Penn's Landing) 104
Tipping 143, 174
Todd, John 54
Todd House **54**
Tomb of the Unknown Soldier 59, **60**
Tours
　children's 170–71
　Fairmount Park 103, **108–109**
　family day in Philadelphia 11
　Germantown 103, **106–107**
　Gettysburg National Military
　　Park **122–3**
　Ghost Tours of Philadelphia 11, 175
　guided 175
　historic Philadelphia day 10
　Lights of Liberty Show 170, 175
　Penn's Landing 103, **104–105**
　Pennsylvania Dutch Country day 11
　Philadelphia Open Studio Tours 34
　Ride the Ducks 170, 175
　shopping day in Philadelphia 10
　Walk Philadelphia 175
Tower Theater 166
Trains 183, 184, 188
　Amtrak 30th Street Station 29, 182,
　　183, 184, 188
　Broad Street Subway 23
　Market Street Subway 23
Travel **182–9**
　air 182–3
　Beyond Philadelphia 113
　bicycles 168, 187

Travel (cont.)
buses 185, 186, 188
cars 184, 187, 189
Center City 69
cruise ships 185
currency exchange 178
disabled travelers 175
ferries 186–7
getting around Philadelphia 186–7
Logan Square and the Museum
District 81
Old City 39
SEPTA 183, 186, 188
Society Hill and Penn's Landing 57
street grid 186
taxis 187
trains 183, 184, 188
traveler's checks 178
travel insurance 177
walking 186
Travelers Aid Society 175
Treaty of Paris 20
Tree Carpet (Philadelphia Museum
of Art) 91
Trenton **126**
hotels 141
Trenton Battle Monument (Trenton)
126
Trent, William 126
Trump, Donald 127
Turnpikes and toll roads 189
Tweeter Center (Camden Waterfront)
101, 163, 166
Two Liberty Place *see* Liberty Place

U

Ulysses (James Joyce) 77
Underground Railroad 60
Dobbin House Tavern (Gettysburg)
120
Johnson House (Germantown) 107
United Airlines 182
University of Pennsylvania and
University City 93, **96–7**
University of Pennsylvania Museum
of Archaeology and Anthropology
26, **97**
University of the Arts 165
UPS 181
Upsala (Germantown) 107
US Airways 182
US Constitution 20, 21, **48–9**, 53
signing of 42
US Mint 19, 40, **46**
US Pro Cycling Championship 33

V

Valley Forge 21, 94, 129
hotels 141
Valley Forge Golf Club 168
Valley Forge National Historic
Park **129**
biking path 168
van Cleave, Joos 90
King Francis I 90
van der Weyden, Rogier 90
van Eyck, Jan 90
*St. Francis of Assisi Receiving the
Stigmata* 90
van Gogh, Vincent 88, 90, 98
The Postman 98
Sunflowers 88, 90
Van Pelt Auditorium (Philadelphia
Museum of Art) 88
Verizon Hall (Kimmel Center for the
Performing Arts) 164

Veteran's Day (public holiday) 35
VF Outlet Village 157
Victorian architecture 29
Academy of Music 29, **76**
Athenaeum 29
Cathedral of Saints Peter and
Paul **84**
Ebenezer Maxwell House 29, 107
Pennsylvania Academy of the Fine
Arts 23, **74–5**
Vietnam War Memorial 105
Virginia Memorial (Gettysburg
National Military Park) 122
VISA
ATMs 178
credit card 177, 178
Vocal arts and choirs 165
Von Steuben, Baron Friedrich 34
Von Steuben Day Gala and Parade 34

W

Wachovia Bank 178
Wachovia Complex 163, 166
Wade, Jennie 121
Walesa, Lech 63
Walking 186
Walking tours
Fairmount Park 103, **108–109**
Germantown 103, **106–107**
Ghost Tours of Philadelphia 11, 175
Lights of Liberty Show 170, 175
Penn's Landing, 103, **104–105**
Walk Philadelphia 175
Walk Philadelphia, tour 175
Walnut Lane Golf Club 168
Walnut Street Theatre 164
Walter, Thomas Ustick 62
Walt Whitman Bridge 66, 104
Walt Whitman House **101**
Wanamaker building 70, 155
organ recital 70, 155
Wanamaker, Rodman 78
Warfield Ridge (Gettysburg National
Military Park) 122
Washington Crossing Historic Park **126**
Washington Crossing, restaurants 153
Washington Crossing the Delaware
River Reenactment 35
Washington, George 19, 20, 31, 43,
55, 62, 94, 103
Battle of Brandywine 129
Battle of Trenton 126
crossing the Delaware River 21, 126
Deshler-Morris House 28, 103, 106
statues 14, 31, 48, 59, 60, 86
Valley Forge 129
Washington Square 18, 30, 31, **60**
Waterfront Museum (Independence
Seaport Museum) 64
Weather
rainfall 34
snowfall 34
sunshine 33
temperature 35
Welcome 18, 55
Welcome Park 31, **55**, 104
Welcome Spring (Longwood
Gardens) 35
Wesley, John 51
West, Benjamin 27, 74, 128
*Christ Healing the Sick in the
Temple* 67
Wetherill, John Price 45
The Wheatfield (Gettysburg
National Military Park) 123
Wheatland (Lancaster) 114

White, Bishop William 52, 54, 61
White House *see* Deshler-Morris House
Whitman, Walt 101
Leaves of Grass 101
Wilbur Chocolate Candy Store and
Museum (Lititz) 114
Willing, Elizabeth 63
Wills, David 121
Wills House and Lincoln Room
Museum (Gettysburg) 121
Wilma Theater 163, 164
Winter activities and sports 168, 169
Winter in Philadelphia 35
Winterthur Museum **128**
Wissahickon Creek 30
Wissahickon Gorge 30, 95
hiking and biking trails 168
Wister, John 106
Wister, Sally 106
Women's fashion 158
Woodford (Fairmount Park) 109
Woodmere Art Museum (Chestnut
Hill) 95
Wood, Naomi 109
Woolley, Edmond 42
Workshop on the Water (Independence
Seaport Museum) 64
World music 166
Wren, Christopher 28
Wright, John 114
Wyck House and Garden
(Germantown) 107
Wyeth, Andrew 129
Wyeth, Jamie 129
Wyeth, N.C. 129

Y

Yellow fever epidemic 19, 21, 106
mass graves at Washington Square
cemetery 60
Yellow Pages directory 180
York **124**

Z

Zoos
Philadelphia Zoo **96**, 171
Tastykake Children's Zoo 171

Acknowledgments

MAIN CONTRIBUTOR

Richard Varr spent a part of his childhood in Philadelphia and returned to the area in 1999. A former television and newspaper reporter, he now writes for newspapers, magazines, and websites, including Porthole Cruise Magazine and onboard publications of several cruise lines.

FACTCHECKER

Scott Walker

PROOFREADER

Word-by-Word

INDEXER

Jyoti Dhar

DK LONDON

PUBLISHER Douglas Amrine
PUBLISHING MANAGER Lucinda Cooke
MANAGING ART EDITOR Kate Poole
SENIOR DESIGNER Tessa Bindloss
SENIOR CARTOGRAPHIC EDITOR Casper Morris
SENIOR DTP DESIGNER Jason Little
DK PICTURE LIBRARY Martin Copeland,
Romaine Werblow
PRODUCTION CONTROLLER Louise Daly

ADDITIONAL PHOTOGRAPHY

Shaen Adey, Paul Bricknell, Geoff Dann, Steve Gorton, Dave King, Andrew Leyerle, Tim Mann, Ray Moller, Stephen Oliver, Ian O'Leary, Tim Ridley, Clive Streeter, Scott Suchman, Matthew Ward, Jerry Young.

DORLING KINDERSLEY would like to thank the following people whose contributions and assistance have made the preparation of this book possible.

CARTOGRAPHY

Back Endpaper reproduced with permission from SEPTA.

SPECIAL ASSISTANCE

The Barnes Foundation: Henry Butler; Independence National Historical Park: Superintendent; Gettysburg Convention & Visitors Bureau: Stacey Fox; Greater Philadelphia Tourism Marketing Corporation: Paula Butler, Kristen Ciappa, Meryl Levitz, Cara Schneider, Donna Schorr; National Liberty Museum: Amanda Hall; Pennsylvania Convention Center Authority: Patti Spaniak; Pennsylvania Dutch Convention & Visitors Bureau: Cara O'Donnell; Philadelphia Academy of the Fine Arts: Laura Blumenthal, Gene Castellano, Robert Cozzolino, Barbara Katus, Michelle McCaffrey; Philadelphia Convention & Visitors Bureau: Ellen Kornfeld, Marissa Phillip; Philadelphia Museum of Art: Holly Frisbee, Rachel Udell; Philadelphia Water Department: Ed Grusheski; Rodin Museum: John Zarobell.

PHOTOGRAPHY PERMISSIONS

Dorling Kindersley would like to thank the following for their assistance and permission to photograph at their establishments:

Academy of Natural Sciences, Atwater Kent Museum, Bishop White House, City Tavern, College of Physicians of Philadelphia/Mütter Museum, Civil War & Underground Railroad Museum of Philadelphia, Eastern State Penitentiary, Ebenezer Maxwell House, Confederate Memorial Hall, New Orleans, Gettysburg National Military Park Visitor Center and Cyclorama Center, Independence Hall, Independence Seaport Museum, Landis Valley Museum, National Constitutional Center, Pennyslvania Academy of the Fine Arts, People's Place Quilt Museum, Reading Terminal Market as well as all the state and national parks, churches, hotels, restaurants, shops, museums, galleries, and other sights too numerous to thank individually.

PICTURE CREDITS

t = top; tl = top left; tlc = top left center;
tc = top center; tr = top right; trc = top right center;
cla = center left above; ca = center above; cra = center right above; cl = center left; c = center; cr = center right; clb = center left below; cb = center below; crb = center right below; bl = bottom left; b = bottom; bc = bottom center; bcl = bottom center left; br = bottom right.

Every effort has been made to trace the copyright holders and we apologize for any unintentional omissions. We would be pleased to insert the appropriate acknowledgments in any subsequent edition of this publication.

Works of art have been reproduced with the permission of the following copyright holders:

© ARS, NY and DACS, London 2005 84b, *Irish Memorial* by Glenna Goodacre 104cr, *Frank Rizzo* by Diane Keller 97br, *Horticulture Mural* by David McShane 87bc, *L'Ouverture* by Ulrick Jean Pierre 51tc, Cover of *The Saturday Evening Post* (June 28, 1958) by Norman Rockwell 27ca.

The publishers would like to thank the following individuals, companies, and picture libraries for their kind permission to reproduce their photographs:

ALAMY: Bernie Epstein 115t; Jeff Greenberg 115bl; Andre Jenny 42tl, 100b; Dennis MacDonald 144cla.

THE BARNES FOUNDATION: 99tl.

BRIDGEMAN ART LIBRARY: © The Barnes Foundation, Merion, Pennsylvania, USA *Postman* 1889 (oil on canvas) by Vincent van Gogh (1853–90) 98tr; *Gardanne* 1885–86 (oil on canvas) by Paul Cezanne (1839–1906) 98cl; *After the Concert* 1877 (oil on canvas) by Pierre-Auguste Renoir (1841–1919) 99cra; *Card Players and Girl* 1890–92 (oil on canvas) by Paul Cezanne (1839–1906) 99crb.

CLIVEDEN (A NATIONAL TRUST PROPERTY): 21cra, 107br.
CORBIS: 9(inset), 13tl, 18t, 20tr, 21cr, 22crb, 23t, 33bc, 37(inset), 38, 83cra, 111(inset), 173(inset), 185b, 189tl; Dave Bartuff 39t, 40tr; Bettmann 8–9, 17ca, 17bl,

19ca, 19crb, 19bc, 21tl, 21br, 22t, 22bl, 22br, 23bc, 40cla, 53br, 131(inset); Dennis Degnan 80; Kevin Fleming 92; Rose Hartman 61br; Robert Holmes 36–37; Catherine Karnow 175tr; Kelly-Mooney Photography 127b; Bob Krist 68, 172-3, 188bc; Francis G. Mayer 16, 20-21c, 63br, Mary Ann McDonald 115crb; Charles O'Rear 46b; Philadelphia Museum of Art: *Peaceable Kingdom* by Edward Hicks (1780–1849) 18crb, 88tr, *Sunflowers* by Vincent van Gogh (1853–90) 88cl, 89cla, *The Nativity* by Paolo Schiavo (1397–1478) 89crb, *Miss Blanche Hurlbert* by Thomas Eakins (1844–1916) 89bl, 90tl, *Dormition of the Virgin* (1427) by Fra Angelico (1387-1455) 90cl, *Jester Vase* (1894) by Marc-Louis-Emmanuel Solon (1835-1913) Joseph E. Temple Fund 90bc, *The Staircase Group* (1795) by Charles Willson Peale (1741-1827) The George W. Elkins Collection 90br; 91tl, *Bird Tree* (1800–1830) Bequest of Lisa Norris Elkins (Mrs. William M. Elkins) 91c, *Gala Ensemble* Italy (late 19th to early 20th century) Bequest of Helen P. McMullen 91b; PictureNet 113 tr; PoodlesRock 20cl, 20br; Bill Ross 2–3, 127t; Joseph Sohm: Visions of America 21crb, 42bl, 48c; Joseph Sohm- ChromoSohm Inc. 43cla; David H. Wells 83br, 102.

CORBIS SABA: Erik Freeland 23crb;

FAIRMOUNT WATERWORKS & INTERPRETIVE CENTER: 171bl
FRANKLIN INSTITUTE SCIENCE MUSEUM: 26cb
FREE LIBRARY OF PHILADELPHIA: 18bl, 19br, 21bc.

GETTYSBURG CONVENTION & VISITORS BUREAU: Paul Witt 123cl, 123br.
GREATER PHILADELPHIA TOURISM MARKETING CORPORATION: 133bl, R.Kennedy 44cra; C. Ridgeway 25ca.
GREYHOUND LINES, INC.: 185tl.

MASTERFILE: David Zimmerman 110–111.

NATIONAL CONSTITUTION CENTER: 48tr.
NATIONAL MUSEUM OF AMERICAN JEWISH HISTORY: 27cr, 41t.

PENNYSLAVANIA ACADEMY OF THE FINE ARTS: 27tl, 74tr, 75cra, 75crb, *The Cello Player* (1896) by Thomas Eakins Oil on canvas. 64 1/4 x 48 1/8 inches. Accession no:1897.3. Joseph E. Temple Fund 74cl, *The Fox Hunt* by Winslow Homer Oil on canvas. 38 x 68 1/2 inches. Accession no: 1894.4. Joseph E. Temple Fund 74br, *Pantocrator* (2002) Oil on linen (triptych) 87 7/8 x 193 3/4 inches. Accession no:

2033.7.a-c by Vincent Desiderio 75tl.
PENNYSLAVANIA DUTCH CONVENTION & VISITORS BUREAU: 11br, 34cla, 112b, 118b; K. Baum 113b.
PHILADELPHIA CONVENTION & VISITORS BUREAU: ©Alma de Cuba PR 166c; ©Barnes Foundation 25cra, 99bl; ©Camden Riversharks Baseball/David Brady 169t; ©Cuba Libre Restaurant & Rum Bar/Mimi Janosy 142br; Melvin Epps 58cl; © Independence Seaport Museum/Rusty Kennedy 65cra; ©The Inn at the Union League of Philadelphia 70tr; ©National Constitution Center/Scott Frances Ltd. 25cb, 40cl, 48bl, 49tl, 49cr; Jim McWilliams 32cla, 34br, 168b, 170b, 184t; ©Pennyslavania Academy of the Fine Arts/Rick Echelmeyer 24; ©Pennyslavania Ballet/Steve Belkowitz 164c; ©Pennyslavania Horticultural Society/Rob Ikeler 32br; Jon Perlmutter 30cla; ©Philadelphia International Airport/ Richard McMullin 182b; ©Philadelphia Office of the City Representative 33cra; ©Philadelphia Orchestra/Eric Sellen 162b; ©The Plaza and The Court at King of Prussia 155b; ©PR Le Bec-Fin 143b; ©Ritz Carlton, Philadelphia 132b; Edward Savaria Jr. 10tc, 25bl, 35cla, 35br, 46c, 70cl, 70b, 71crb, 101b, 142cl, 143tl, 158tr, 160cla, 163tl, 170cla; 190tc ©Sheraton University City 133tl; Anthony Sinagoga 41crb, 44cl, 158bl ©Valley Forge Convention & Visitors Bureau 170t; ©Westin Philadelphia 132t.

PHILLIES: 32tc
PURE: 167tr

RICHARD VARR: 43cr.

WYK HOUSE AND GARDEN: 106t.

Front endpaper: All special photography except CORBIS : cr, Dennis Degnan tl, Kevin Fleming tr, Bob Krist bl; MASTERFILE: David Zimmerman cl.

JACKET:
Front - Alamy Images: ImagesState bl; Corbis:Dennis Degnan main image; courtesy of www.hexsigns.com: design ©Jacob Zook bc; ©Philadelphia Convention and Visitors Bureau: Anthony Sinagoga c. Back - DK Images: Demetrio Carassco tl, br. Spine - Corbis: Dennis Degnan.

All other images © Dorling Kindersley. For more information see www.dkimages.com

---

SPECIAL EDITIONS OF DK TRAVEL GUIDES

DK Travel Guides can be purchased in bulk quantities at discounted prices for use in promotions or as premiums. We are also able to offer special editions and personalized jackets, corporate imprints, and excerpts from all of our books, tailored specifically to meet your own needs.

To find out more, please contact:
(in the United States) **SpecialSales@dk.com**
(in the UK) **Sarah.Burgess@dk.com**
(in Canada) DK Special Sales at **general@tourmaline.ca**
(in Australia)
business.development@pearson.com.au